ALMOST CRYING

MAKO TAKAHASHI

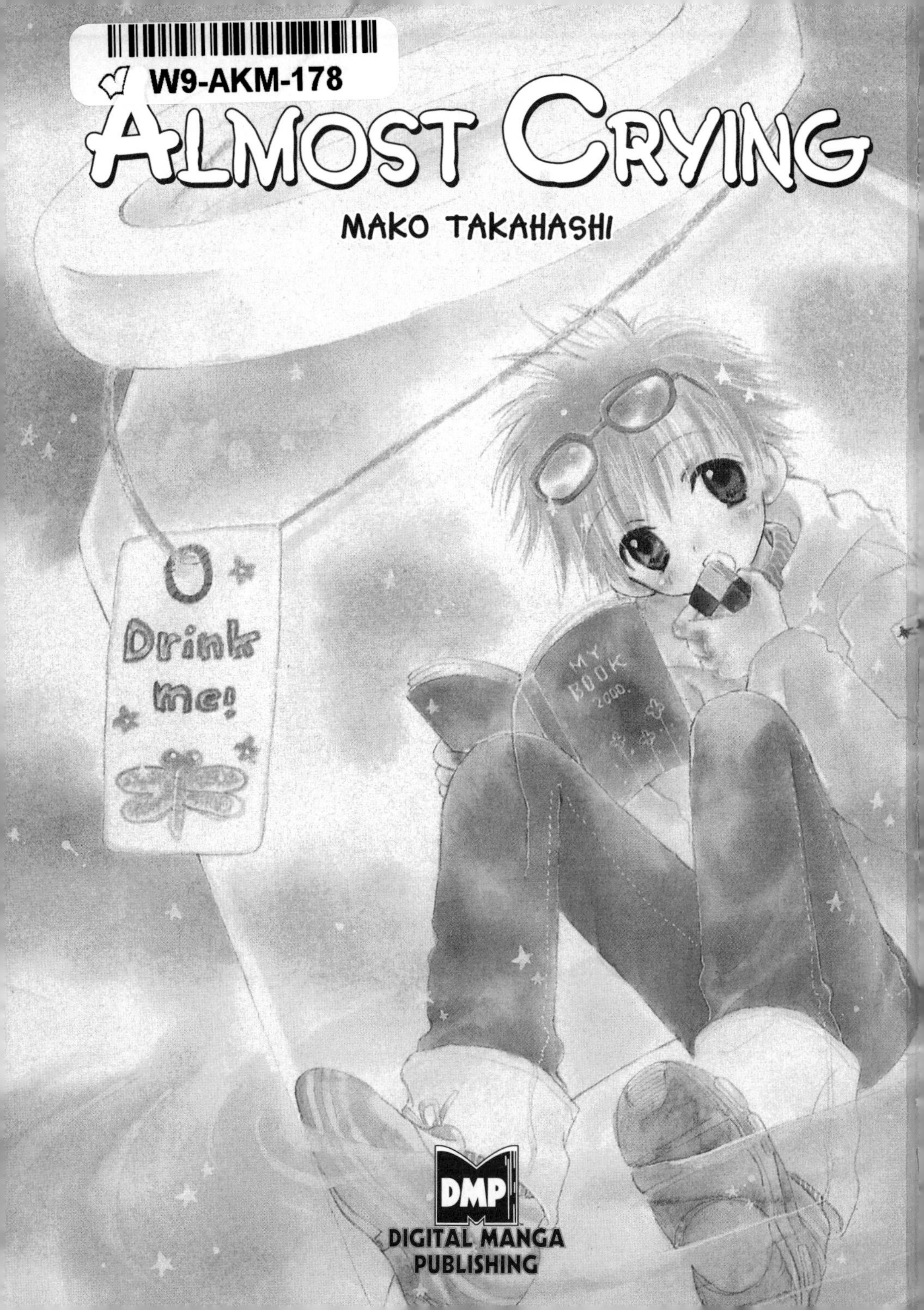
Drink me!
MY BOOK 2000.

DMP
DIGITAL MANGA PUBLISHING

ALMOST CRYING

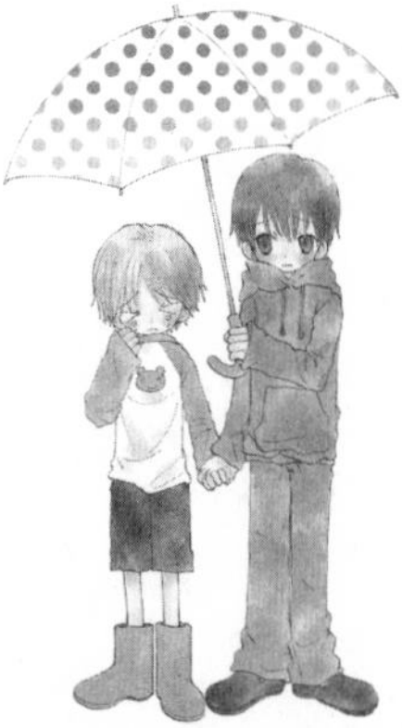

Translation — Sachiko Sato
Lettering — Replibooks
Graphic Design — Wendy Lee
Editing — Bambi Eloriaga
Editor in Chief — Fred Lui
Publisher — Hikaru Sasahara

English Edition Published by
DIGITAL MANGA PUBLISHING
A division of DIGITAL MANGA, Inc.
1487 W 178th Street, Suite 300
Gardena, CA 90248

www.dmpbooks.com

First Edition: March 2006
ISBN: 1-56970-909-2

1 3 5 7 9 10 8 6 4 2

Printed in China

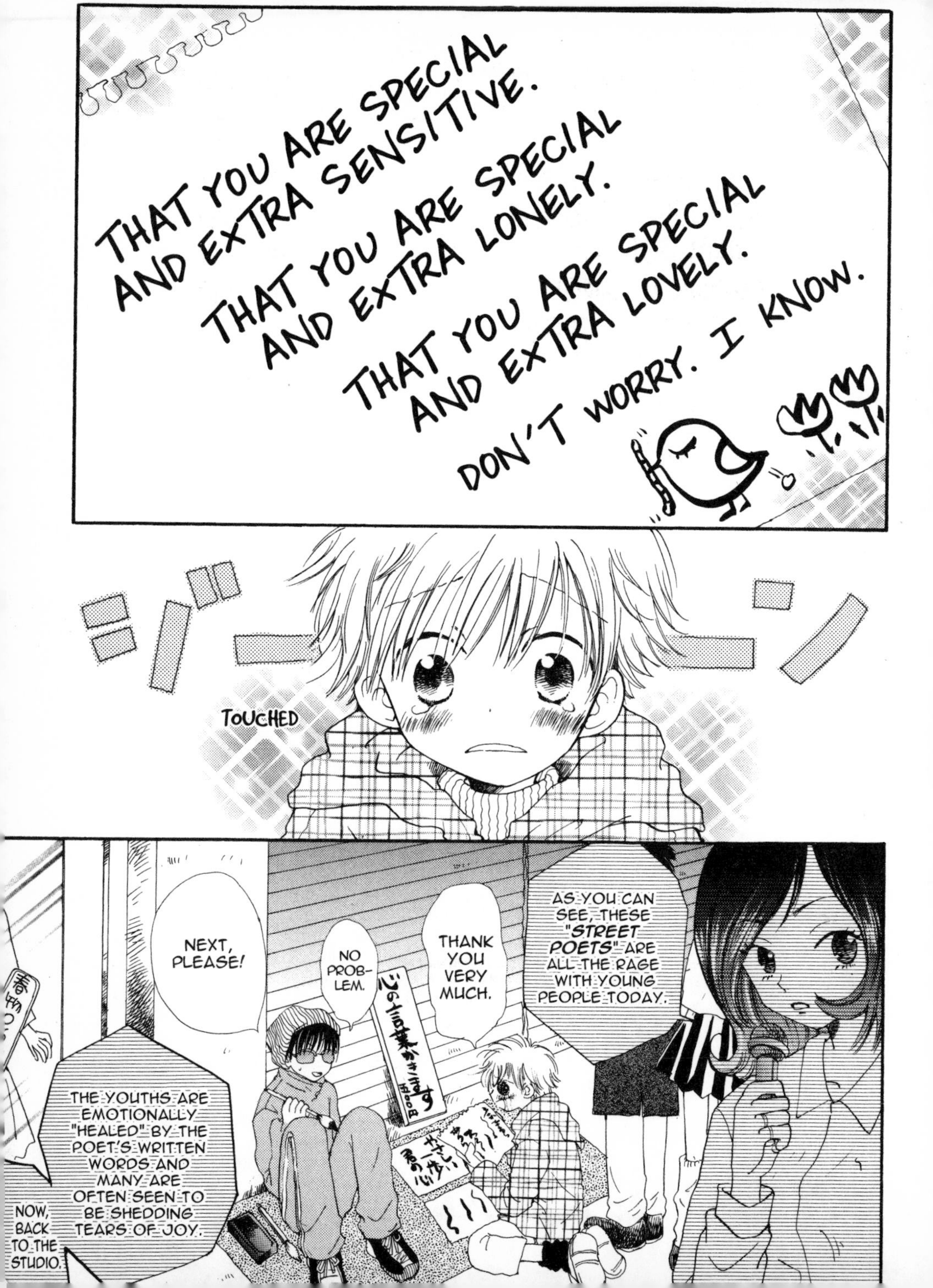
THAT YOU ARE SPECIAL AND EXTRA SENSITIVE.
THAT YOU ARE SPECIAL AND EXTRA LONELY.
THAT YOU ARE SPECIAL AND EXTRA LOVELY.
DON'T WORRY. I KNOW.
TOUCHED
AS YOU CAN SEE, THESE "STREET POETS" ARE ALL THE RAGE WITH YOUNG PEOPLE TODAY.
THANK YOU VERY MUCH.
NO PROB-LEM.
NEXT, PLEASE!
THE YOUTHS ARE EMOTIONALLY "HEALED" BY THE POET'S WRITTEN WORDS AND MANY ARE OFTEN SEEN TO BE SHEDDING TEARS OF JOY.
NOW, BACK TO THE STUDIO.

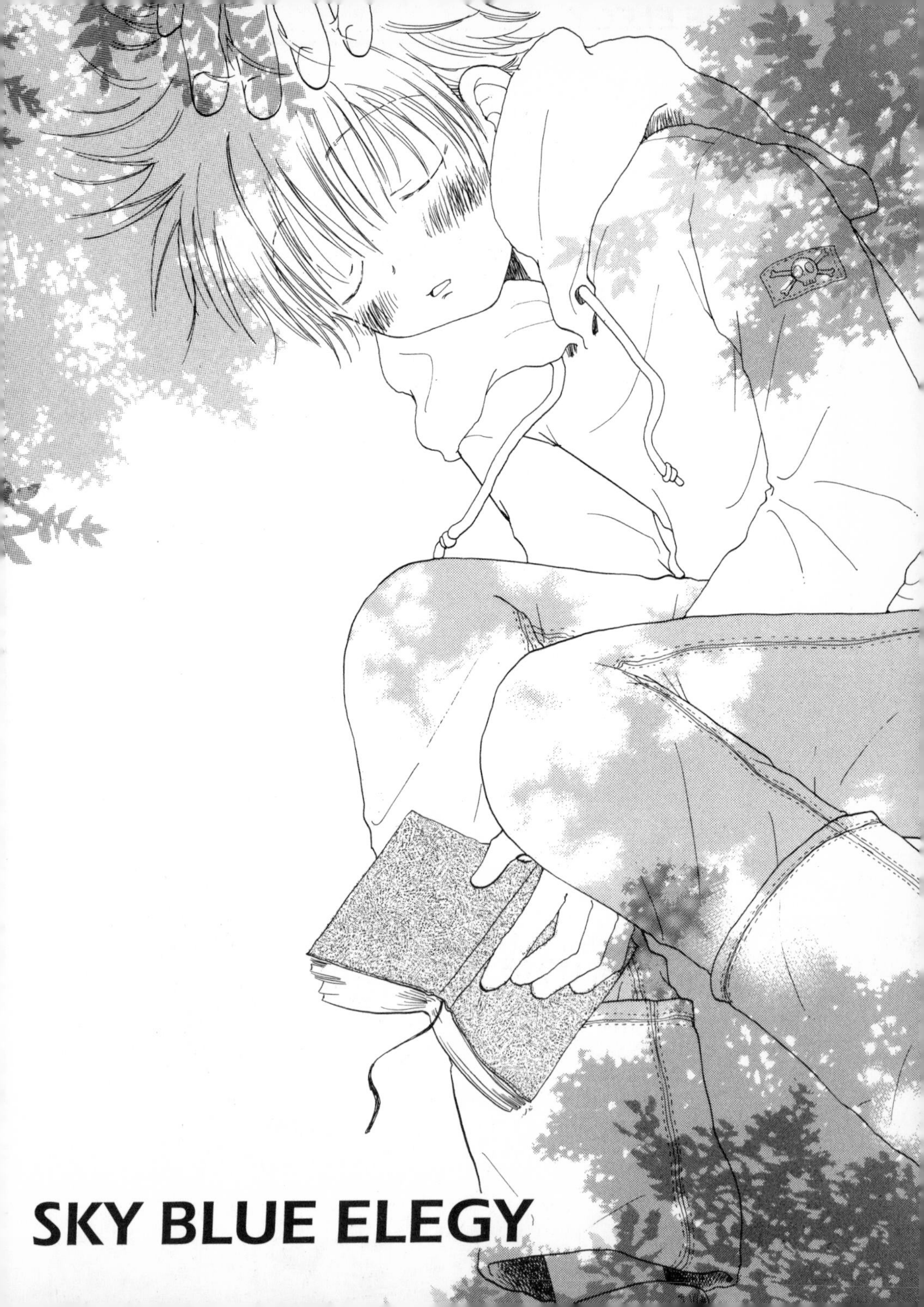

SKY BLUE ELEGY

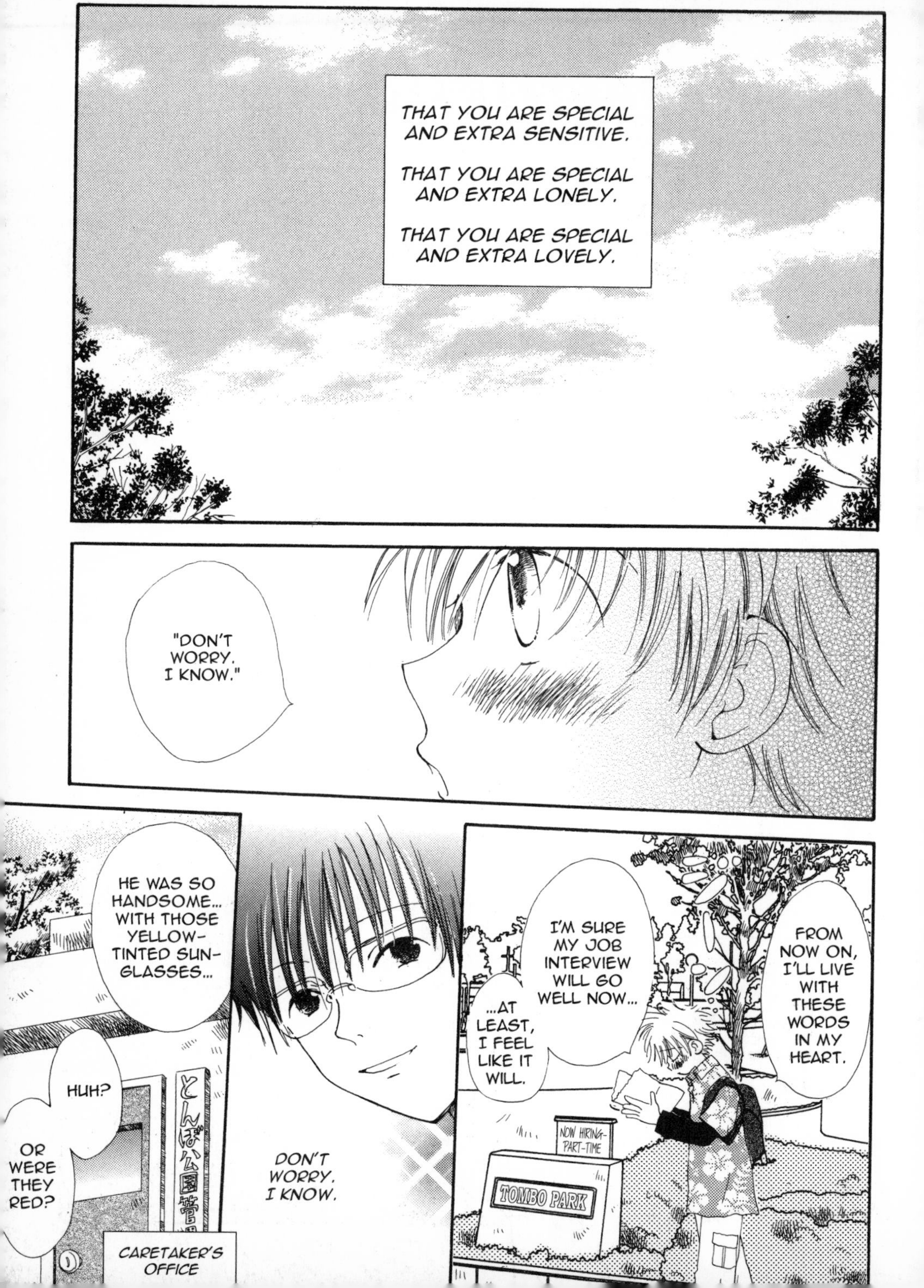
THAT YOU ARE SPECIAL AND EXTRA SENSITIVE.
THAT YOU ARE SPECIAL AND EXTRA LONELY.
THAT YOU ARE SPECIAL AND EXTRA LOVELY.
"DON'T WORRY. I KNOW."
FROM NOW ON, I'LL LIVE WITH THESE WORDS IN MY HEART.
I'M SURE MY JOB INTERVIEW WILL GO WELL NOW...
...AT LEAST, I FEEL LIKE IT WILL.
NOW HIRING- PART-TIME
TOMBO PARK
DON'T WORRY. I KNOW.
HE WAS SO HANDSOME... WITH THOSE YELLOW-TINTED SUN-GLASSES...
HUH?
OR WERE THEY RED?
CARETAKER'S OFFICE

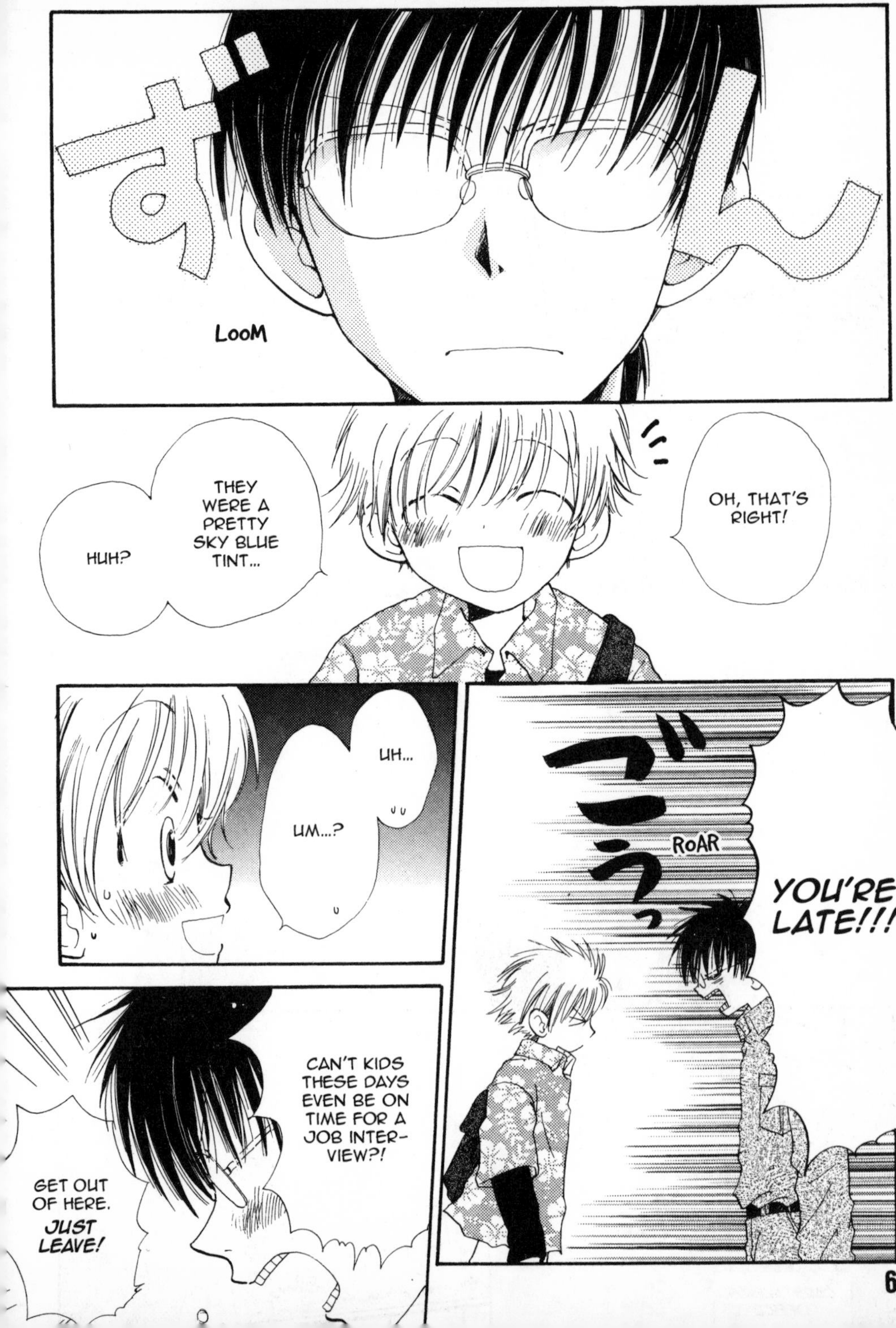
ず～ん
LOOM
OH, THAT'S RIGHT!
THEY WERE A PRETTY SKY BLUE TINT...
HUH?
ごうっ
ROAR
YOU'RE LATE!!!
UH...
UM...?
CAN'T KIDS THESE DAYS EVEN BE ON TIME FOR A JOB INTER-VIEW?!
GET OUT OF HERE.
JUST LEAVE!

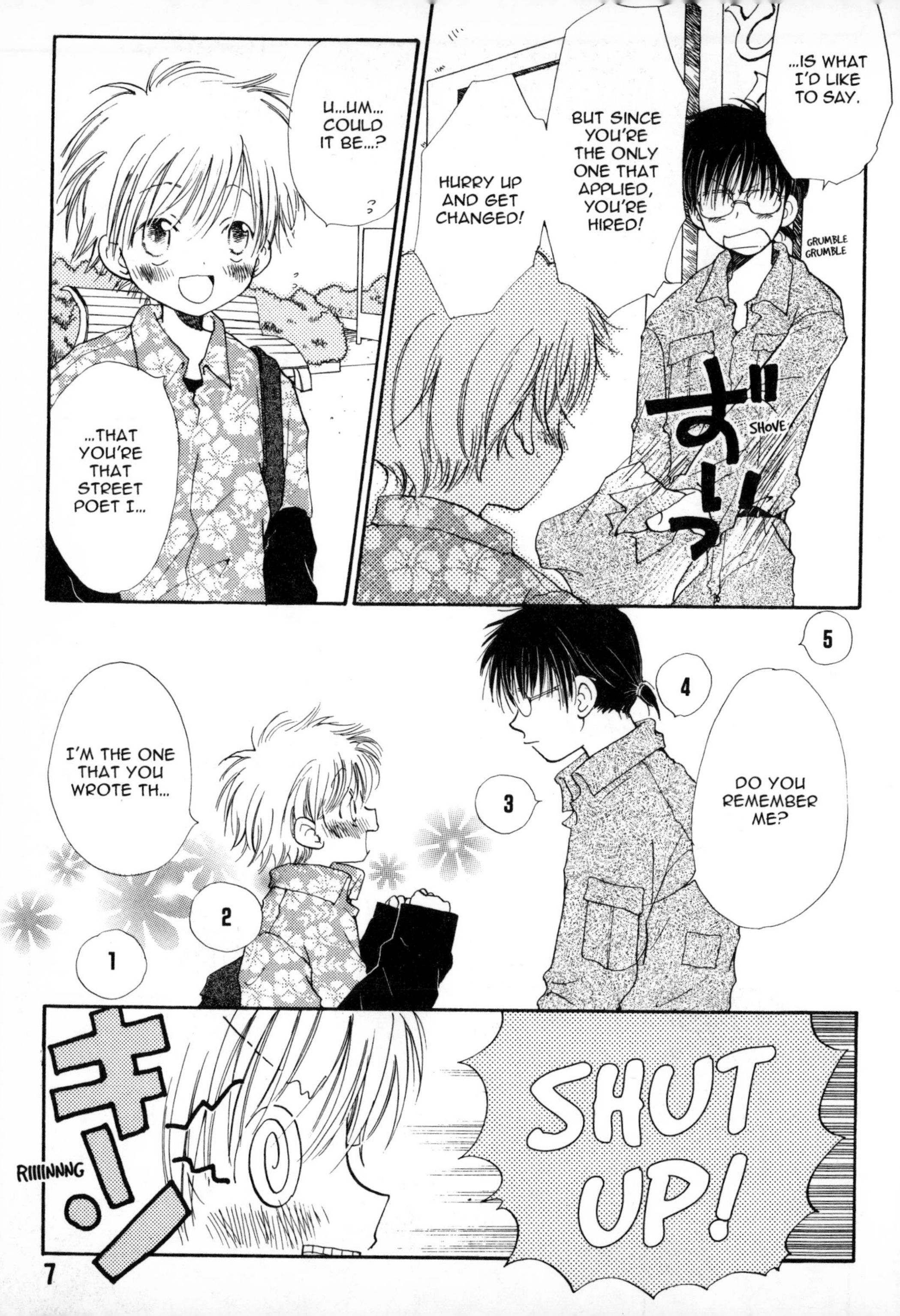

...IS WHAT I'D LIKE TO SAY.
BUT SINCE YOU'RE THE ONLY ONE THAT APPLIED, YOU'RE HIRED!
HURRY UP AND GET CHANGED!
GRUMBLE GRUMBLE
SHOVE
U...UM... COULD IT BE...?
...THAT YOU'RE THAT STREET POET I...
DO YOU REMEMBER ME?
5
4
3
I'M THE ONE THAT YOU WROTE TH...
2
1
SHUT UP!
RIIIINNNG

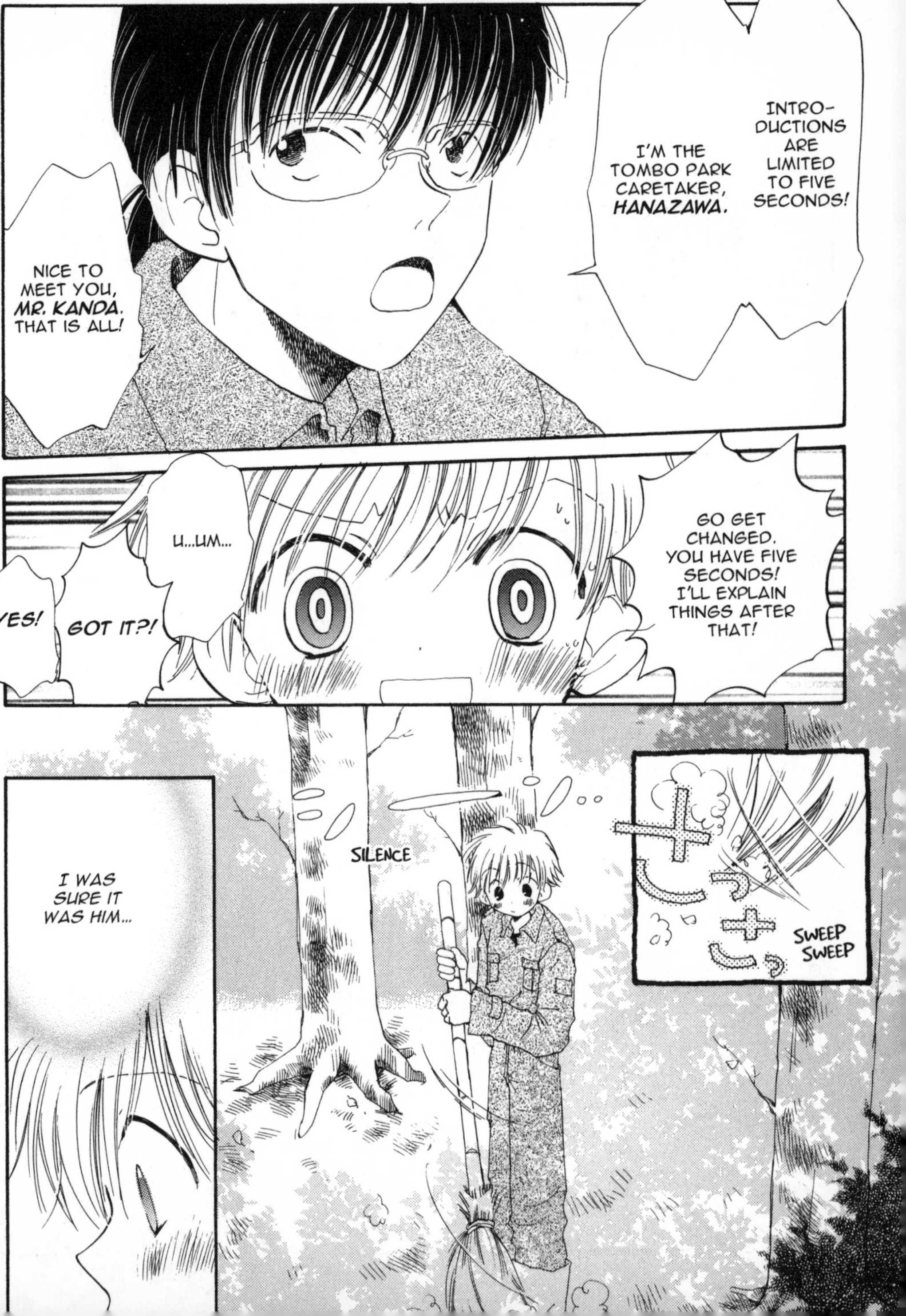
INTRO-DUCTIONS ARE LIMITED TO FIVE SECONDS!
I'M THE TOMBO PARK CARETAKER, HANAZAWA.
NICE TO MEET YOU, MR. KANDA. THAT IS ALL!
GO GET CHANGED. YOU HAVE FIVE SECONDS! I'LL EXPLAIN THINGS AFTER THAT!
U...UM...
GOT IT?!
YES!
SWEEP SWEEP
SILENCE
I WAS SURE IT WAS HIM...

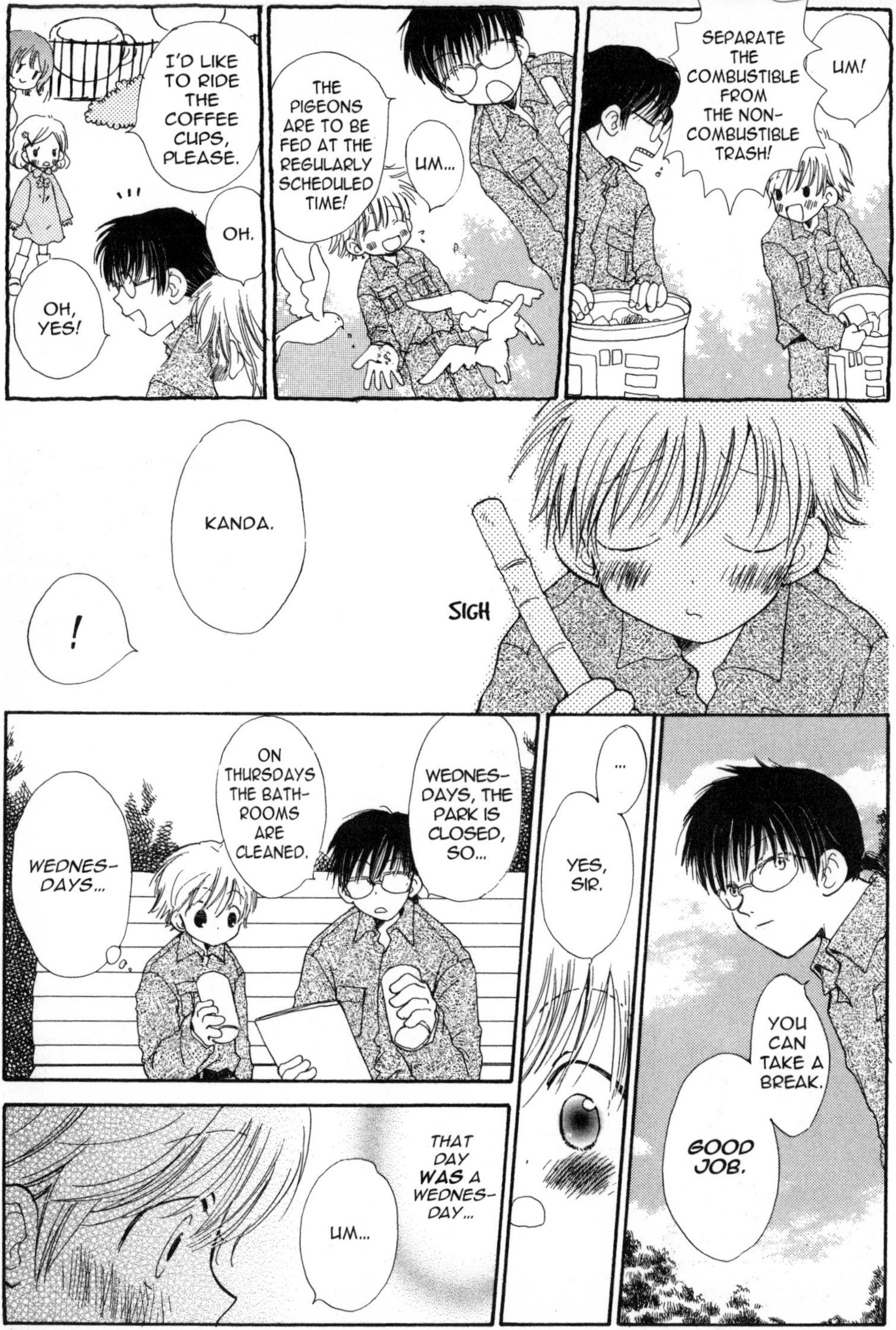
SEPARATE THE COMBUSTIBLE FROM THE NON-COMBUSTIBLE TRASH!
UM!
THE PIGEONS ARE TO BE FED AT THE REGULARLY SCHEDULED TIME!
UM...
I'D LIKE TO RIDE THE COFFEE CUPS, PLEASE.
OH.
OH, YES!
SIGH
KANDA.
!
YOU CAN TAKE A BREAK.
GOOD JOB.
...
YES, SIR.
WEDNES-DAYS, THE PARK IS CLOSED, SO...
ON THURSDAYS THE BATH-ROOMS ARE CLEANED.
WEDNES-DAYS...
THAT DAY WAS A WEDNES-DAY...
UM...

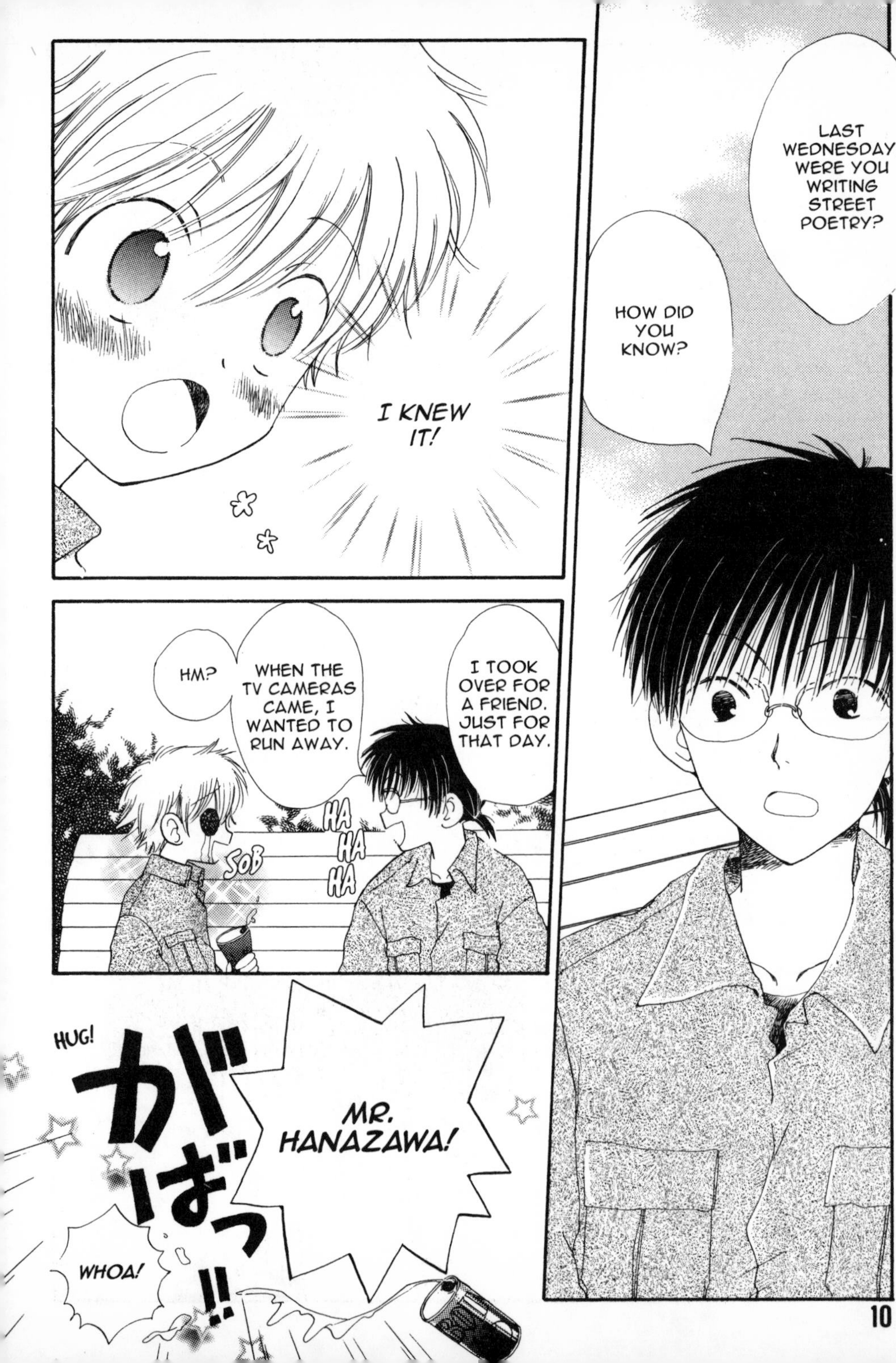
LAST WEDNESDAY, WERE YOU WRITING STREET POETRY?
HOW DID YOU KNOW?
I KNEW IT!
I TOOK OVER FOR A FRIEND. JUST FOR THAT DAY.
WHEN THE TV CAMERAS CAME, I WANTED TO RUN AWAY.
HM?
HA HA HA
SOB
MR. HANAZAWA!
HUG!
がばっ!!
WHOA!

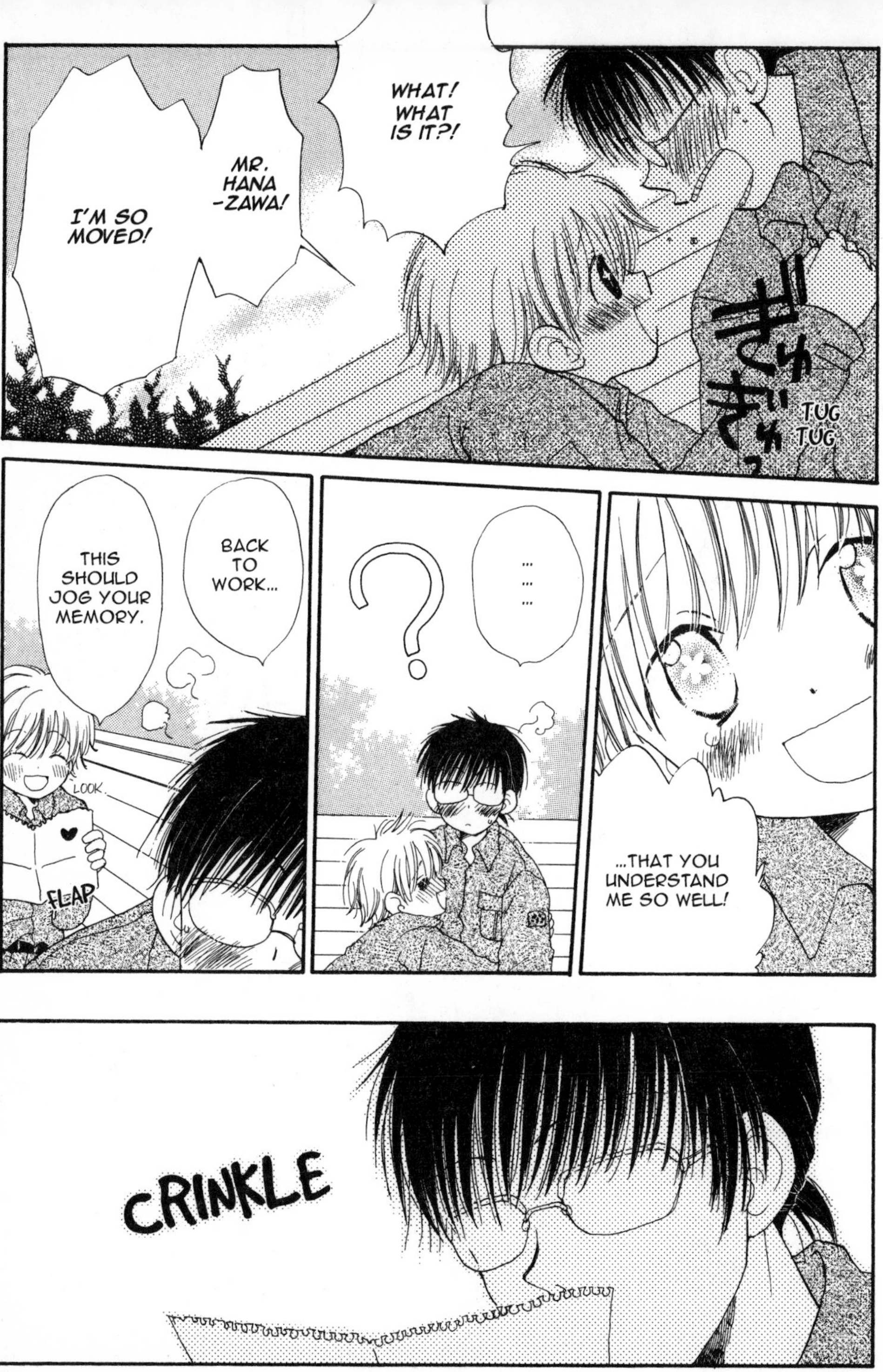
WHAT! WHAT IS IT?!
MR. HANA-ZAWA!
I'M SO MOVED!
TUG TUG
...THAT YOU UNDERSTAND ME SO WELL!
...
...
...
BACK TO WORK...
THIS SHOULD JOG YOUR MEMORY.
LOOK.
FLAP
CRINKLE

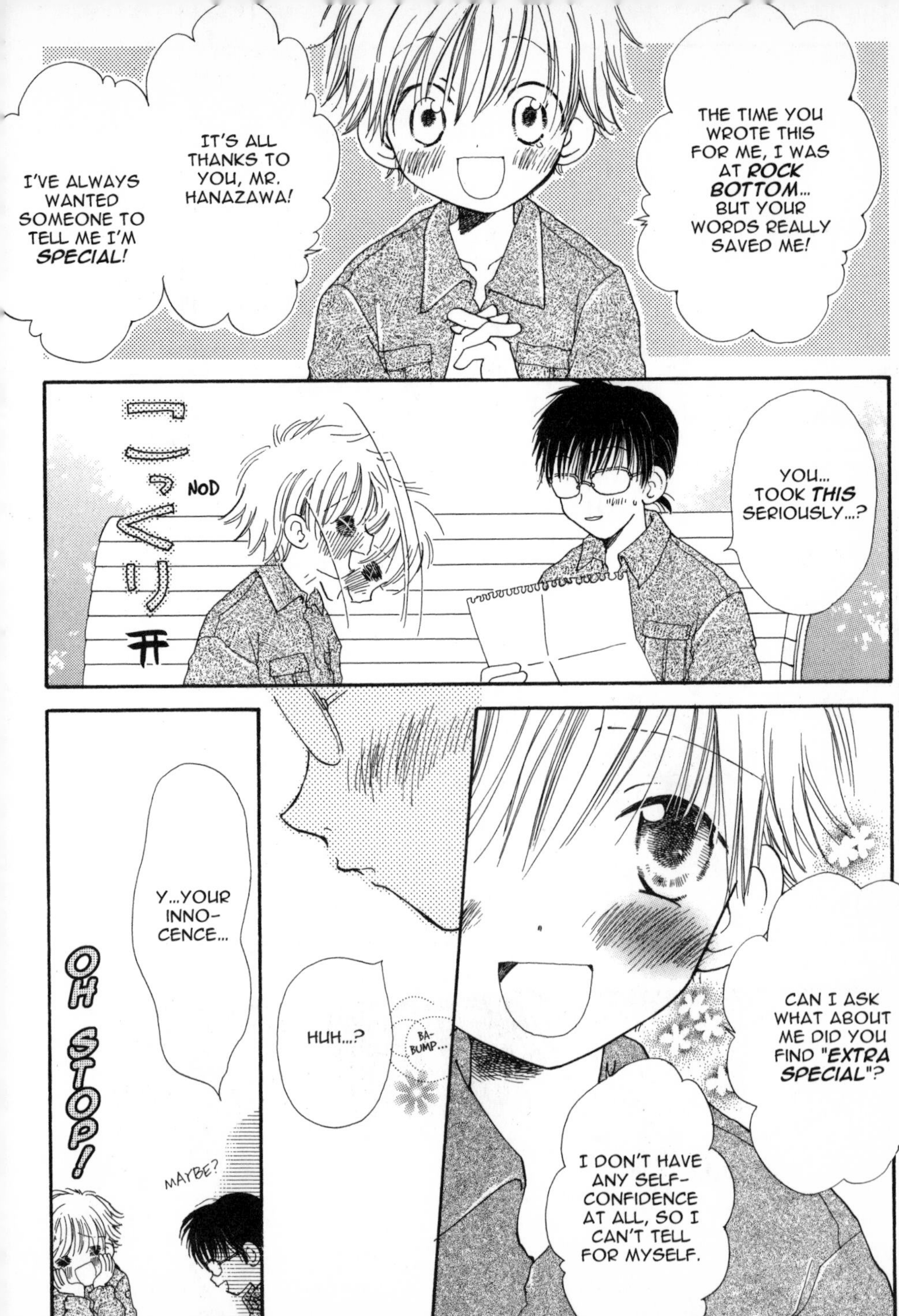
THE TIME YOU WROTE THIS FOR ME, I WAS AT ROCK BOTTOM... BUT YOUR WORDS REALLY SAVED ME!
IT'S ALL THANKS TO YOU, MR. HANAZAWA!
I'VE ALWAYS WANTED SOMEONE TO TELL ME I'M SPECIAL!
YOU... TOOK THIS SERIOUSLY...?
NOD
CAN I ASK WHAT ABOUT ME DID YOU FIND "EXTRA SPECIAL"?
I DON'T HAVE ANY SELF-CONFIDENCE AT ALL, SO I CAN'T TELL FOR MYSELF.
HUH...?
BA-BUMP...
Y...YOUR INNO-CENCE...
OH STOP!
MAYBE?

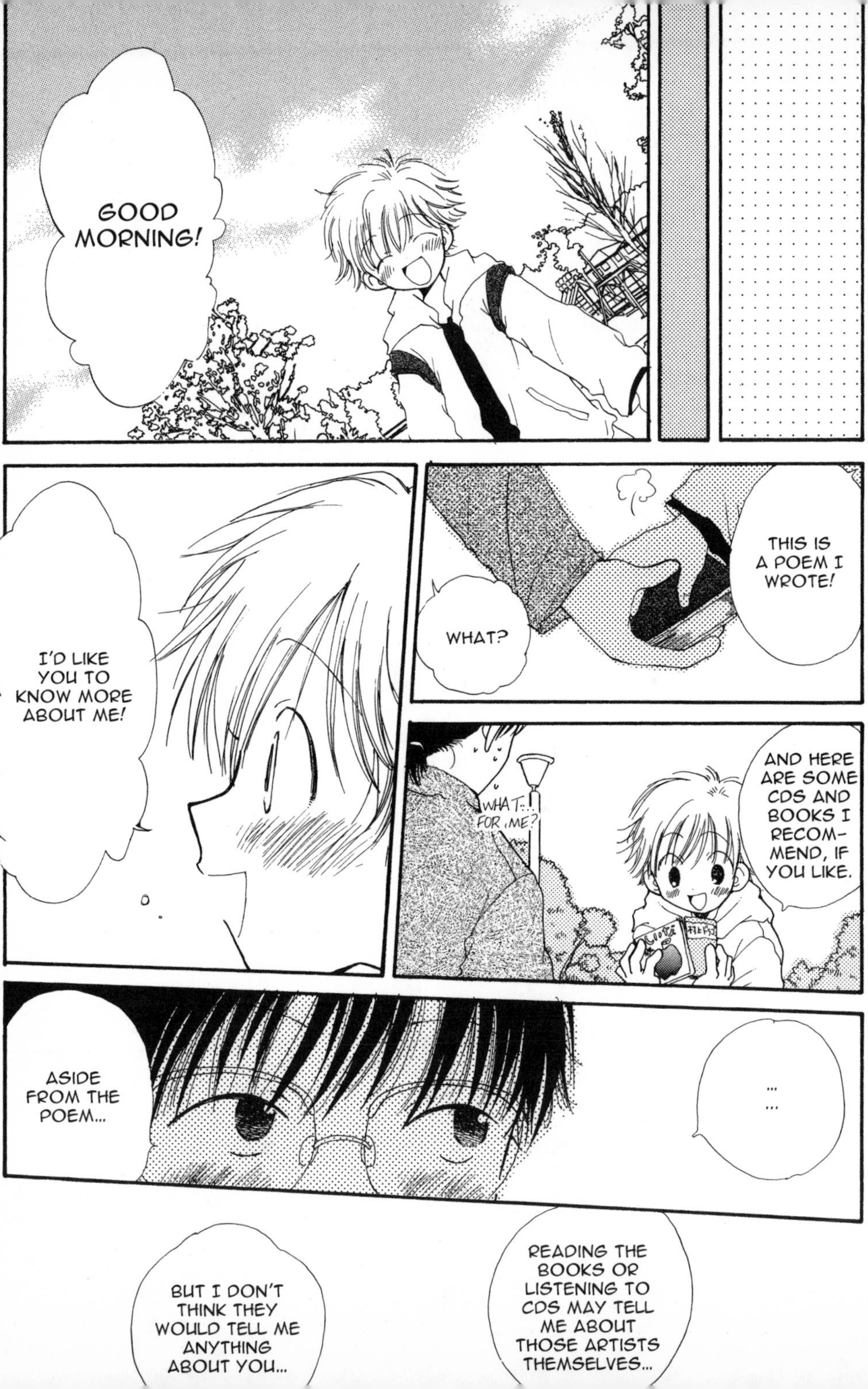
GOOD MORNING!
THIS IS A POEM I WROTE!
WHAT?
AND HERE ARE SOME CDS AND BOOKS I RECOMMEND, IF YOU LIKE.
WHAT... FOR ME?
I'D LIKE YOU TO KNOW MORE ABOUT ME!
... ...
ASIDE FROM THE POEM...
READING THE BOOKS OR LISTENING TO CDS MAY TELL ME ABOUT THOSE ARTISTS THEMSELVES...
BUT I DON'T THINK THEY WOULD TELL ME ANYTHING ABOUT YOU...

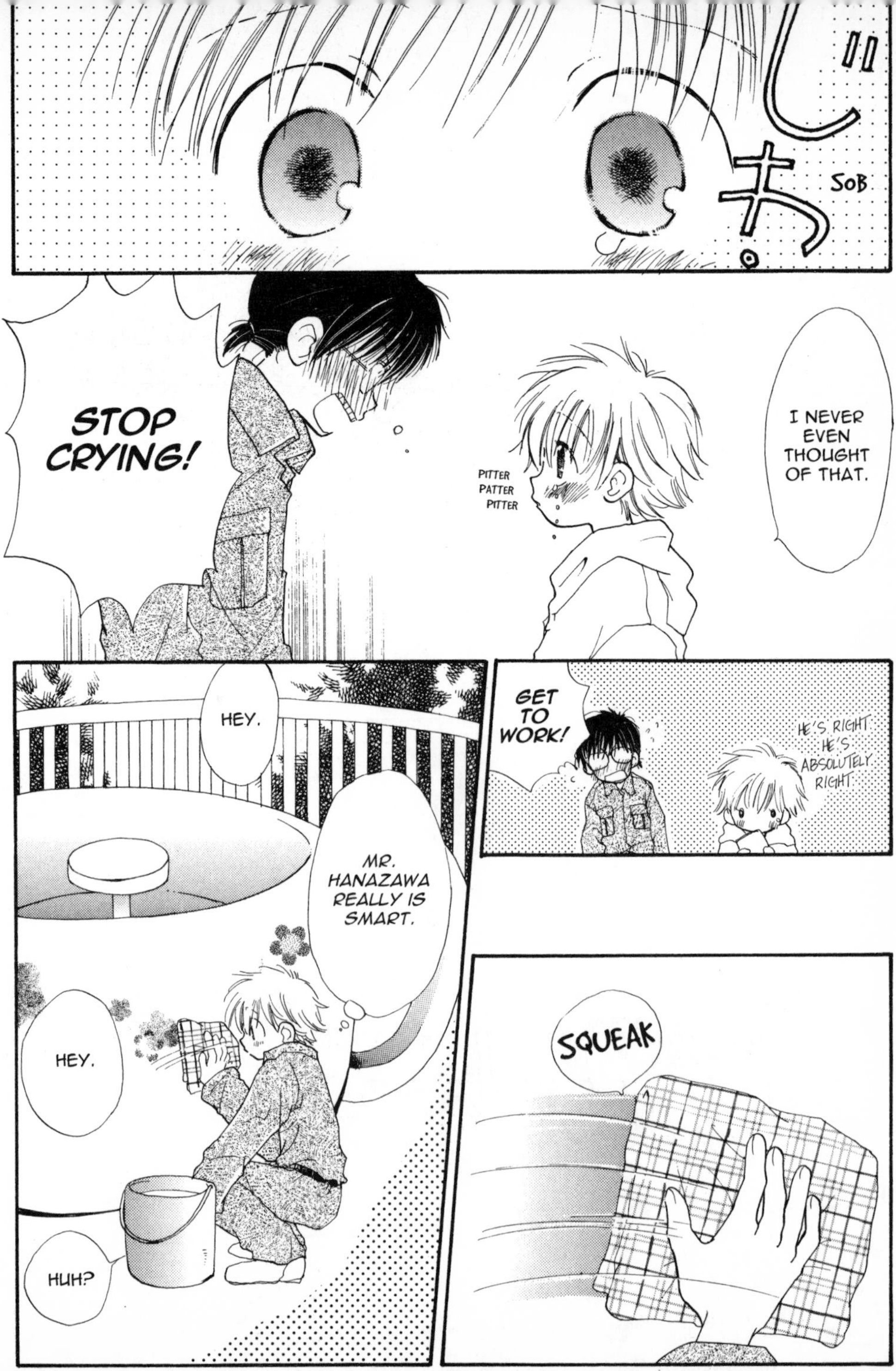
しお。
SOB
I NEVER EVEN THOUGHT OF THAT.
PITTER PATTER PITTER
STOP CRYING!
GET TO WORK!
HE'S RIGHT. HE'S ABSOLUTELY RIGHT.
SQUEAK
HEY.
MR. HANAZAWA REALLY IS SMART.
HEY.
HUH?

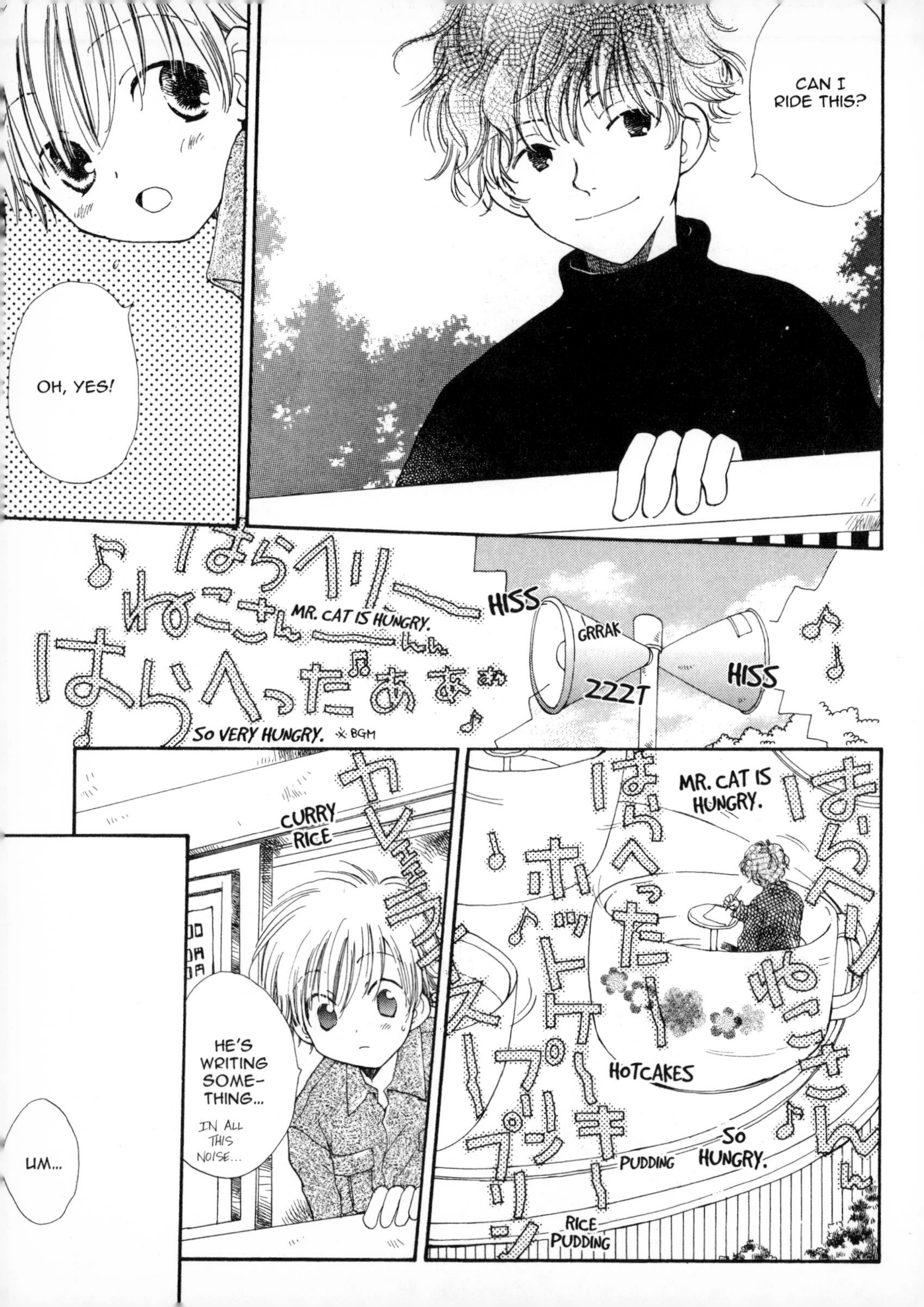
CAN I RIDE THIS?
OH, YES!
MR. CAT IS HUNGRY.
HISS
GRRAK
ZZZT
HISS
SO VERY HUNGRY.
※BGM
MR. CAT IS HUNGRY.
HOTCAKES
SO HUNGRY.
PUDDING
RICE PUDDING
CURRY RICE
HE'S WRITING SOMETHING...
IN ALL THIS NOISE...
UM...

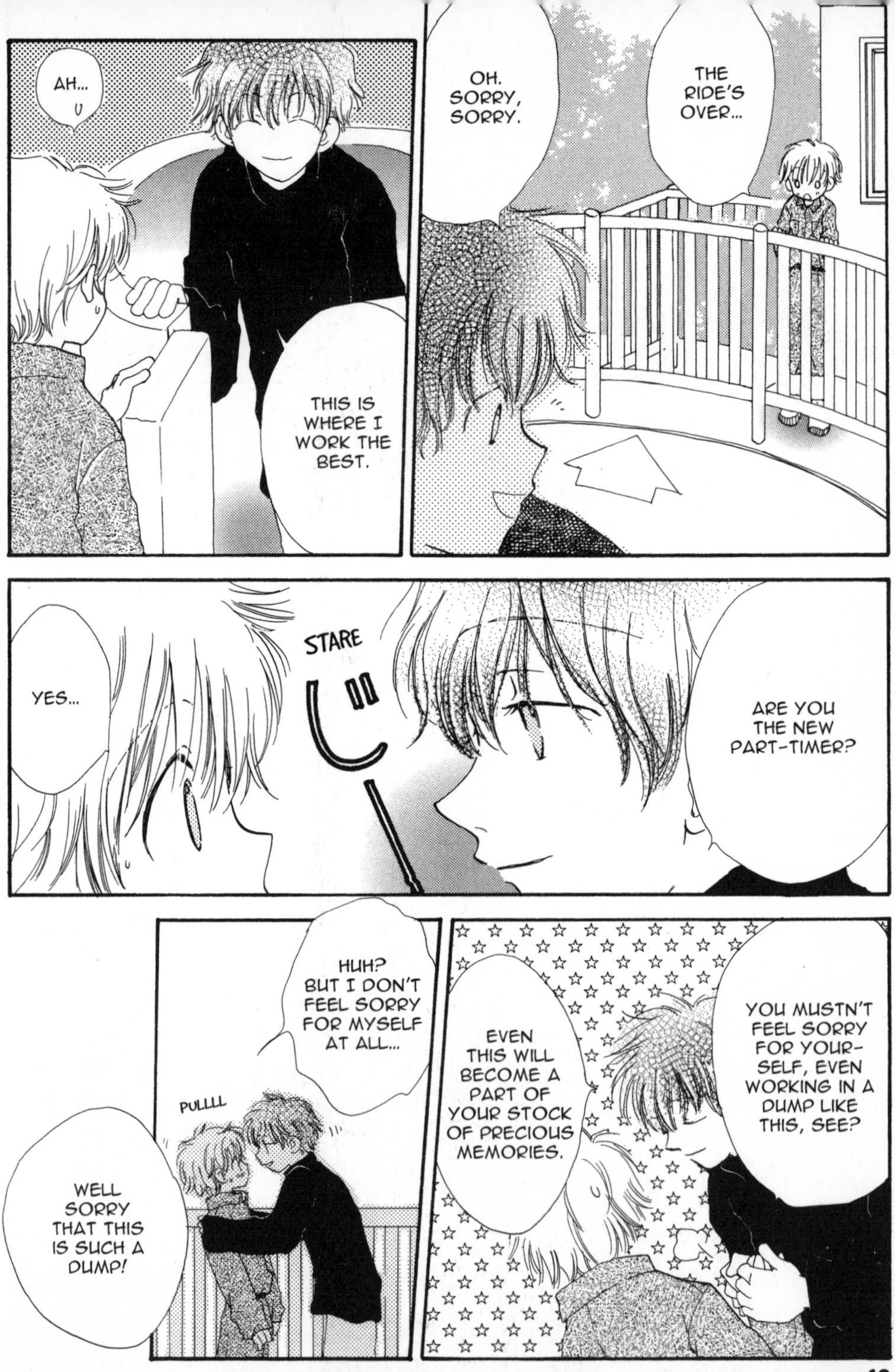
THE RIDE'S OVER...
OH. SORRY, SORRY.
AH...
THIS IS WHERE I WORK THE BEST.
ARE YOU THE NEW PART-TIMER?
STARE
YES...
YOU MUSTN'T FEEL SORRY FOR YOURSELF, EVEN WORKING IN A DUMP LIKE THIS, SEE?
EVEN THIS WILL BECOME A PART OF YOUR STOCK OF PRECIOUS MEMORIES.
HUH? BUT I DON'T FEEL SORRY FOR MYSELF AT ALL...
PULLLL
WELL SORRY THAT THIS IS SUCH A DUMP!

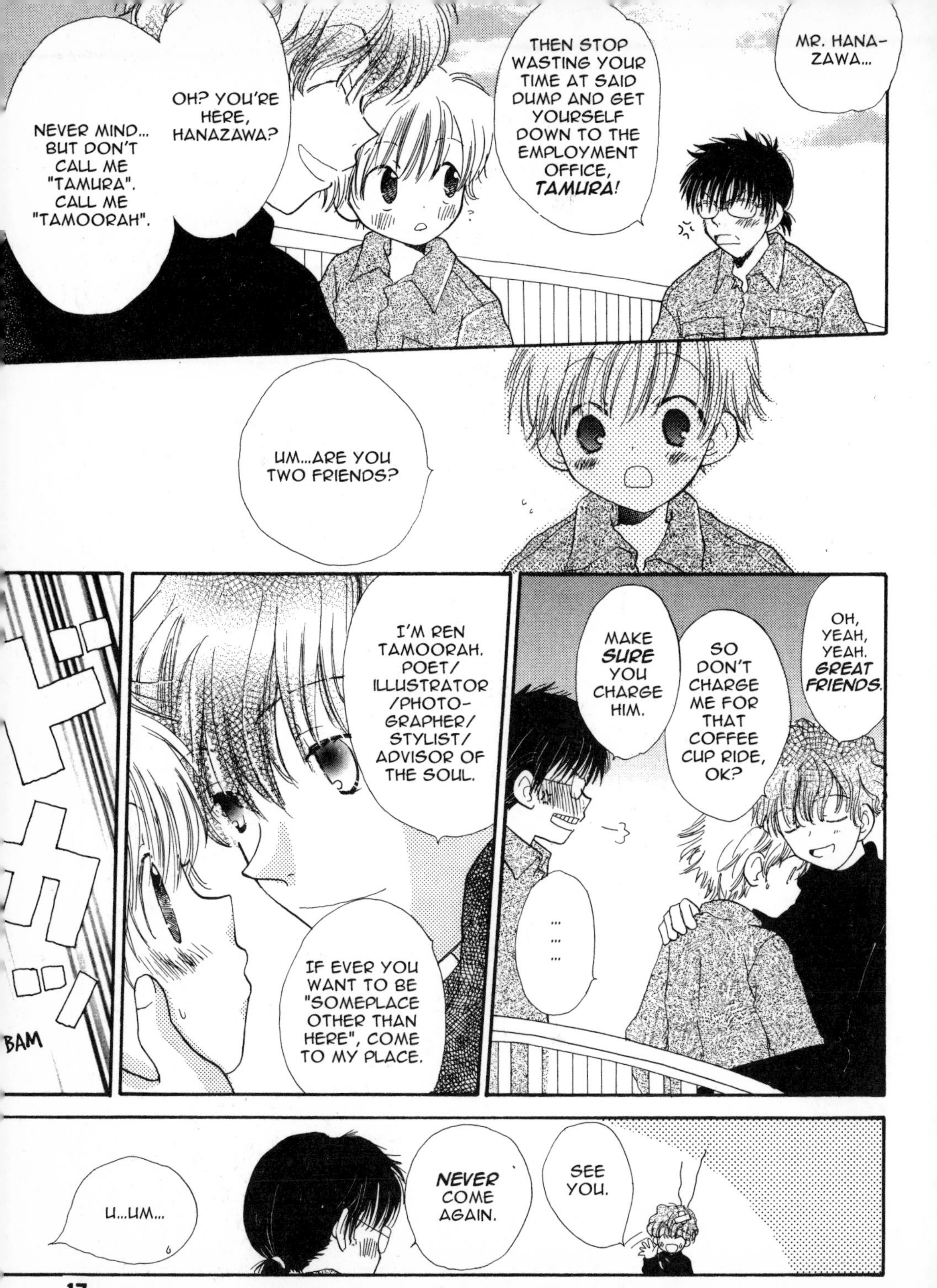
MR. HANA-ZAWA...
THEN STOP WASTING YOUR TIME AT SAID DUMP AND GET YOURSELF DOWN TO THE EMPLOYMENT OFFICE, ***TAMURA!***
OH? YOU'RE HERE, HANAZAWA?
NEVER MIND... BUT DON'T CALL ME "TAMURA". CALL ME "TAMOORAH".
UM...ARE YOU TWO FRIENDS?
OH, YEAH, YEAH. ***GREAT FRIENDS.***
SO DON'T CHARGE ME FOR THAT COFFEE CUP RIDE, OK?
MAKE ***SURE*** YOU CHARGE HIM.
... ...
I'M REN TAMOORAH. POET/ ILLUSTRATOR /PHOTO-GRAPHER/ STYLIST/ ADVISOR OF THE SOUL.
IF EVER YOU WANT TO BE "SOMEPLACE OTHER THAN HERE", COME TO MY PLACE.
BAM
SEE YOU.
NEVER COME AGAIN.
U...UM...

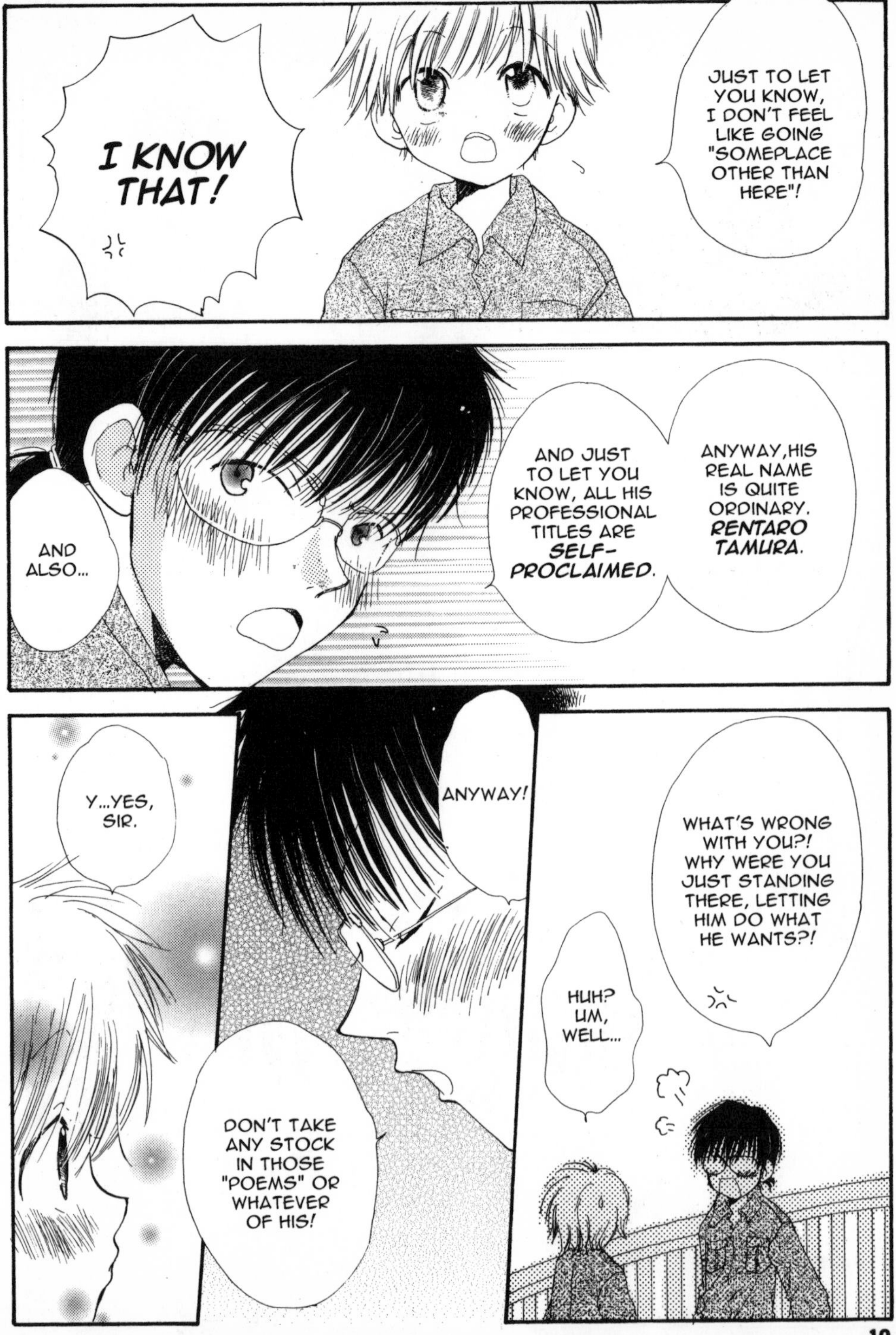
JUST TO LET YOU KNOW, I DON'T FEEL LIKE GOING "SOMEPLACE OTHER THAN HERE"!
I KNOW THAT!
ANYWAY, HIS REAL NAME IS QUITE ORDINARY. RENTARO TAMURA.
AND JUST TO LET YOU KNOW, ALL HIS PROFESSIONAL TITLES ARE SELF-PROCLAIMED.
AND ALSO...
WHAT'S WRONG WITH YOU?! WHY WERE YOU JUST STANDING THERE, LETTING HIM DO WHAT HE WANTS?!
HUH? UM, WELL...
ANYWAY!
DON'T TAKE ANY STOCK IN THOSE "POEMS" OR WHATEVER OF HIS!
Y...YES, SIR.

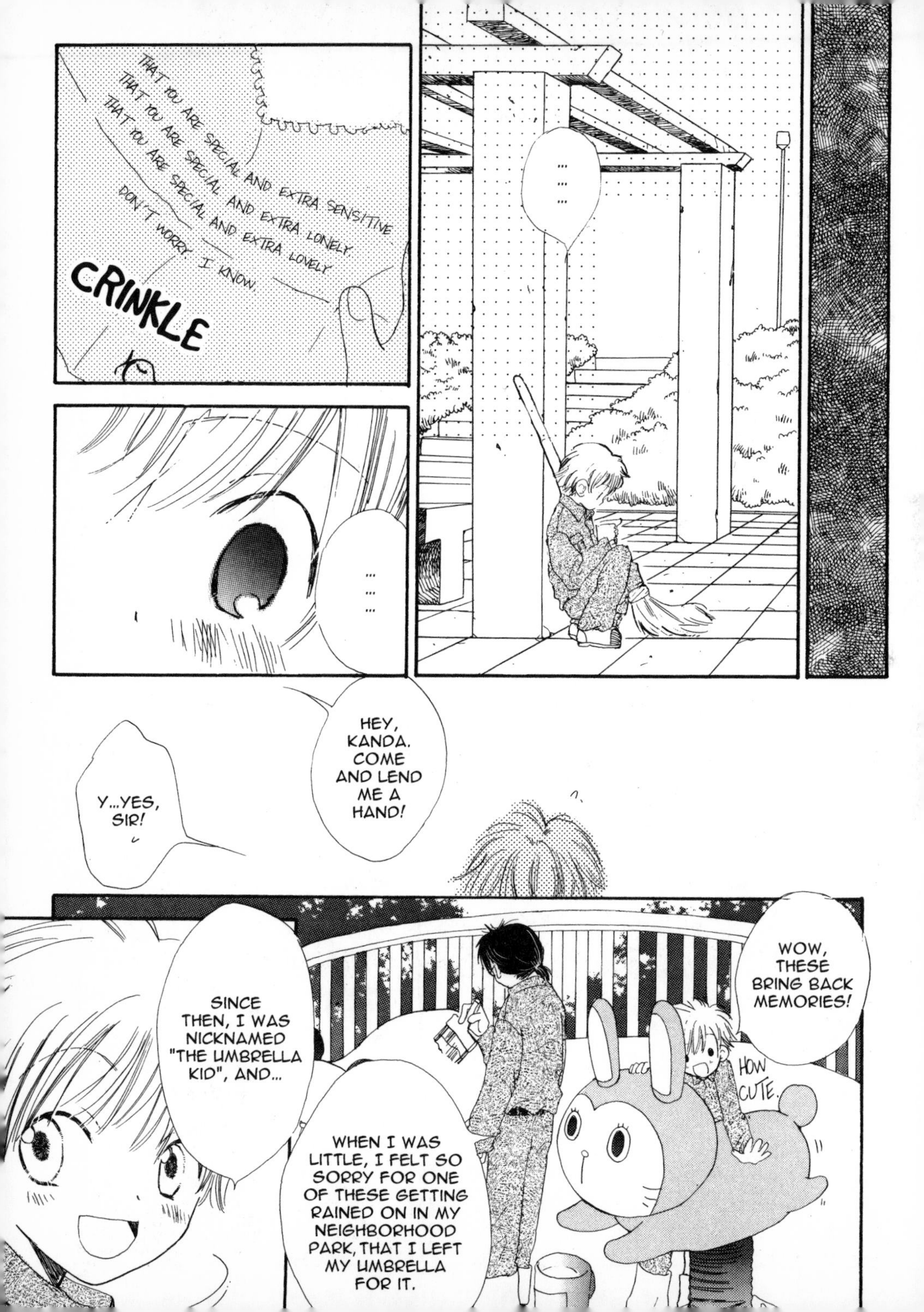
...
...
...
THAT YOU ARE SPECIAL AND EXTRA SENSITIVE
THAT YOU ARE SPECIAL AND EXTRA LONELY
THAT YOU ARE SPECIAL AND EXTRA LONELY
DON'T WORRY. I KNOW.
CRINKLE
...
...
...
HEY, KANDA. COME AND LEND ME A HAND!
Y...YES, SIR!
WOW, THESE BRING BACK MEMORIES!
HOW CUTE.
WHEN I WAS LITTLE, I FELT SO SORRY FOR ONE OF THESE GETTING RAINED ON IN MY NEIGHBORHOOD PARK, THAT I LEFT MY UMBRELLA FOR IT.
SINCE THEN, I WAS NICKNAMED "THE UMBRELLA KID", AND...

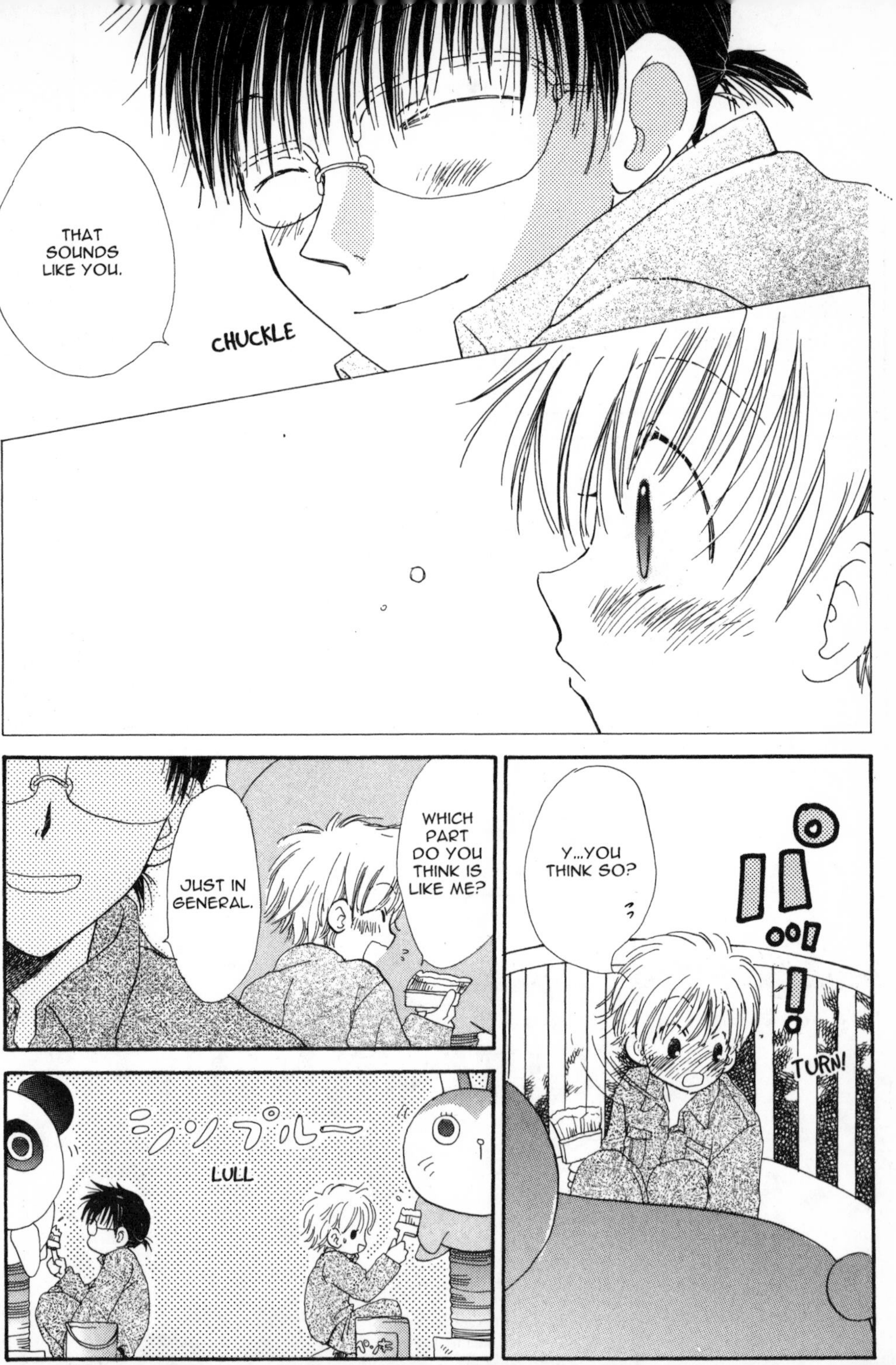
THAT SOUNDS LIKE YOU.
CHUCKLE
Y...YOU THINK SO?
TURN!
WHICH PART DO YOU THINK IS LIKE ME?
JUST IN GENERAL.
LULL

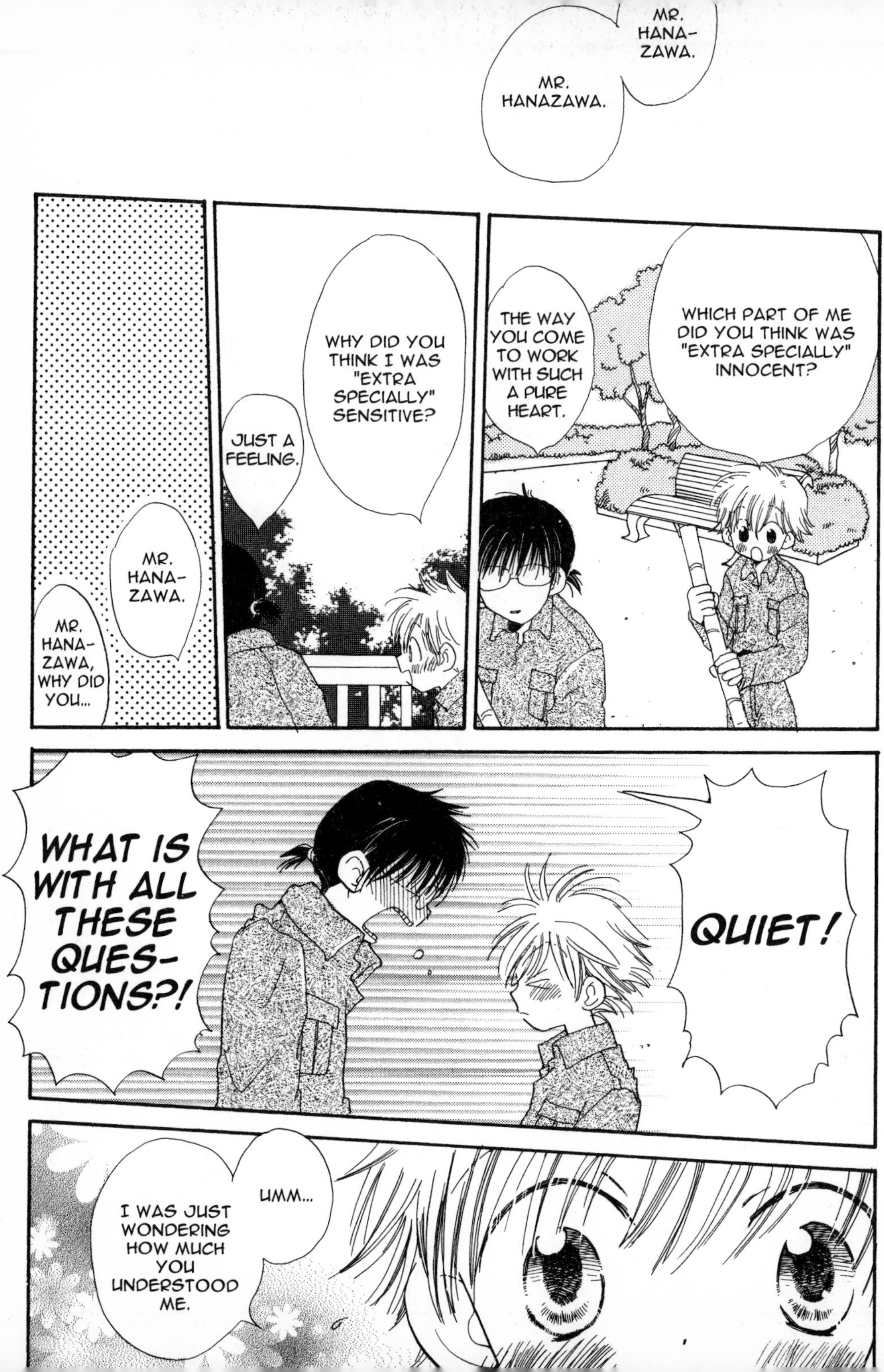
MR. HANA-ZAWA.
MR. HANAZAWA.
WHICH PART OF ME DID YOU THINK WAS "EXTRA SPECIALLY" INNOCENT?
THE WAY YOU COME TO WORK WITH SUCH A PURE HEART.
WHY DID YOU THINK I WAS "EXTRA SPECIALLY" SENSITIVE?
JUST A FEELING.
MR. HANA-ZAWA.
MR. HANA-ZAWA, WHY DID YOU...
QUIET!
WHAT IS WITH ALL THESE QUES-TIONS?!
UMM...
I WAS JUST WONDERING HOW MUCH YOU UNDERSTOOD ME.

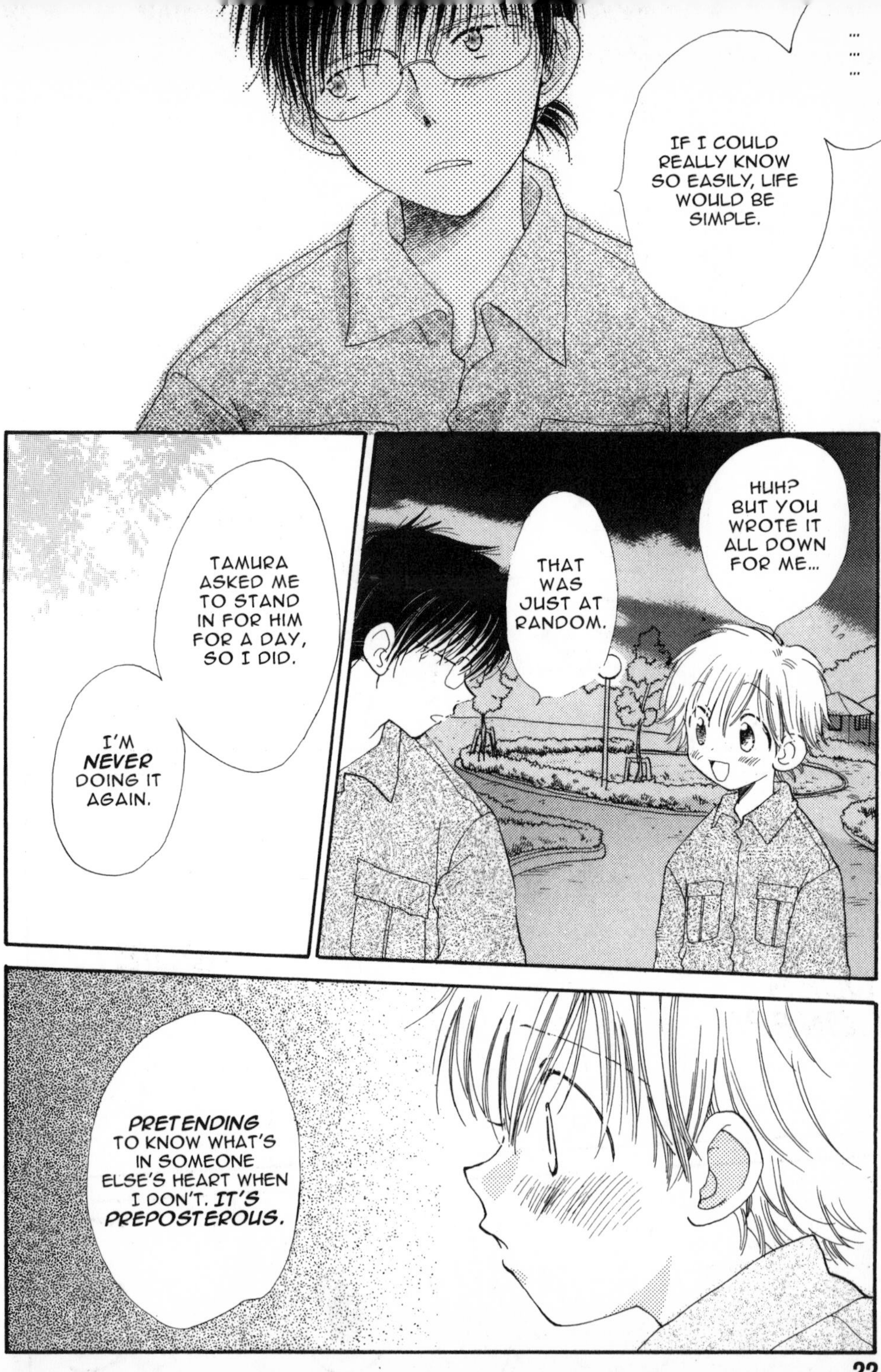

....
IF I COULD REALLY KNOW SO EASILY, LIFE WOULD BE SIMPLE.
HUH? BUT YOU WROTE IT ALL DOWN FOR ME...
THAT WAS JUST AT RANDOM.
TAMURA ASKED ME TO STAND IN FOR HIM FOR A DAY, SO I DID.
I'M *NEVER* DOING IT AGAIN.
PRETENDING TO KNOW WHAT'S IN SOMEONE ELSE'S HEART WHEN I DON'T. *IT'S PREPOSTEROUS.*

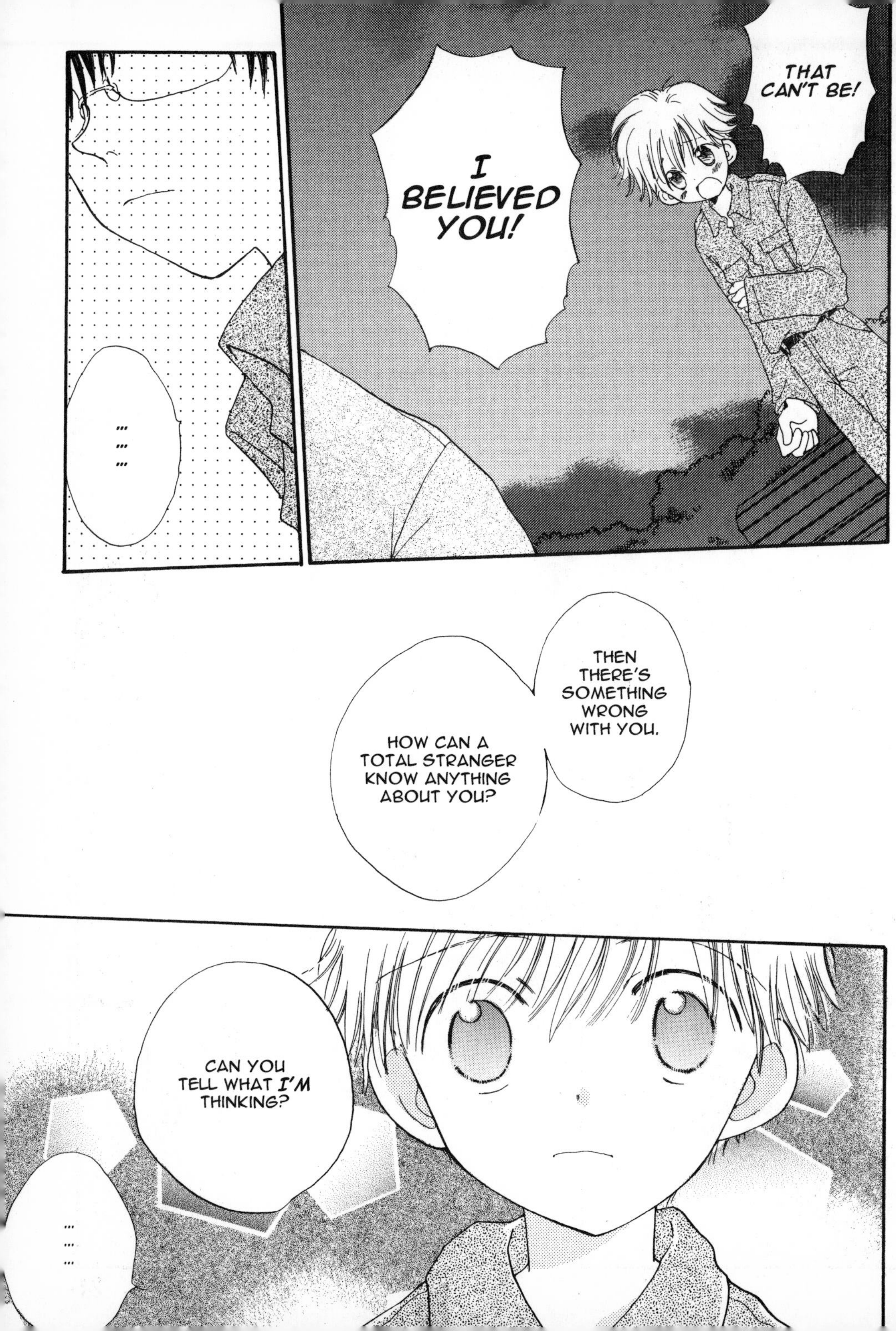
THAT CAN'T BE!
I BELIEVED YOU!
...
...
...
THEN THERE'S SOMETHING WRONG WITH YOU.
HOW CAN A TOTAL STRANGER KNOW ANYTHING ABOUT YOU?
CAN YOU TELL WHAT *I'M* THINKING?
...
...
...

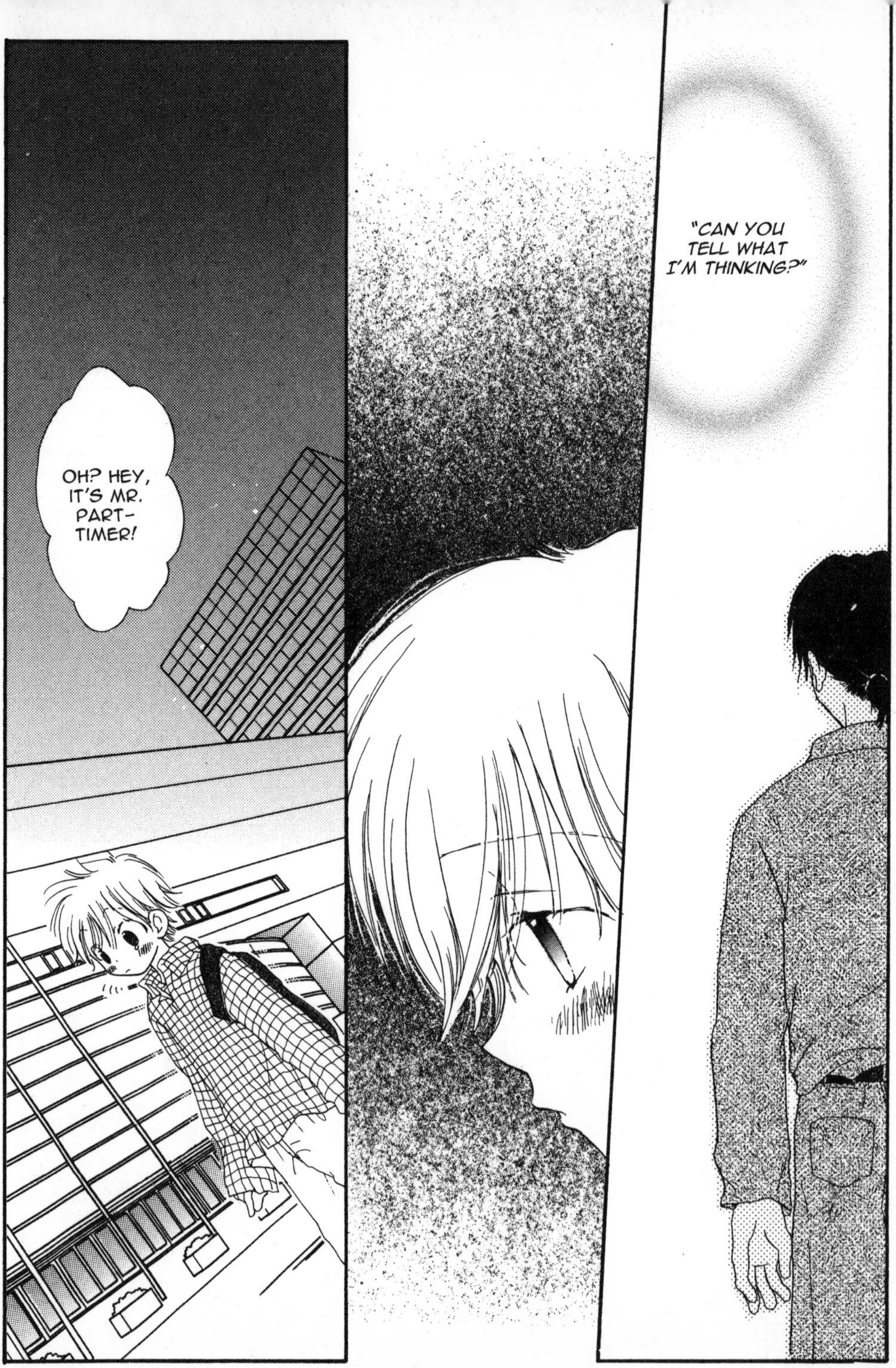
"CAN YOU TELL WHAT I'M THINKING?"
OH? HEY, IT'S MR. PART-TIMER!

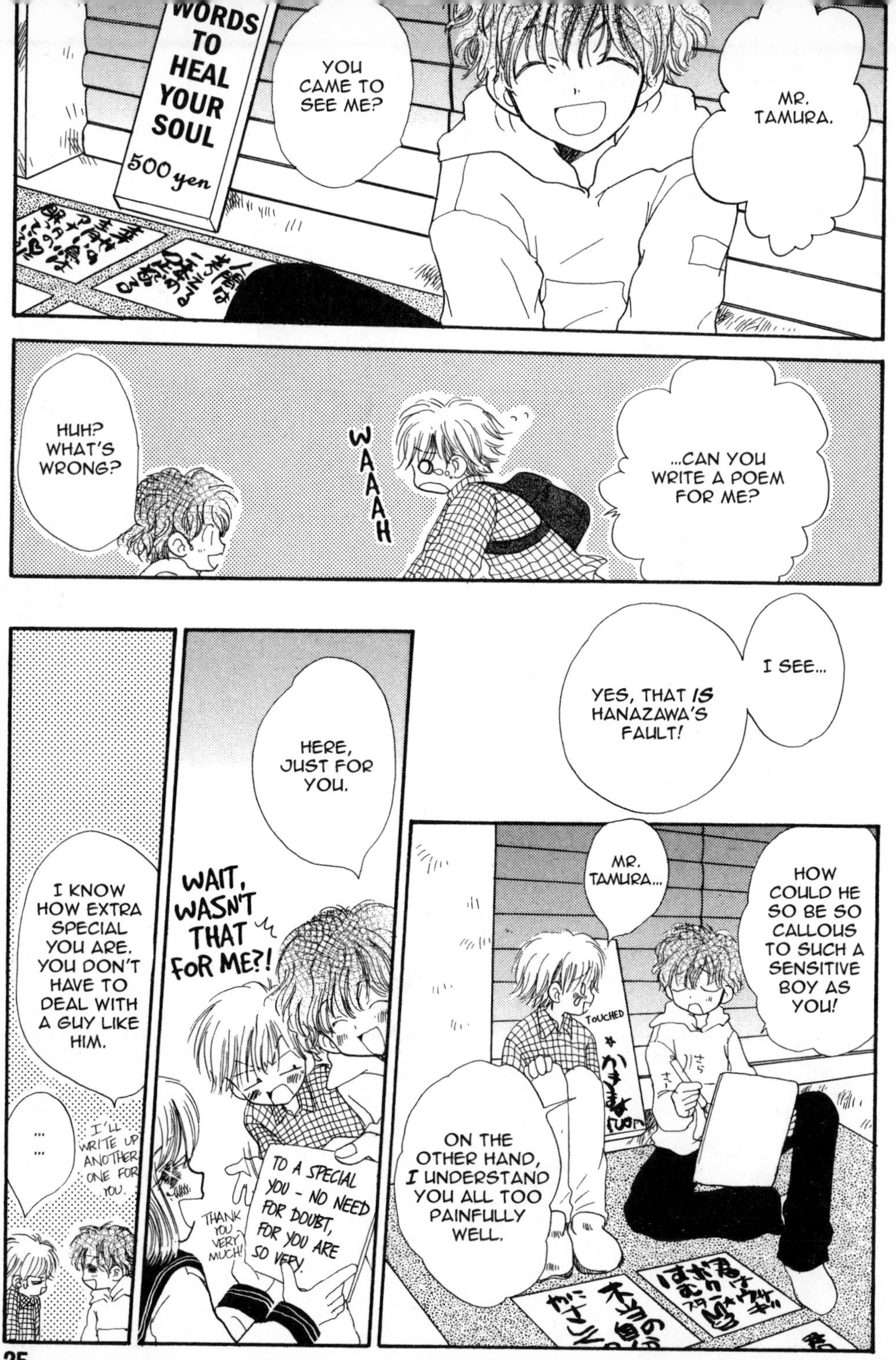
MR. TAMURA.
YOU CAME TO SEE ME?
WORDS TO HEAL YOUR SOUL
500 yen
...CAN YOU WRITE A POEM FOR ME?
WAAAAH
HUH? WHAT'S WRONG?
I SEE...
YES, THAT *IS* HANAZAWA'S FAULT!
HOW COULD HE SO BE SO CALLOUS TO SUCH A SENSITIVE BOY AS YOU!
MR. TAMURA...
TOUCHED
ON THE OTHER HAND, *I* UNDERSTAND YOU ALL TOO PAINFULLY WELL.
HERE, JUST FOR YOU.
WAIT, WASN'T THAT FOR ME?!
TO A SPECIAL YOU - NO NEED FOR DOUBT, FOR YOU ARE SO VERY.
THANK YOU VERY MUCH!
I KNOW HOW EXTRA SPECIAL YOU ARE. YOU DON'T HAVE TO DEAL WITH A GUY LIKE HIM.
I'LL WRITE UP ANOTHER ONE FOR YOU.
... ...

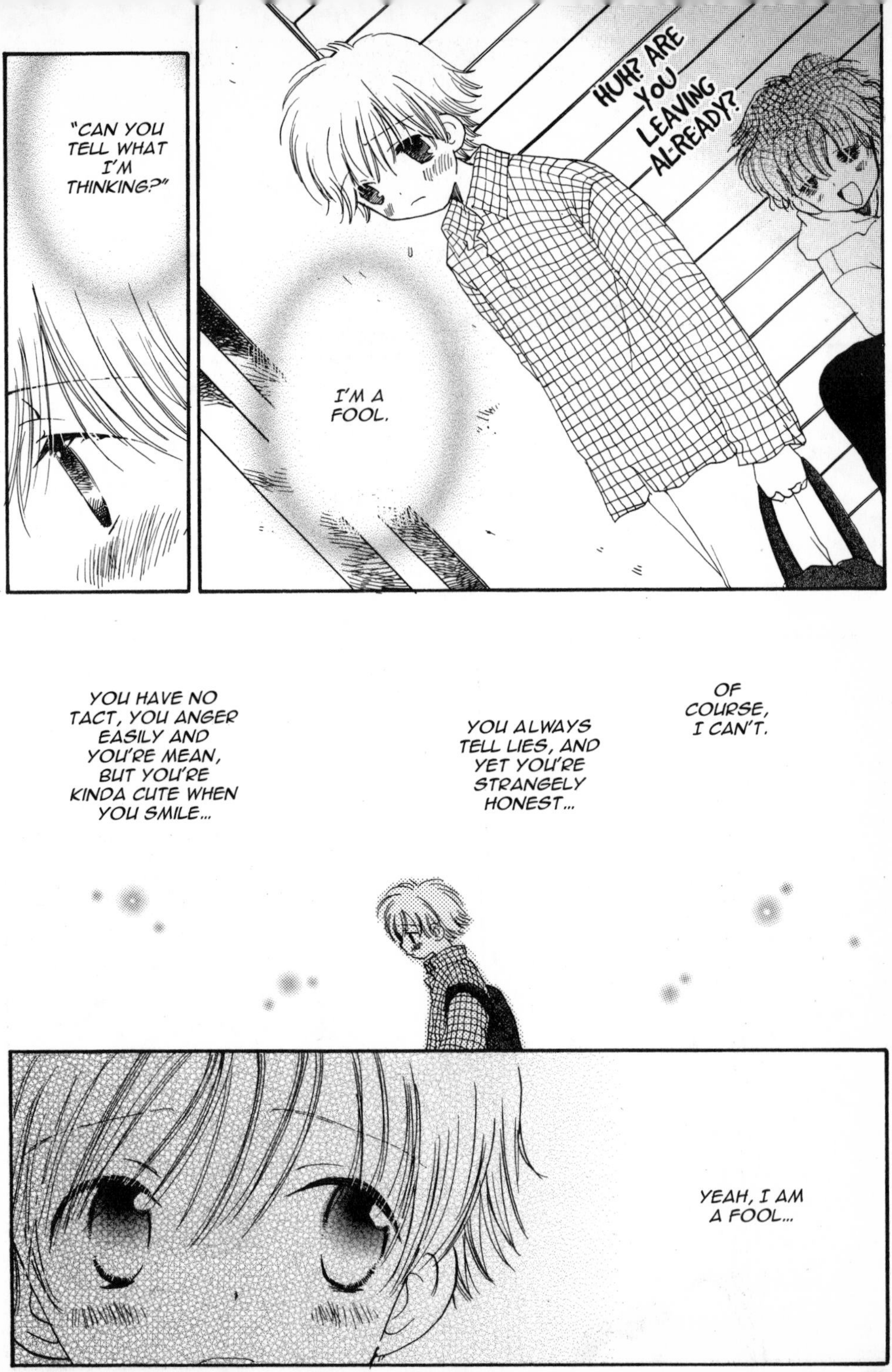
HUH? ARE YOU LEAVING AL-READY?
I'M A FOOL.
"CAN YOU TELL WHAT I'M THINKING?"
OF COURSE, I CAN'T.
YOU ALWAYS TELL LIES, AND YET YOU'RE STRANGELY HONEST...
YOU HAVE NO TACT, YOU ANGER EASILY AND YOU'RE MEAN, BUT YOU'RE KINDA CUTE WHEN YOU SMILE...
YEAH, I AM A FOOL...

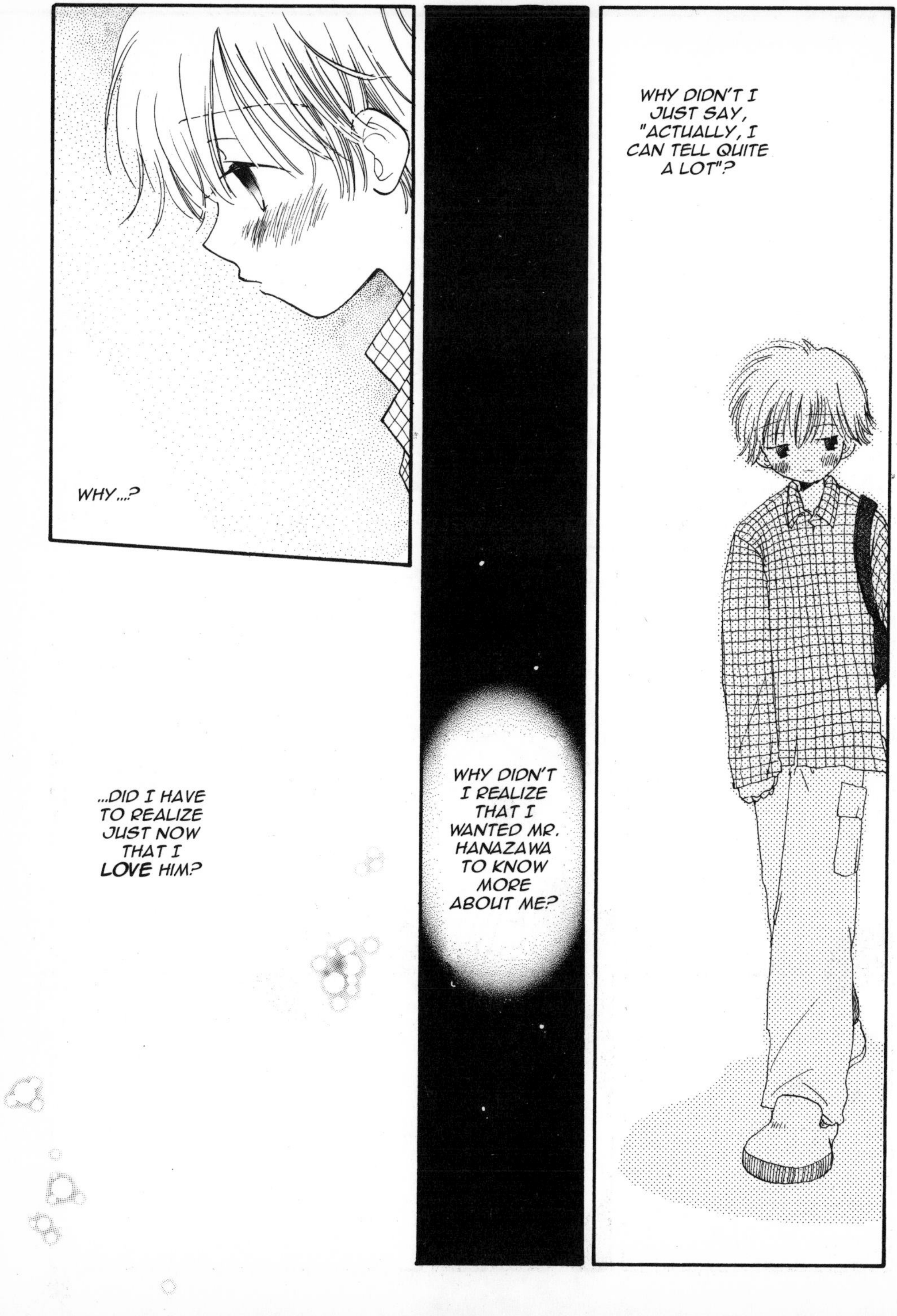
WHY DIDN'T I JUST SAY, "ACTUALLY, I CAN TELL QUITE A LOT"?
WHY DIDN'T I REALIZE THAT I WANTED MR. HANAZAWA TO KNOW MORE ABOUT ME?
WHY...?
...DID I HAVE TO REALIZE JUST NOW THAT I **LOVE** HIM?

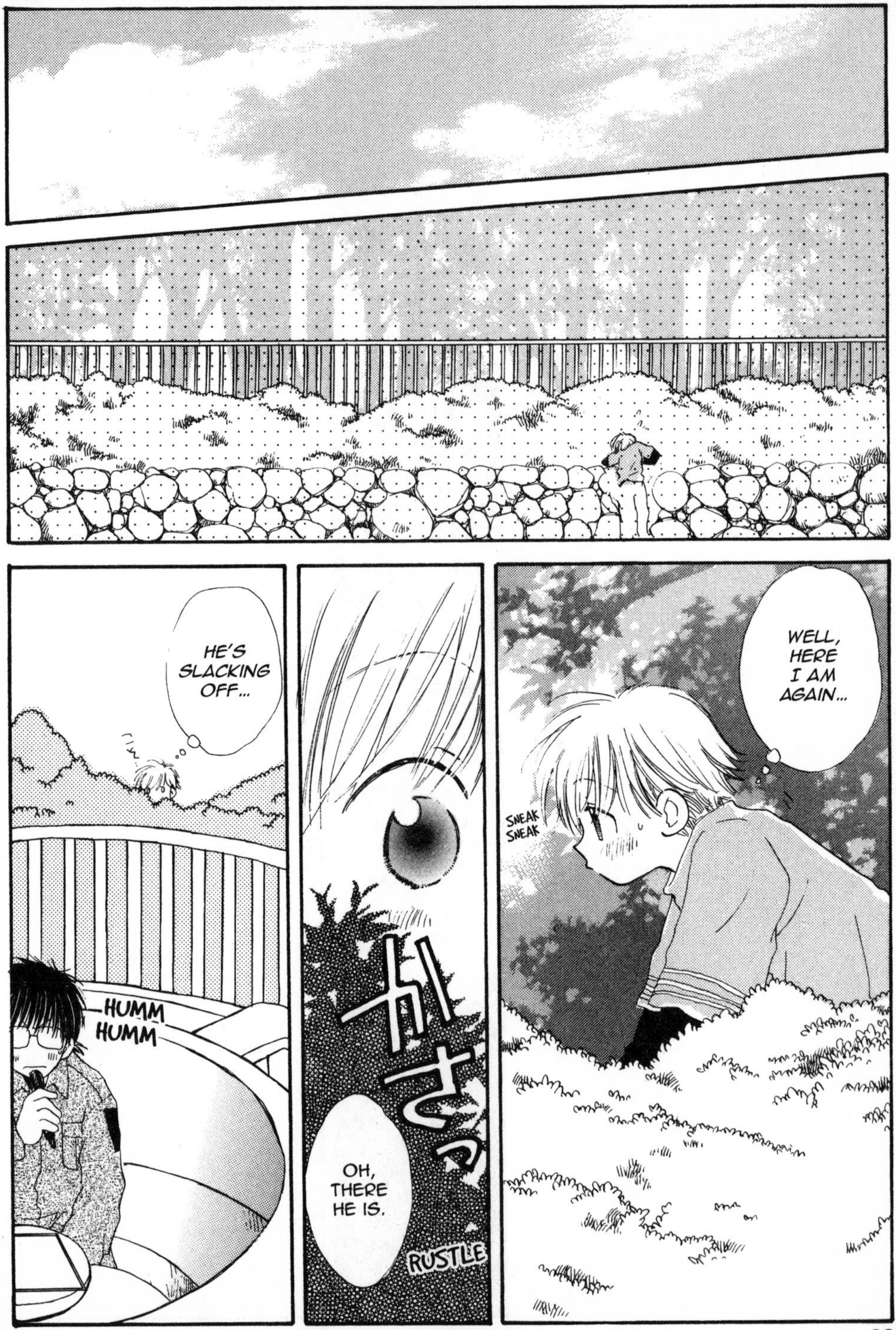
WELL, HERE I AM AGAIN...
SNEAK SNEAK
かさっ
OH, THERE HE IS.
RUSTLE
HE'S SLACKING OFF...
HUMM HUMM

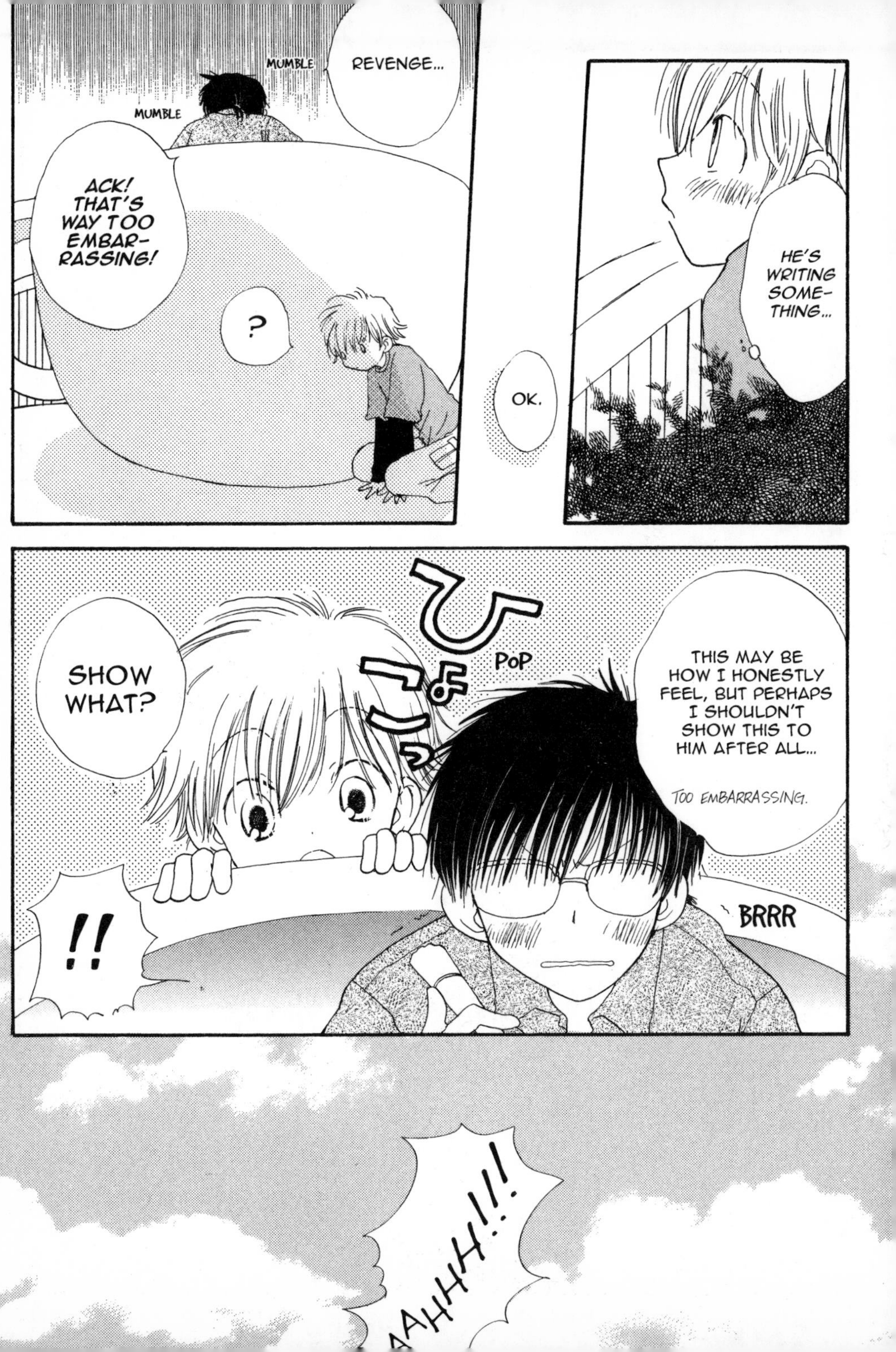
HE'S WRITING SOME-THING...
OK.
REVENGE...
MUMBLE
MUMBLE
ACK! THAT'S WAY TOO EMBAR-RASSING!
?
THIS MAY BE HOW I HONESTLY FEEL, BUT PERHAPS I SHOULDN'T SHOW THIS TO HIM AFTER ALL...
TOO EMBARRASSING.
BRRR
POP
ひょこっ
SHOW WHAT?
!!
AAHH!!!

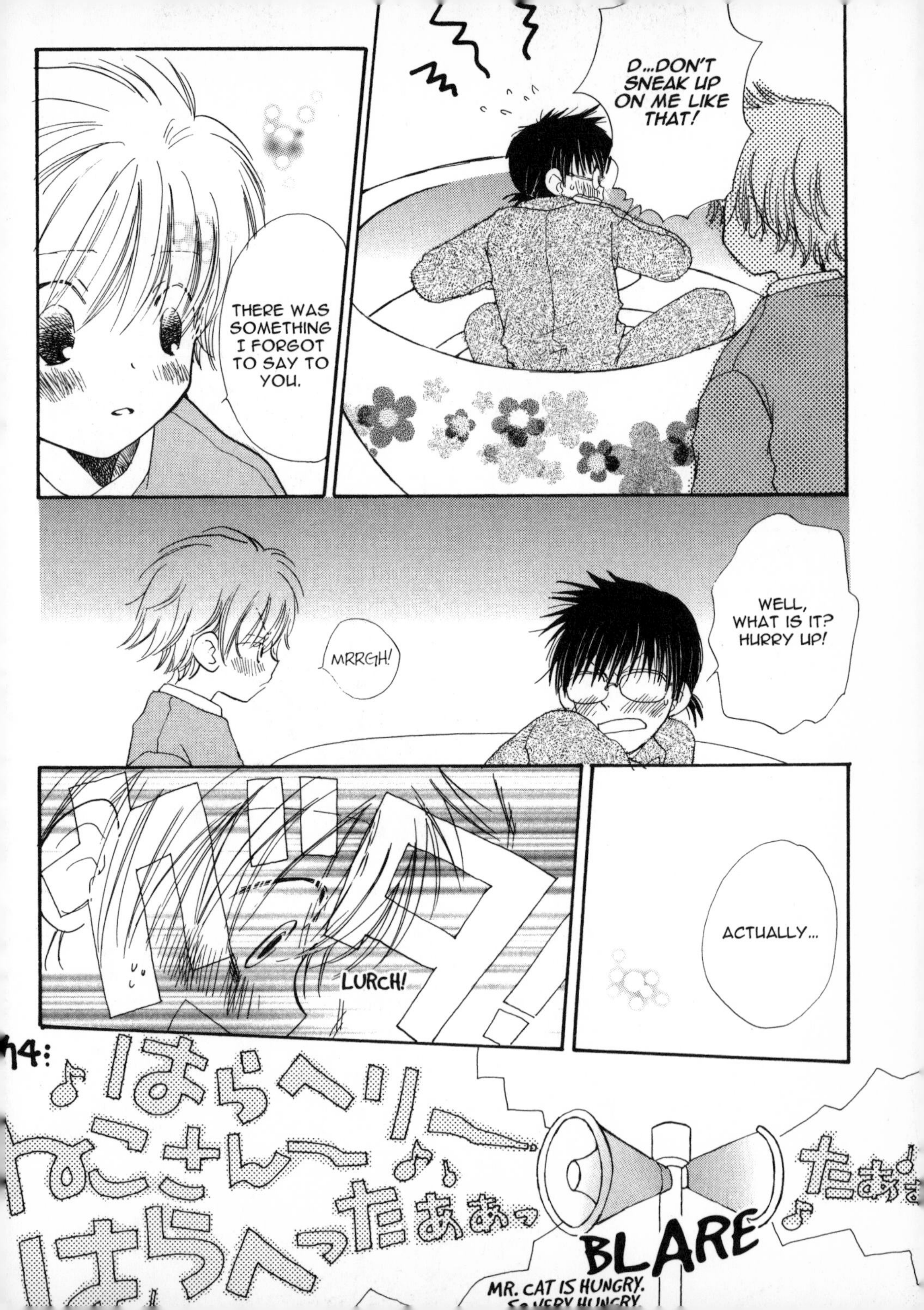
D...DON'T SNEAK UP ON ME LIKE THAT!
THERE WAS SOMETHING I FORGOT TO SAY TO YOU.
WELL, WHAT IS IT? HURRY UP!
MRRGH!
ACTUALLY...
LURCH!
はらへり〜
はらへったあぁっ
BLARE
MR. CAT IS HUNGRY.

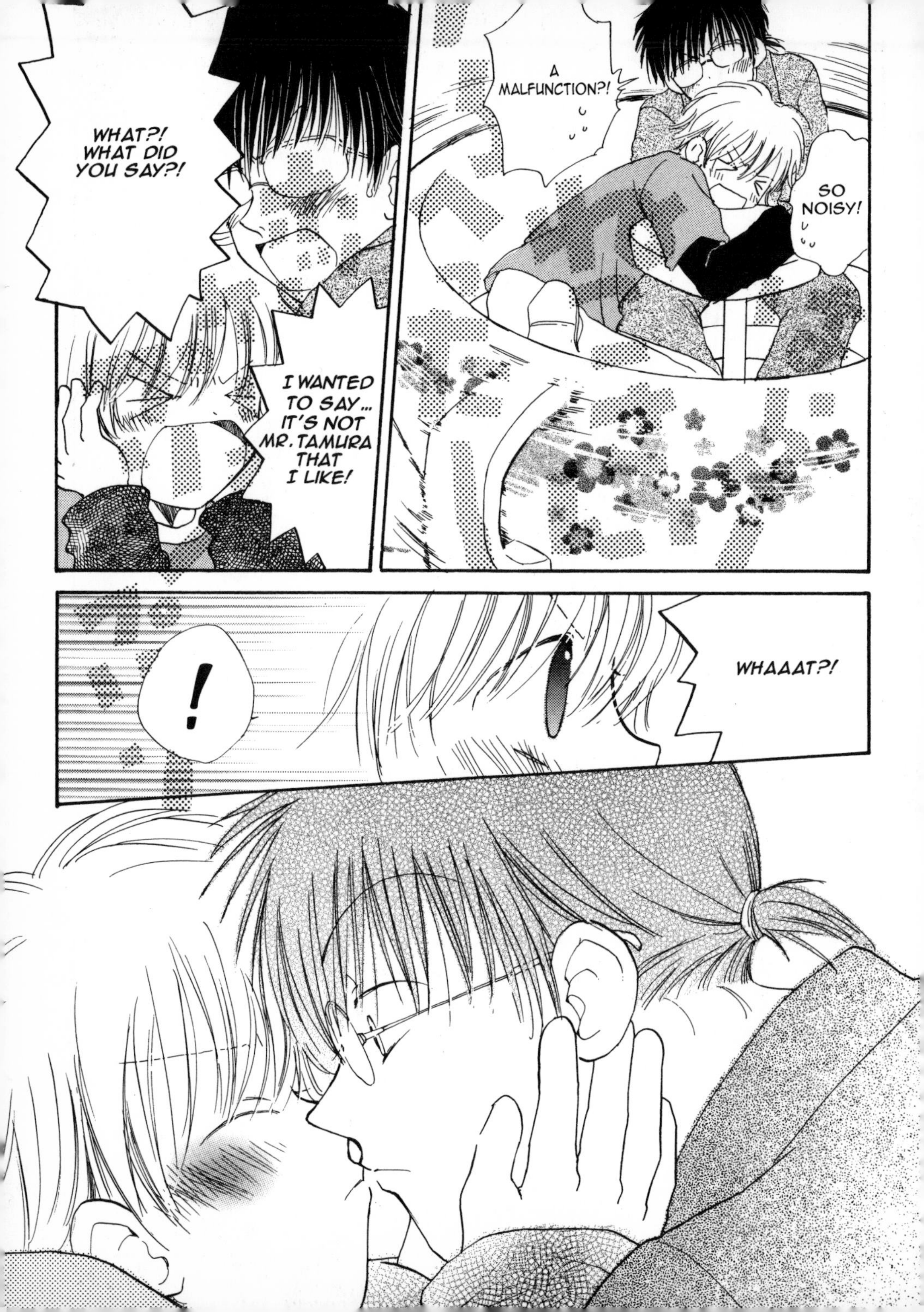
A MALFUNCTION?!
SO NOISY!
WHAT?! WHAT DID YOU SAY?!
I WANTED TO SAY... IT'S NOT MR. TAMURA THAT I LIKE!
WHAAAT?!
!

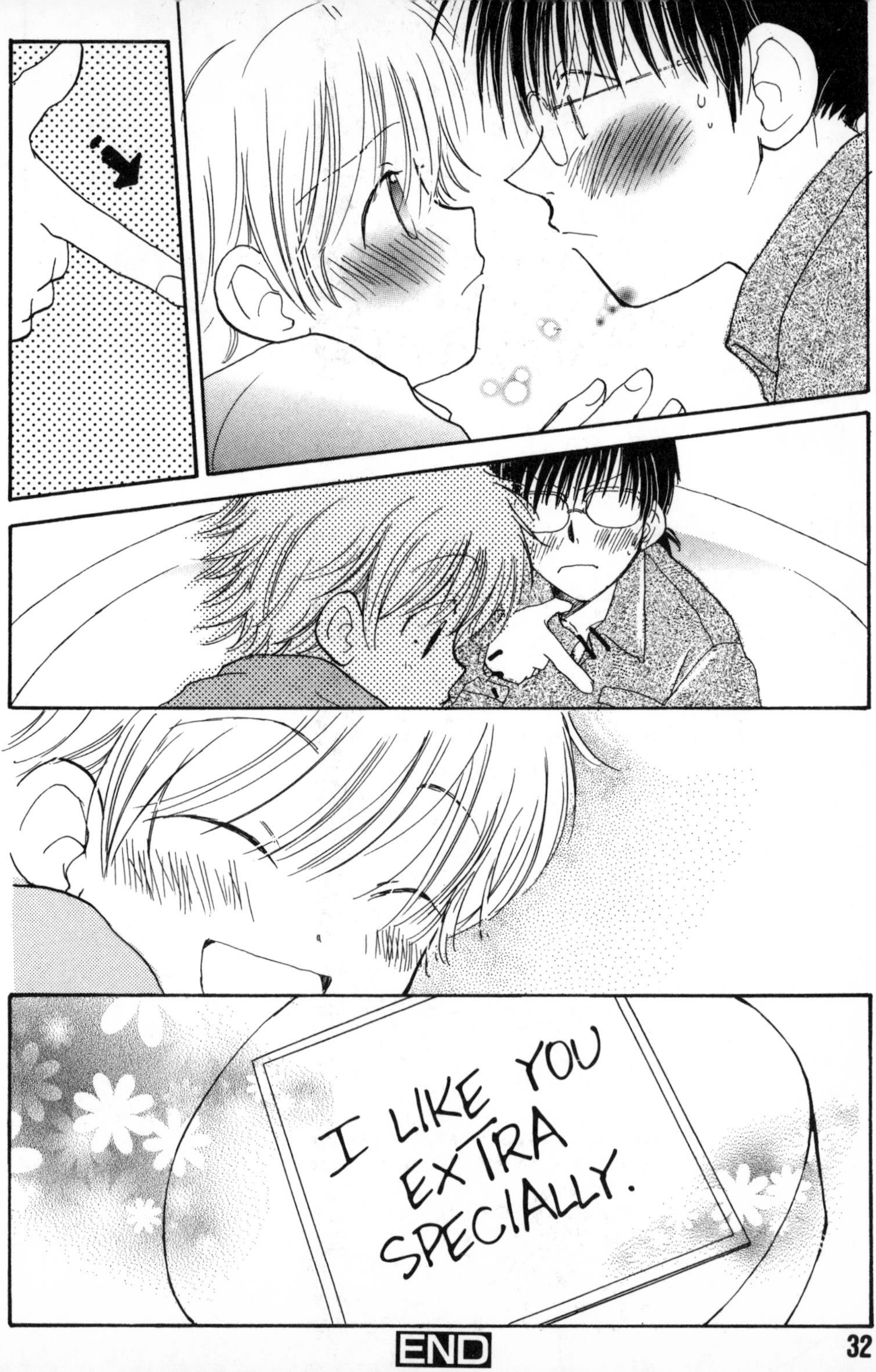
I LIKE YOU EXTRA SPECIALLY.
END

THE MER-PRINCE

THE LITTLE MERMAID'S BROTHERS AND SISTERS CAME TO HELP HER. "NOW, WITH THIS KNIFE, STAB THE PRINCE'S HEART."

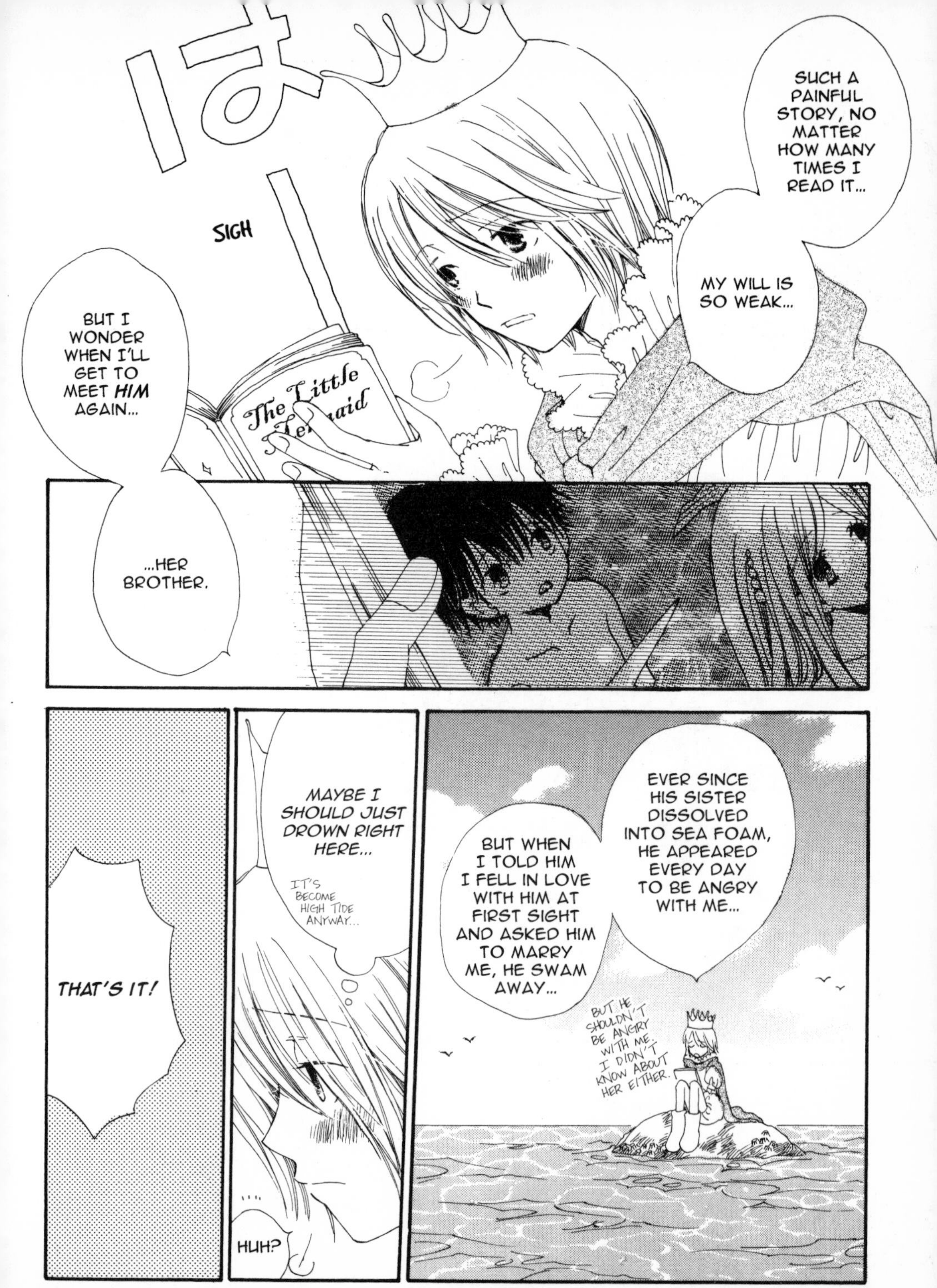
SUCH A PAINFUL STORY, NO MATTER HOW MANY TIMES I READ IT...
MY WILL IS SO WEAK...
は
SIGH
BUT I WONDER WHEN I'LL GET TO MEET HIM AGAIN...
The Little Mermaid
...HER BROTHER.
EVER SINCE HIS SISTER DISSOLVED INTO SEA FOAM, HE APPEARED EVERY DAY TO BE ANGRY WITH ME...
BUT WHEN I TOLD HIM I FELL IN LOVE WITH HIM AT FIRST SIGHT AND ASKED HIM TO MARRY ME, HE SWAM AWAY...
BUT HE SHOULDN'T BE ANGRY WITH ME. I DIDN'T KNOW ABOUT HER EITHER.
MAYBE I SHOULD JUST DROWN RIGHT HERE...
IT'S BECOME HIGH TIDE ANYWAY...
...
HUH?
THAT'S IT!

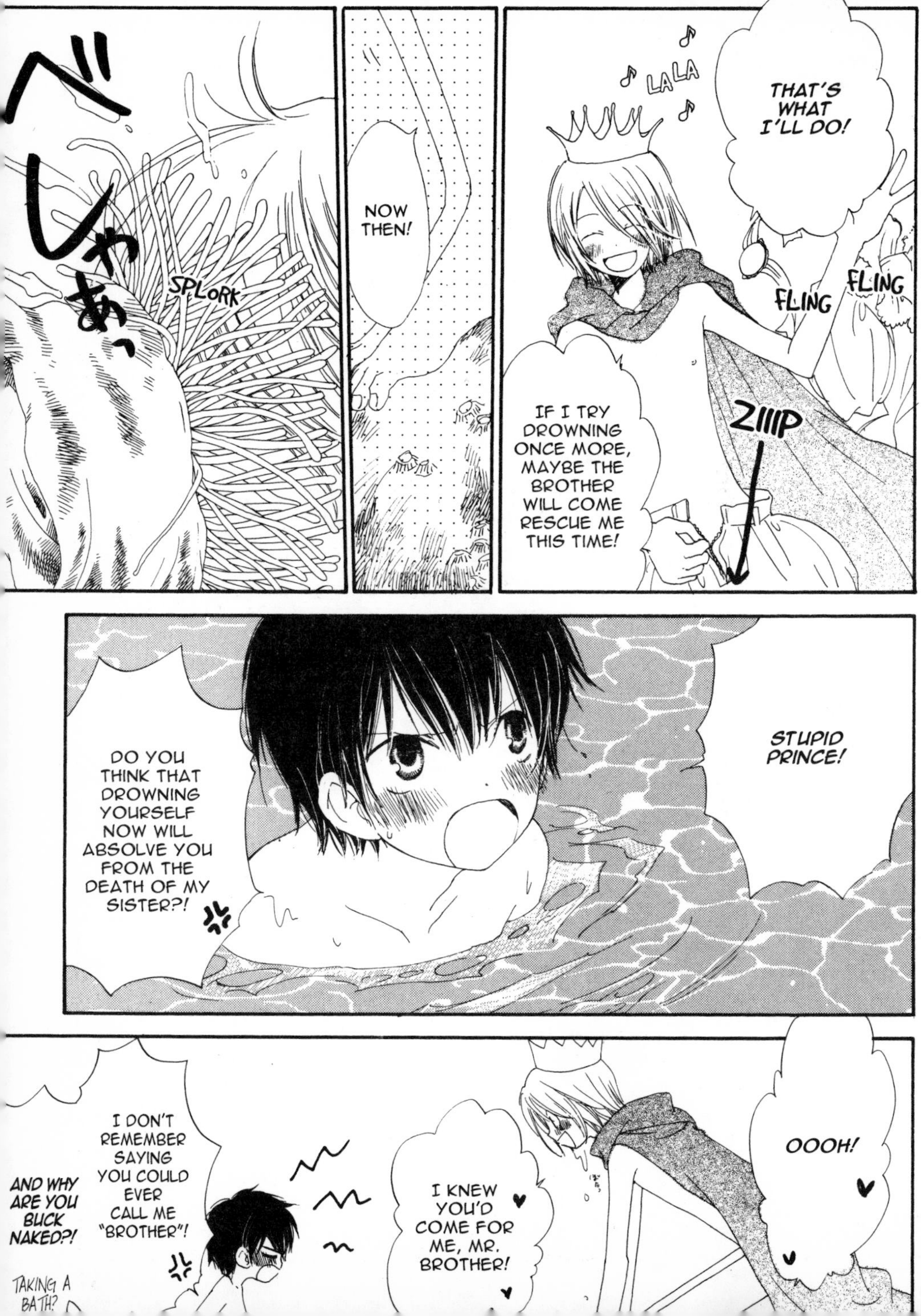
THAT'S WHAT I'LL DO!
LA LA
FLING
FLING
IF I TRY DROWNING ONCE MORE, MAYBE THE BROTHER WILL COME RESCUE ME THIS TIME!
ZIIIP
NOW THEN!
べしゃあ
SPLORK
STUPID PRINCE!
DO YOU THINK THAT DROWNING YOURSELF NOW WILL ABSOLVE YOU FROM THE DEATH OF MY SISTER?!
OOOH!
I KNEW YOU'D COME FOR ME, MR. BROTHER!
I DON'T REMEMBER SAYING YOU COULD EVER CALL ME "BROTHER"!
AND WHY ARE YOU BUCK NAKED?!
TAKING A BATH?

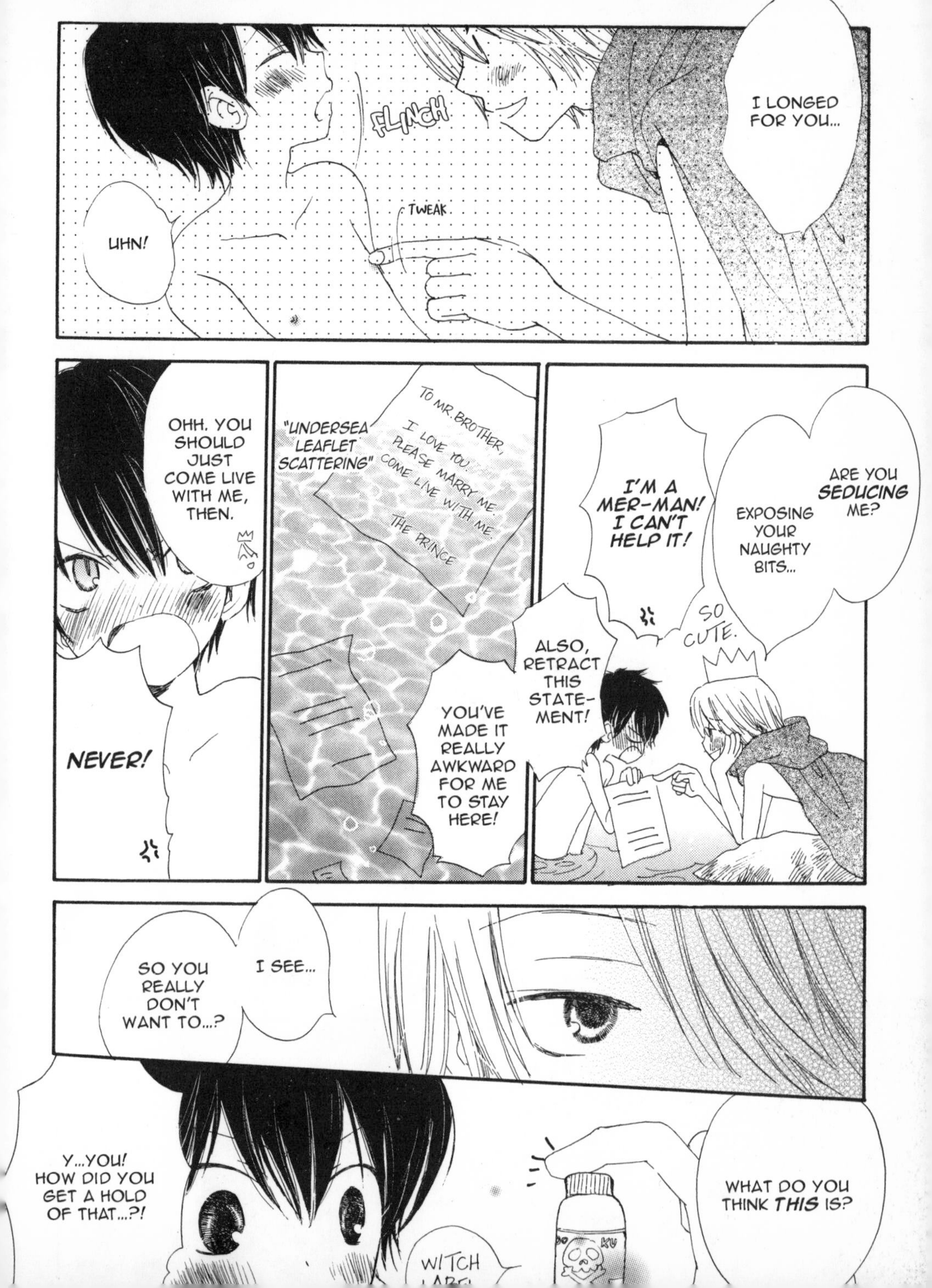
I LONGED FOR YOU...
FLINCH
TWEAK
UHN!
ARE YOU SEDUCING ME?
EXPOSING YOUR NAUGHTY BITS...
I'M A MER-MAN! I CAN'T HELP IT!
SO CUTE.
ALSO, RETRACT THIS STATEMENT!
YOU'VE MADE IT REALLY AWKWARD FOR ME TO STAY HERE!
TO MR. BROTHER, I LOVE YOU. PLEASE MARRY ME. COME LIVE WITH ME. THE PRINCE
"UNDERSEA LEAFLET SCATTERING"
OHH. YOU SHOULD JUST COME LIVE WITH ME, THEN.
NEVER!
I SEE...
SO YOU REALLY DON'T WANT TO...?
WHAT DO YOU THINK THIS IS?
Y...YOU! HOW DID YOU GET A HOLD OF THAT...?!
WITCH

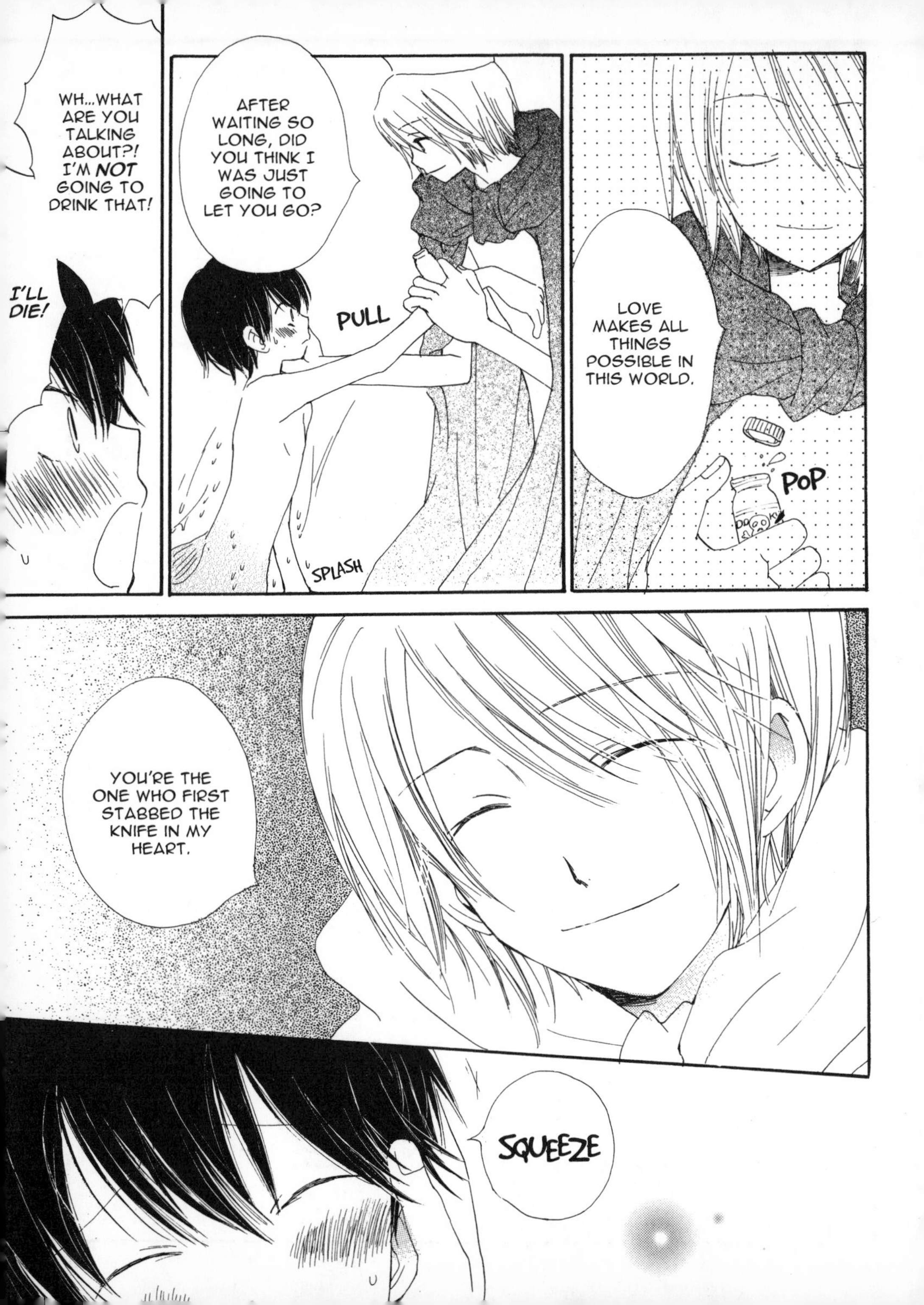
LOVE MAKES ALL THINGS POSSIBLE IN THIS WORLD.
POP
AFTER WAITING SO LONG, DID YOU THINK I WAS JUST GOING TO LET YOU GO?
PULL
SPLASH
WH...WHAT ARE YOU TALKING ABOUT?! I'M **NOT** GOING TO DRINK THAT!
I'LL DIE!
YOU'RE THE ONE WHO FIRST STABBED THE KNIFE IN MY HEART.
SQUEEZE

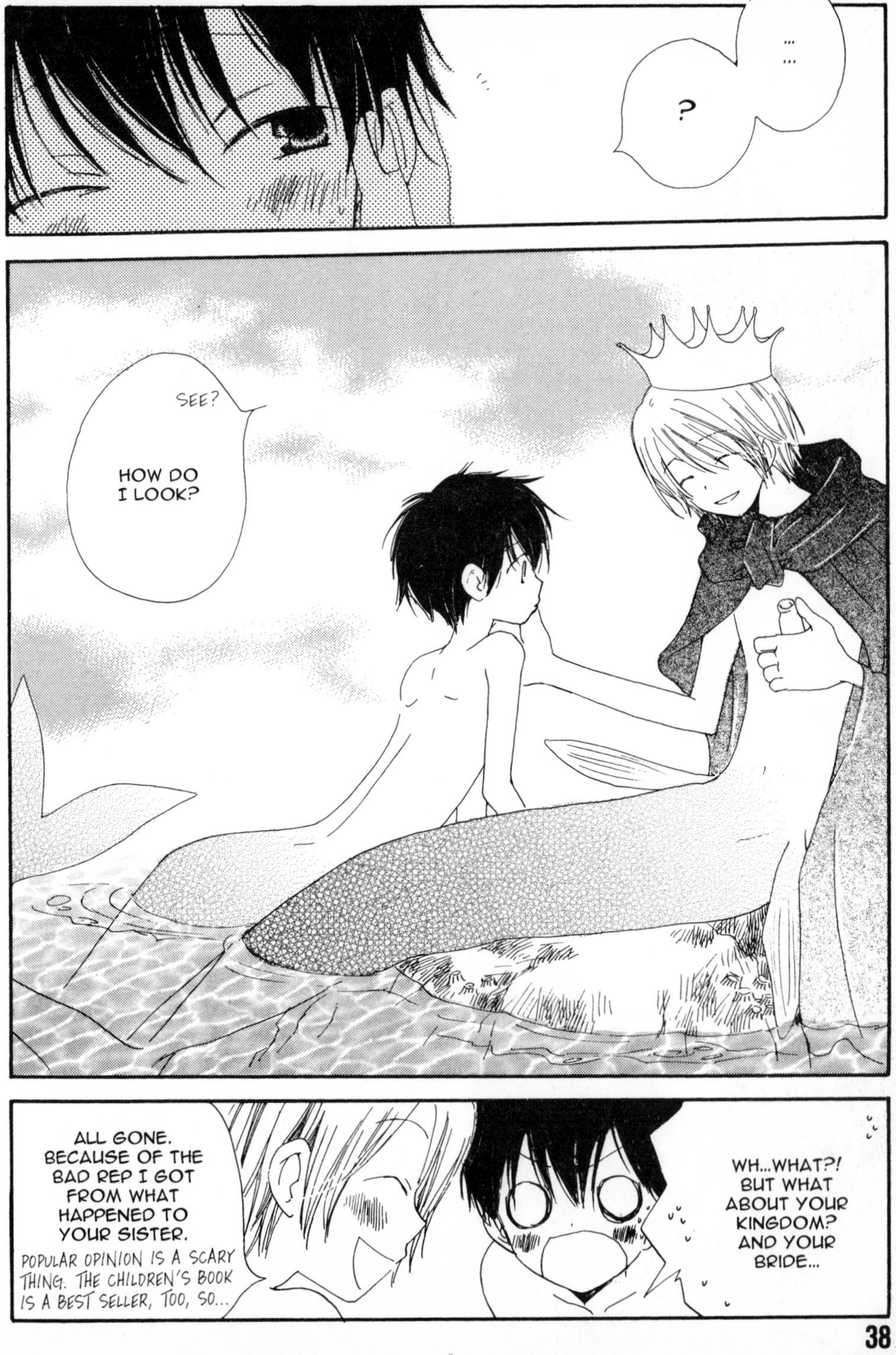
...
...
?
SEE?
HOW DO I LOOK?
WH...WHAT?! BUT WHAT ABOUT YOUR KINGDOM? AND YOUR BRIDE...
ALL GONE. BECAUSE OF THE BAD REP I GOT FROM WHAT HAPPENED TO YOUR SISTER.
POPULAR OPINION IS A SCARY THING. THE CHILDREN'S BOOK IS A BEST SELLER, TOO, SO...

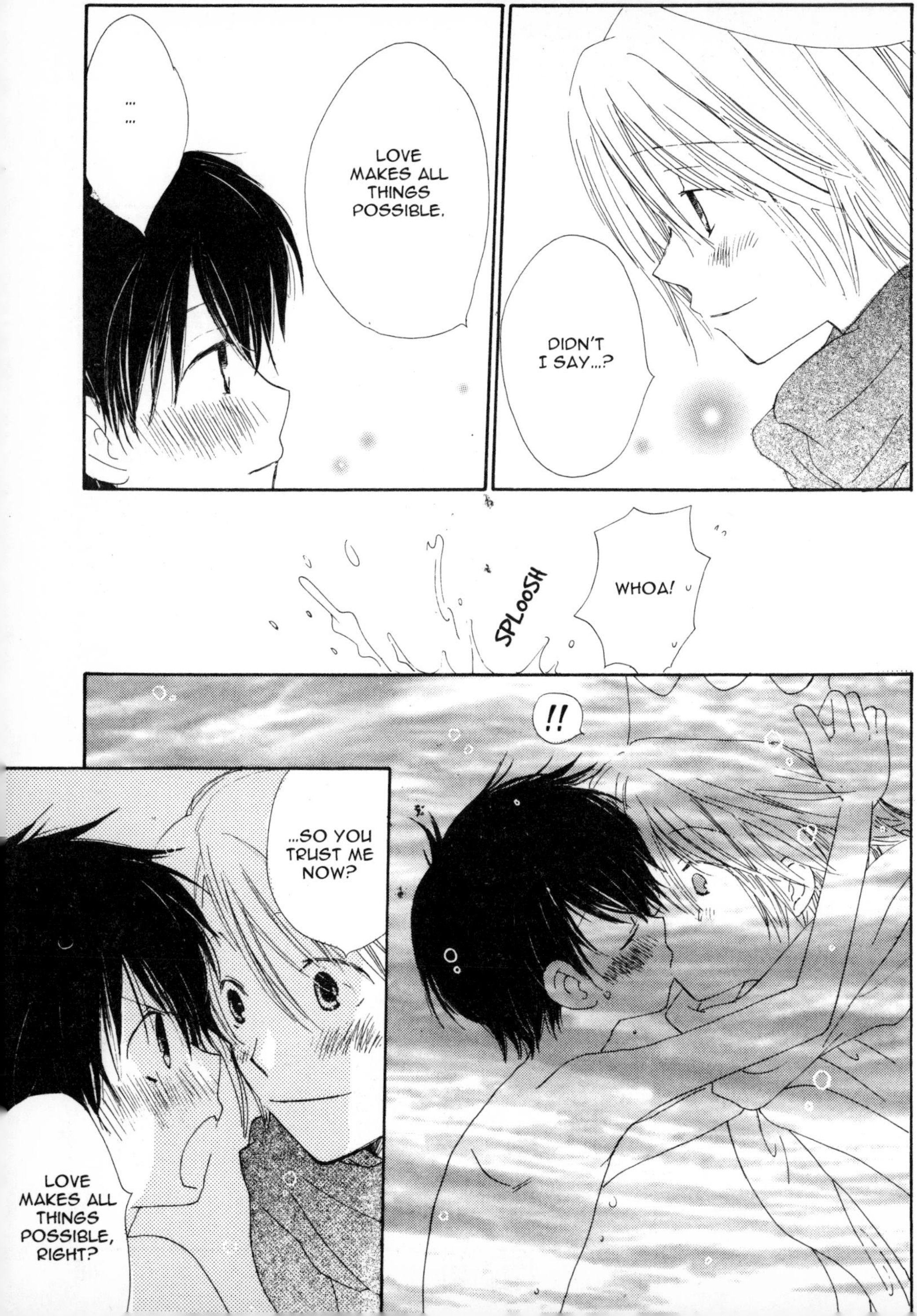
DIDN'T I SAY...?
LOVE MAKES ALL THINGS POSSIBLE.
......
WHOA!
SPLOOSH
!!
...SO YOU TRUST ME NOW?
LOVE MAKES ALL THINGS POSSIBLE, RIGHT?

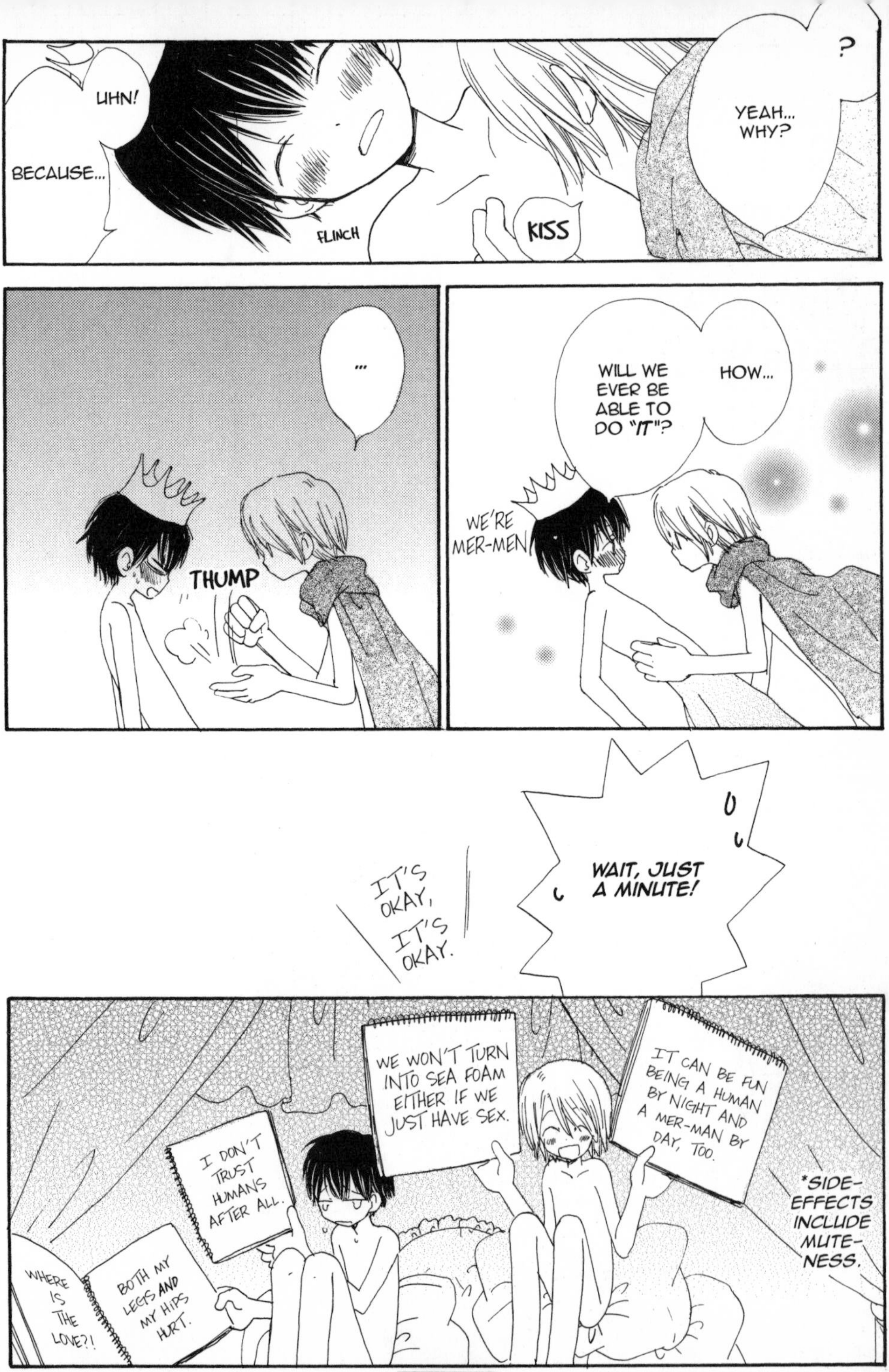
?
YEAH... WHY?
KISS
UHN!
BECAUSE...
FLINCH
HOW...
WILL WE EVER BE ABLE TO DO "IT"?
WE'RE MER-MEN
...
THUMP
WAIT, JUST A MINUTE!
IT'S OKAY, IT'S OKAY.
IT CAN BE FUN BEING A HUMAN BY NIGHT AND A MER-MAN BY DAY, TOO.
*SIDE-EFFECTS INCLUDE MUTE-NESS.
WE WON'T TURN INTO SEA FOAM EITHER IF WE JUST HAVE SEX.
I DON'T TRUST HUMANS AFTER ALL.
BOTH MY LEGS AND MY HIPS HURT.
WHERE IS THE LOVE?!

END

MILK ROBOT

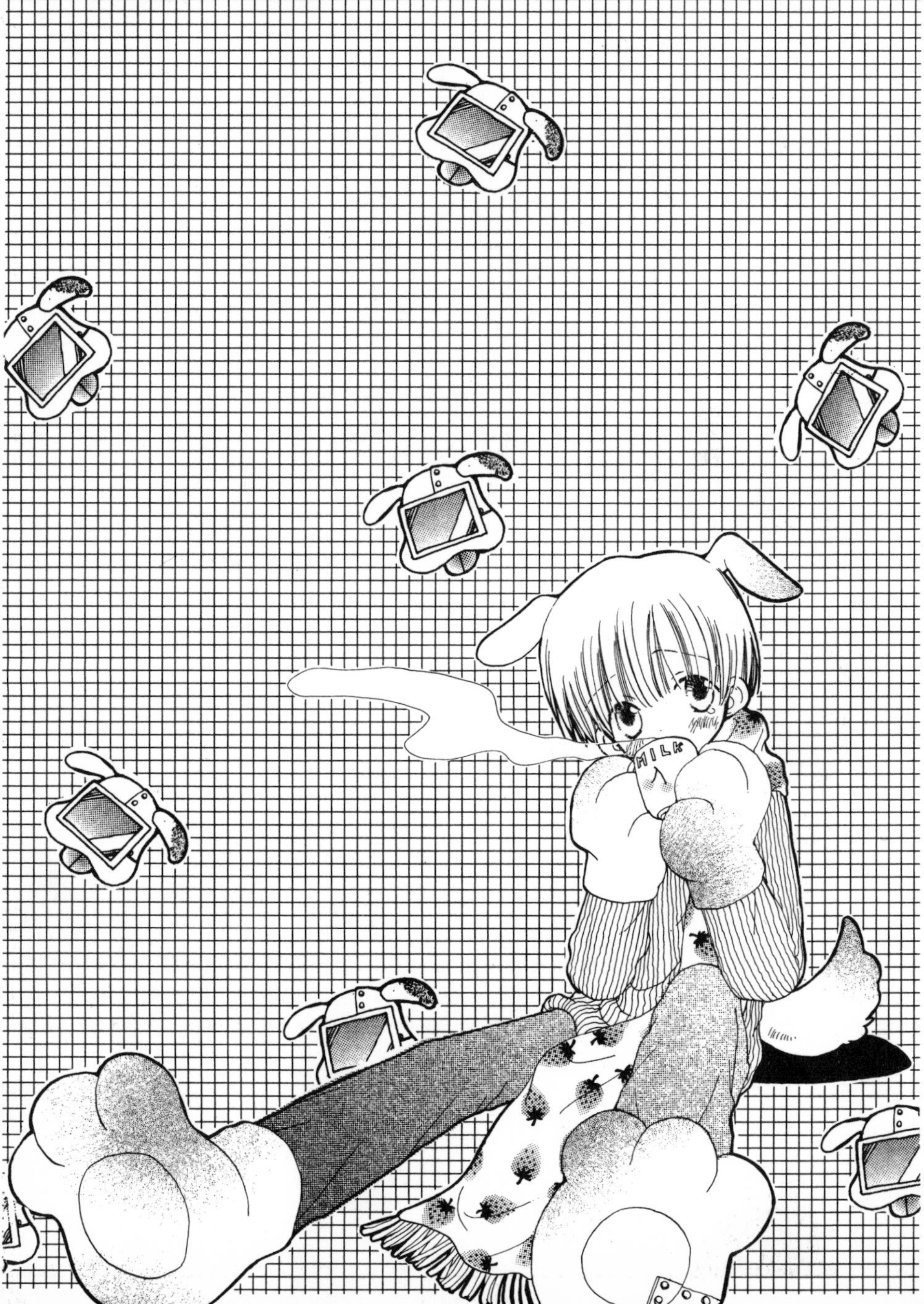
MILK

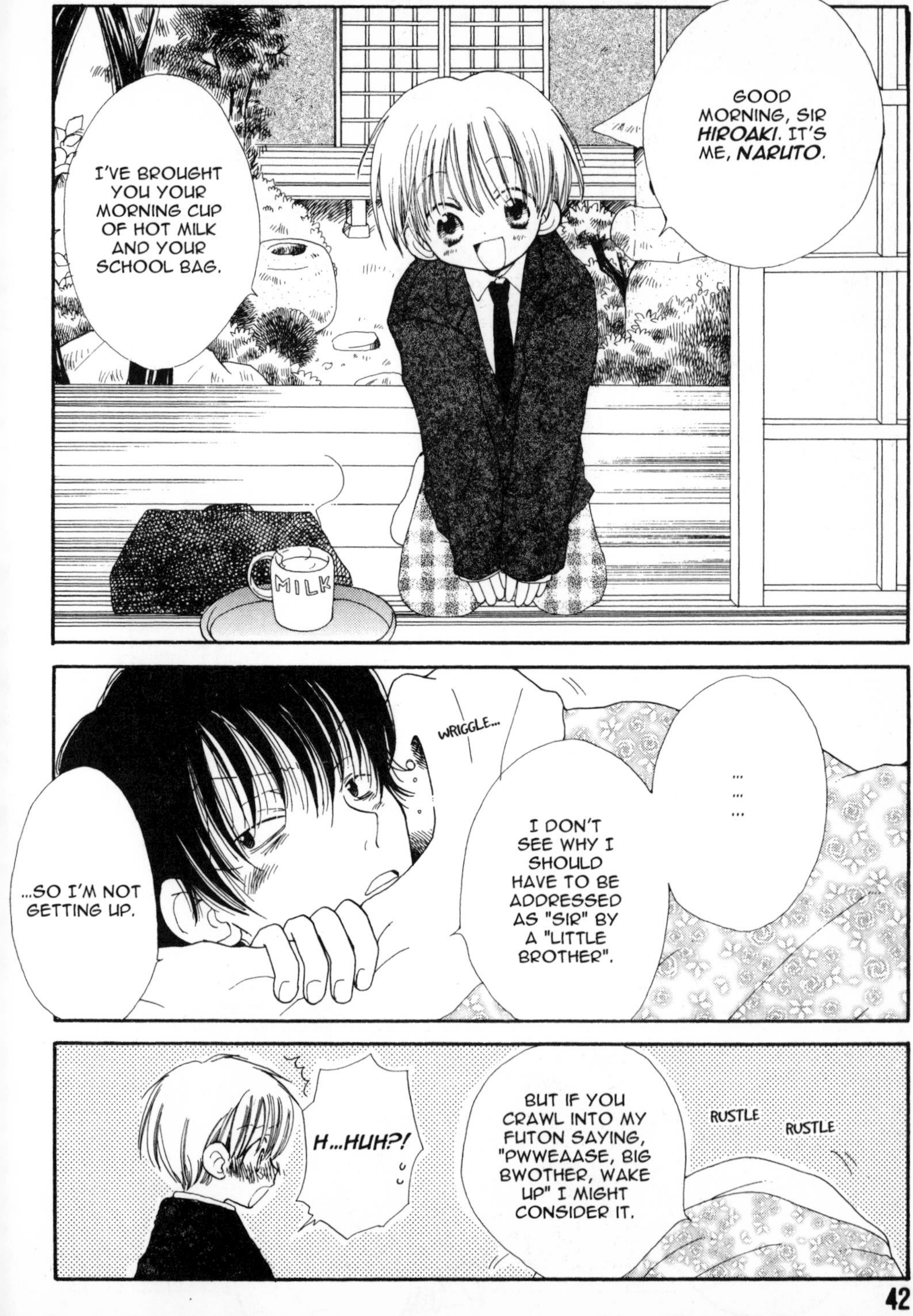
GOOD MORNING, SIR HIROAKI. IT'S ME, NARUTO.
I'VE BROUGHT YOU YOUR MORNING CUP OF HOT MILK AND YOUR SCHOOL BAG.
MILK
... ...
WRIGGLE...
I DON'T SEE WHY I SHOULD HAVE TO BE ADDRESSED AS "SIR" BY A "LITTLE BROTHER".
...SO I'M NOT GETTING UP.
RUSTLE
RUSTLE
BUT IF YOU CRAWL INTO MY FUTON SAYING, "PWWEAASE, BIG BWOTHER, WAKE UP" I MIGHT CONSIDER IT.
H...HUH?!

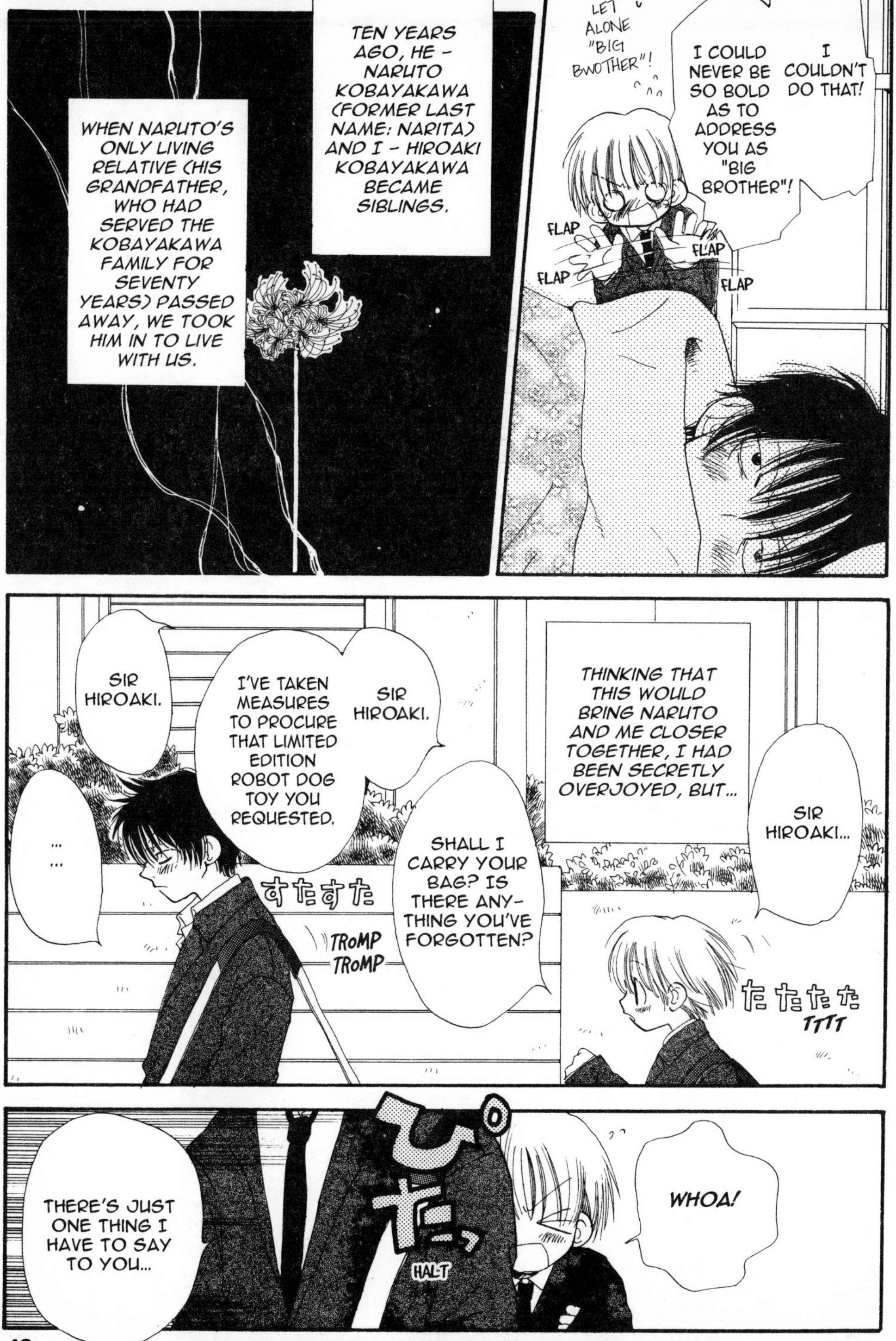

I COULDN'T DO THAT!
I COULD NEVER BE SO BOLD AS TO ADDRESS YOU AS "BIG BROTHER"!
LET ALONE "BIG BWOTHER"!
FLAP
FLAP
FLAP
FLAP
TEN YEARS AGO, HE - NARUTO KOBAYAKAWA (FORMER LAST NAME: NARITA) AND I - HIROAKI KOBAYAKAWA BECAME SIBLINGS.
WHEN NARUTO'S ONLY LIVING RELATIVE (HIS GRANDFATHER, WHO HAD SERVED THE KOBAYAKAWA FAMILY FOR SEVENTY YEARS) PASSED AWAY, WE TOOK HIM IN TO LIVE WITH US.
SIR HIROAKI...
たたたた
TTTT
THINKING THAT THIS WOULD BRING NARUTO AND ME CLOSER TOGETHER, I HAD BEEN SECRETLY OVERJOYED, BUT...
SHALL I CARRY YOUR BAG? IS THERE ANY-THING YOU'VE FORGOTTEN?
SIR HIROAKI.
I'VE TAKEN MEASURES TO PROCURE THAT LIMITED EDITION ROBOT DOG TOY YOU REQUESTED.
すたすた
TROMP TROMP
SIR HIROAKI.
... ...
WHOA!
ぴたっ
HALT
THERE'S JUST ONE THING I HAVE TO SAY TO YOU...

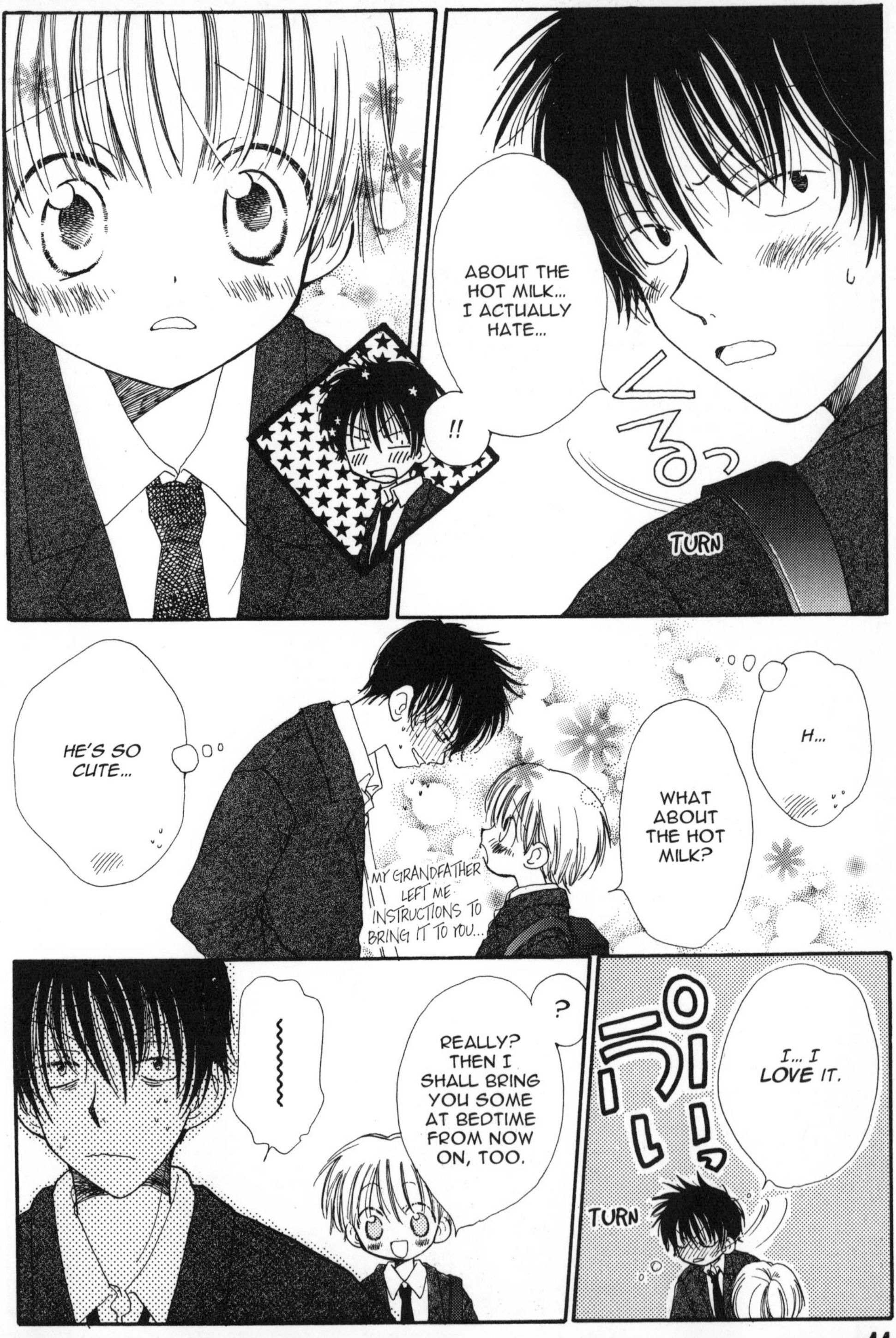
ABOUT THE HOT MILK... I ACTUALLY HATE...
くるっ
TURN
!!
H...
WHAT ABOUT THE HOT MILK?
MY GRANDFATHER LEFT ME INSTRUCTIONS TO BRING IT TO YOU...
HE'S SO CUTE...
ぷいっ
I... I LOVE IT.
TURN
?
REALLY? THEN I SHALL BRING YOU SOME AT BEDTIME FROM NOW ON, TOO.
~~~
~~~

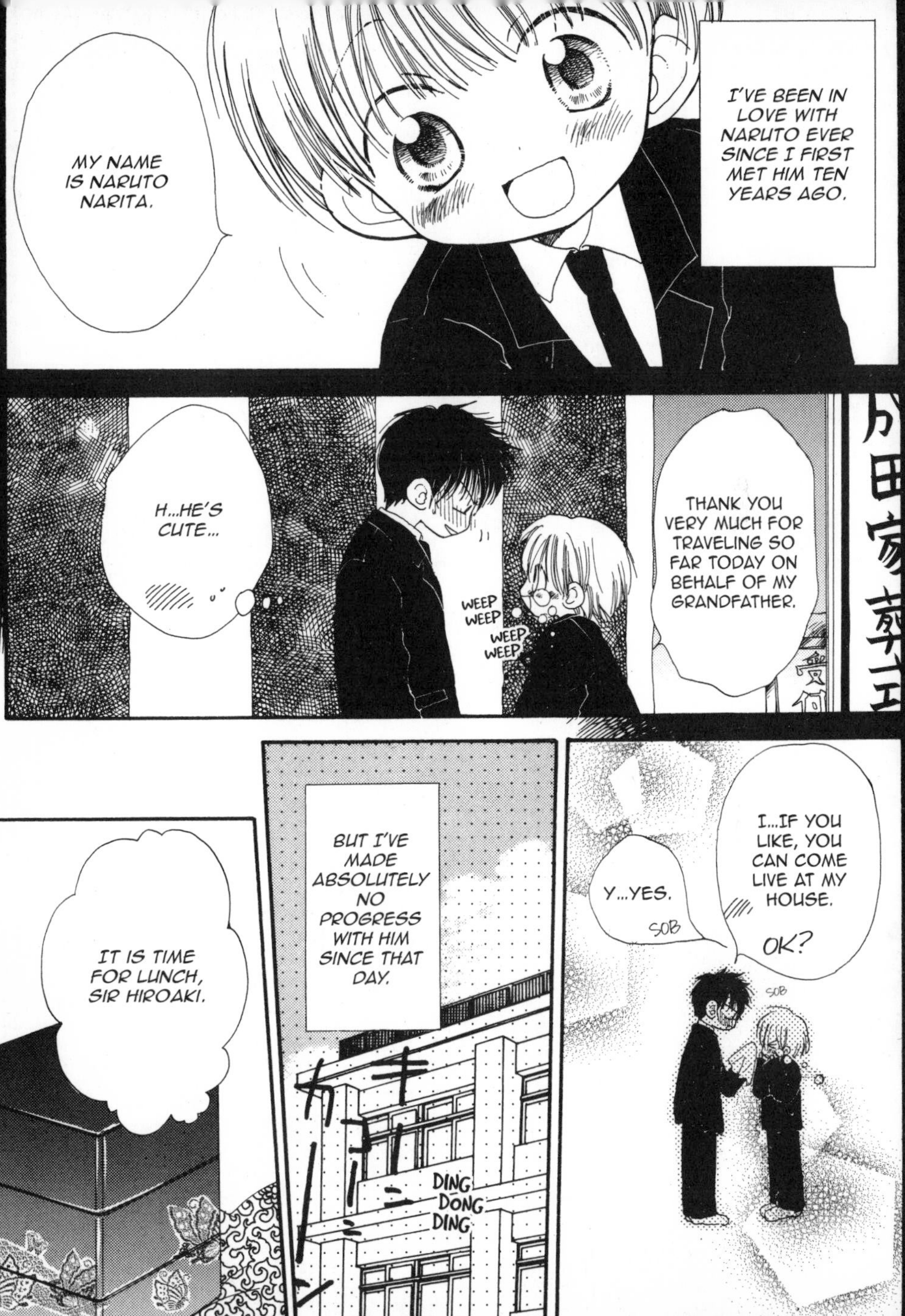
I'VE BEEN IN LOVE WITH NARUTO EVER SINCE I FIRST MET HIM TEN YEARS AGO.
MY NAME IS NARUTO NARITA.
THANK YOU VERY MUCH FOR TRAVELING SO FAR TODAY ON BEHALF OF MY GRANDFATHER.
WEEP WEEP WEEP WEEP
H...HE'S CUTE...
I...IF YOU LIKE, YOU CAN COME LIVE AT MY HOUSE.
OK?
Y...YES.
SOB
SOB
BUT I'VE MADE ABSOLUTELY NO PROGRESS WITH HIM SINCE THAT DAY.
DING DONG DING
IT IS TIME FOR LUNCH, SIR HIROAKI.

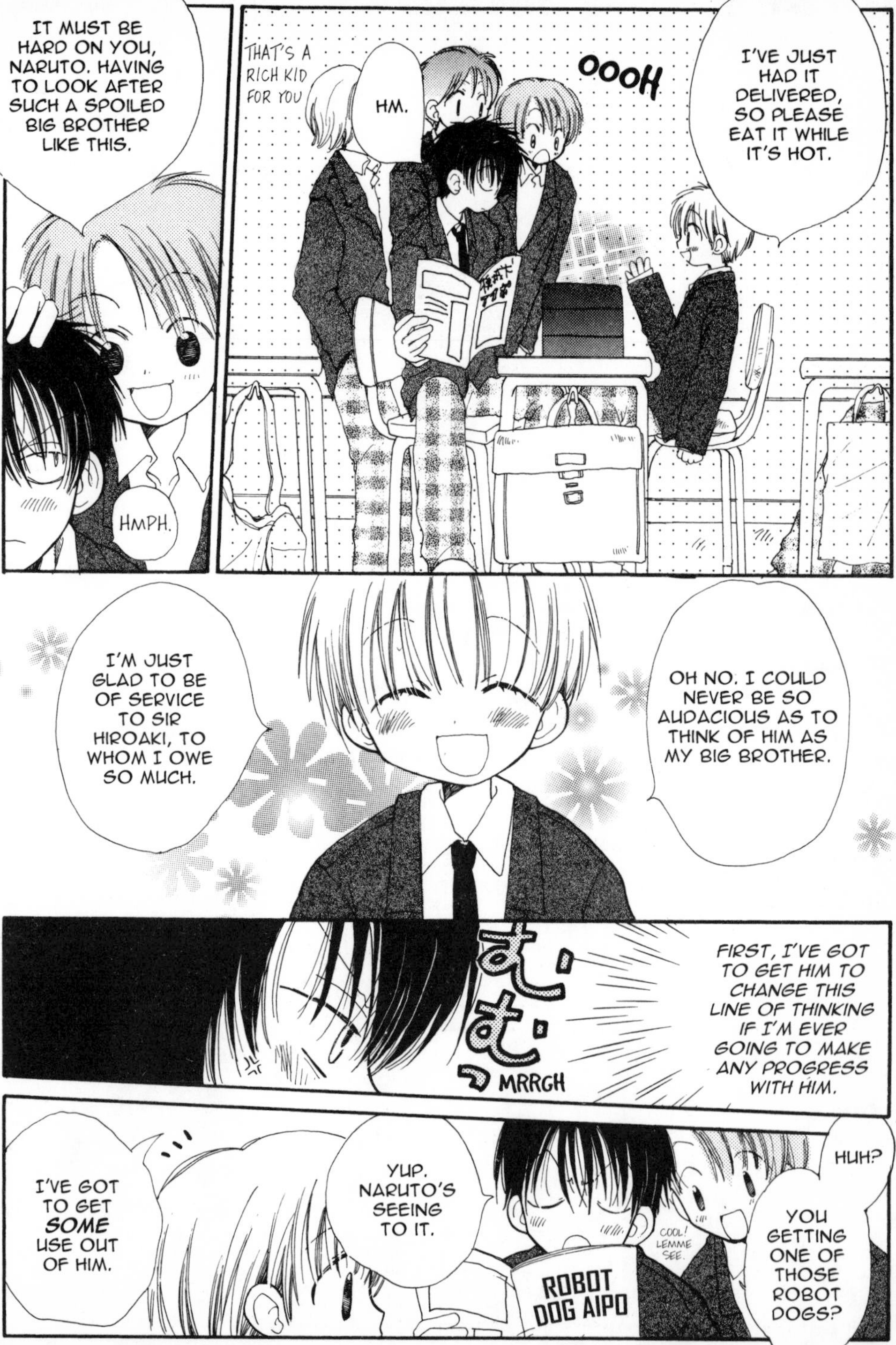
I'VE JUST HAD IT DELIVERED, SO PLEASE EAT IT WHILE IT'S HOT.
OOOH
HM.
THAT'S A RICH KID FOR YOU
IT MUST BE HARD ON YOU, NARUTO. HAVING TO LOOK AFTER SUCH A SPOILED BIG BROTHER LIKE THIS.
HMPH.
OH NO. I COULD NEVER BE SO AUDACIOUS AS TO THINK OF HIM AS MY BIG BROTHER.
I'M JUST GLAD TO BE OF SERVICE TO SIR HIROAKI, TO WHOM I OWE SO MUCH.
FIRST, I'VE GOT TO GET HIM TO CHANGE THIS LINE OF THINKING IF I'M EVER GOING TO MAKE ANY PROGRESS WITH HIM.
むむっ
MRRGH
HUH?
YOU GETTING ONE OF THOSE ROBOT DOGS?
COOL! LEMME SEE.
ROBOT DOG AIPO
YUP. NARUTO'S SEEING TO IT.
I'VE GOT TO GET SOME USE OUT OF HIM.

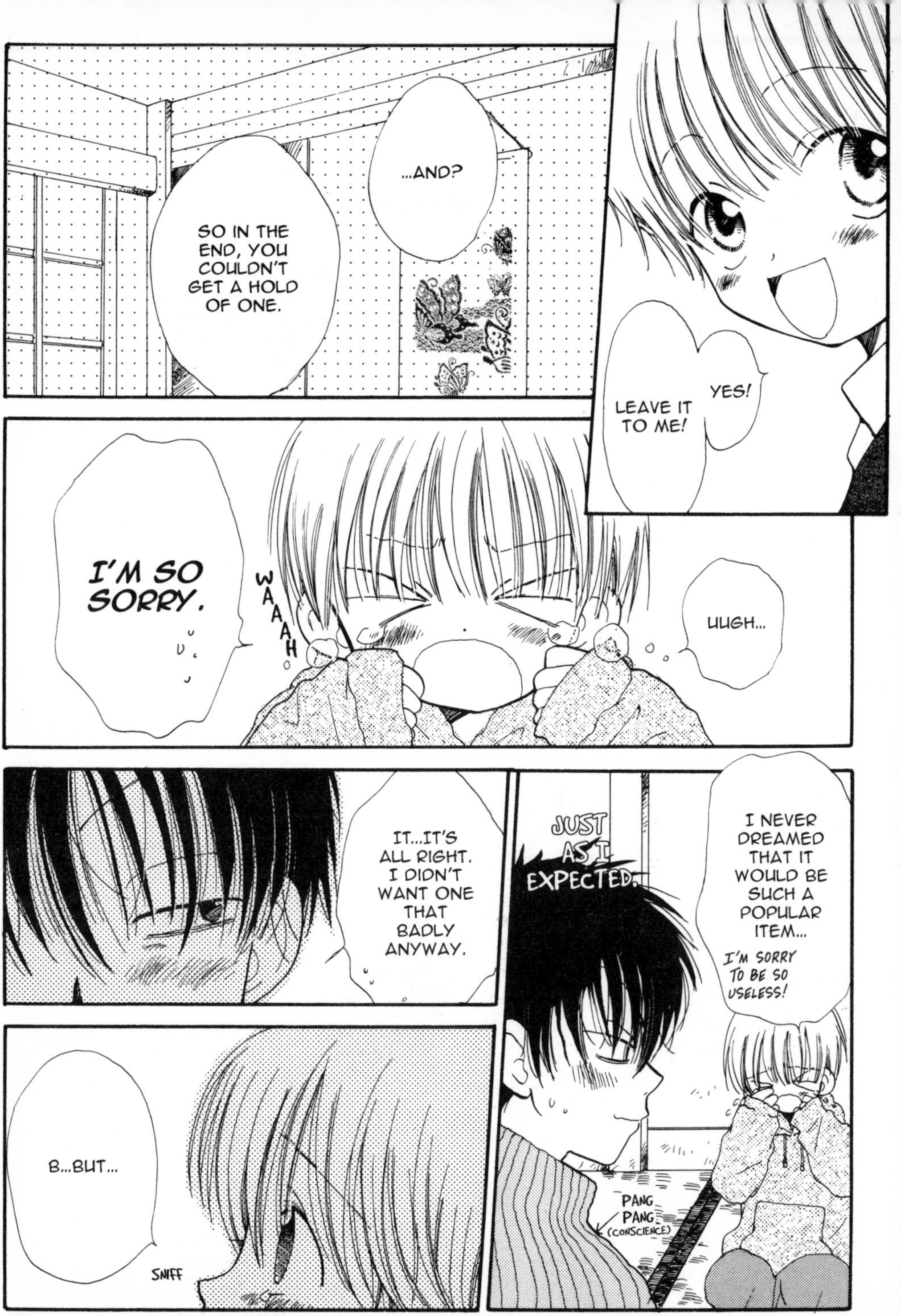
YES!
LEAVE IT TO ME!
...AND?
SO IN THE END, YOU COULDN'T GET A HOLD OF ONE.
UUGH...
WAAAAH
I'M SO SORRY.
I NEVER DREAMED THAT IT WOULD BE SUCH A POPULAR ITEM...
I'M SORRY TO BE SO USELESS!
JUST AS I EXPECTED.
PANG PANG (CONSCIENCE)
IT...IT'S ALL RIGHT. I DIDN'T WANT ONE THAT BADLY ANYWAY.
B...BUT...
SNIFF

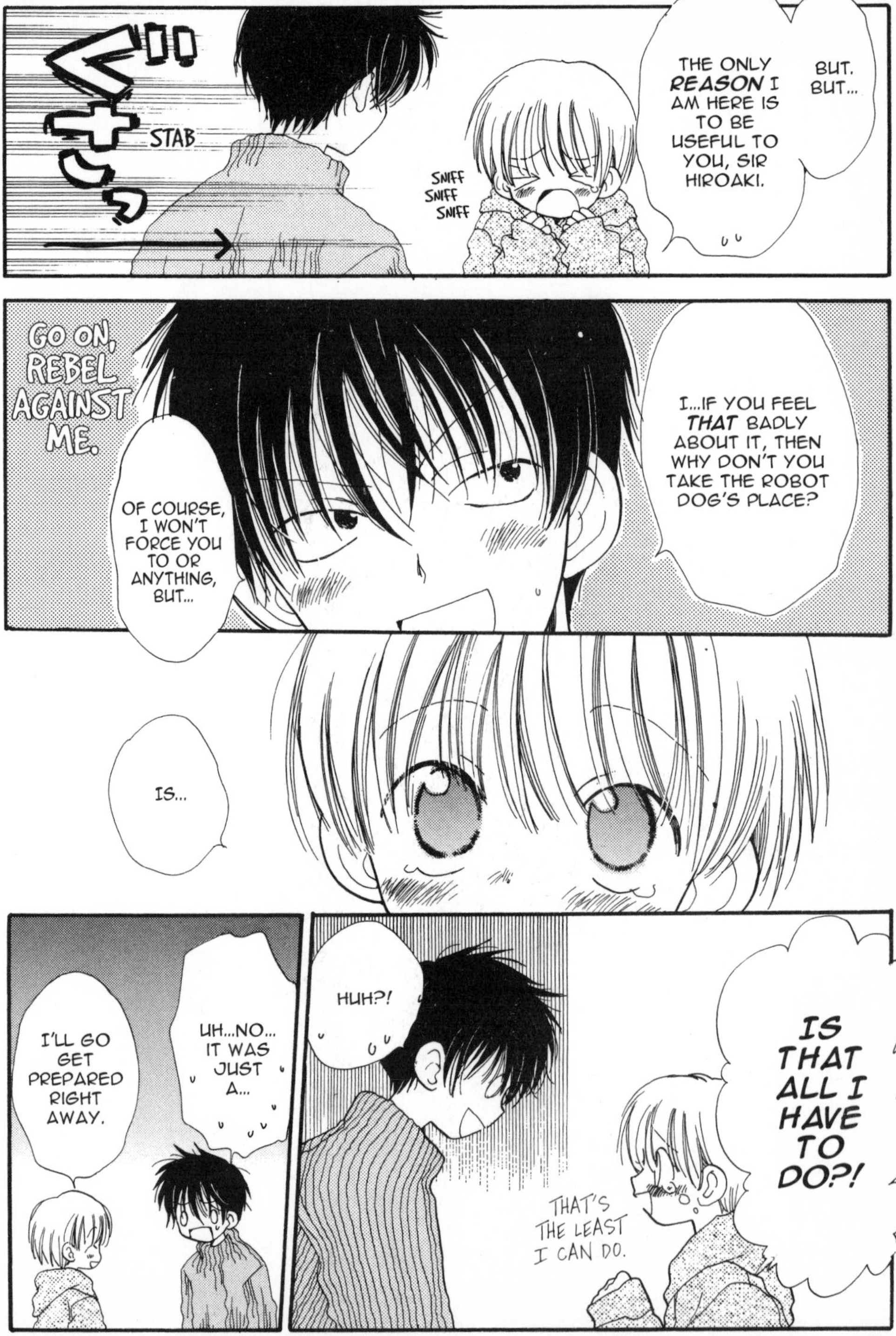
BUT. BUT...
THE ONLY REASON I AM HERE IS TO BE USEFUL TO YOU, SIR HIROAKI.
SNIFF SNIFF SNIFF
STAB
I...IF YOU FEEL THAT BADLY ABOUT IT, THEN WHY DON'T YOU TAKE THE ROBOT DOG'S PLACE?
OF COURSE, I WON'T FORCE YOU TO OR ANYTHING, BUT...
GO ON, REBEL AGAINST ME.
IS...
IS THAT ALL I HAVE TO DO?!
THAT'S THE LEAST I CAN DO.
HUH?!
UH...NO... IT WAS JUST A...
I'LL GO GET PREPARED RIGHT AWAY.

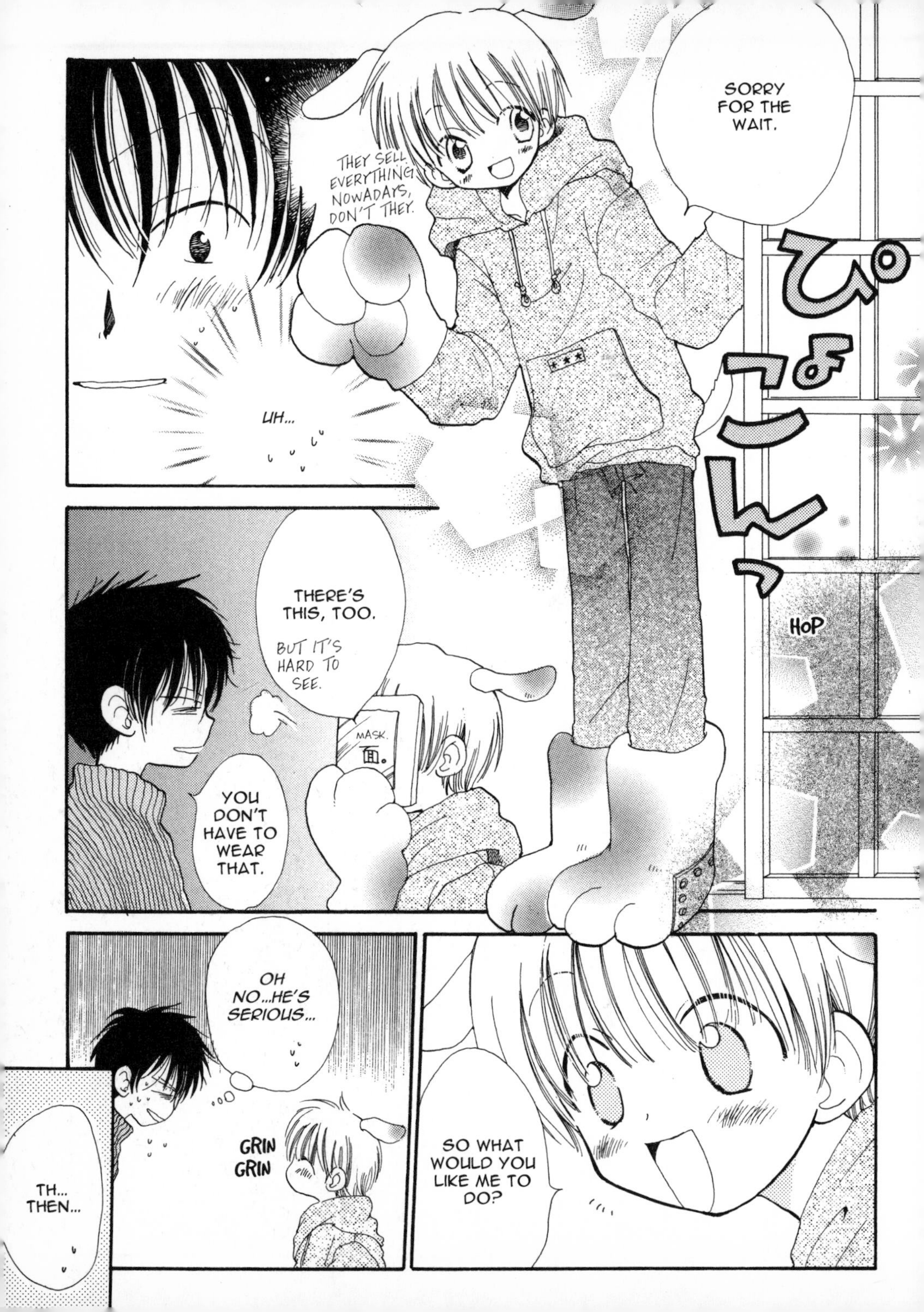
SORRY FOR THE WAIT.
THEY SELL EVERYTHING NOWADAYS, DON'T THEY.
ぴょこんっ
HOP
UH...
THERE'S THIS, TOO.
BUT IT'S HARD TO SEE.
MASK.
面。
YOU DON'T HAVE TO WEAR THAT.
SO WHAT WOULD YOU LIKE ME TO DO?
OH NO...HE'S SERIOUS...
GRIN GRIN
TH... THEN...

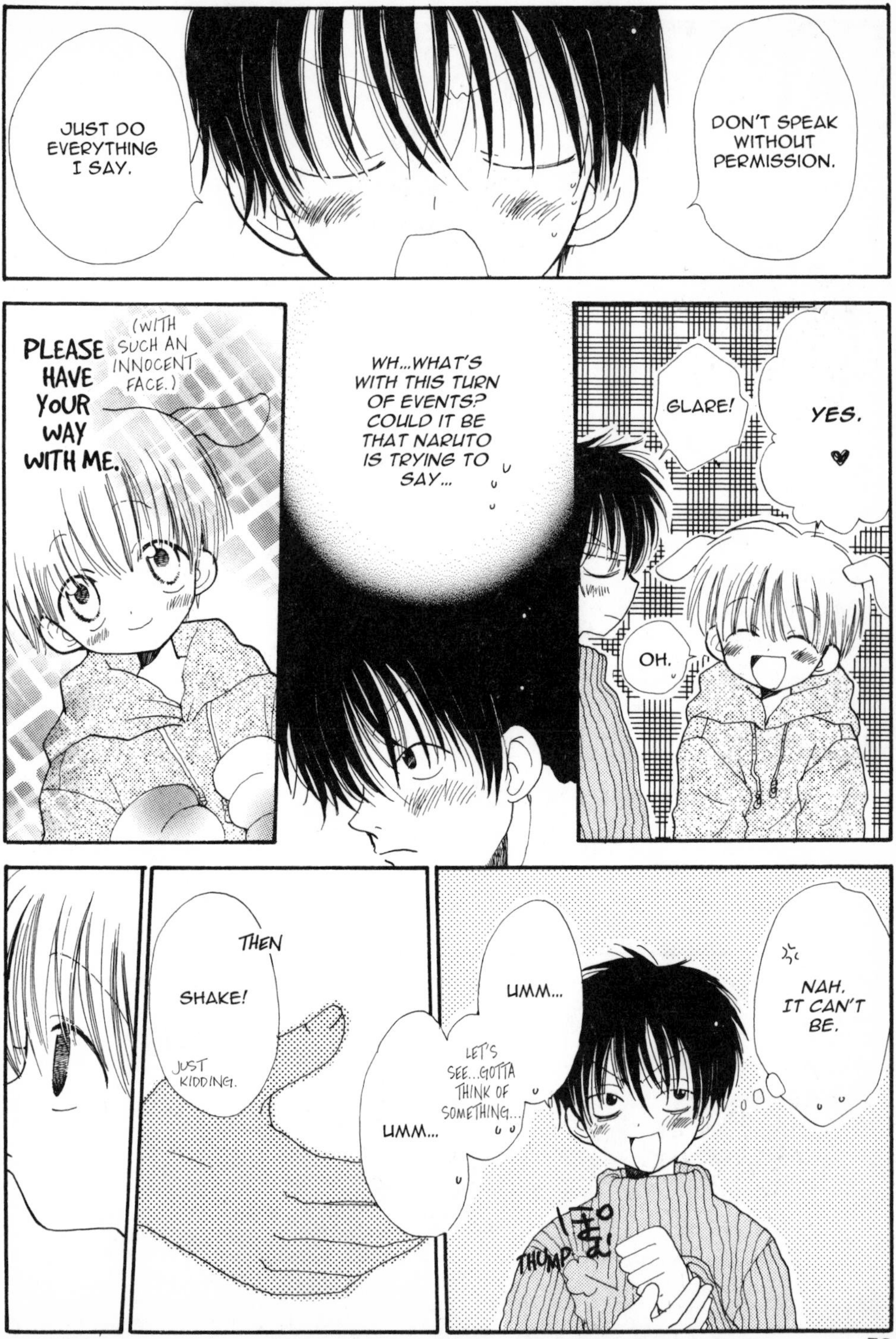
DON'T SPEAK WITHOUT PERMISSION.
JUST DO EVERYTHING I SAY.
YES. ♥
GLARE!
OH.
WH...WHAT'S WITH THIS TURN OF EVENTS? COULD IT BE THAT NARUTO IS TRYING TO SAY...
PLEASE HAVE YOUR WAY WITH ME.
(WITH SUCH AN INNOCENT FACE.)
NAH. IT CAN'T BE.
UMM...
LET'S SEE...GOTTA THINK OF SOMETHING...
UMM...
THUMP
THEN
SHAKE!
JUST KIDDING.

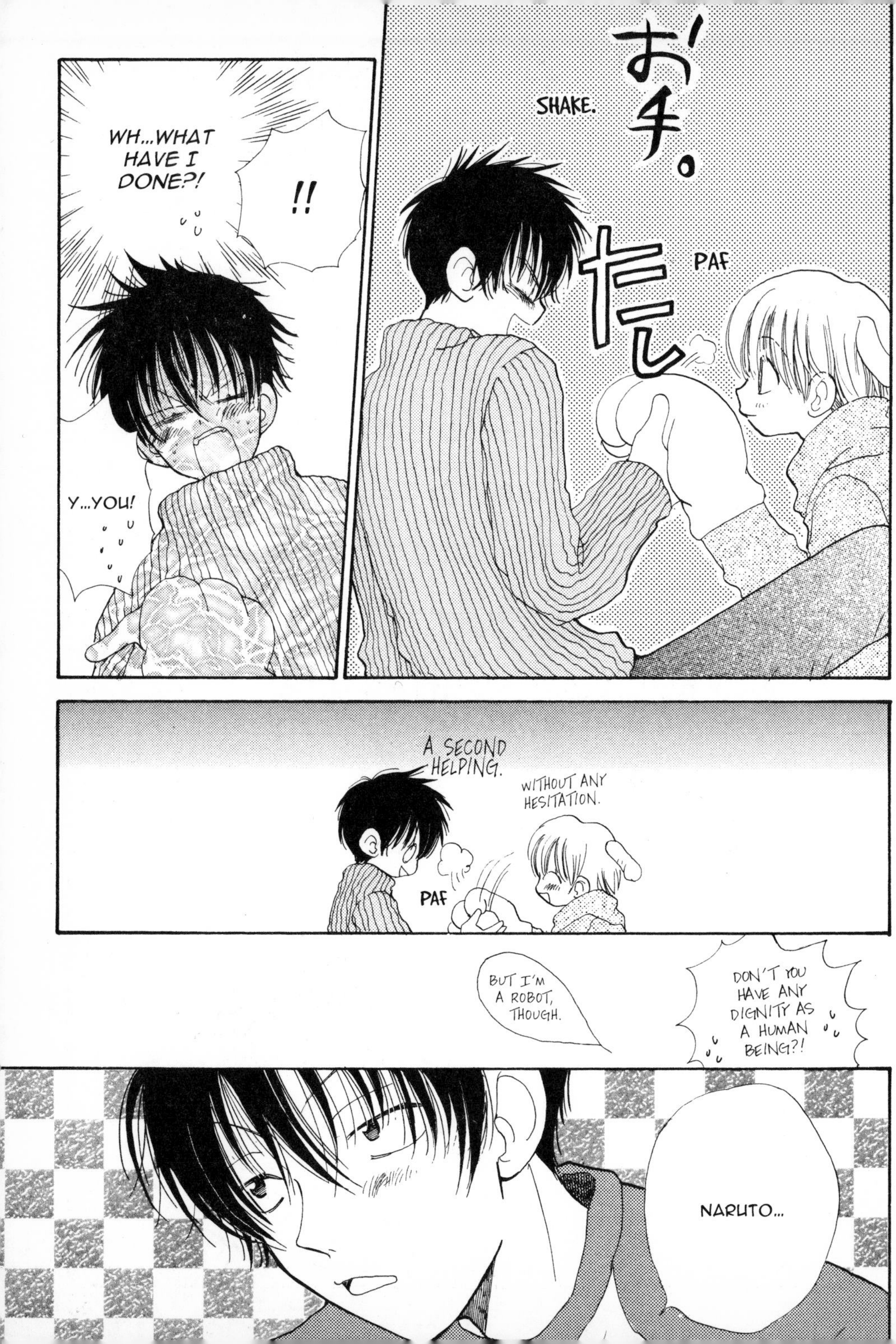
お手。
SHAKE.
たし
PAF
WH...WHAT HAVE I DONE?!
!!
Y...YOU!
A SECOND HELPING.
WITHOUT ANY HESITATION.
PAF
DON'T YOU HAVE ANY DIGNITY AS A HUMAN BEING?!
BUT I'M A ROBOT, THOUGH.
NARUTO...

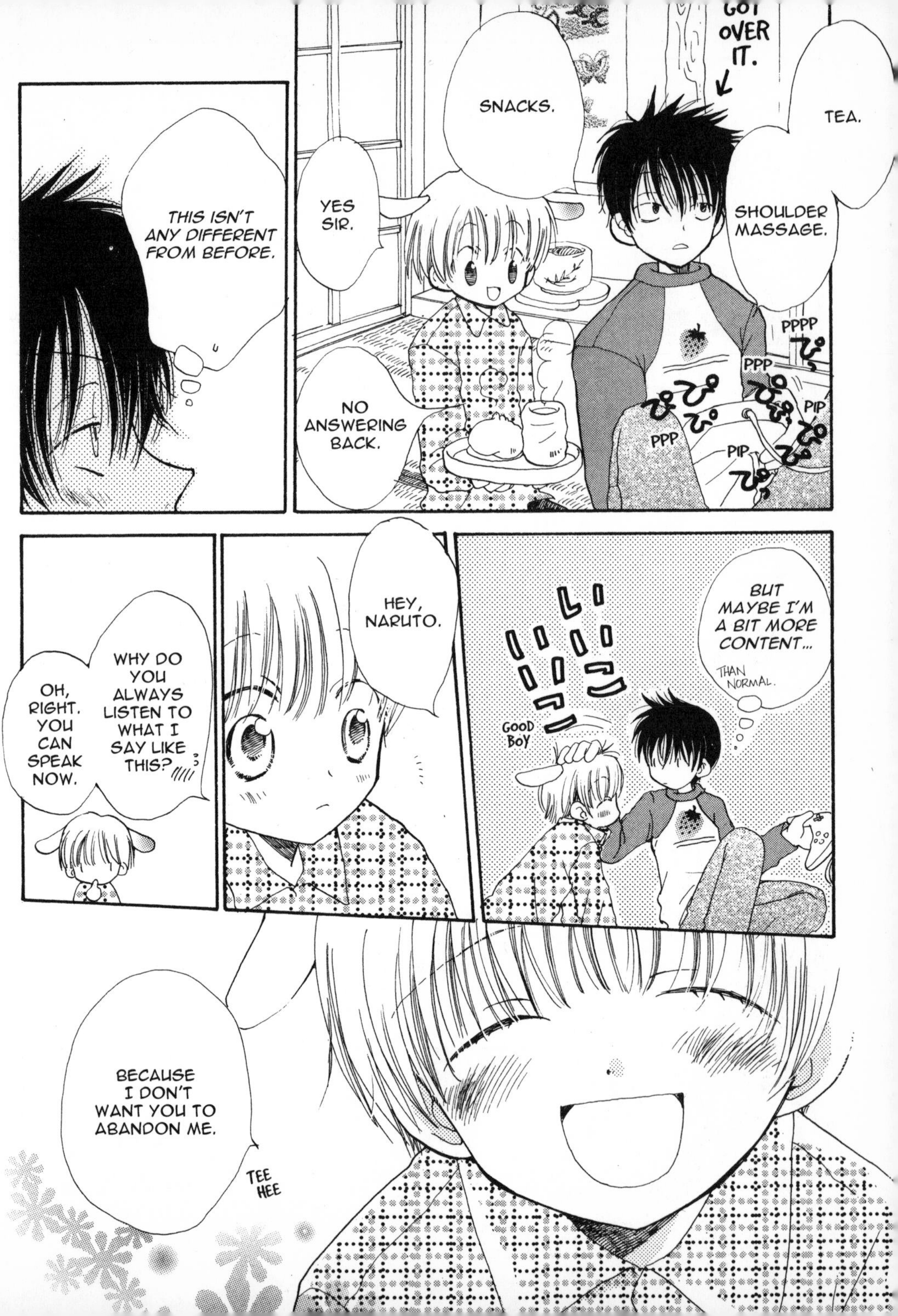
GOT OVER IT.
TEA.
SHOULDER MASSAGE.
SNACKS.
YES SIR.
PPPP
PPP
PIP
PPP
PIP
NO ANSWERING BACK.
THIS ISN'T ANY DIFFERENT FROM BEFORE.
BUT MAYBE I'M A BIT MORE CONTENT...
THAN NORMAL.
GOOD BOY
HEY, NARUTO.
WHY DO YOU ALWAYS LISTEN TO WHAT I SAY LIKE THIS?
OH, RIGHT. YOU CAN SPEAK NOW.
BECAUSE I DON'T WANT YOU TO ABANDON ME.
TEE HEE

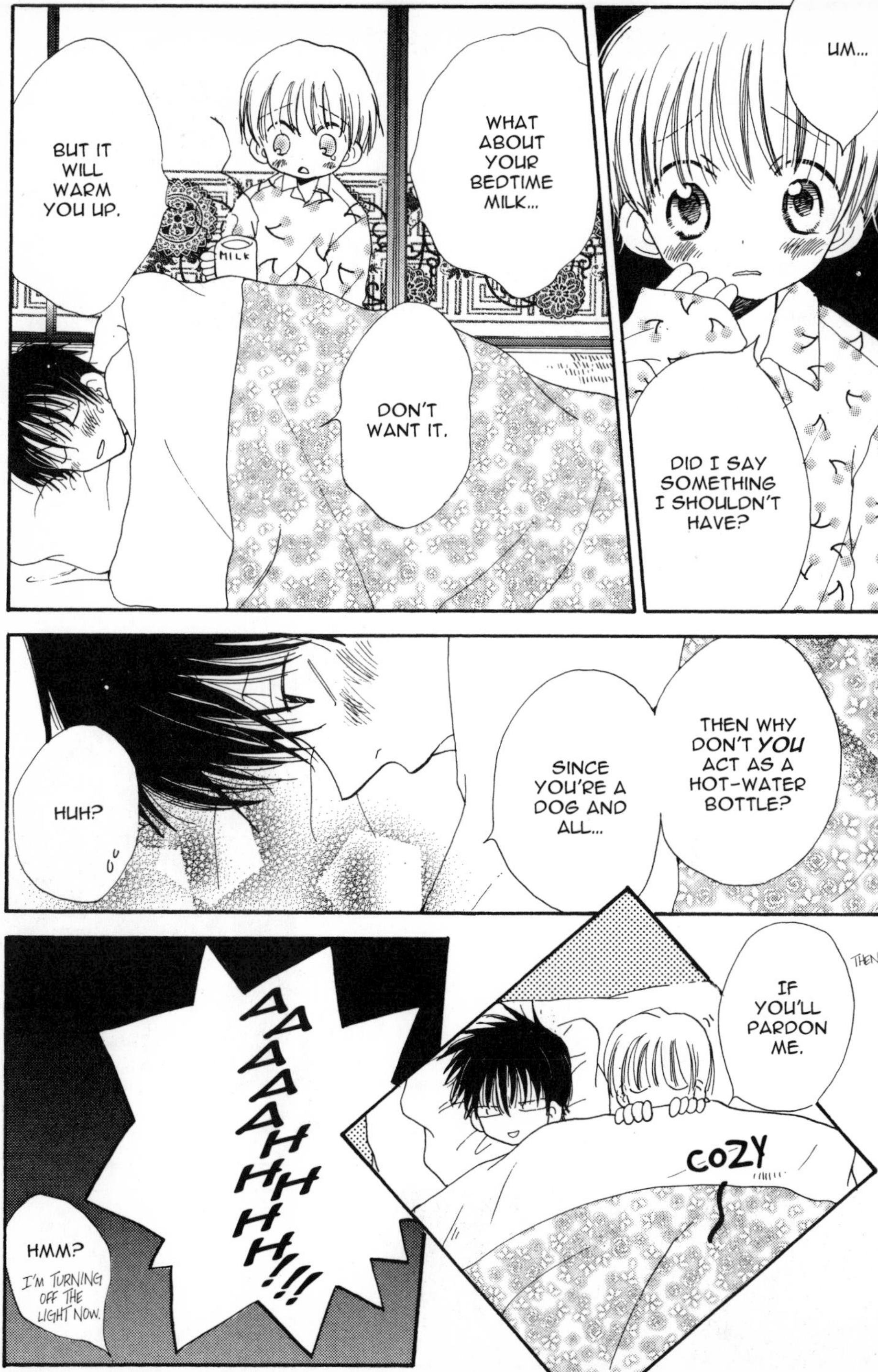

UM...
DID I SAY SOMETHING I SHOULDN'T HAVE?
WHAT ABOUT YOUR BEDTIME MILK...
DON'T WANT IT.
BUT IT WILL WARM YOU UP.
MILK
THEN WHY DON'T *YOU* ACT AS A HOT-WATER BOTTLE?
SINCE YOU'RE A DOG AND ALL...
HUH?
THEN...
IF YOU'LL PARDON ME.
COZY
AAAAAHHHHHH!!!
HMM?
I'M TURNING OFF THE LIGHT NOW.

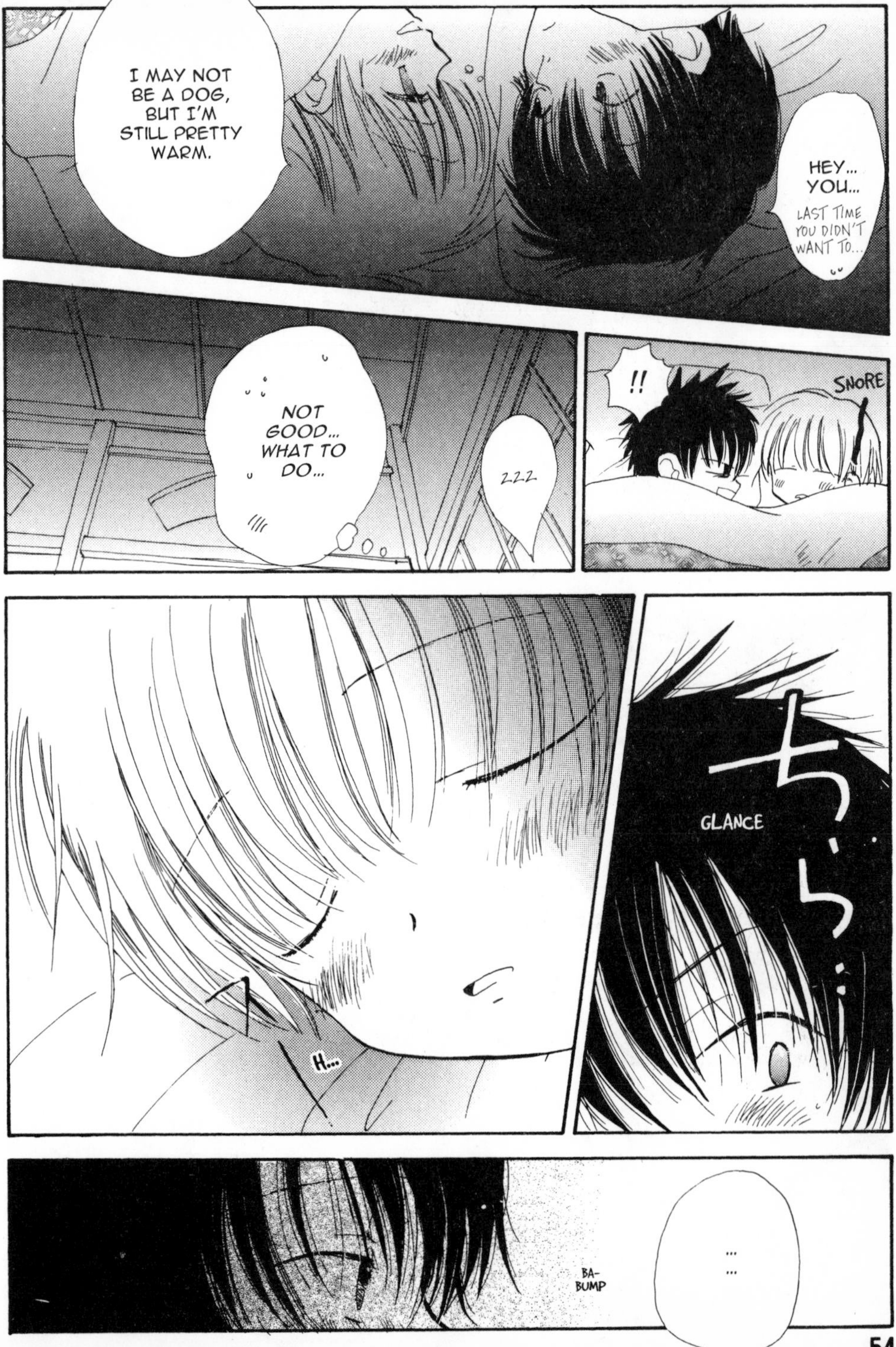
HEY... YOU...
LAST TIME YOU DIDN'T WANT TO...
I MAY NOT BE A DOG, BUT I'M STILL PRETTY WARM.
SNORE
!!
ZZZ
NOT GOOD... WHAT TO DO...
GLANCE
H...
...
...
BA-BUMP

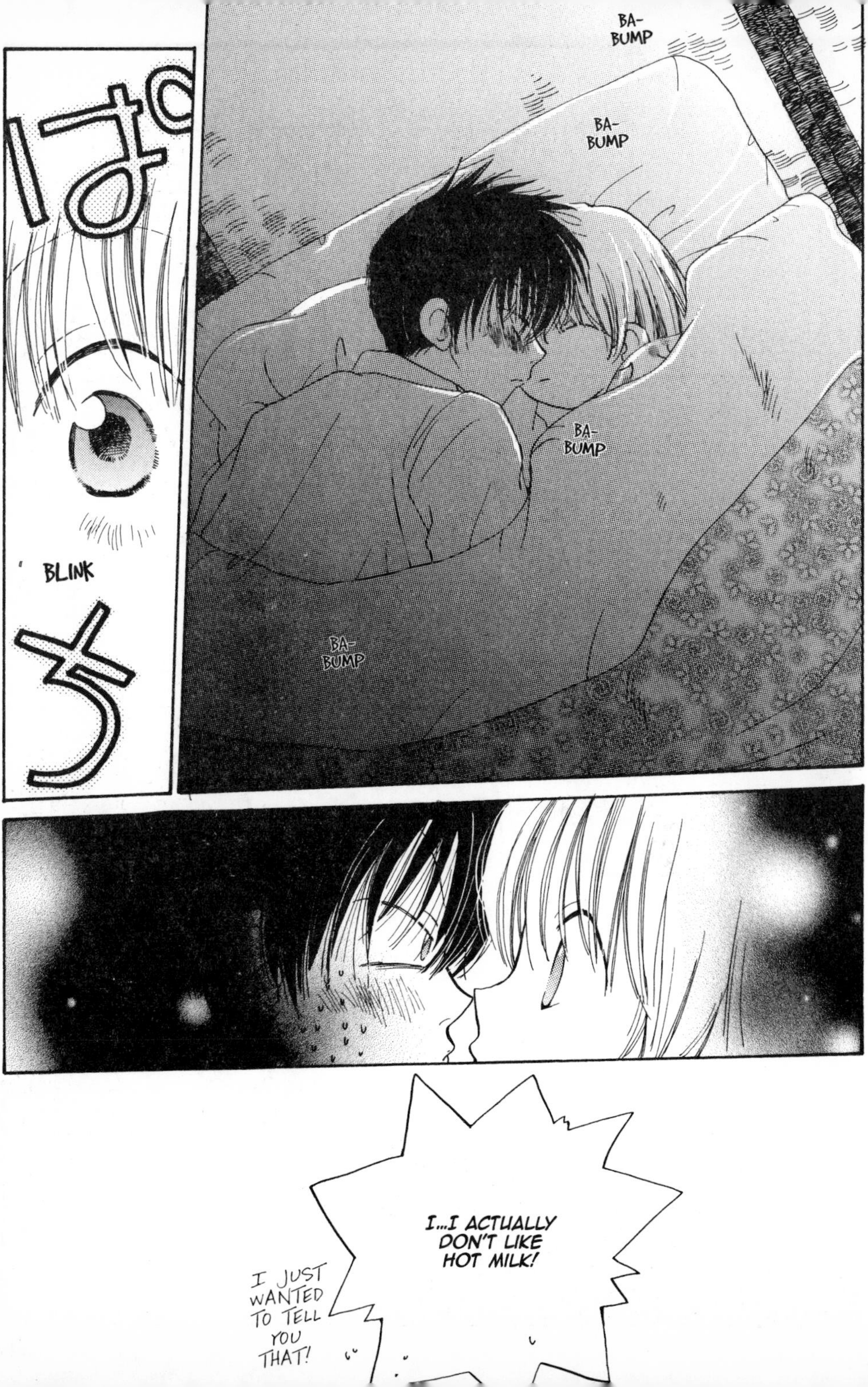
BA-BUMP
BA-BUMP
BA-BUMP
BA-BUMP
ぱち
BLINK
I...I ACTUALLY DON'T LIKE HOT MILK!
I JUST WANTED TO TELL YOU THAT!

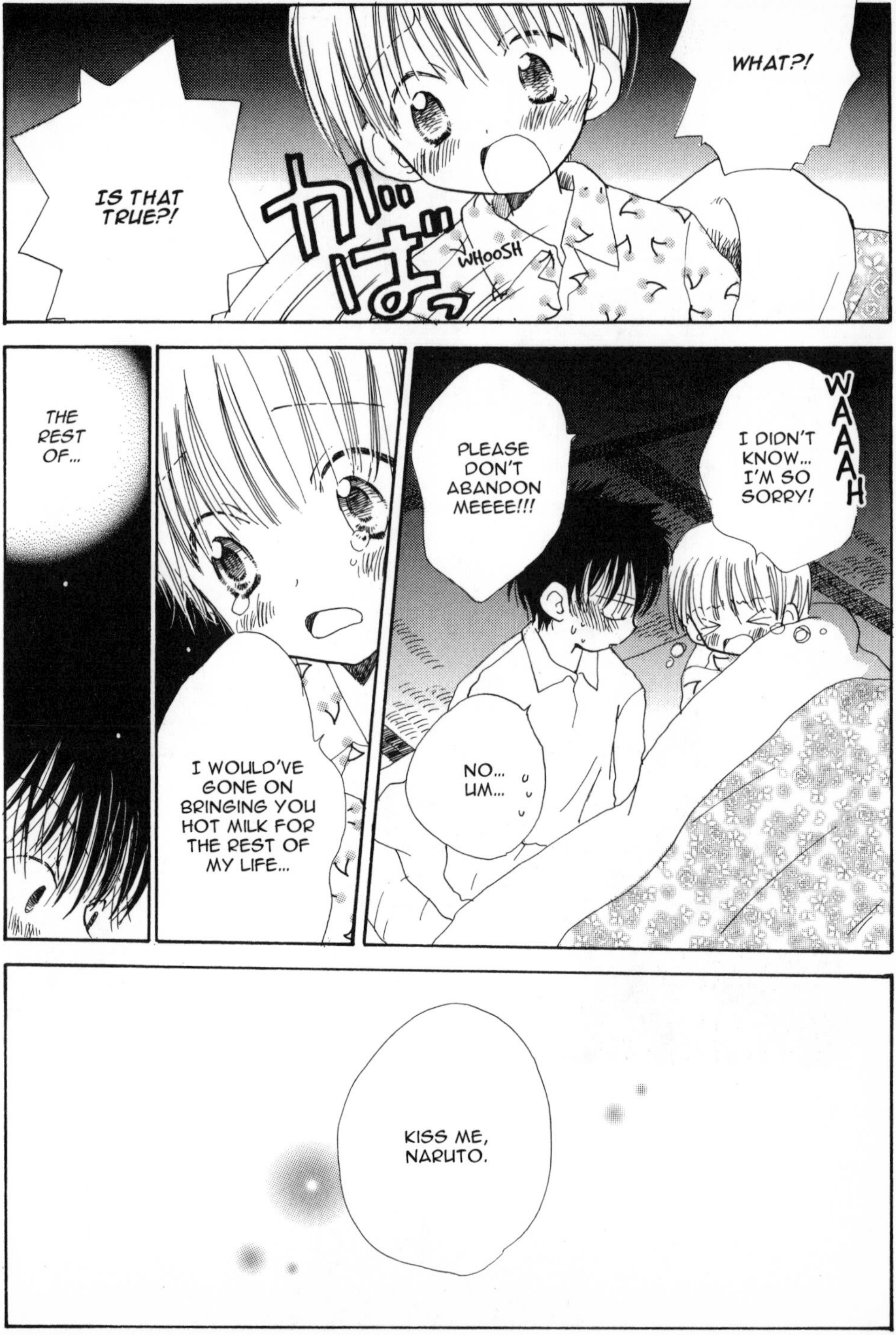
WHAT?!
WHOOSH
IS THAT TRUE?!
WAAAH
I DIDN'T KNOW... I'M SO SORRY!
PLEASE DON'T ABANDON MEEEE!!!
NO... UM...
I WOULD'VE GONE ON BRINGING YOU HOT MILK FOR THE REST OF MY LIFE...
THE REST OF...
KISS ME, NARUTO.

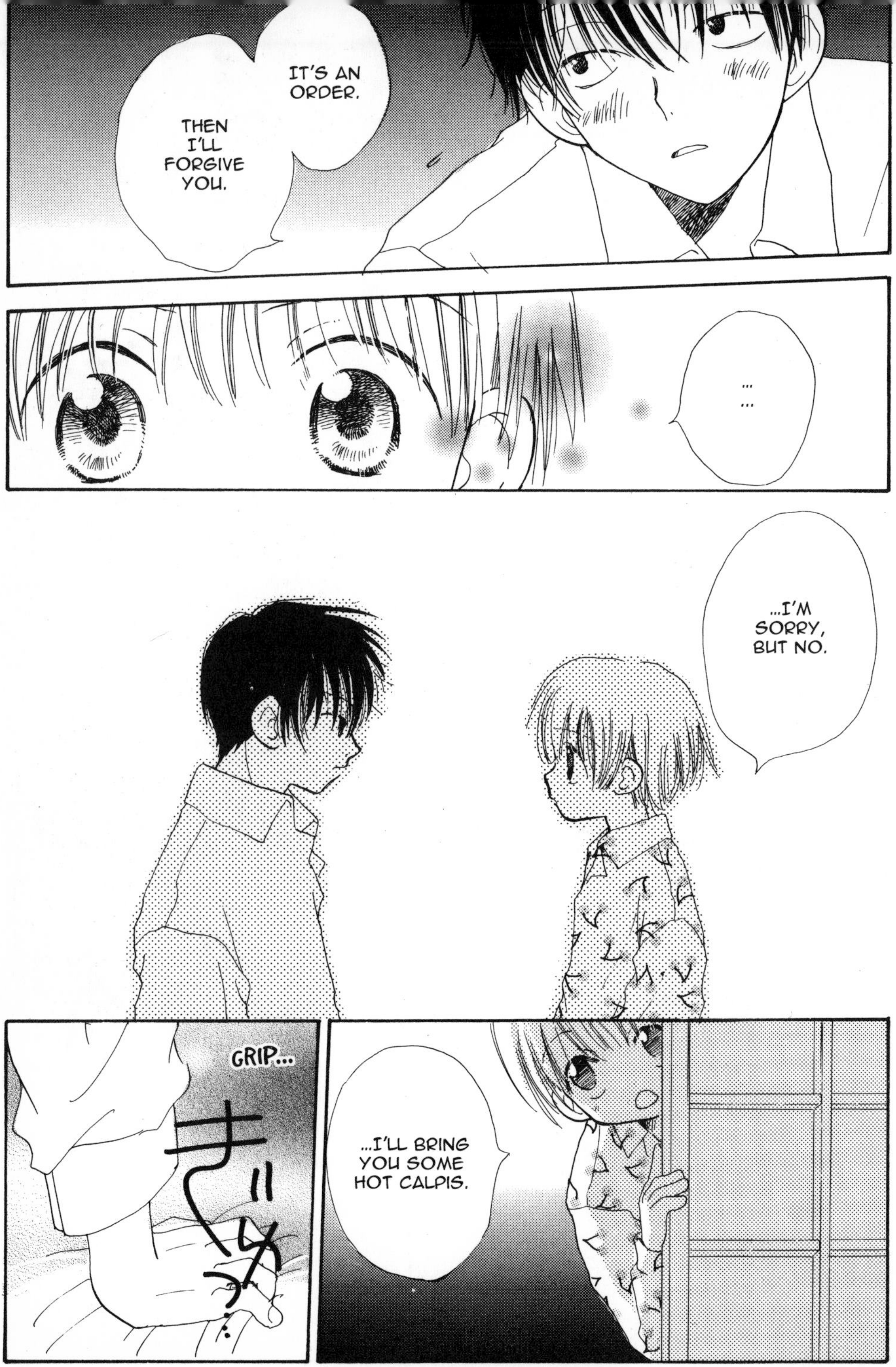
IT'S AN ORDER.
THEN I'LL FORGIVE YOU.
... ...
...I'M SORRY, BUT NO.
...I'LL BRING YOU SOME HOT CALPIS.
GRIP...

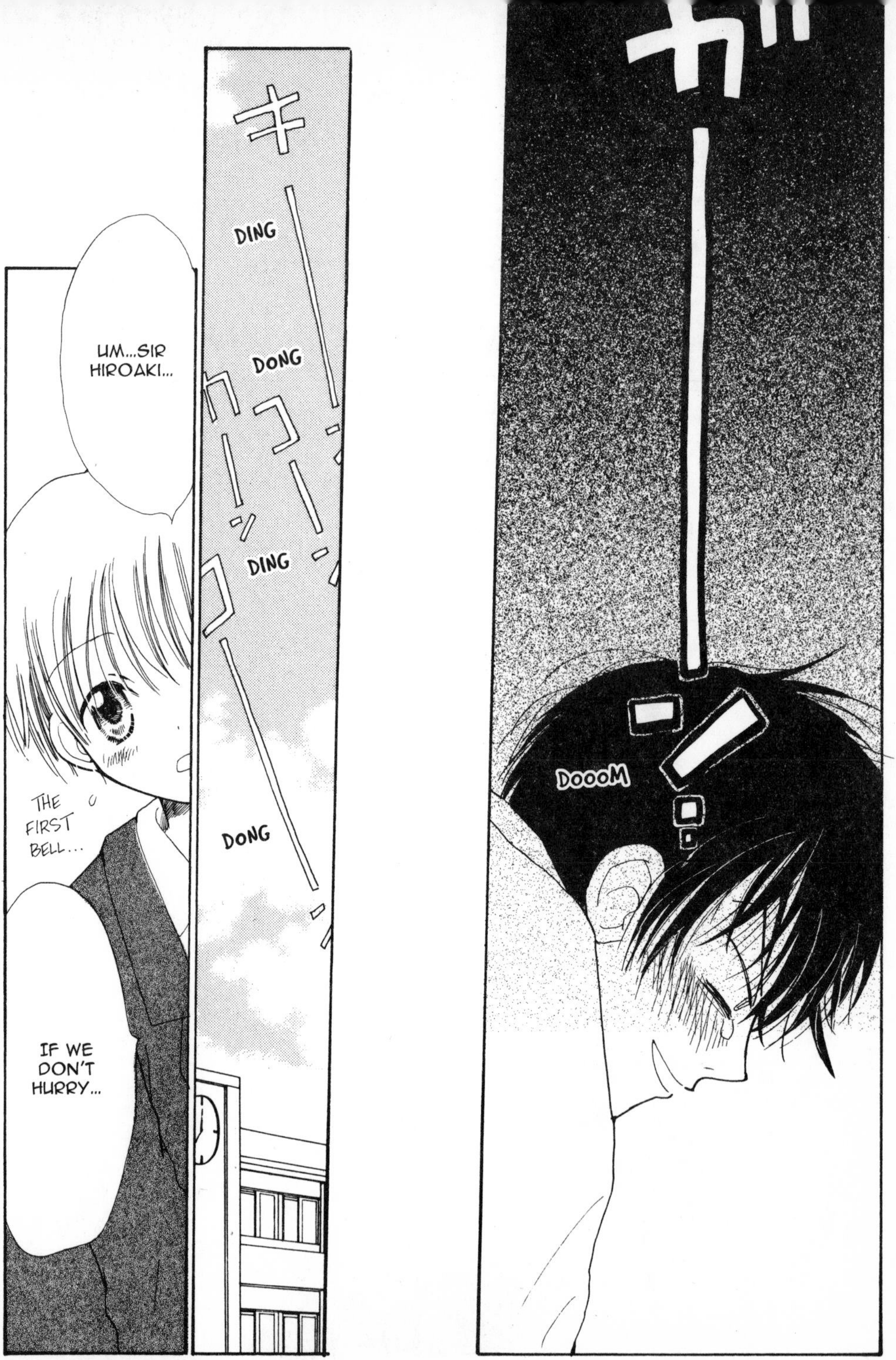
ガーン
DoooM
キーンコーンカーンコーン
DING
DONG
DING
DONG
UM...SIR HIROAKI...
THE FIRST BELL...
IF WE DON'T HURRY...

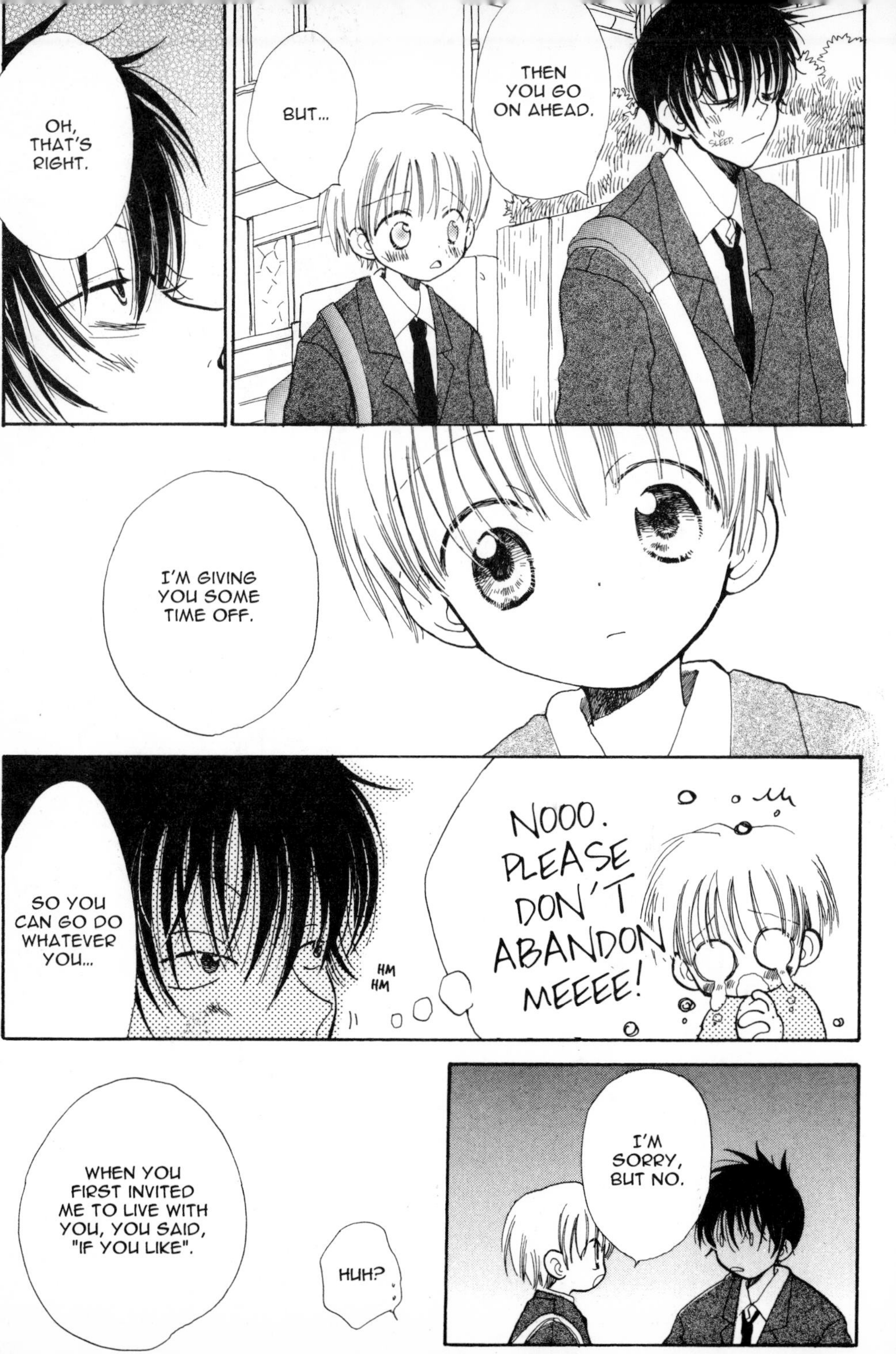
THEN YOU GO ON AHEAD.
NO SLEEP.
BUT...
OH, THAT'S RIGHT.
I'M GIVING YOU SOME TIME OFF.
SO YOU CAN GO DO WHATEVER YOU...
HM HM
NOOO. PLEASE DON'T ABANDON MEEEE!
I'M SORRY, BUT NO.
HUH?
WHEN YOU FIRST INVITED ME TO LIVE WITH YOU, YOU SAID, "IF YOU LIKE".

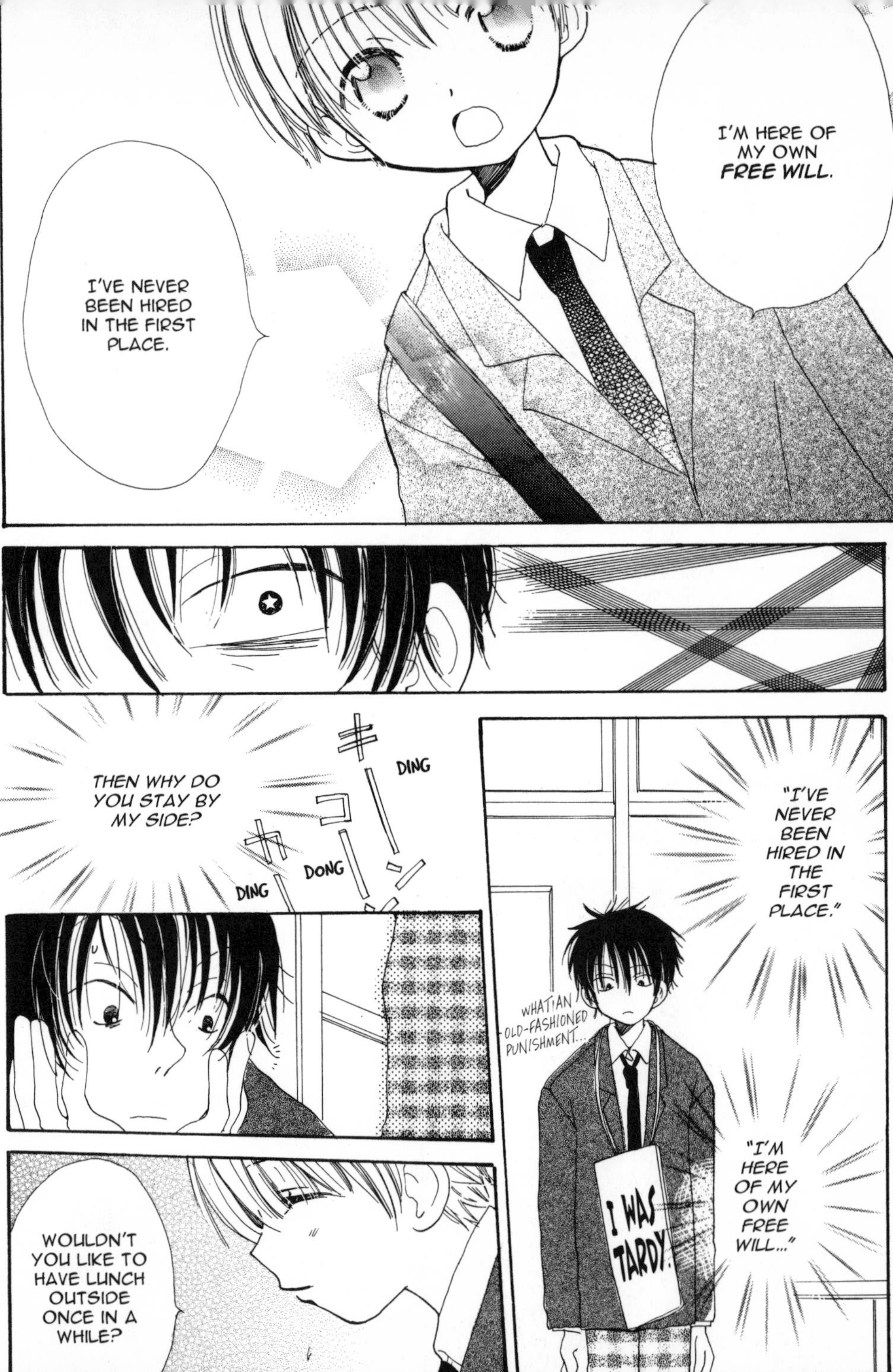
I'M HERE OF MY OWN FREE WILL.
I'VE NEVER BEEN HIRED IN THE FIRST PLACE.
"I'VE NEVER BEEN HIRED IN THE FIRST PLACE."
"I'M HERE OF MY OWN FREE WILL..."
WHAT AN OLD-FASHIONED PUNISHMENT...
I WAS TARDY.
THEN WHY DO YOU STAY BY MY SIDE?
DING
DONG
DING
WOULDN'T YOU LIKE TO HAVE LUNCH OUTSIDE ONCE IN A WHILE?

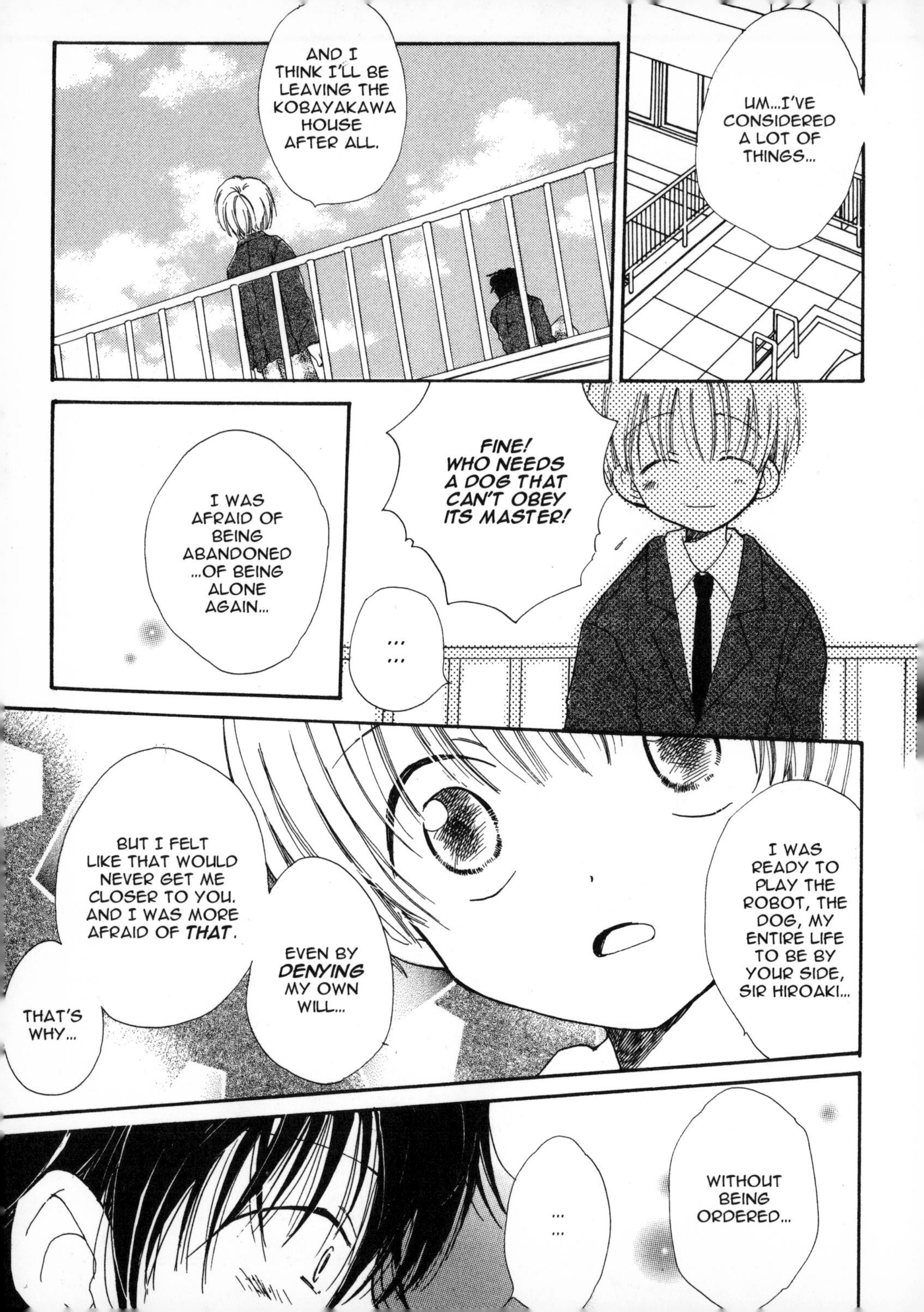
UM...I'VE CONSIDERED A LOT OF THINGS...
AND I THINK I'LL BE LEAVING THE KOBAYAKAWA HOUSE AFTER ALL.
FINE! WHO NEEDS A DOG THAT CAN'T OBEY ITS MASTER!
......
I WAS AFRAID OF BEING ABANDONED ...OF BEING ALONE AGAIN...
I WAS READY TO PLAY THE ROBOT, THE DOG, MY ENTIRE LIFE TO BE BY YOUR SIDE, SIR HIROAKI...
EVEN BY ***DENYING*** MY OWN WILL...
BUT I FELT LIKE THAT WOULD NEVER GET ME CLOSER TO YOU. AND I WAS MORE AFRAID OF ***THAT***.
THAT'S WHY...
WITHOUT BEING ORDERED...
......

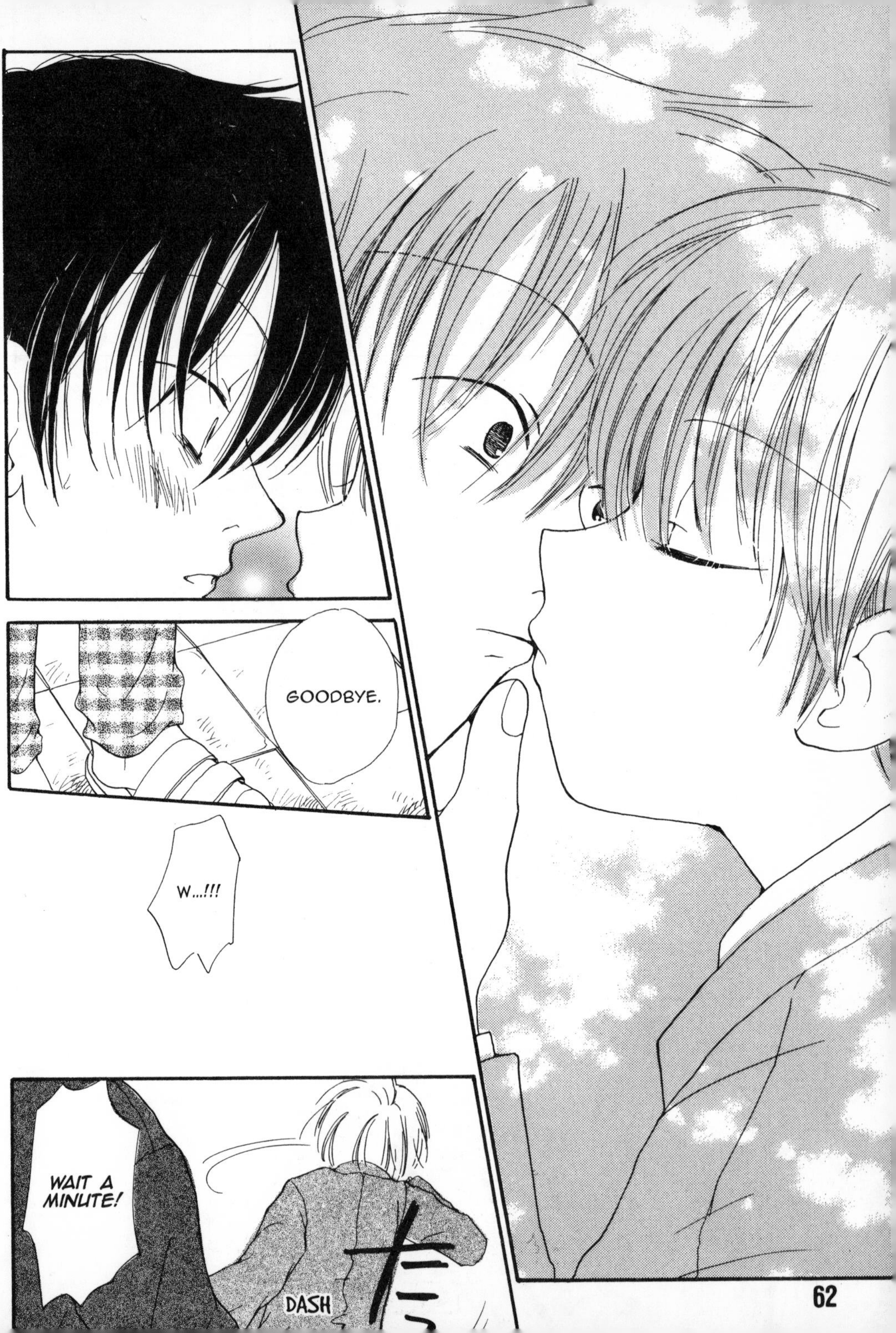
GOODBYE.
W...!!!
WAIT A MINUTE!
DASH

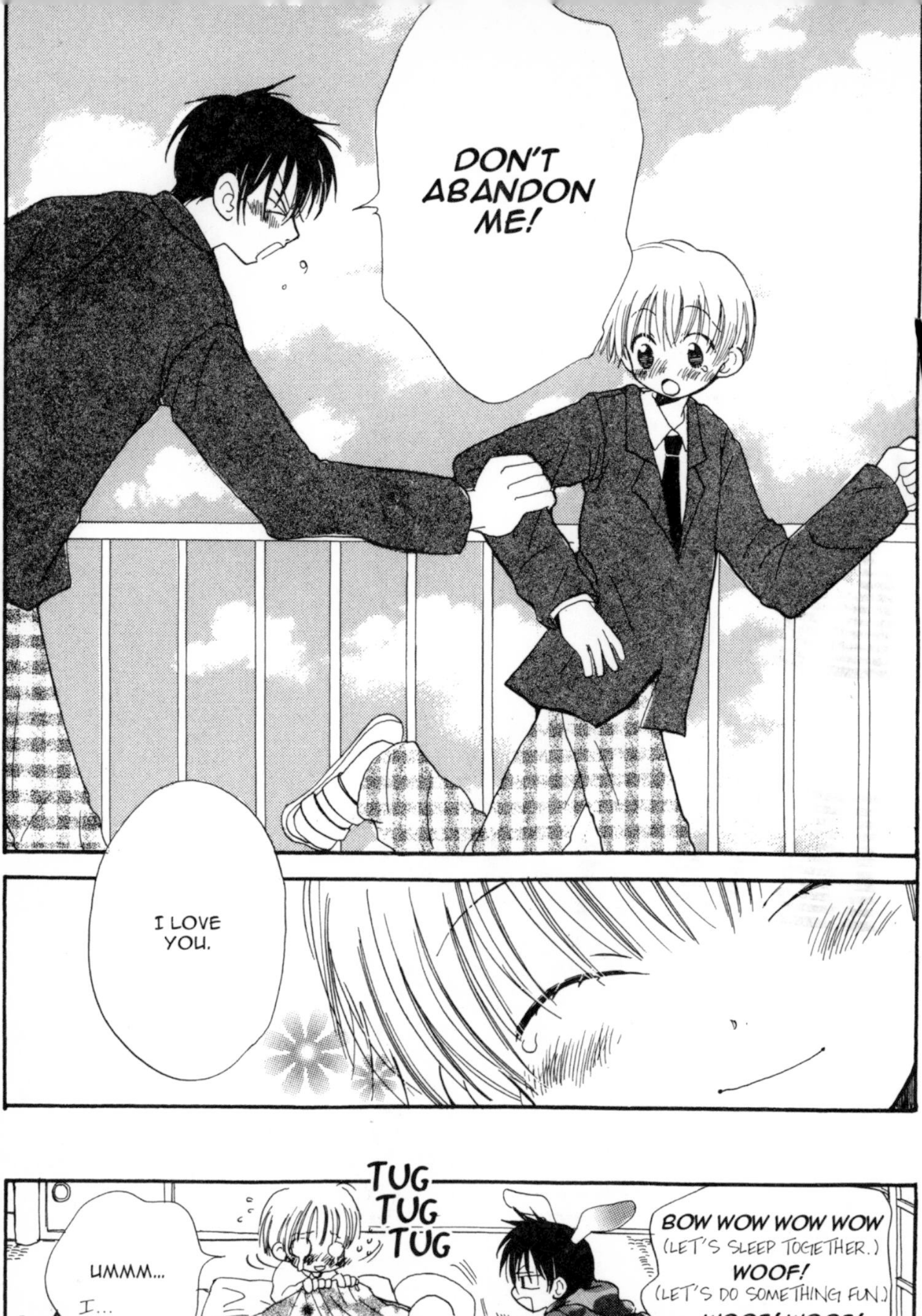
DON'T ABANDON ME!
I LOVE YOU.
BOW WOW WOW WOW (LET'S SLEEP TOGETHER.) WOOF! (LET'S DO SOMETHING FUN.) WOOF! WOOF! (YOU DON'T WANT ME AS A BIG BROTHER, RIGHT?)
TUG TUG TUG
UMMM... I...

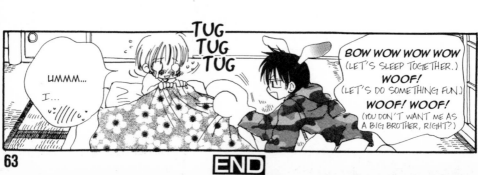

END

SECOND HAND

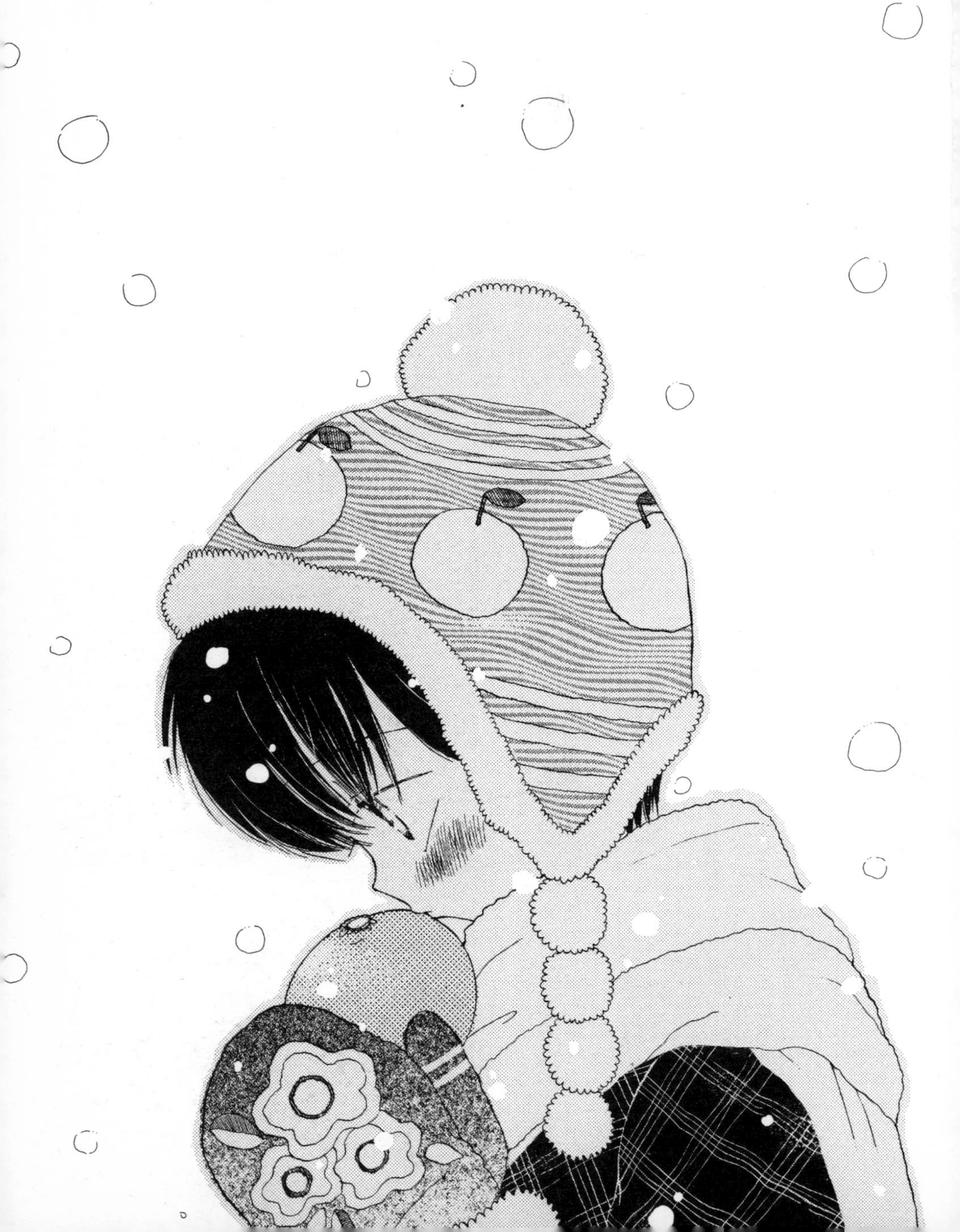

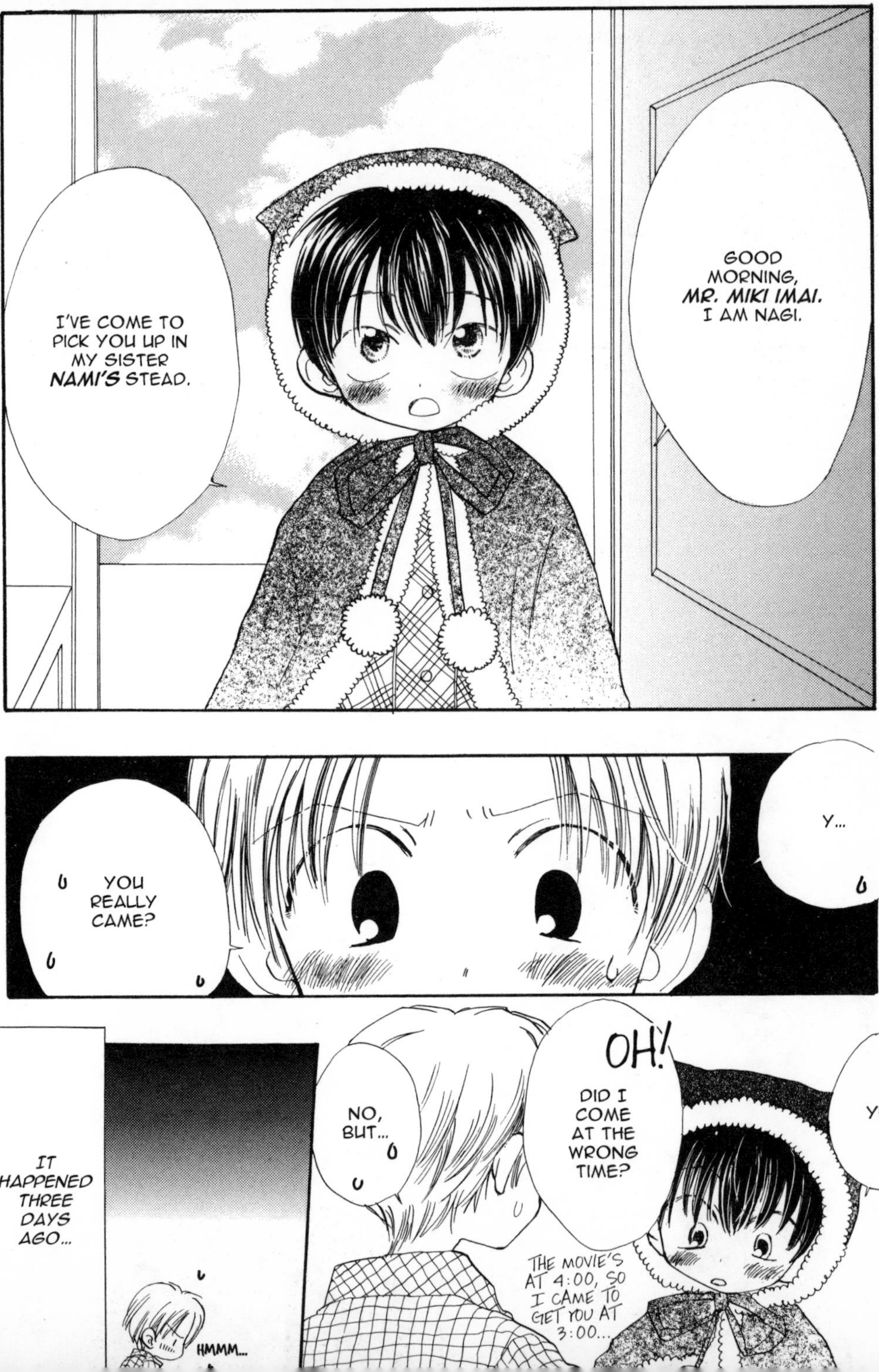
GOOD MORNING, MR. MIKI IMAI. I AM NAGI.
I'VE COME TO PICK YOU UP IN MY SISTER NAMI'S STEAD.
Y...
YOU REALLY CAME?
YES.
OH! DID I COME AT THE WRONG TIME?
NO, BUT...
THE MOVIE'S AT 4:00, SO I CAME TO GET YOU AT 3:00...
IT HAPPENED THREE DAYS AGO...
HMMM...

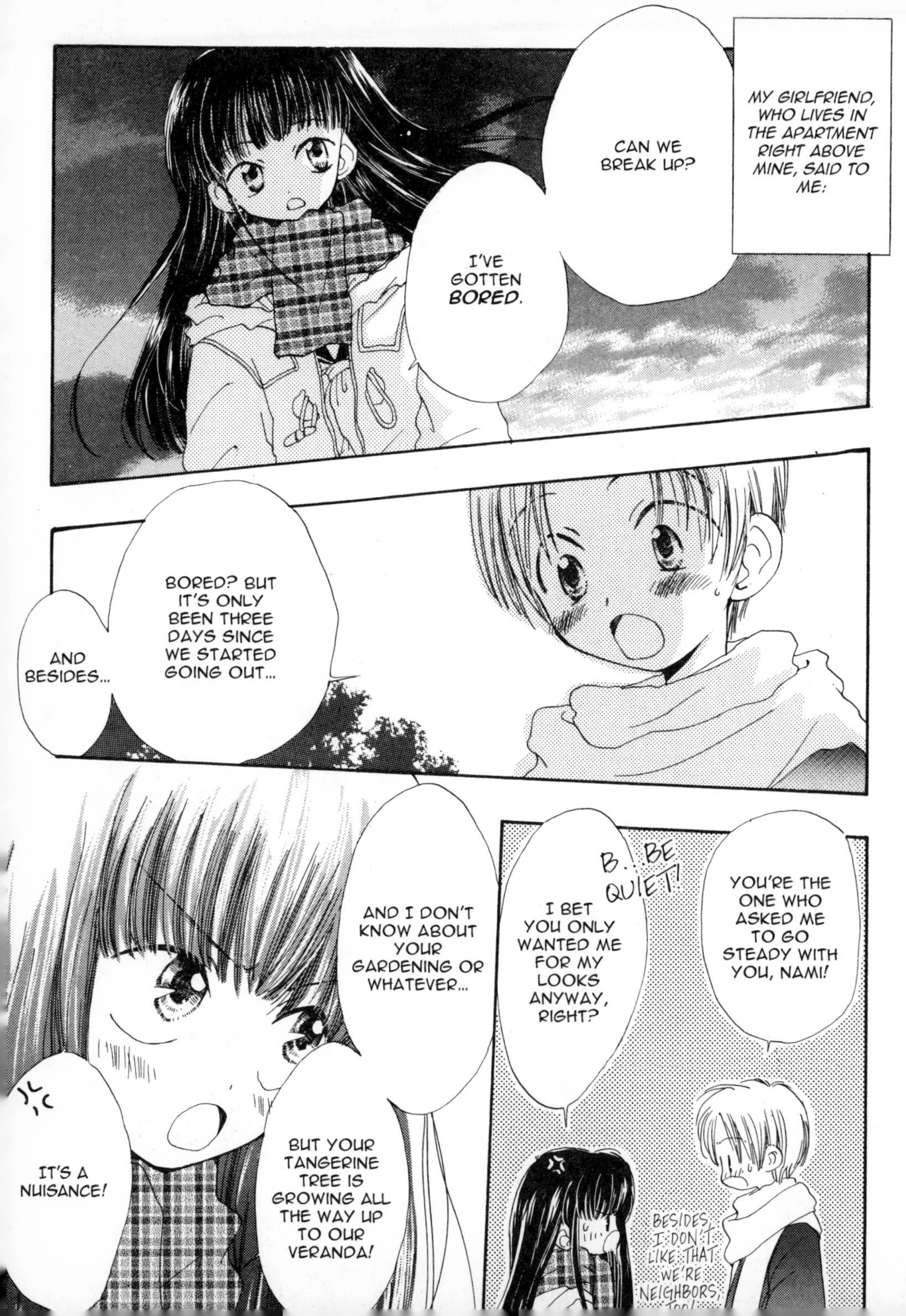
MY GIRLFRIEND, WHO LIVES IN THE APARTMENT RIGHT ABOVE MINE, SAID TO ME:
CAN WE BREAK UP?
I'VE GOTTEN BORED.
BORED? BUT IT'S ONLY BEEN THREE DAYS SINCE WE STARTED GOING OUT...
AND BESIDES...
YOU'RE THE ONE WHO ASKED ME TO GO STEADY WITH YOU, NAMI!
B...BE QUIET!
I BET YOU ONLY WANTED ME FOR MY LOOKS ANYWAY, RIGHT?
BESIDES, I DON'T LIKE THAT WE'RE NEIGHBORS, TOO!
AND I DON'T KNOW ABOUT YOUR GARDENING OR WHATEVER...
BUT YOUR TANGERINE TREE IS GROWING ALL THE WAY UP TO OUR VERANDA!
IT'S A NUISANCE!

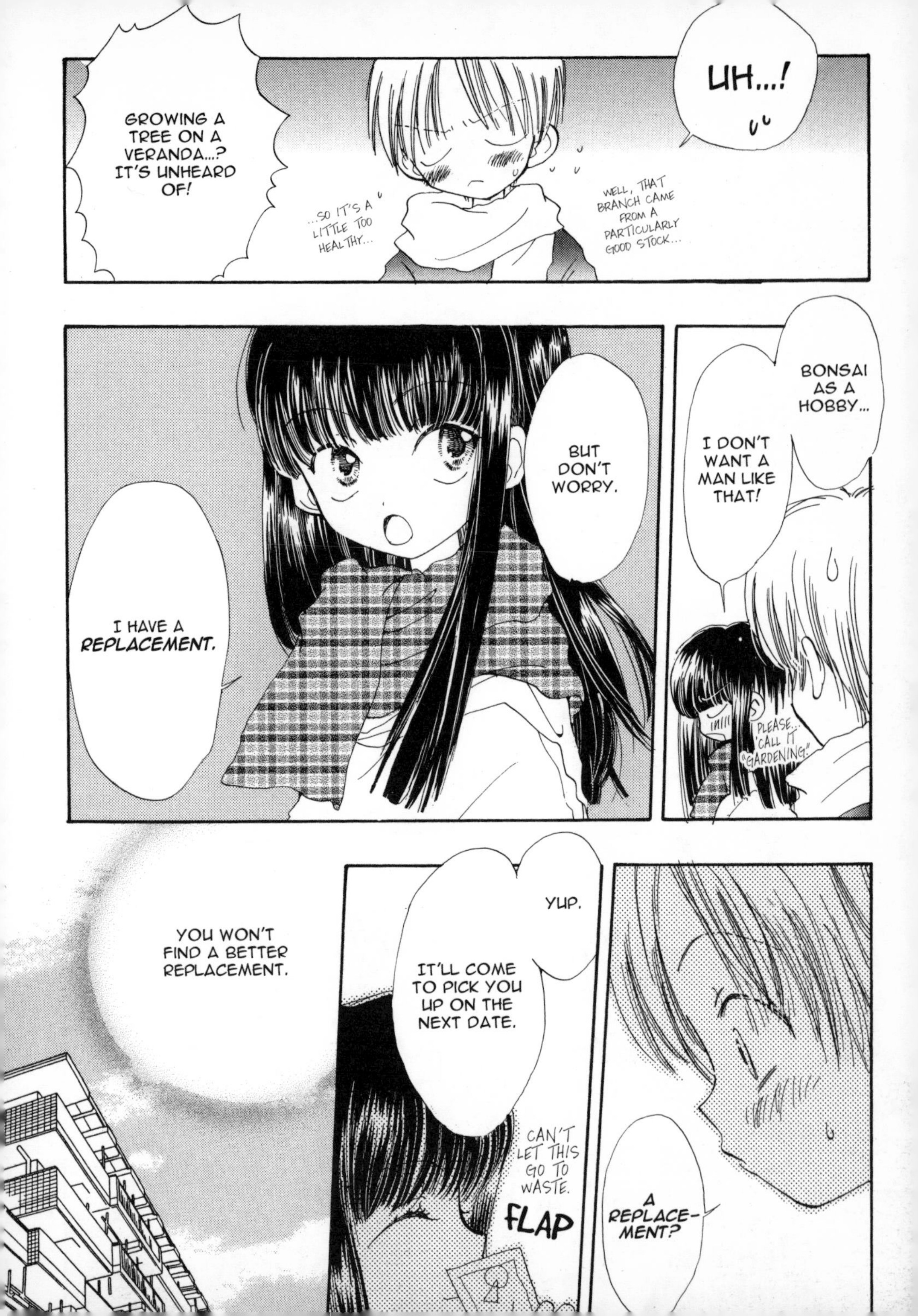
UH...!
WELL, THAT BRANCH CAME FROM A PARTICULARLY GOOD STOCK...
...SO IT'S A LITTLE TOO HEALTHY...
GROWING A TREE ON A VERANDA...? IT'S UNHEARD OF!
BONSAI AS A HOBBY...
I DON'T WANT A MAN LIKE THAT!
PLEASE... CALL IT "GARDENING."
BUT DON'T WORRY.
I HAVE A REPLACEMENT.
A REPLACE-MENT?
YUP.
IT'LL COME TO PICK YOU UP ON THE NEXT DATE.
CAN'T LET THIS GO TO WASTE.
FLAP
YOU WON'T FIND A BETTER REPLACEMENT.

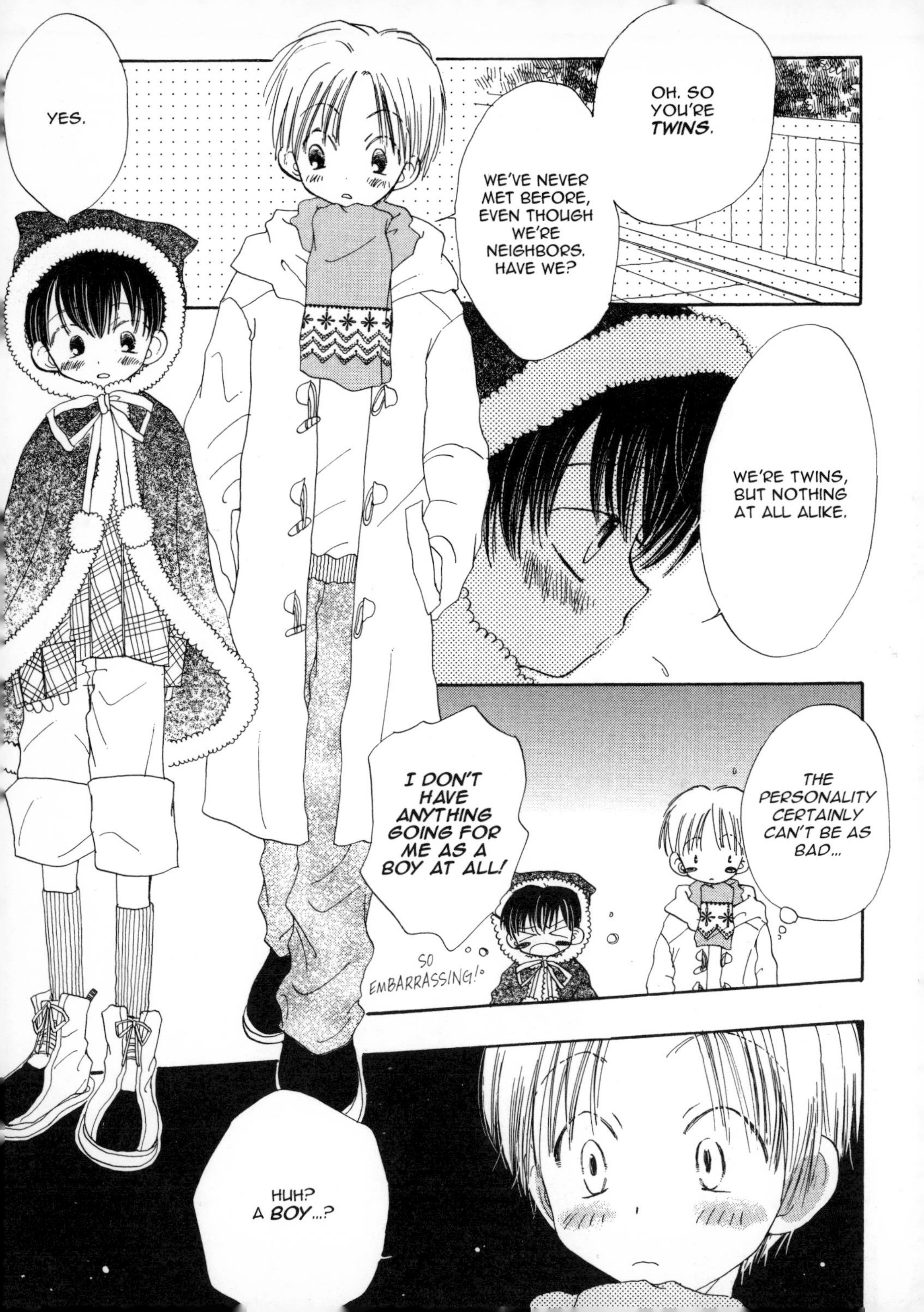

OH. SO YOU'RE *TWINS*.
WE'VE NEVER MET BEFORE, EVEN THOUGH WE'RE NEIGHBORS. HAVE WE?
YES.
WE'RE TWINS, BUT NOTHING AT ALL ALIKE.
THE PERSONALITY CERTAINLY CAN'T BE AS BAD...
I DON'T HAVE ANYTHING GOING FOR ME AS A BOY AT ALL!
SO EMBARRASSING!
HUH? A *BOY*...?

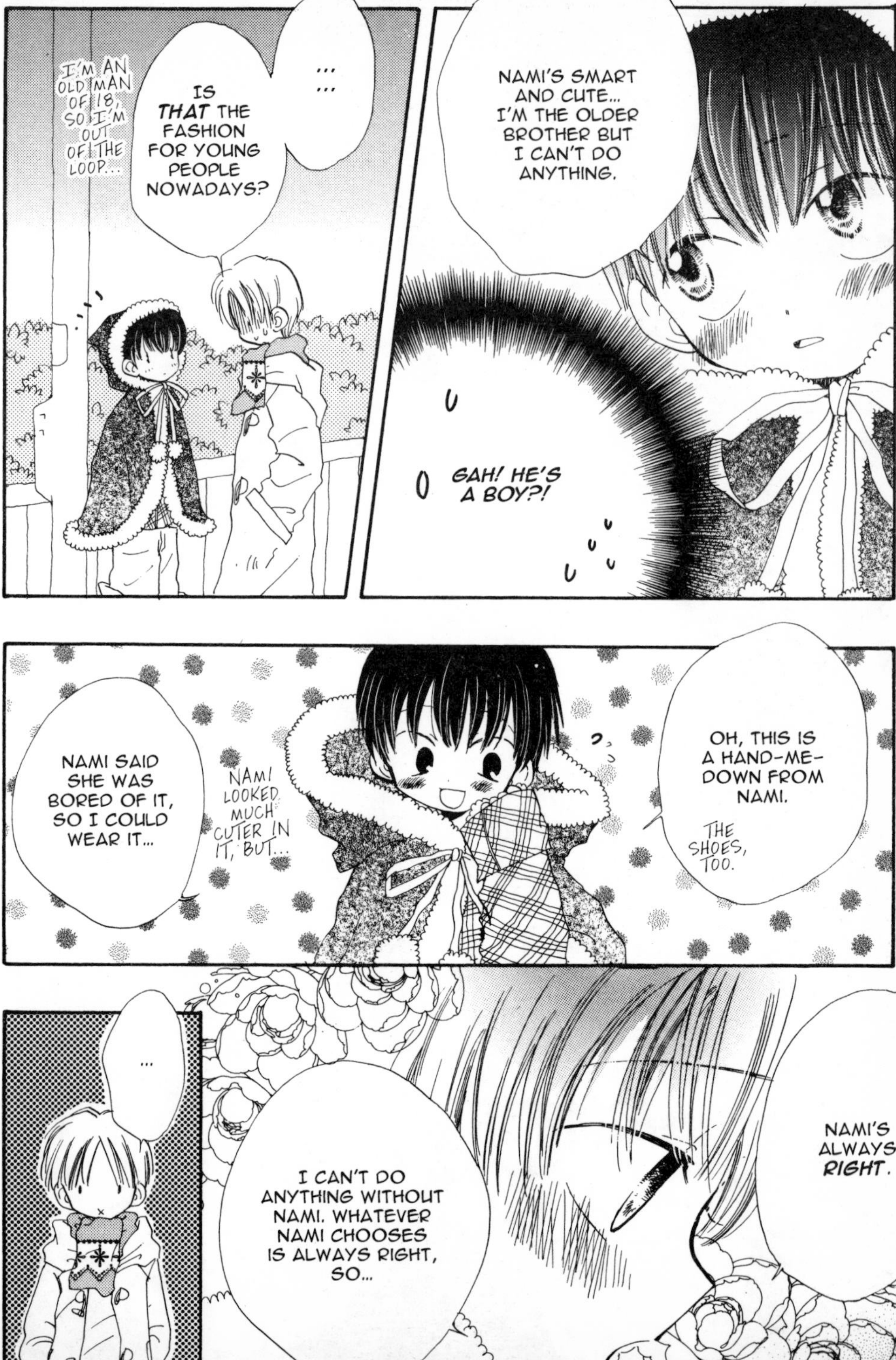
NAMI'S SMART AND CUTE... I'M THE OLDER BROTHER BUT I CAN'T DO ANYTHING.
GAH! HE'S A BOY?!
... ...
IS THAT THE FASHION FOR YOUNG PEOPLE NOWADAYS?
I'M AN OLD MAN OF 18, SO I'M OUT OF THE LOOP...
OH, THIS IS A HAND-ME-DOWN FROM NAMI.
THE SHOES, TOO.
NAMI LOOKED MUCH CUTER IN IT, BUT...
NAMI SAID SHE WAS BORED OF IT, SO I COULD WEAR IT...
NAMI'S ALWAYS RIGHT.
I CAN'T DO ANYTHING WITHOUT NAMI. WHATEVER NAMI CHOOSES IS ALWAYS RIGHT, SO...
...

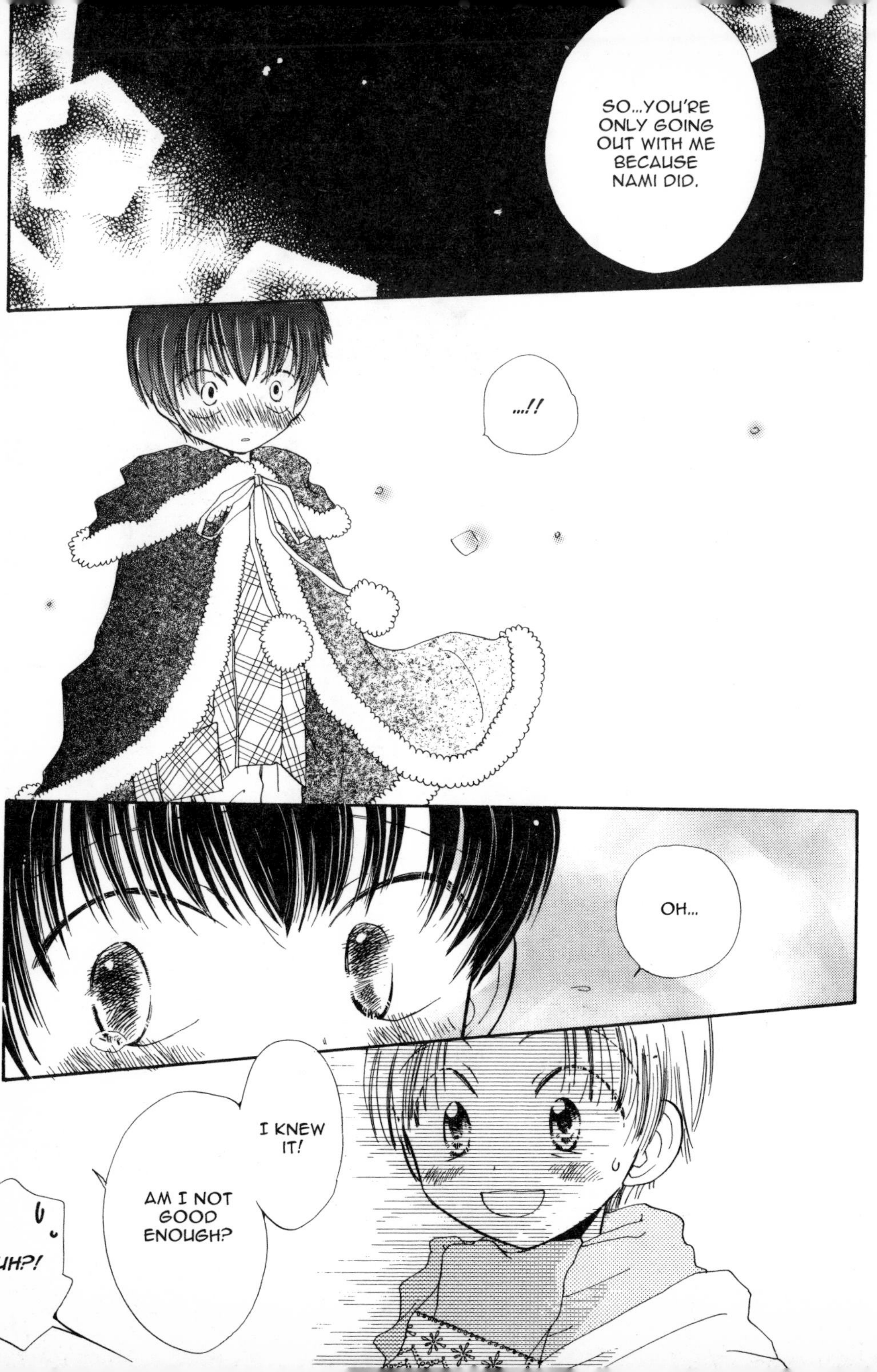
SO...YOU'RE ONLY GOING OUT WITH ME BECAUSE NAMI DID.
...!!
OH...
I KNEW IT!
AM I NOT GOOD ENOUGH?
HUH?!

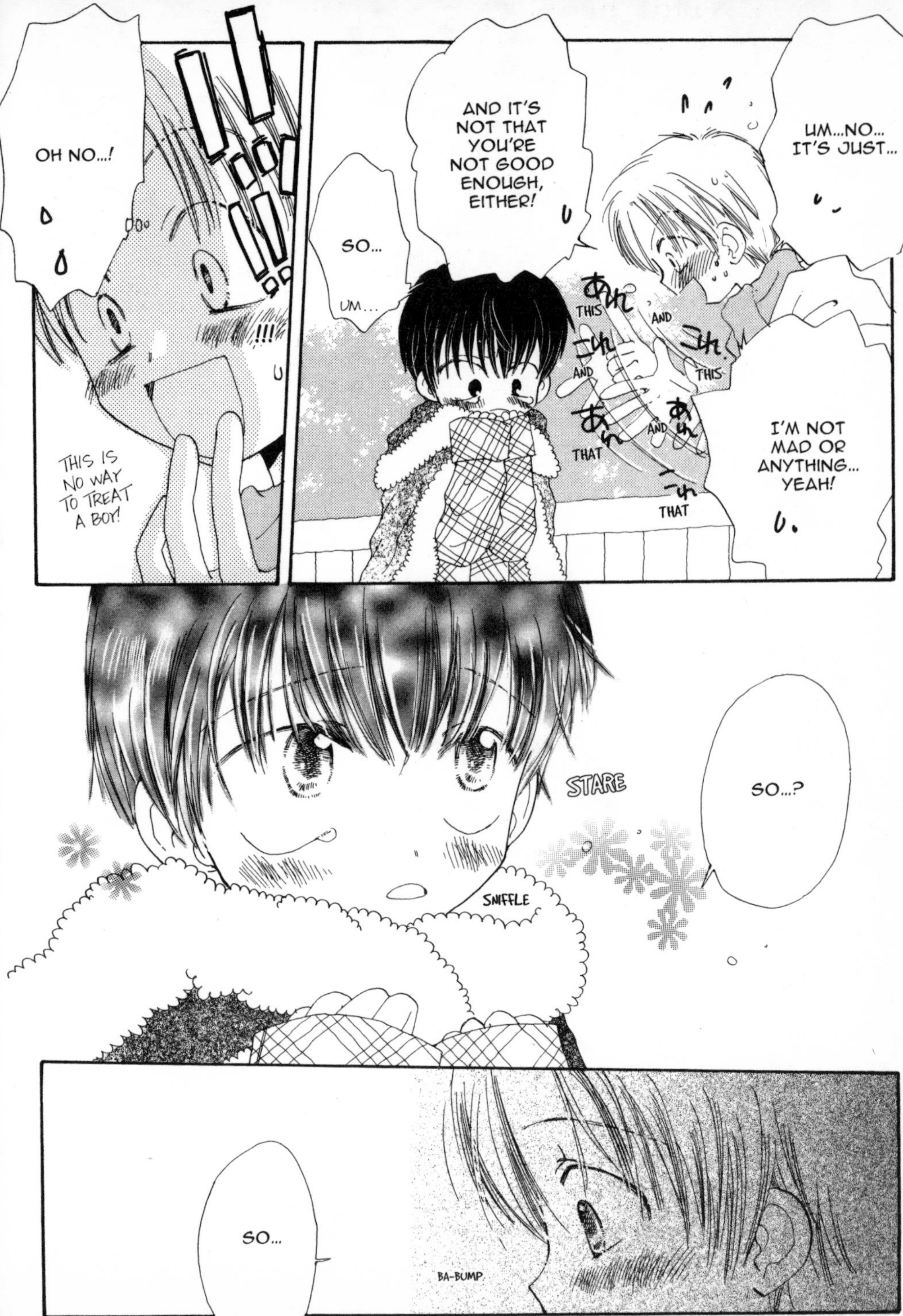
UM...NO... IT'S JUST...
AND IT'S NOT THAT YOU'RE NOT GOOD ENOUGH, EITHER!
I'M NOT MAD OR ANYTHING... YEAH!
SO...
UM...
これ THIS
あれ THIS
AND
これ AND
あれ AND
あれ THAT
これ THAT
OH NO...!
THIS IS NO WAY TO TREAT A BOY!
SO...?
STARE
SNIFFLE
SO...
BA-BUMP

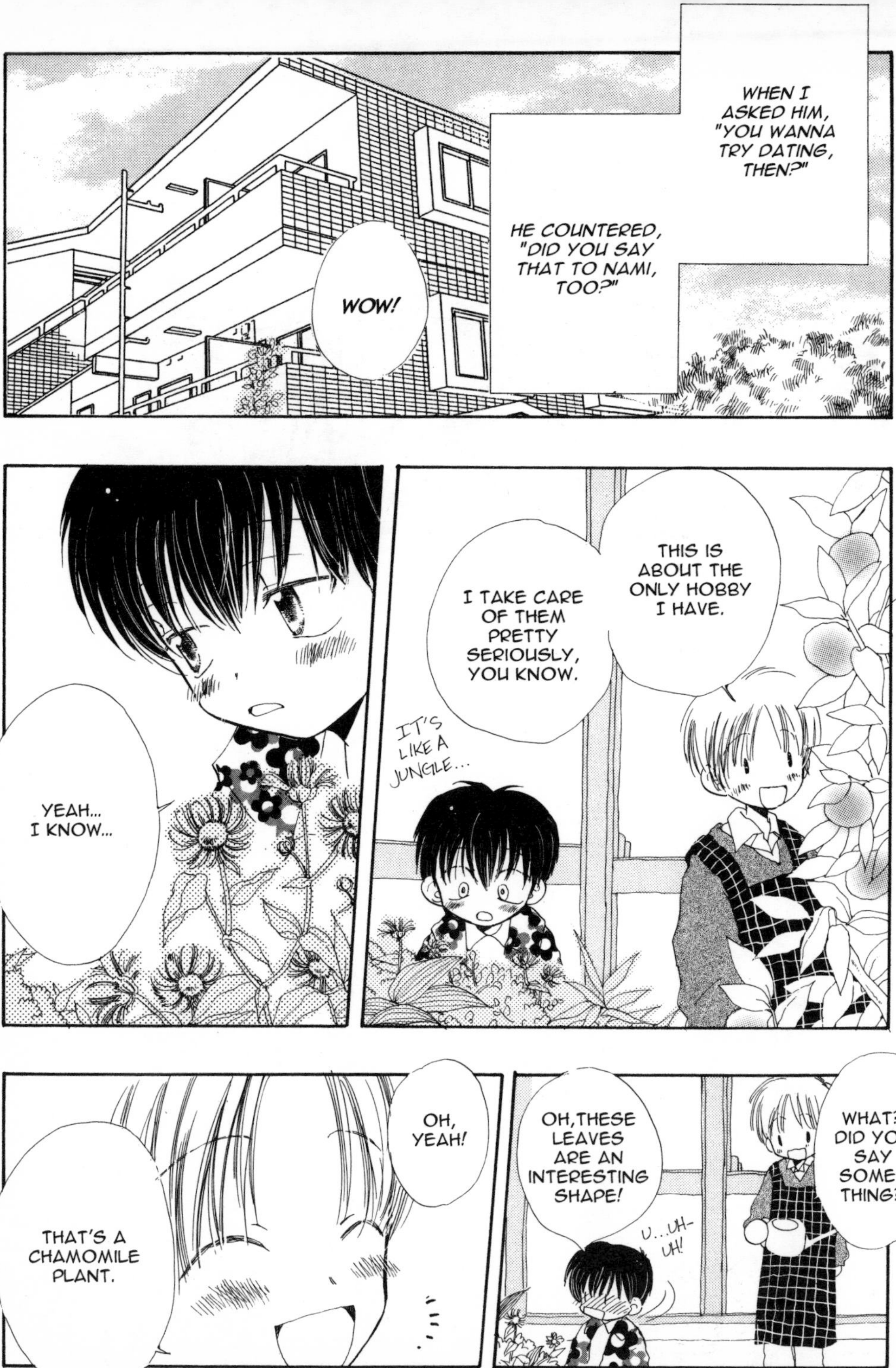
WHEN I ASKED HIM, "YOU WANNA TRY DATING, THEN?"
HE COUNTERED, "DID YOU SAY THAT TO NAMI, TOO?"
WOW!
THIS IS ABOUT THE ONLY HOBBY I HAVE.
I TAKE CARE OF THEM PRETTY SERIOUSLY, YOU KNOW.
IT'S LIKE A JUNGLE...
YEAH... I KNOW...
WHAT? DID YOU SAY SOME-THING?
OH, THESE LEAVES ARE AN INTERESTING SHAPE!
U...UH-UH!
OH, YEAH!
THAT'S A CHAMOMILE PLANT.

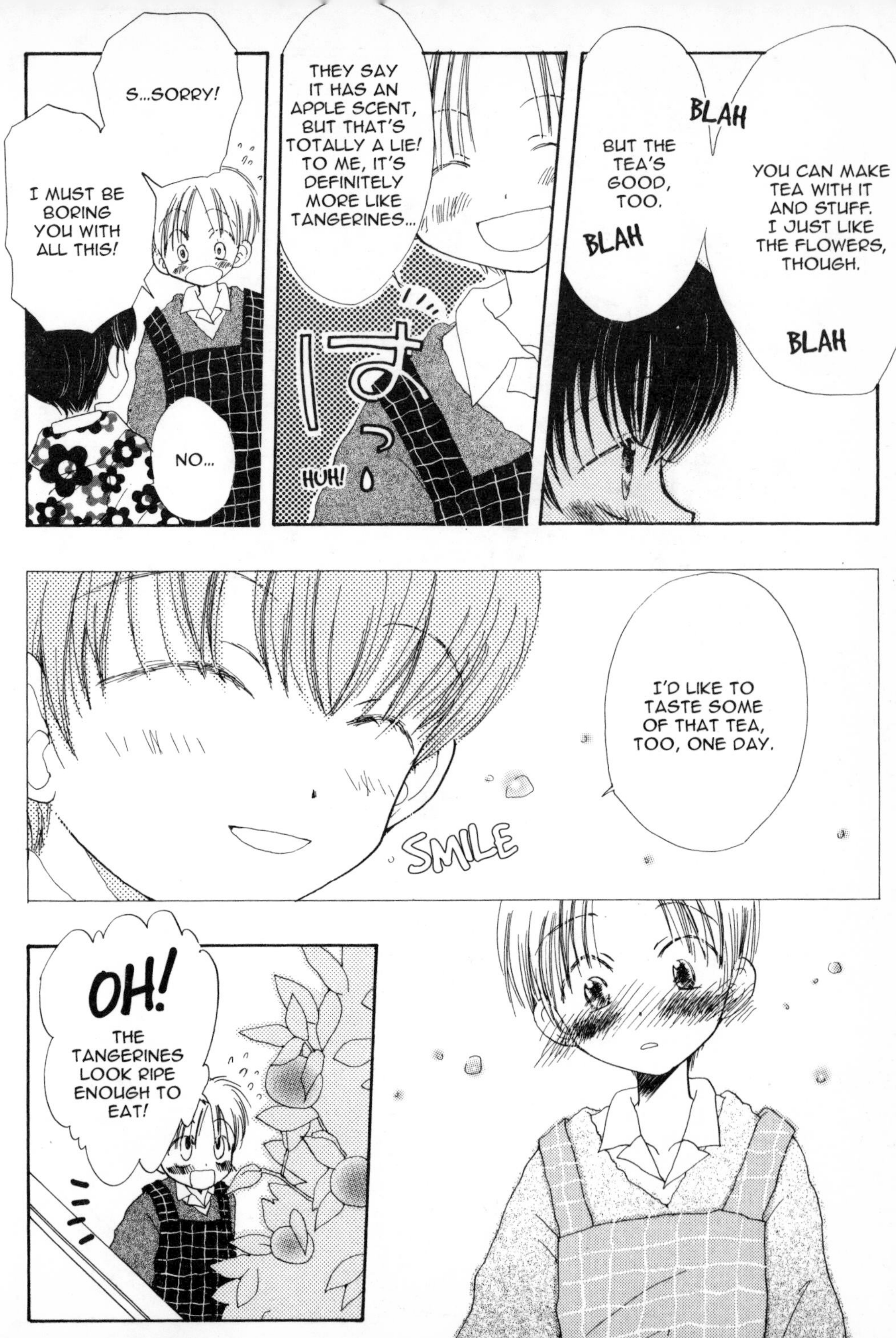

BLAH
YOU CAN MAKE TEA WITH IT AND STUFF. I JUST LIKE THE FLOWERS, THOUGH.
BUT THE TEA'S GOOD, TOO.
BLAH
BLAH
THEY SAY IT HAS AN APPLE SCENT, BUT THAT'S TOTALLY A LIE! TO ME, IT'S DEFINITELY MORE LIKE TANGERINES...
はっ
HUH!
S...SORRY!
I MUST BE BORING YOU WITH ALL THIS!
NO...
I'D LIKE TO TASTE SOME OF THAT TEA, TOO, ONE DAY.
SMILE
OH!
THE TANGERINES LOOK RIPE ENOUGH TO EAT!

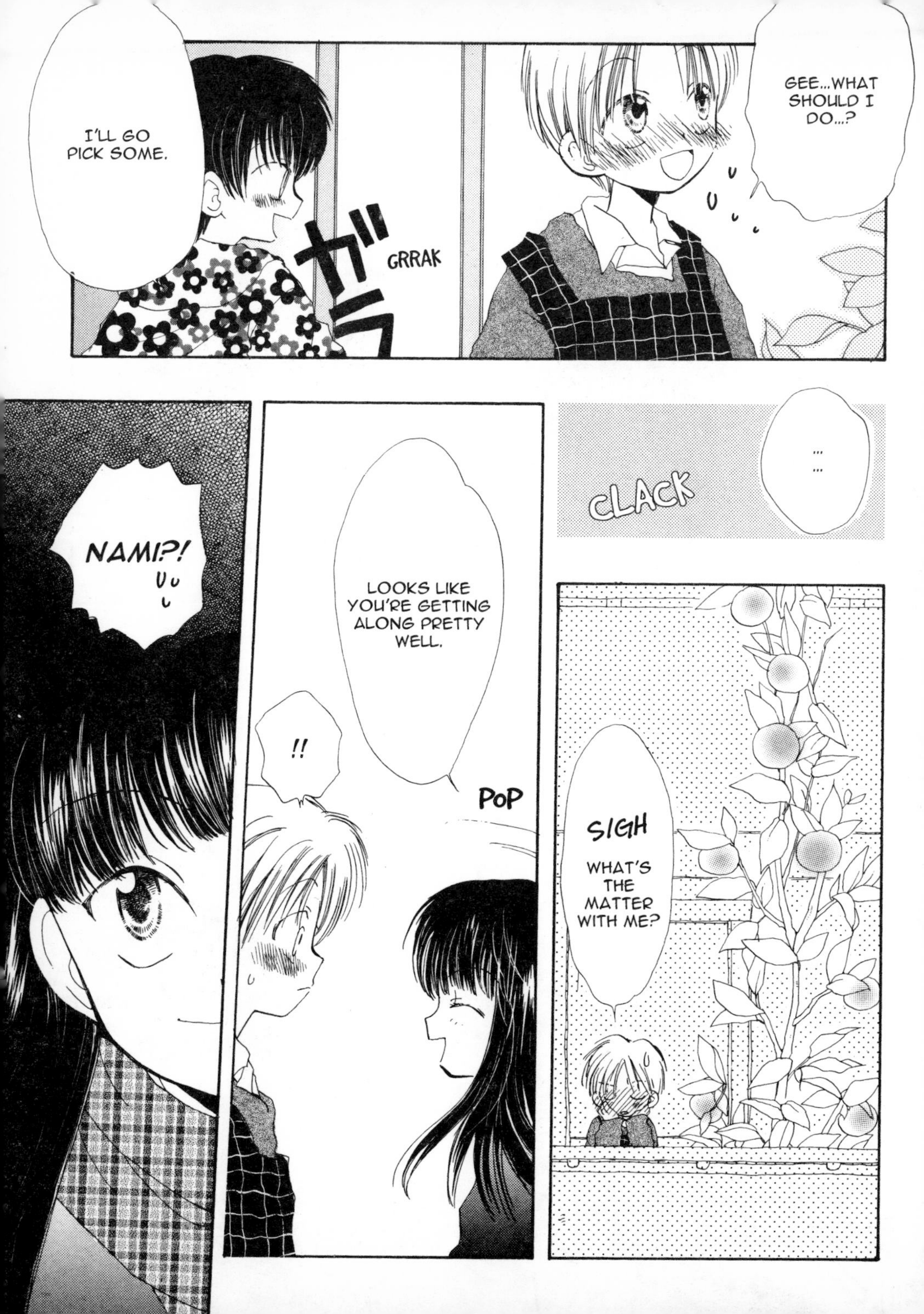
GEE...WHAT SHOULD I DO...?
I'LL GO PICK SOME.
ガラ
GRRAK
CLACK
......
SIGH
WHAT'S THE MATTER WITH ME?
LOOKS LIKE YOU'RE GETTING ALONG PRETTY WELL.
POP
!!
NAMI?!

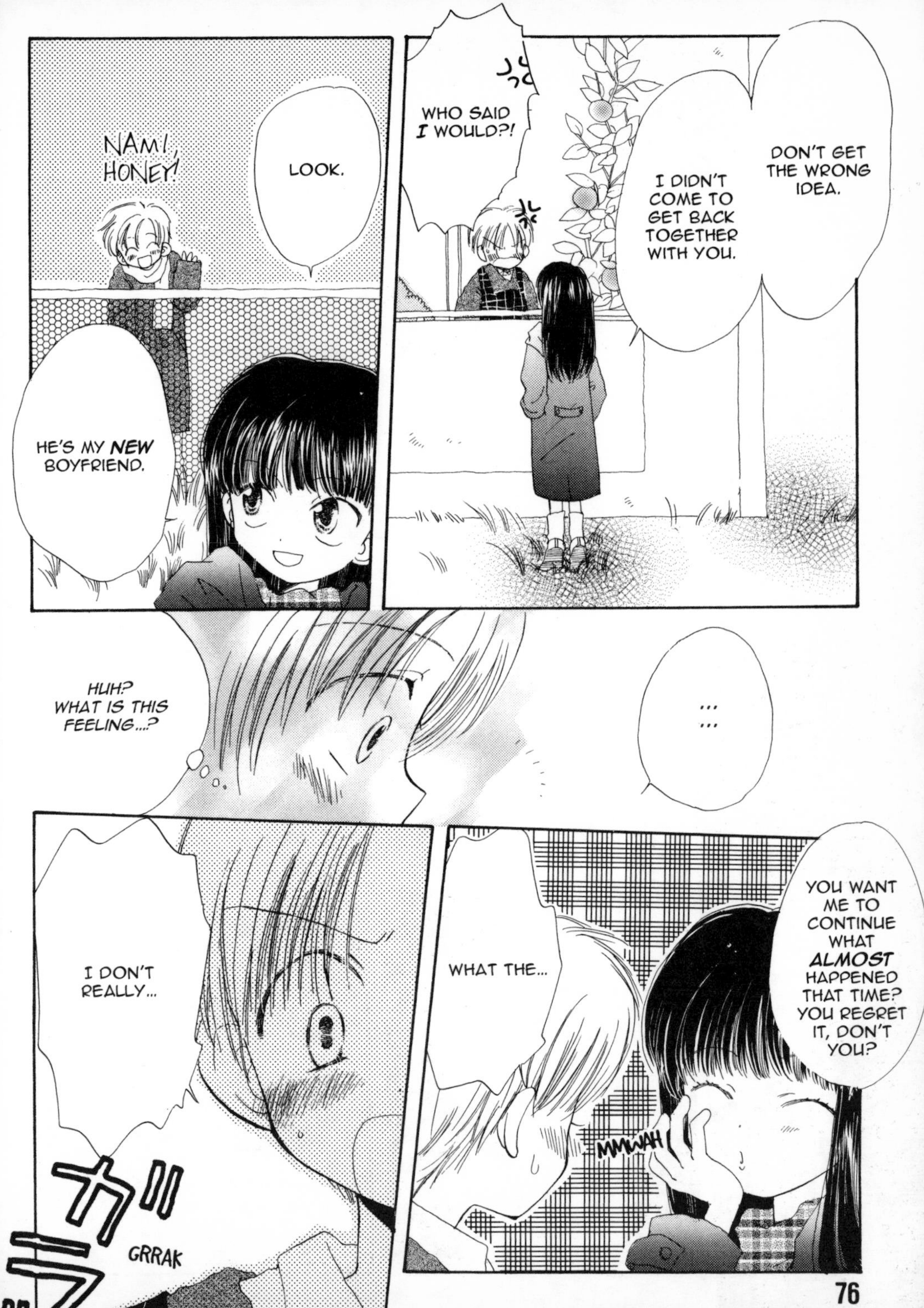
DON'T GET THE WRONG IDEA.
I DIDN'T COME TO GET BACK TOGETHER WITH YOU.
WHO SAID *I* WOULD?!
LOOK.
NAMI, HONEY!
HE'S MY **NEW** BOYFRIEND.
...
...
HUH? WHAT IS THIS FEELING...?
YOU WANT ME TO CONTINUE WHAT **ALMOST** HAPPENED THAT TIME? YOU REGRET IT, DON'T YOU?
MMWAH
WHAT THE...
I DON'T REALLY...
GRRAK

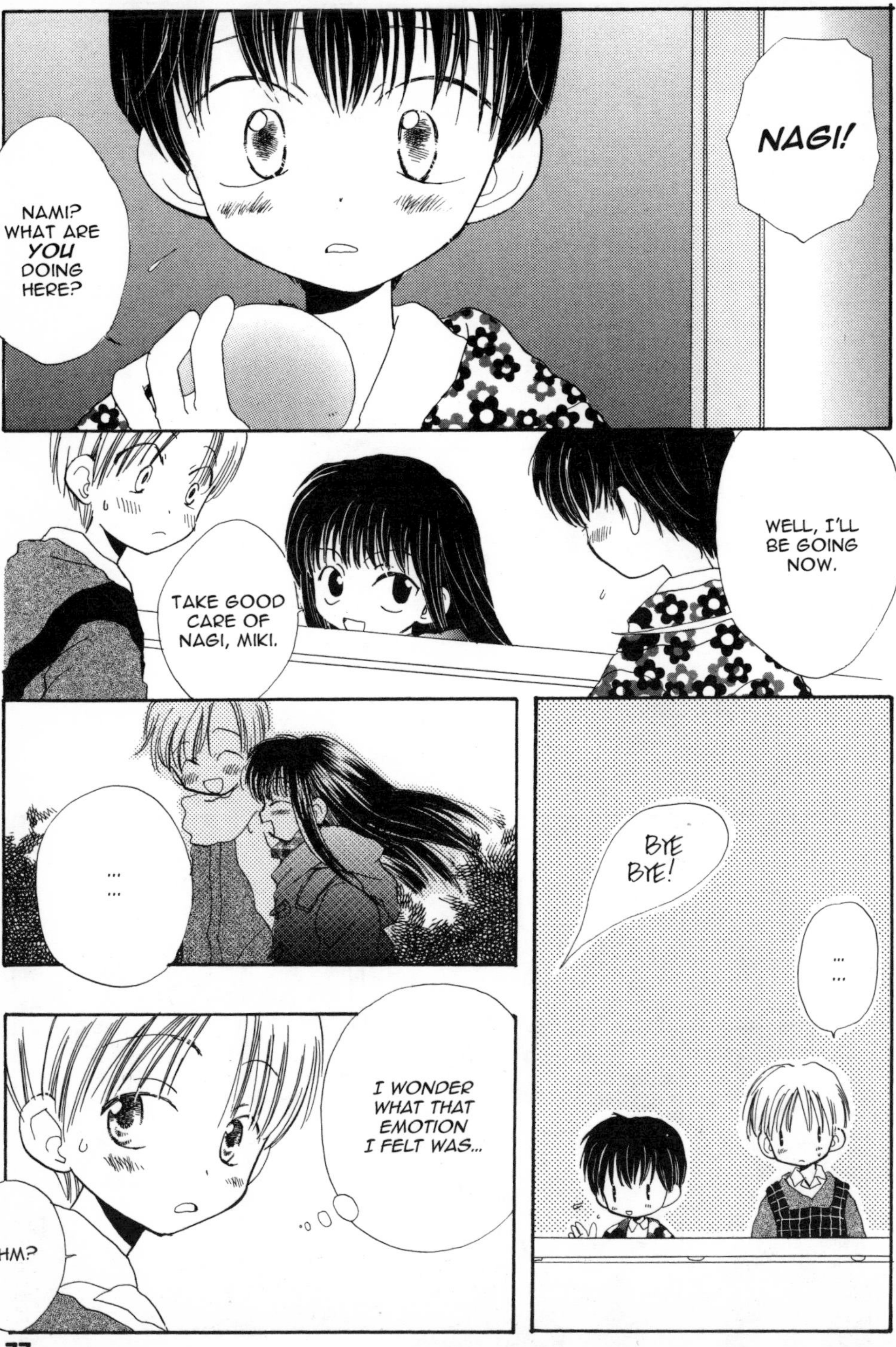
NAGI!
NAMI? WHAT ARE YOU DOING HERE?
WELL, I'LL BE GOING NOW.
TAKE GOOD CARE OF NAGI, MIKI.
BYE BYE!
... ...
... ...
I WONDER WHAT THAT EMOTION I FELT WAS...
HM?

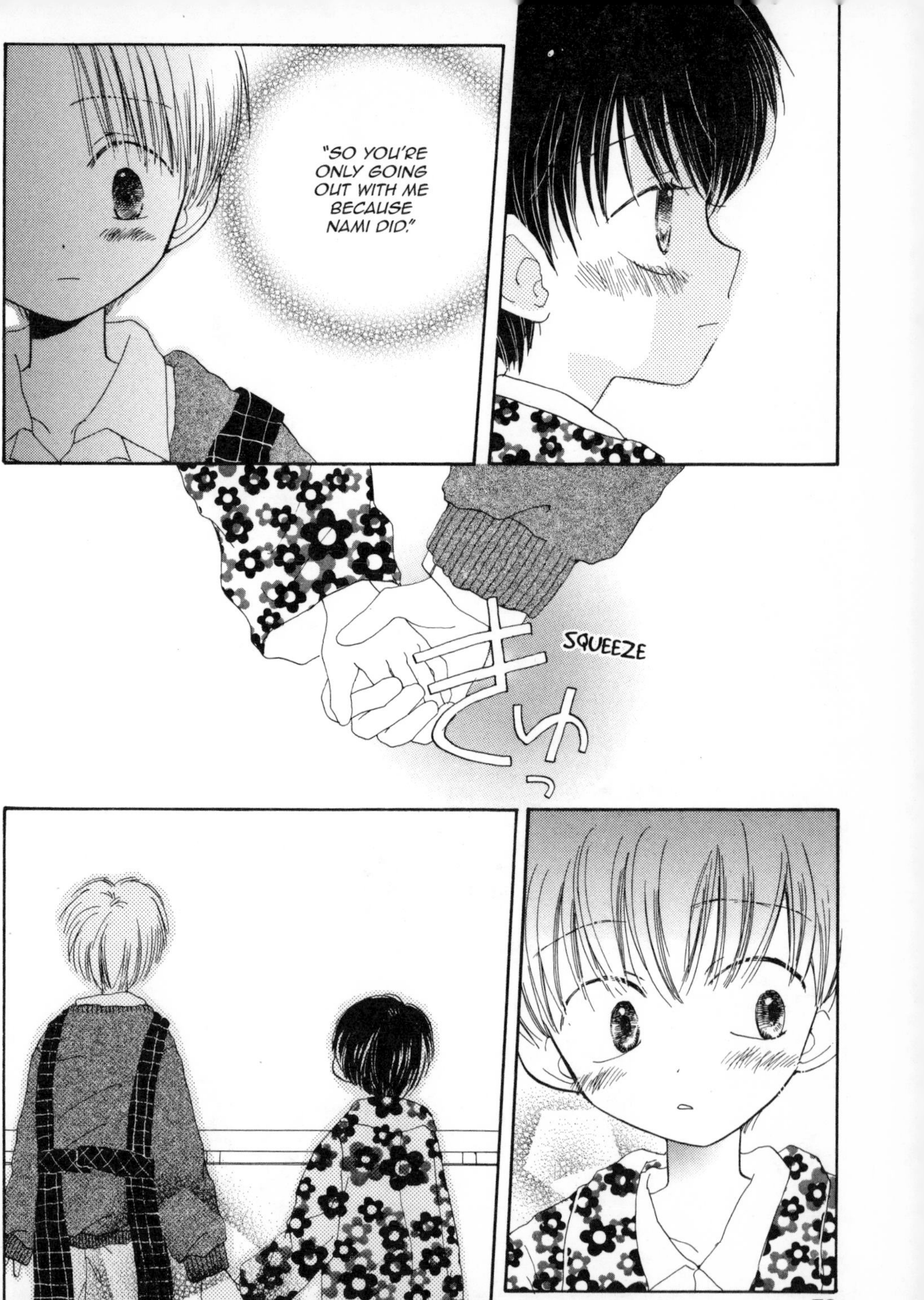
"SO YOU'RE ONLY GOING OUT WITH ME BECAUSE NAMI DID."
きゅっ
SQUEEZE

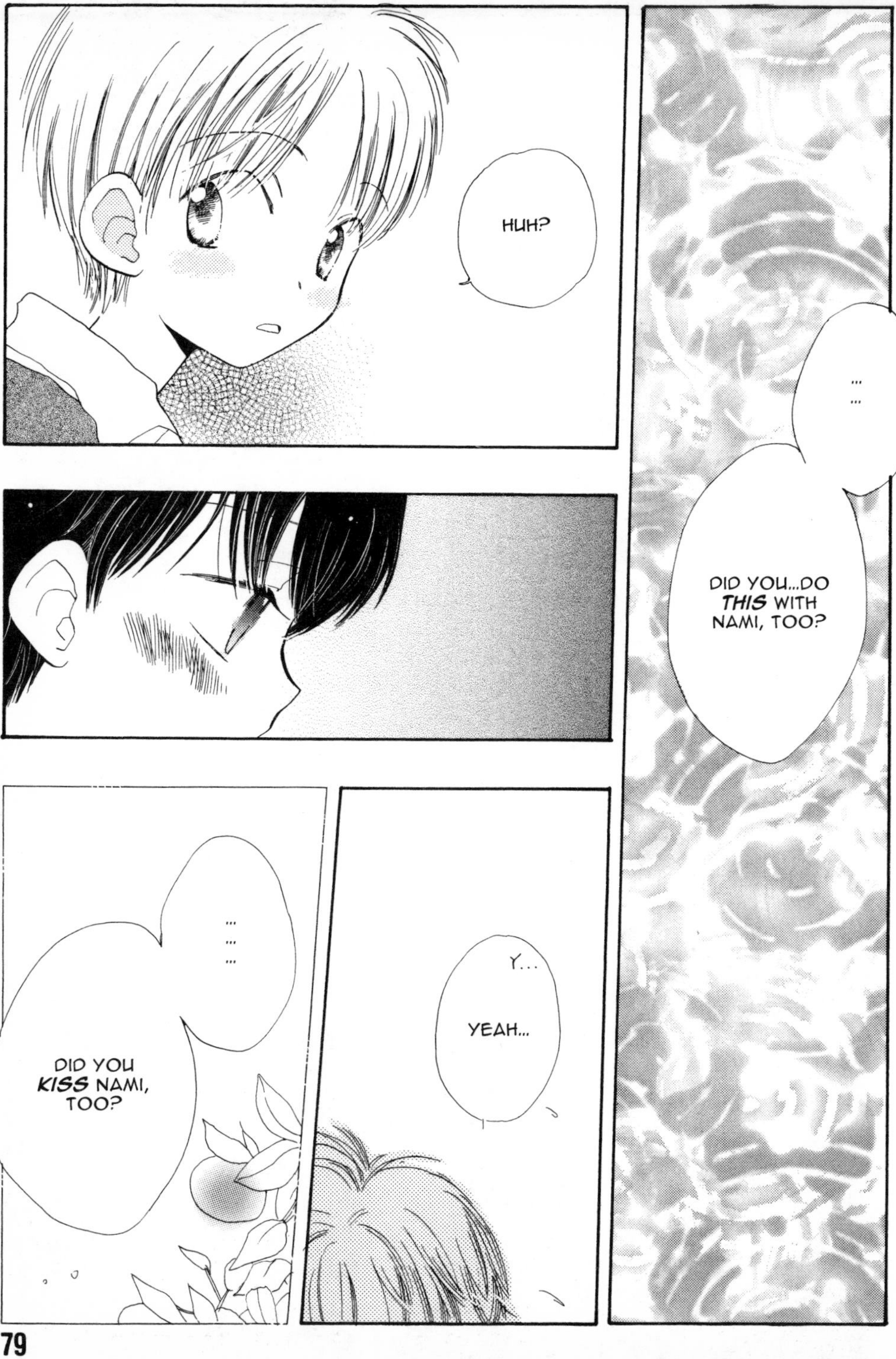
......
DID YOU...DO THIS WITH NAMI, TOO?
HUH?
Y... YEAH...
....
DID YOU KISS NAMI, TOO?

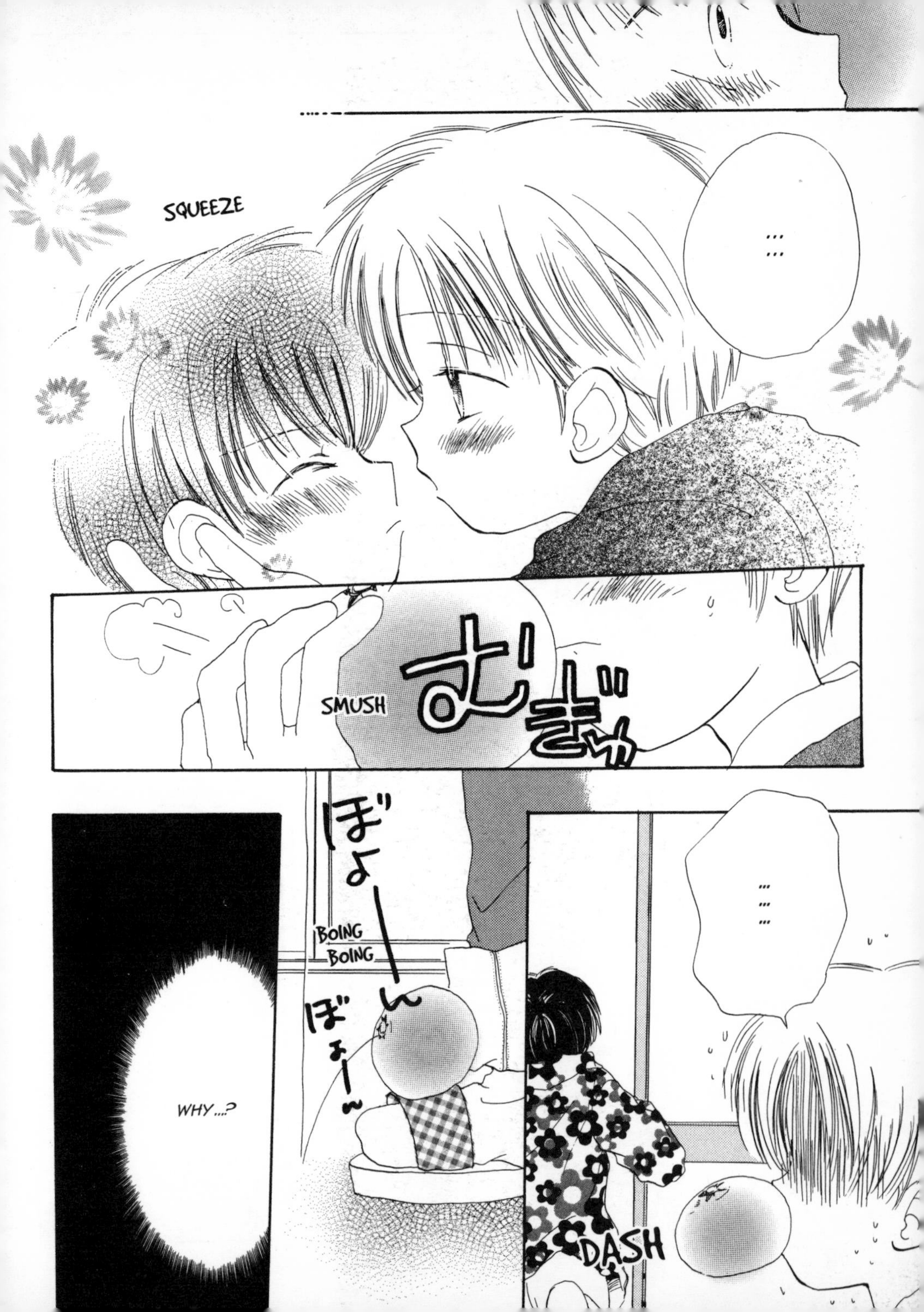

……
SQUEEZE
SMUSH
むぎゅ
……
DASH
ぼよーん
ぼよー〜
BOING
BOING
WHY...?

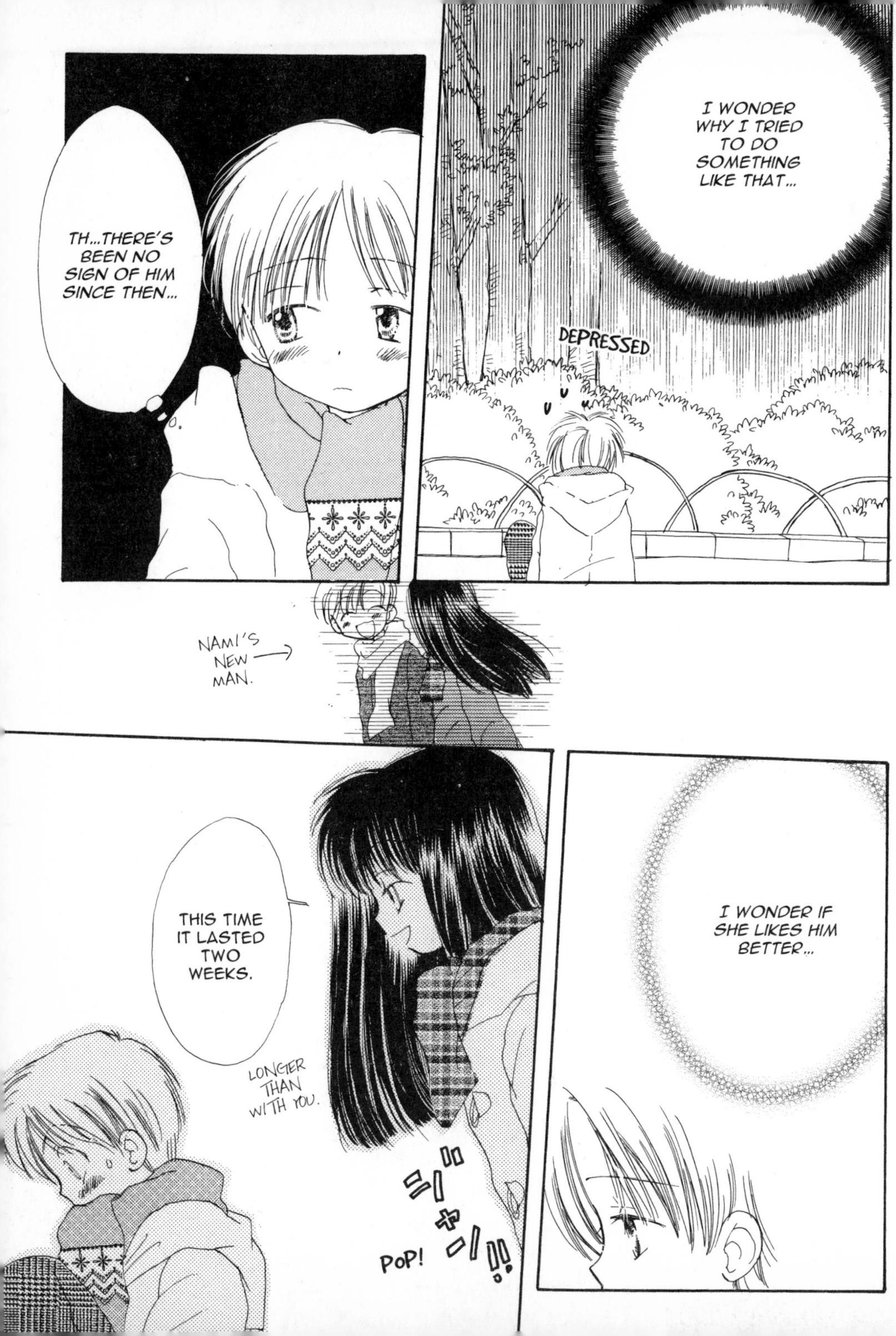
I WONDER WHY I TRIED TO DO SOMETHING LIKE THAT...
DEPRESSED
TH...THERE'S BEEN NO SIGN OF HIM SINCE THEN...
NAMI'S NEW MAN.
I WONDER IF SHE LIKES HIM BETTER...
THIS TIME IT LASTED TWO WEEKS.
LONGER THAN WITH YOU.
POP!

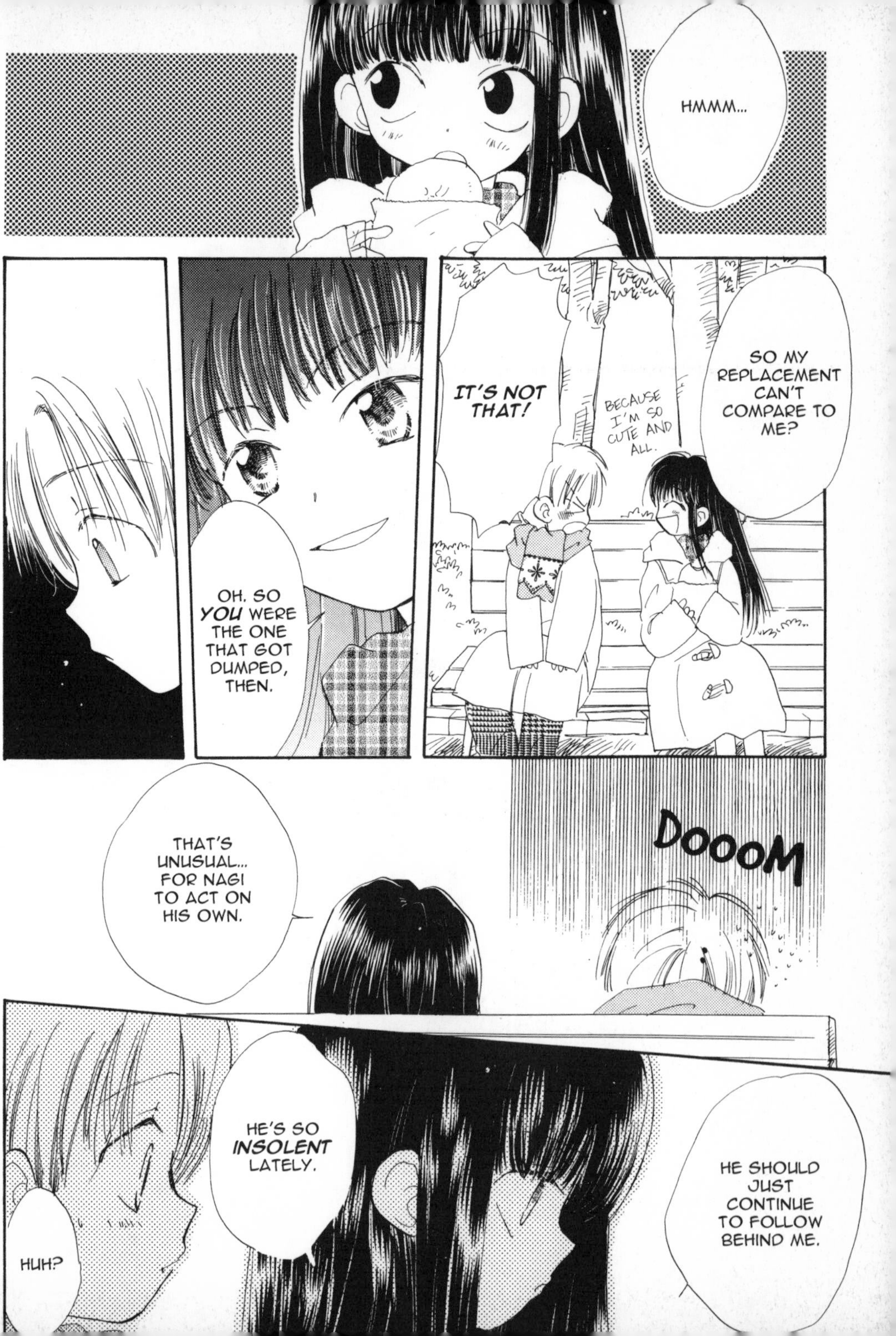
HMMM...
SO MY REPLACEMENT CAN'T COMPARE TO ME?
BECAUSE I'M SO CUTE AND ALL.
IT'S NOT THAT!
OH. SO YOU WERE THE ONE THAT GOT DUMPED, THEN.
DOOOM
THAT'S UNUSUAL... FOR NAGI TO ACT ON HIS OWN.
HE SHOULD JUST CONTINUE TO FOLLOW BEHIND ME.
HE'S SO INSOLENT LATELY.
HUH?

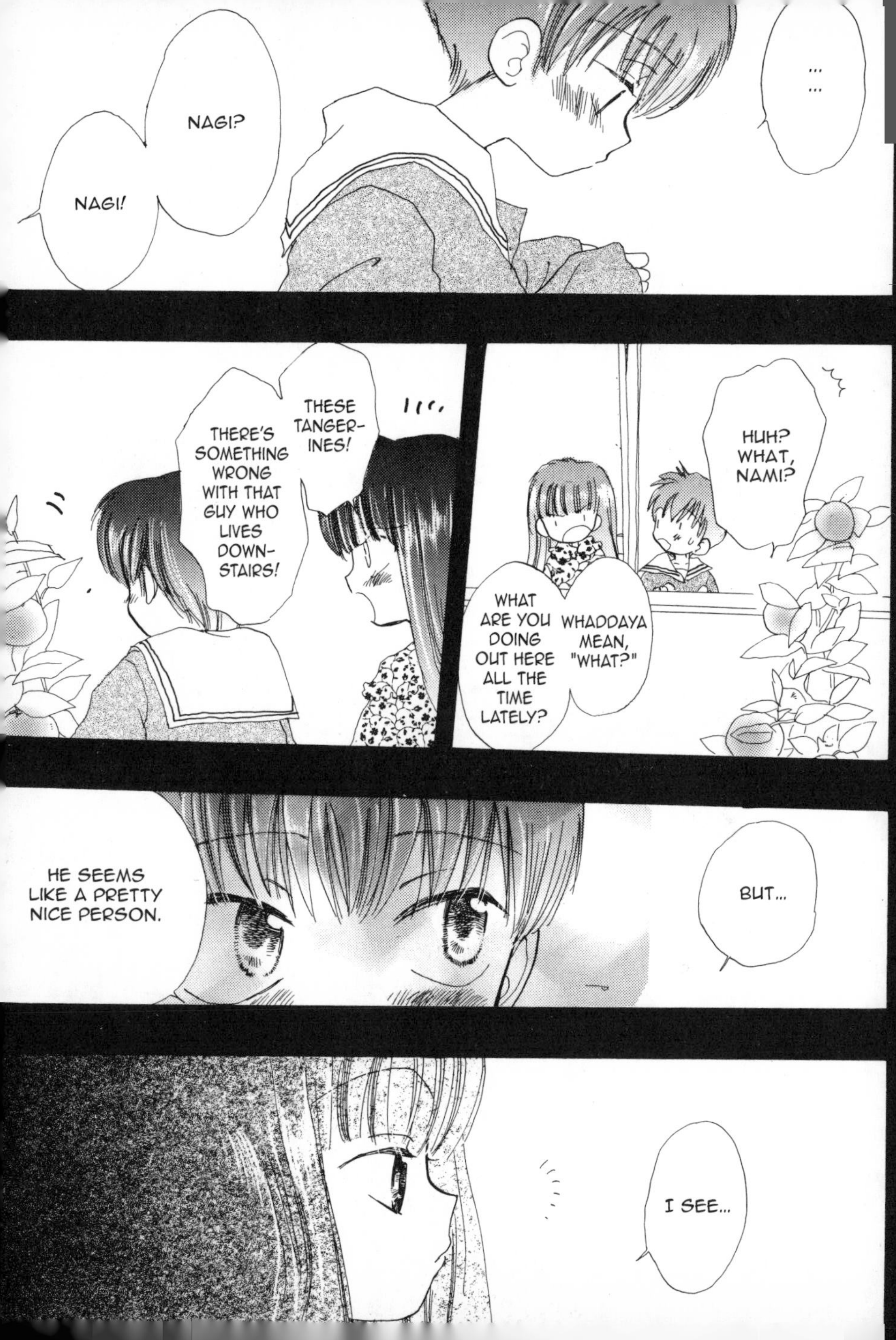
……
……
NAGI?
NAGI!
HUH? WHAT, NAMI?
WHADDAYA MEAN, "WHAT?"
WHAT ARE YOU DOING OUT HERE ALL THE TIME LATELY?
THESE TANGER-INES!
THERE'S SOMETHING WRONG WITH THAT GUY WHO LIVES DOWN-STAIRS!
BUT...
HE SEEMS LIKE A PRETTY NICE PERSON.
I SEE...

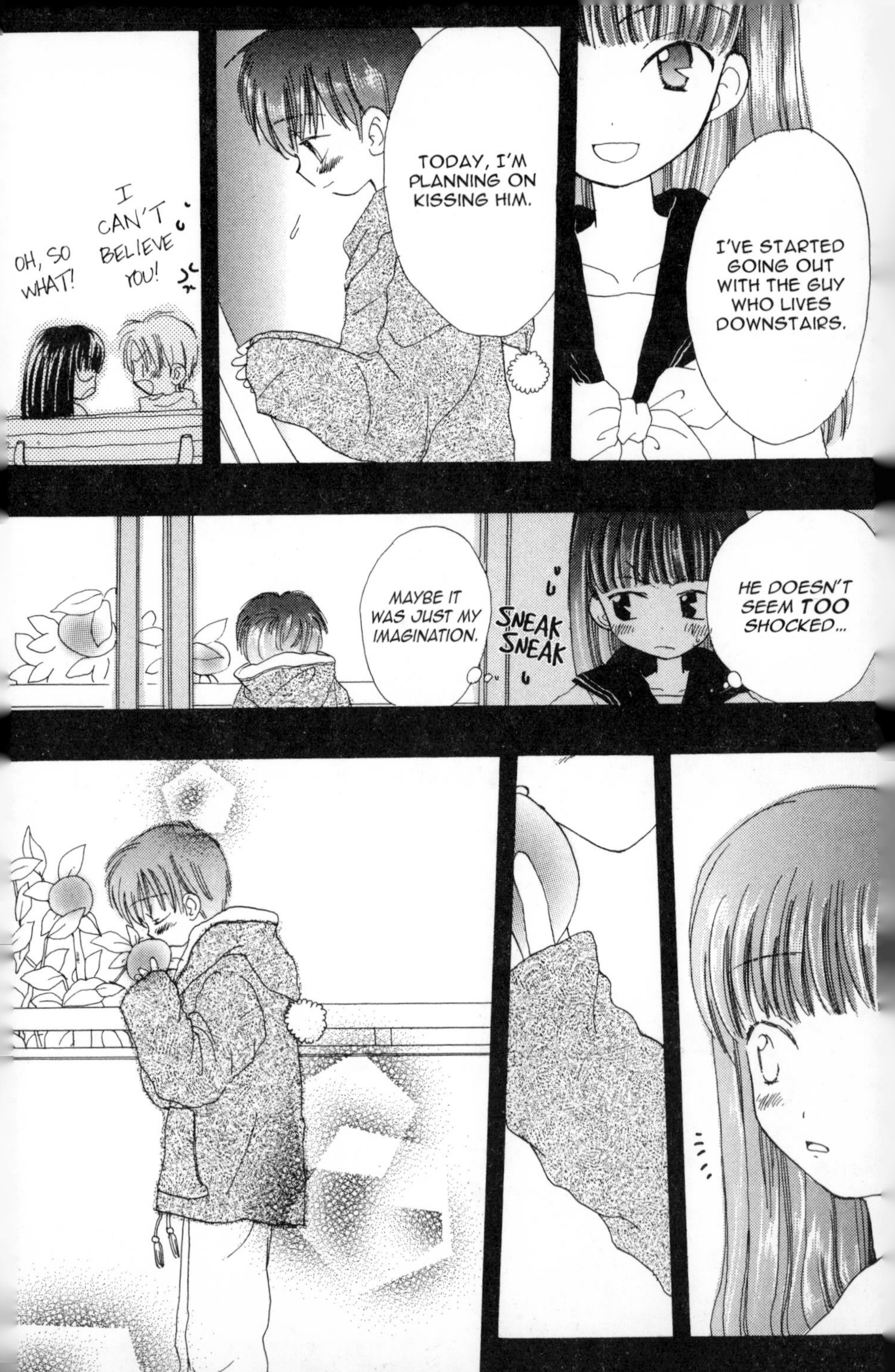
I'VE STARTED GOING OUT WITH THE GUY WHO LIVES DOWNSTAIRS.
TODAY, I'M PLANNING ON KISSING HIM.
I CAN'T BELIEVE YOU!
OH, SO WHAT!
HE DOESN'T SEEM **TOO** SHOCKED...
SNEAK SNEAK
MAYBE IT WAS JUST MY IMAGINATION.

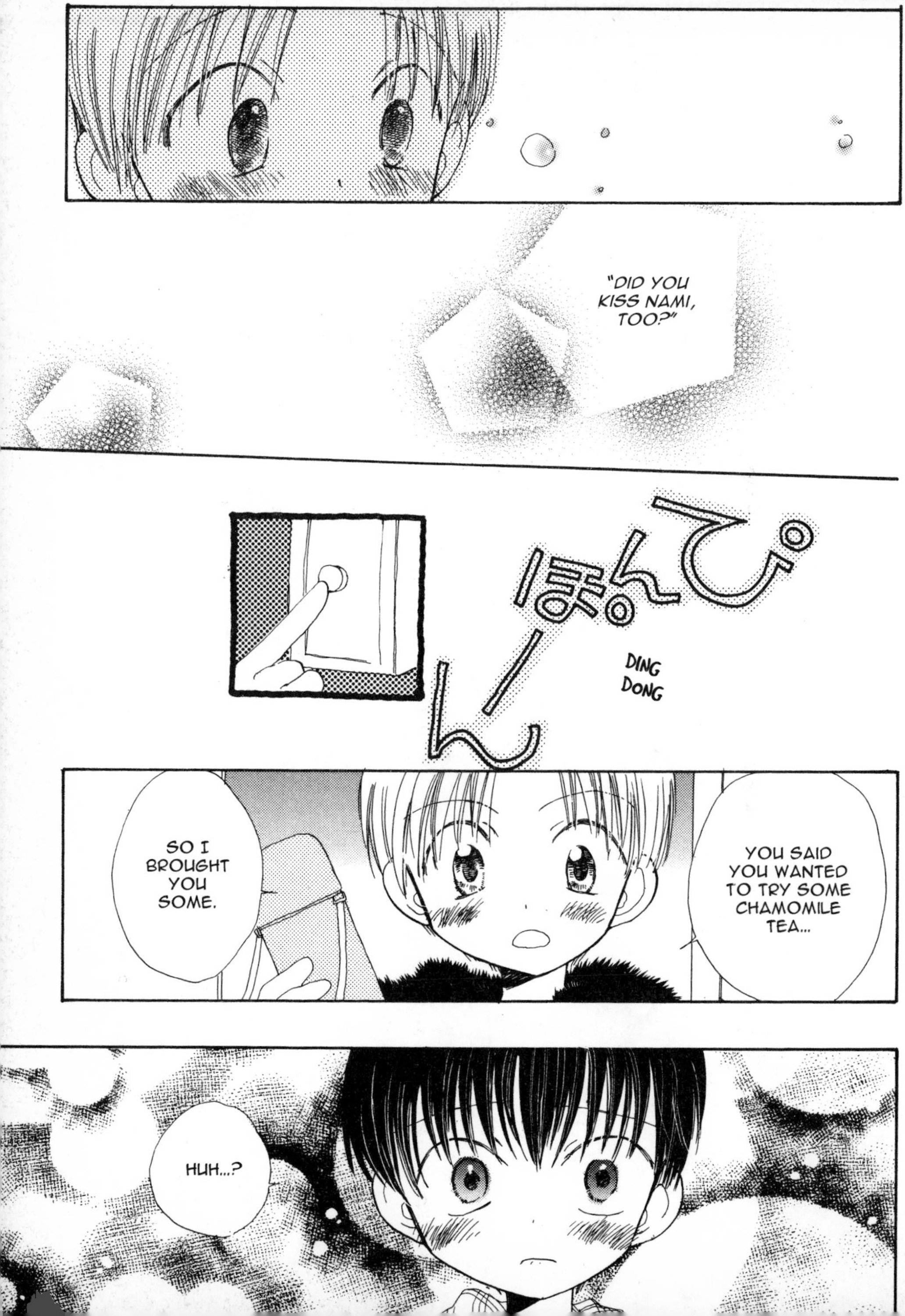
"DID YOU KISS NAMI, TOO?"
ぴんぽーん
DING DONG
YOU SAID YOU WANTED TO TRY SOME CHAMOMILE TEA...
SO I BROUGHT YOU SOME.
HUH...?

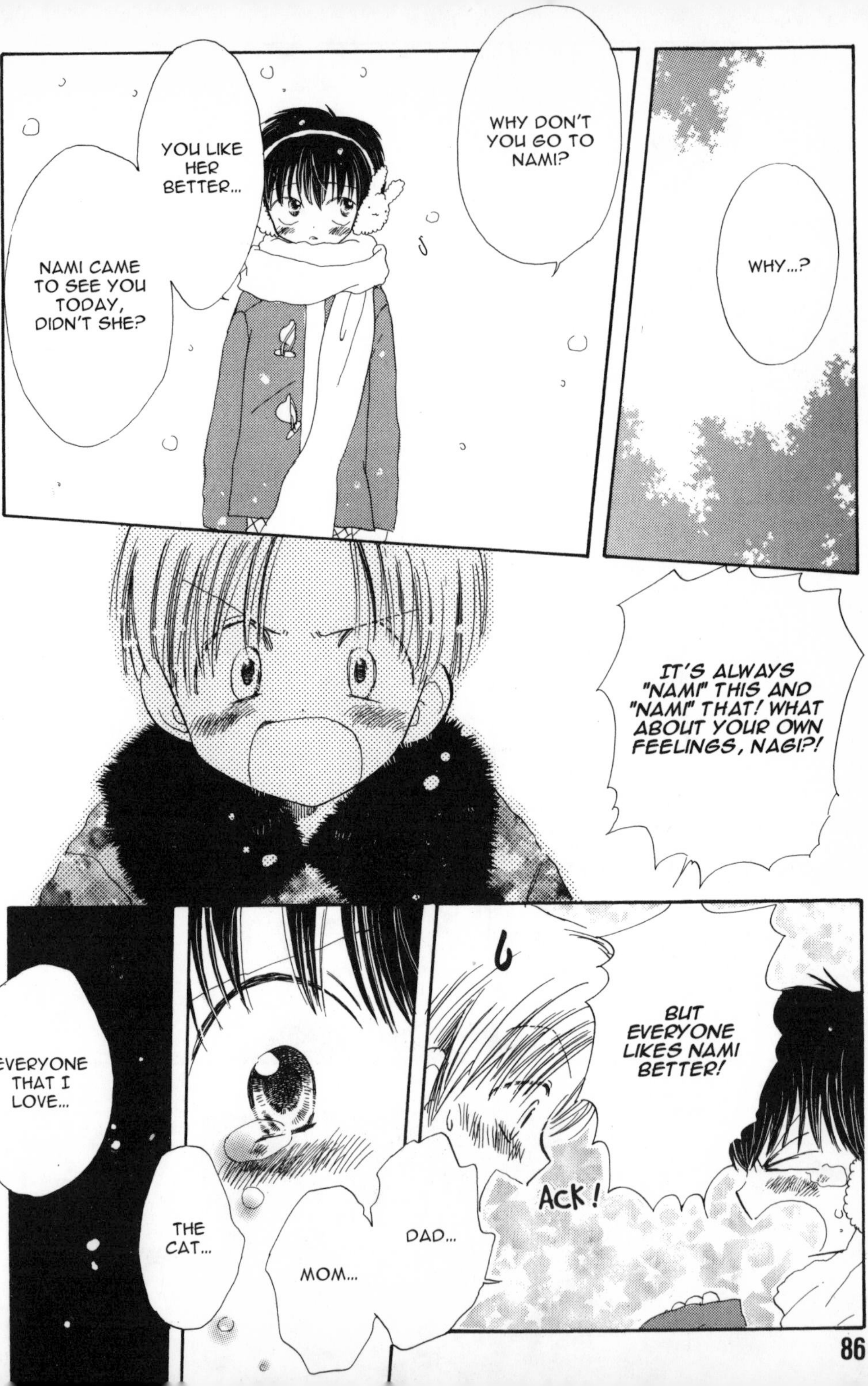
WHY...?
WHY DON'T YOU GO TO NAMI?
YOU LIKE HER BETTER...
NAMI CAME TO SEE YOU TODAY, DIDN'T SHE?
IT'S ALWAYS "NAMI" THIS AND "NAMI" THAT! WHAT ABOUT YOUR OWN FEELINGS, NAGI?!
BUT EVERYONE LIKES NAMI BETTER!
ACK!
DAD...
MOM...
THE CAT...
EVERYONE THAT I LOVE...

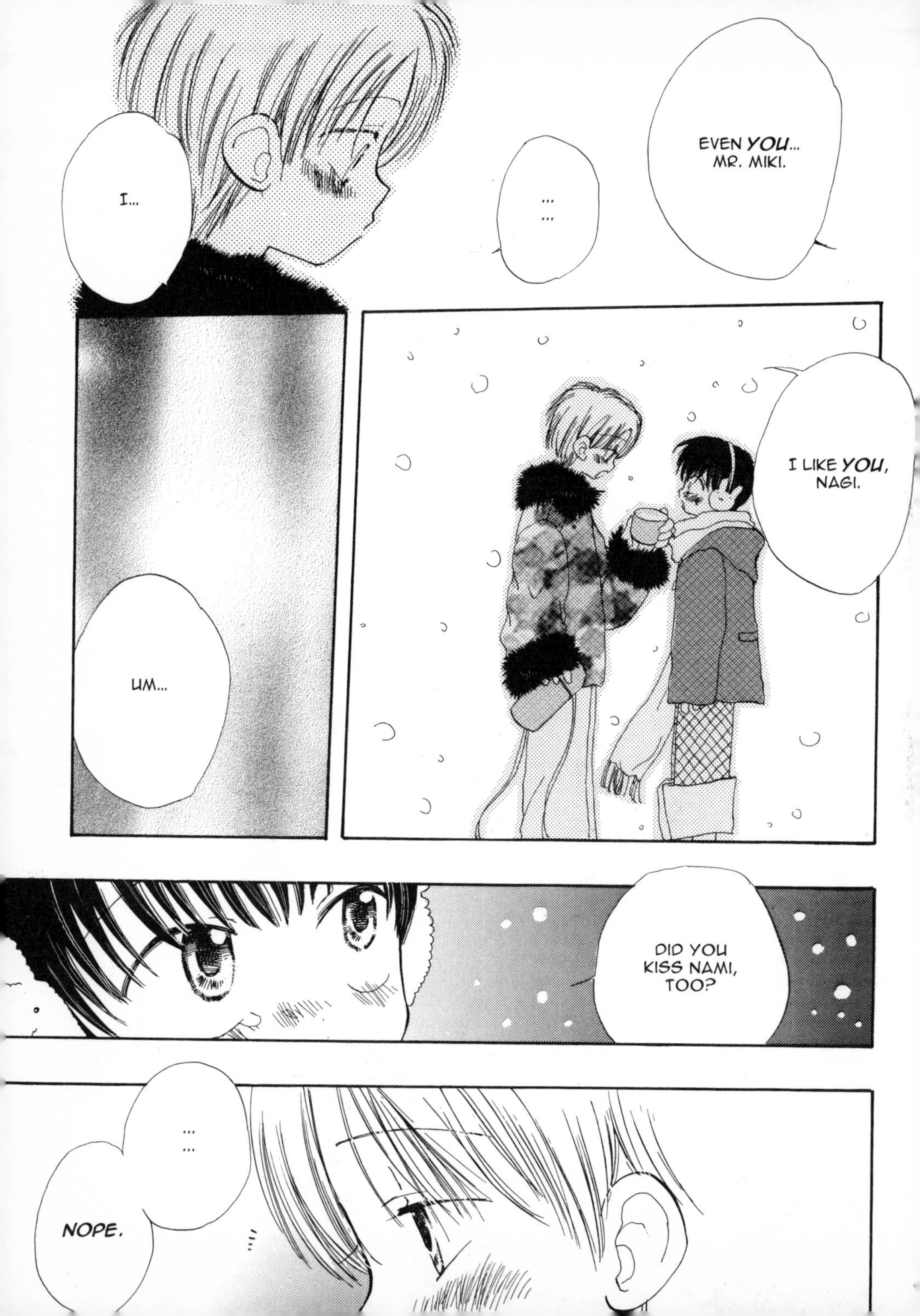
EVEN *YOU*... MR. MIKI.
... ...
I...
I LIKE *YOU*, NAGI.
UM...
DID YOU KISS NAMI, TOO?
... ...
NOPE.

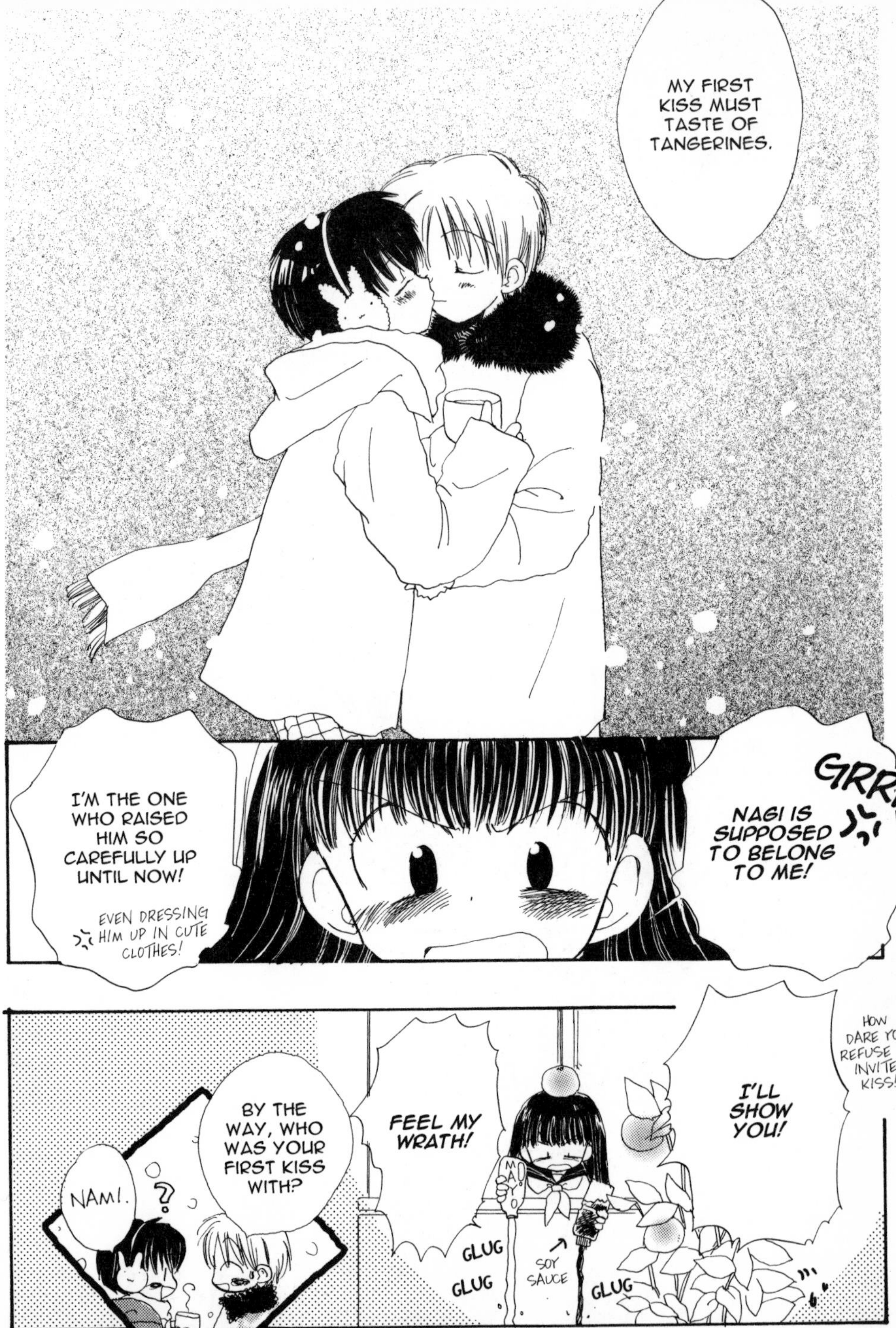
MY FIRST KISS MUST TASTE OF TANGERINES.
GRRR!
NAGI IS SUPPOSED TO BELONG TO ME!
I'M THE ONE WHO RAISED HIM SO CAREFULLY UP UNTIL NOW!
EVEN DRESSING HIM UP IN CUTE CLOTHES!
HOW DARE YOU REFUSE MY INVITED KISS!
I'LL SHOW YOU!
FEEL MY WRATH!
MAYO
SOY SAUCE
GLUG
GLUG
GLUG
BY THE WAY, WHO WAS YOUR FIRST KISS WITH?
NAMI.

END

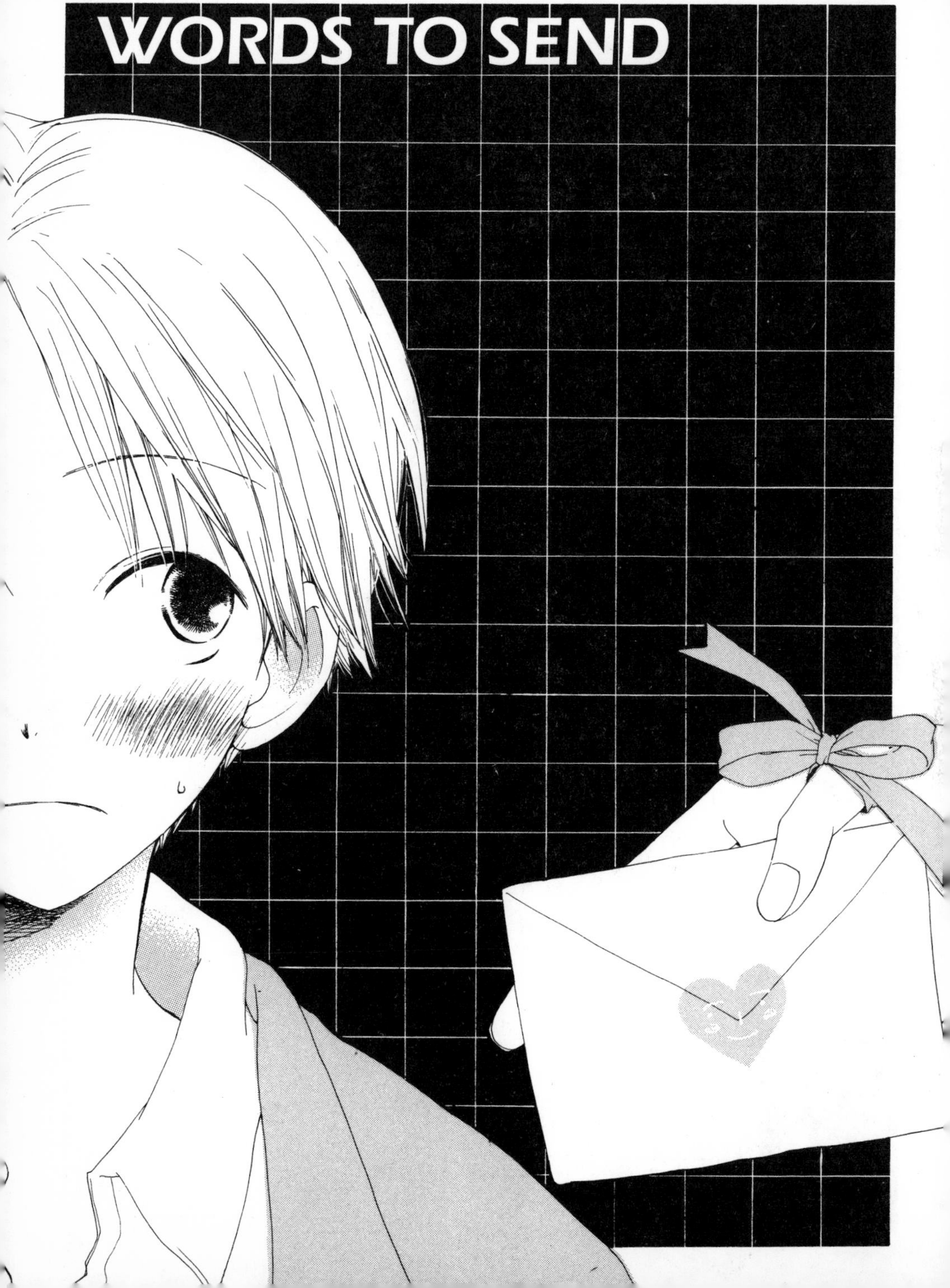
WORDS TO SEND

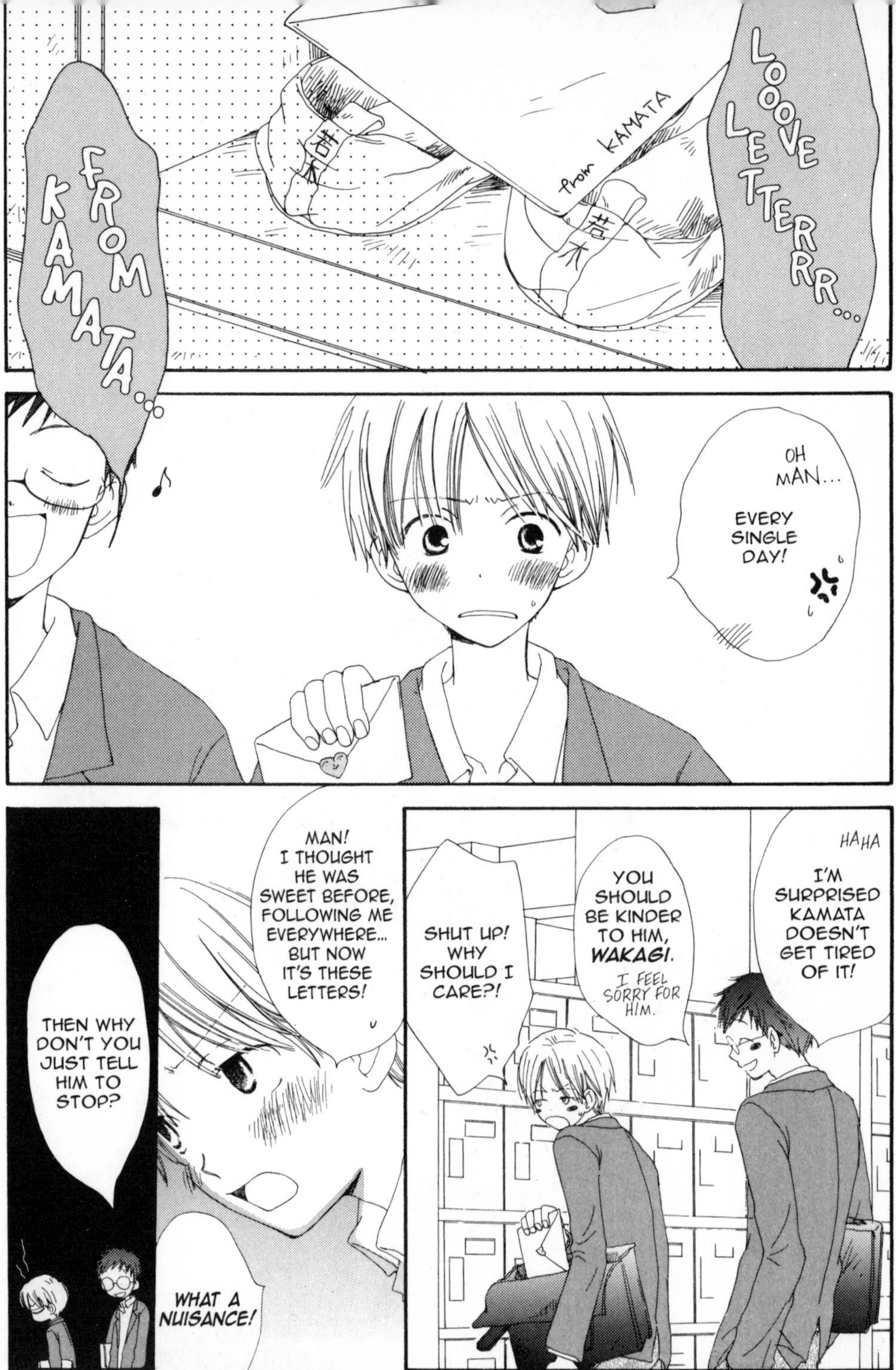
LOOOVE LETTERRR...
from KAMATA
FROM KAMATA...
OH MAN... EVERY SINGLE DAY!
HAHA
I'M SURPRISED KAMATA DOESN'T GET TIRED OF IT!
YOU SHOULD BE KINDER TO HIM, WAKAGI.
I FEEL SORRY FOR HIM.
SHUT UP! WHY SHOULD I CARE?!
MAN! I THOUGHT HE WAS SWEET BEFORE, FOLLOWING ME EVERYWHERE... BUT NOW IT'S THESE LETTERS!
THEN WHY DON'T YOU JUST TELL HIM TO STOP?
WHAT A NUISANCE!

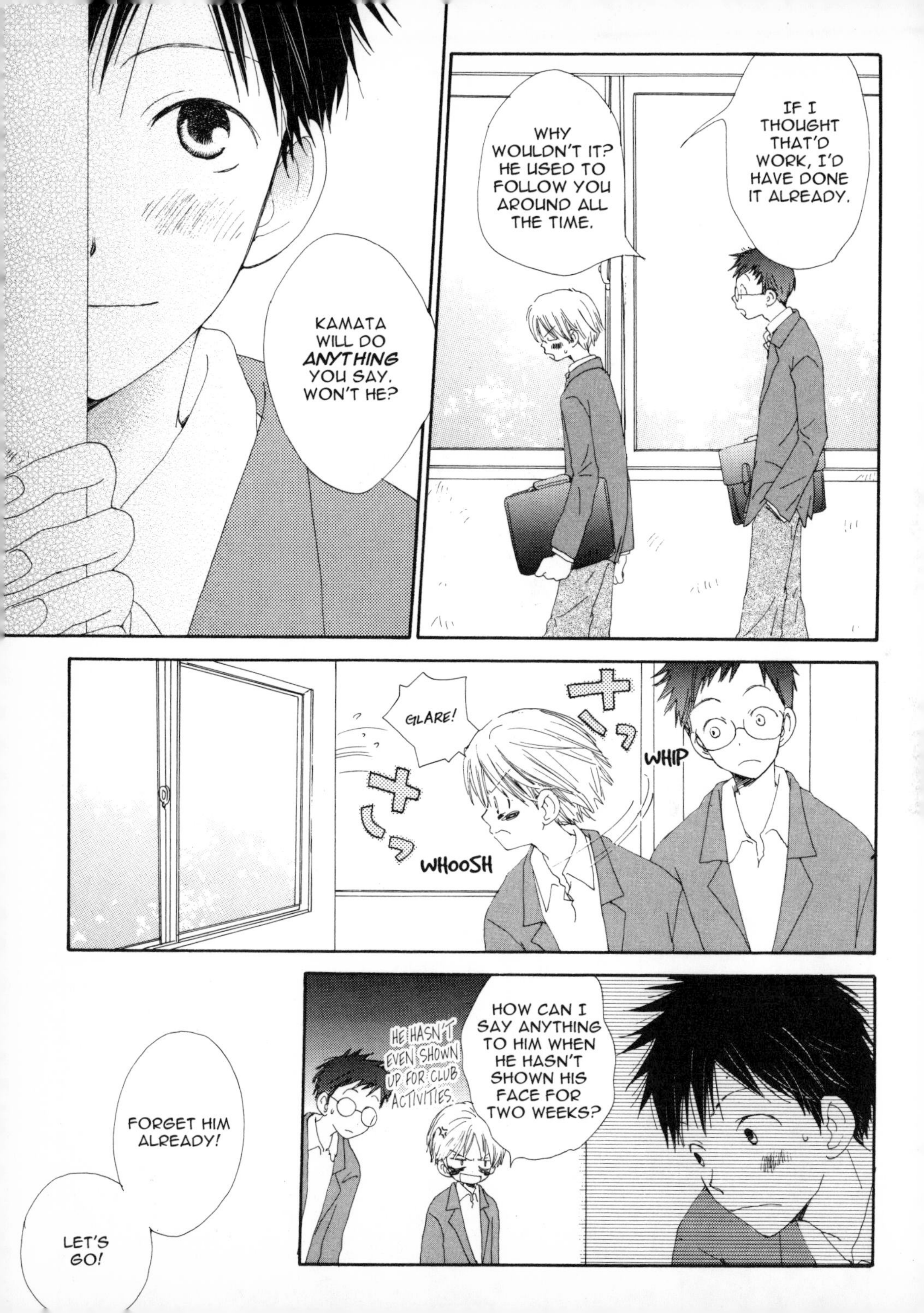
KAMATA WILL DO ANYTHING YOU SAY. WON'T HE?
IF I THOUGHT THAT'D WORK, I'D HAVE DONE IT ALREADY.
WHY WOULDN'T IT? HE USED TO FOLLOW YOU AROUND ALL THE TIME.
WHIP
GLARE!
WHOOSH
HOW CAN I SAY ANYTHING TO HIM WHEN HE HASN'T SHOWN HIS FACE FOR TWO WEEKS?
HE HASN'T EVEN SHOWN UP FOR CLUB ACTIVITIES.
FORGET HIM ALREADY!
LET'S GO!

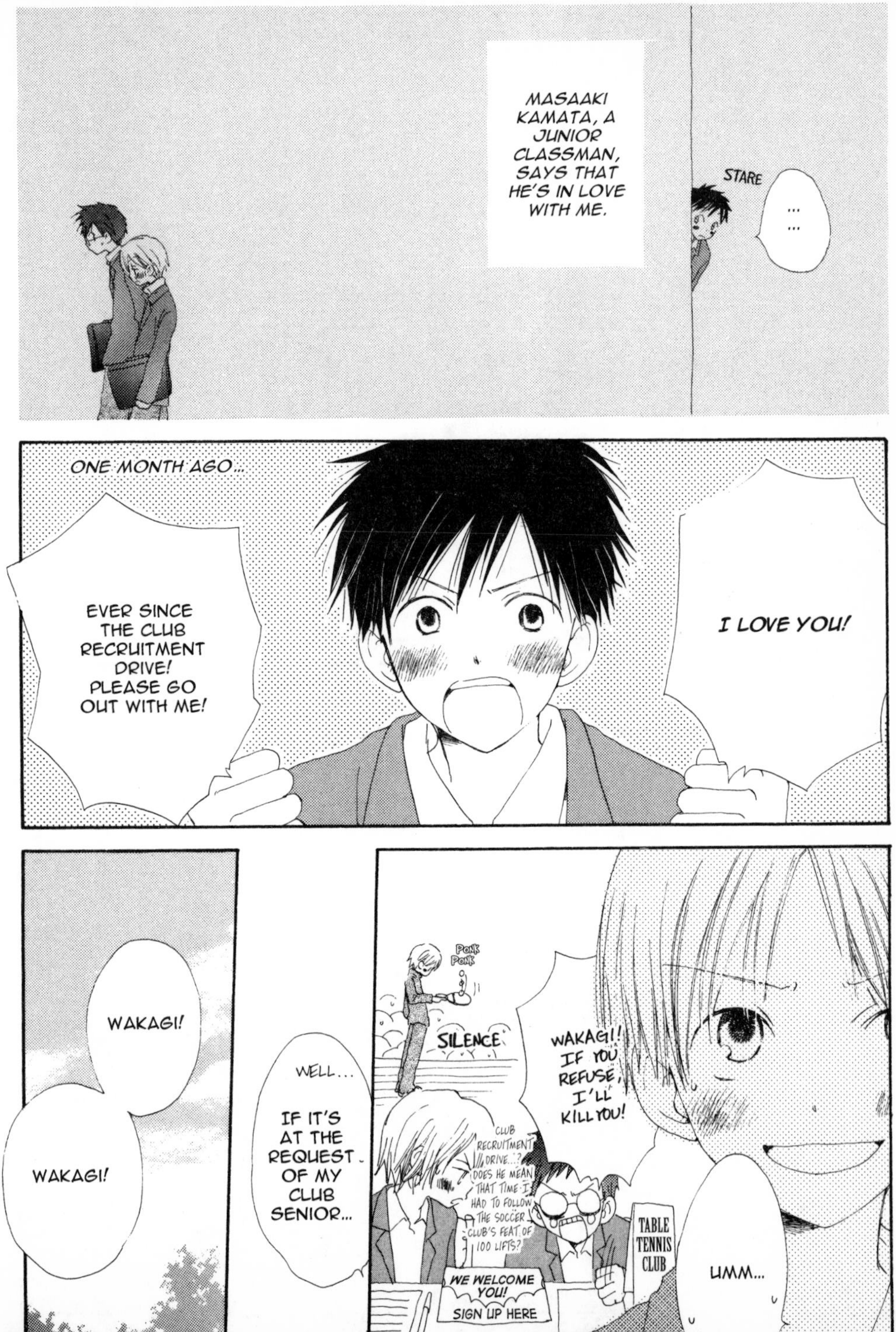
STARE
……
……
MASAAKI KAMATA, A JUNIOR CLASSMAN, SAYS THAT HE'S IN LOVE WITH ME.
ONE MONTH AGO...
I LOVE YOU!
EVER SINCE THE CLUB RECRUITMENT DRIVE! PLEASE GO OUT WITH ME!
WAKAGI!! IF YOU REFUSE, I'LL KILL YOU!
PONK PONK
SILENCE
CLUB RECRUITMENT DRIVE...? DOES HE MEAN THAT TIME I HAD TO FOLLOW THE SOCCER CLUB'S FEAT OF 100 LIFTS?
TABLE TENNIS CLUB
WE WELCOME YOU!
SIGN UP HERE
UMM...
WELL...
IF IT'S AT THE REQUEST OF MY CLUB SENIOR...
WAKAGI!
WAKAGI!

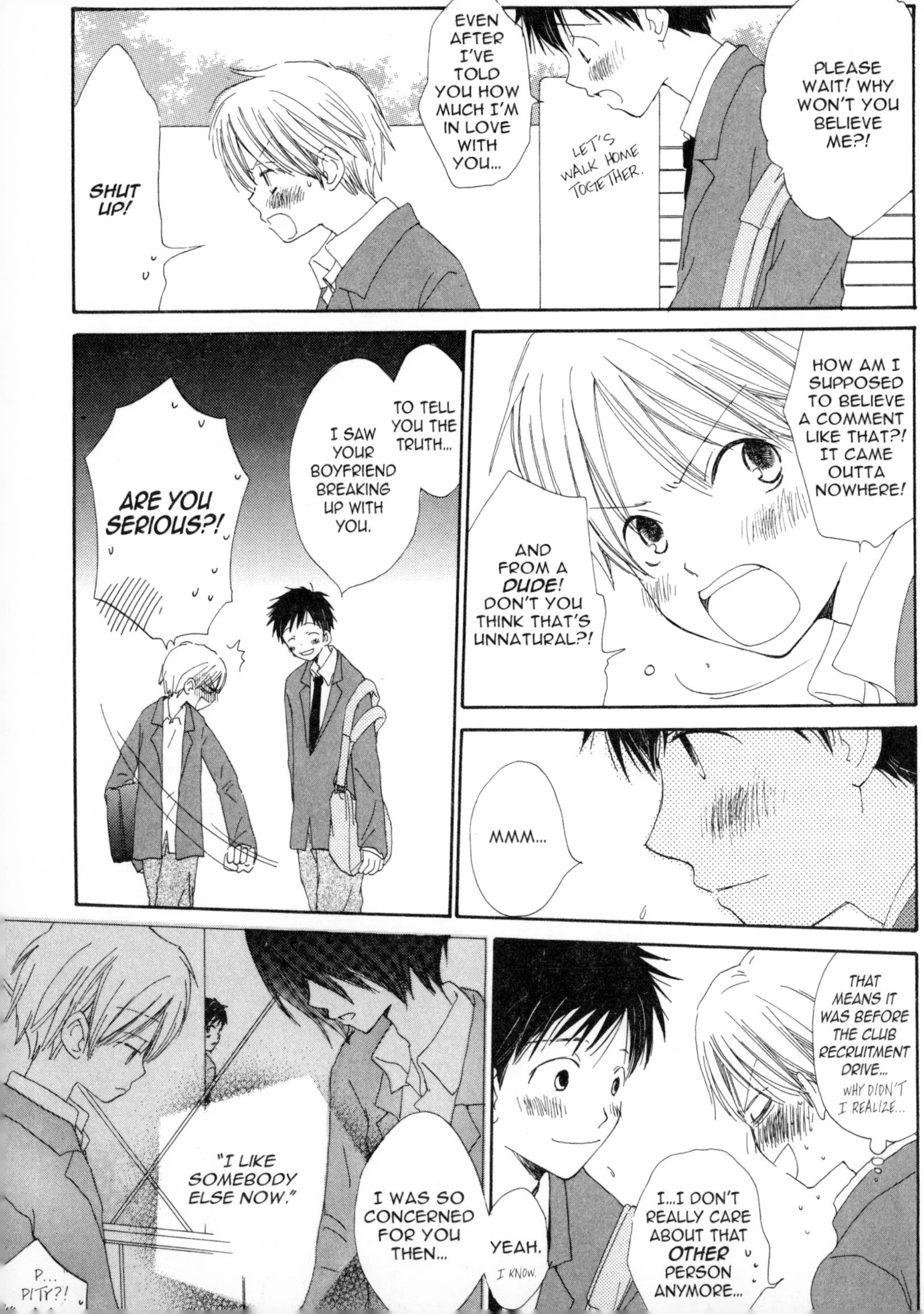
PLEASE WAIT! WHY WON'T YOU BELIEVE ME?!
LET'S WALK HOME TOGETHER.
EVEN AFTER I'VE TOLD YOU HOW MUCH I'M IN LOVE WITH YOU...
SHUT UP!
HOW AM I SUPPOSED TO BELIEVE A COMMENT LIKE THAT?! IT CAME OUTTA NOWHERE!
AND FROM A DUDE! DON'T YOU THINK THAT'S UNNATURAL?!
MMM...
TO TELL YOU THE TRUTH...
I SAW YOUR BOYFRIEND BREAKING UP WITH YOU.
ARE YOU SERIOUS?!
THAT MEANS IT WAS BEFORE THE CLUB RECRUITMENT DRIVE...
WHY DIDN'T I REALIZE...
I...I DON'T REALLY CARE ABOUT THAT OTHER PERSON ANYMORE...
YEAH.
I KNOW.
I WAS SO CONCERNED FOR YOU THEN...
"I LIKE SOMEBODY ELSE NOW."
P... PITY?!

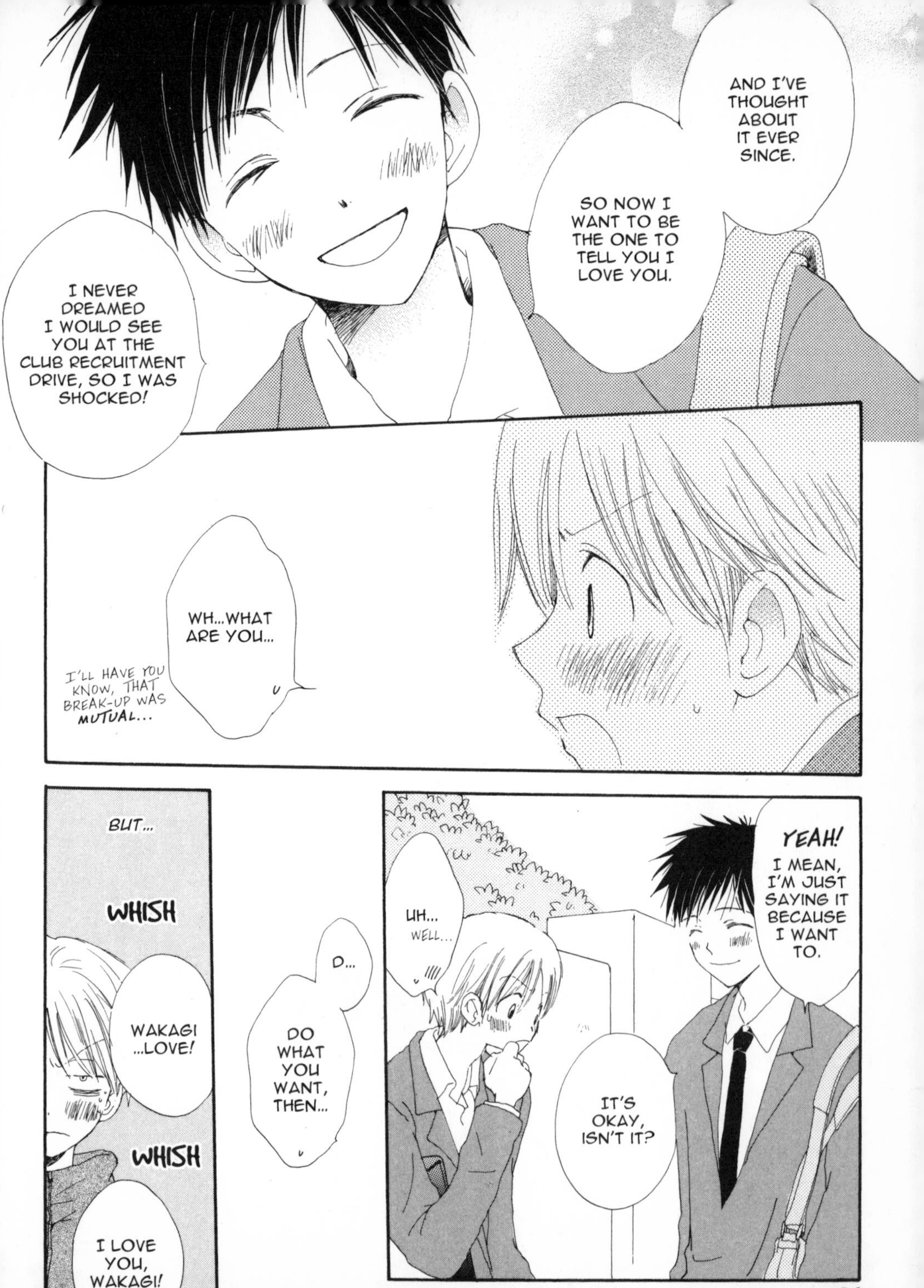
AND I'VE THOUGHT ABOUT IT EVER SINCE.
SO NOW I WANT TO BE THE ONE TO TELL YOU I LOVE YOU.
I NEVER DREAMED I WOULD SEE YOU AT THE CLUB RECRUITMENT DRIVE, SO I WAS SHOCKED!
WH...WHAT ARE YOU...
I'LL HAVE YOU KNOW, THAT BREAK-UP WAS MUTUAL...
YEAH! I MEAN, I'M JUST SAYING IT BECAUSE I WANT TO.
IT'S OKAY, ISN'T IT?
UH... WELL...
D...
DO WHAT YOU WANT, THEN...
BUT...
WHISH
WAKAGI ...LOVE!
WHISH
I LOVE YOU, WAKAGI!

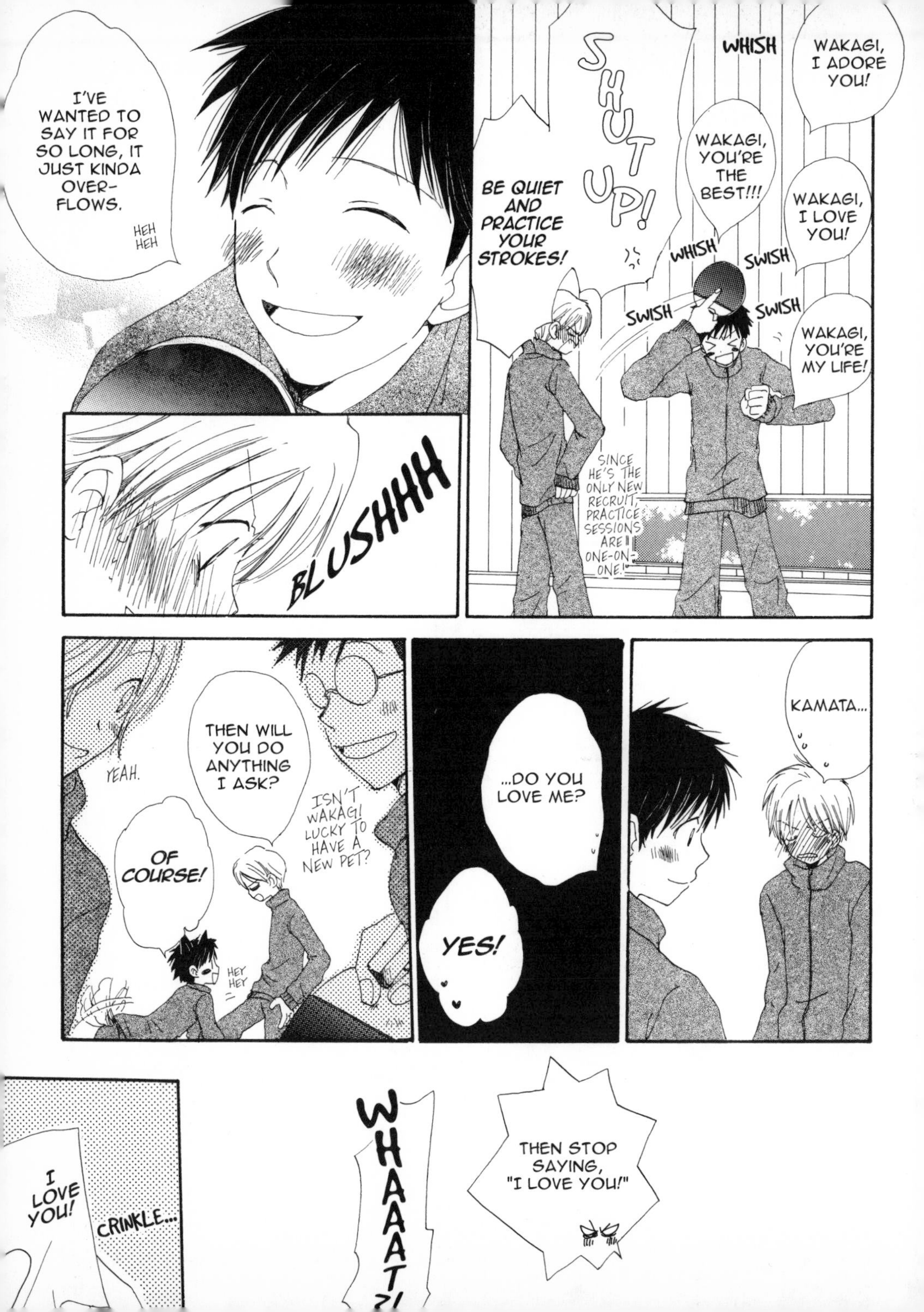
WHISH
WAKAGI, I ADORE YOU!
WAKAGI, YOU'RE THE BEST!!!
SHUT UP!
BE QUIET AND PRACTICE YOUR STROKES!
WAKAGI, I LOVE YOU!
WHISH
SWISH
SWISH
SWISH
WAKAGI, YOU'RE MY LIFE!
SINCE HE'S THE ONLY NEW RECRUIT, PRACTICE SESSIONS ARE ONE-ON-ONE!
I'VE WANTED TO SAY IT FOR SO LONG, IT JUST KINDA OVER-FLOWS.
HEH HEH
BLUSHHH
KAMATA...
...DO YOU LOVE ME?
YES!
THEN WILL YOU DO ANYTHING I ASK?
ISN'T WAKAGI LUCKY TO HAVE A NEW PET?
YEAH.
OF COURSE!
HEY HEY
THEN STOP SAYING, "I LOVE YOU!"
WHAAAT?!
CRINKLE...
I LOVE YOU!

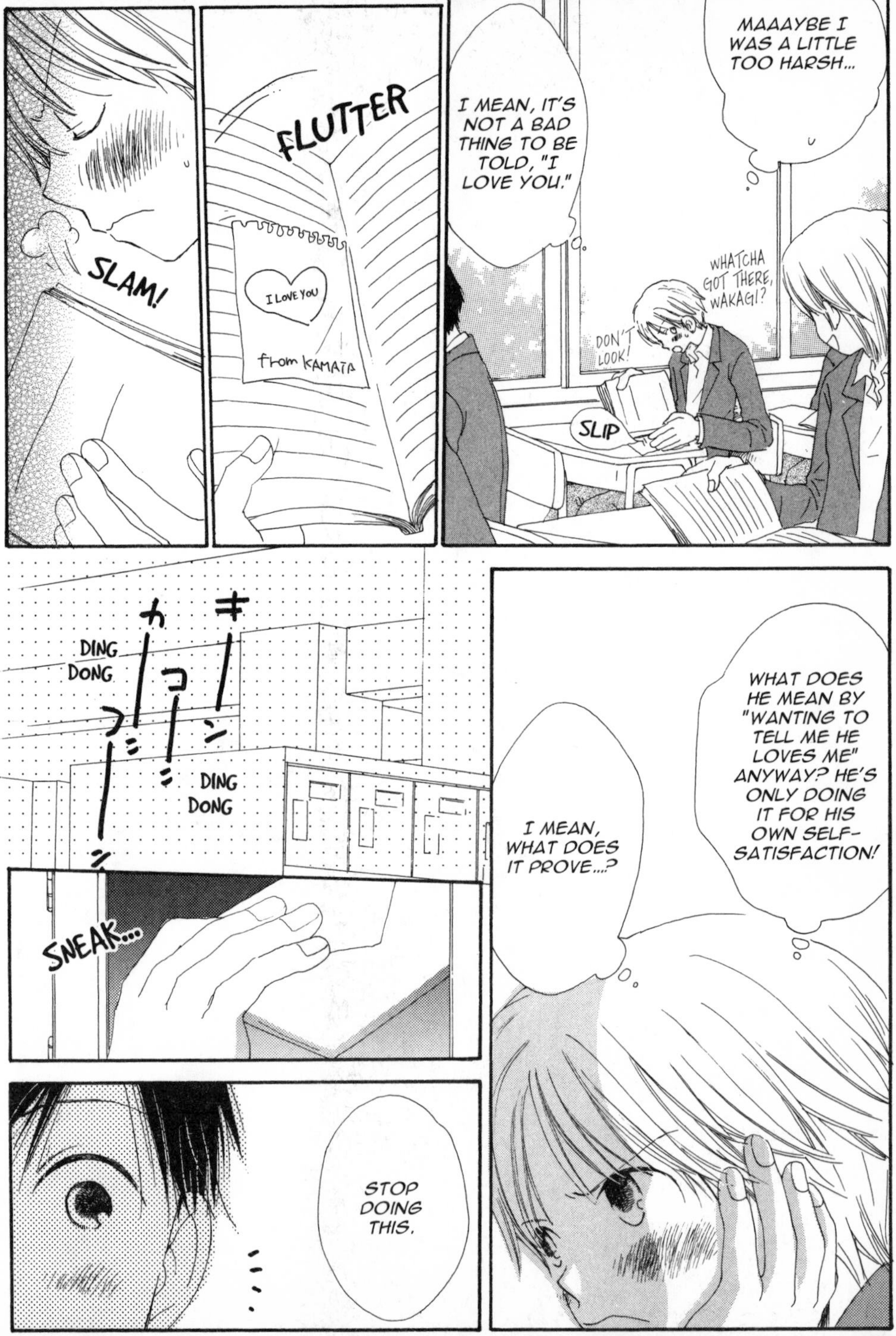
MAAAYBE I WAS A LITTLE TOO HARSH...
I MEAN, IT'S NOT A BAD THING TO BE TOLD, "I LOVE YOU."
WHATCHA GOT THERE, WAKAGI?
DON'T LOOK!
SLIP
FLUTTER
I LOVE YOU
from KAMATA
SLAM!
WHAT DOES HE MEAN BY "WANTING TO TELL ME HE LOVES ME" ANYWAY? HE'S ONLY DOING IT FOR HIS OWN SELF-SATISFACTION!
I MEAN, WHAT DOES IT PROVE...?
キーン
コー
DING DONG
カー
コー
DING DONG
SNEAK...
STOP DOING THIS.
...

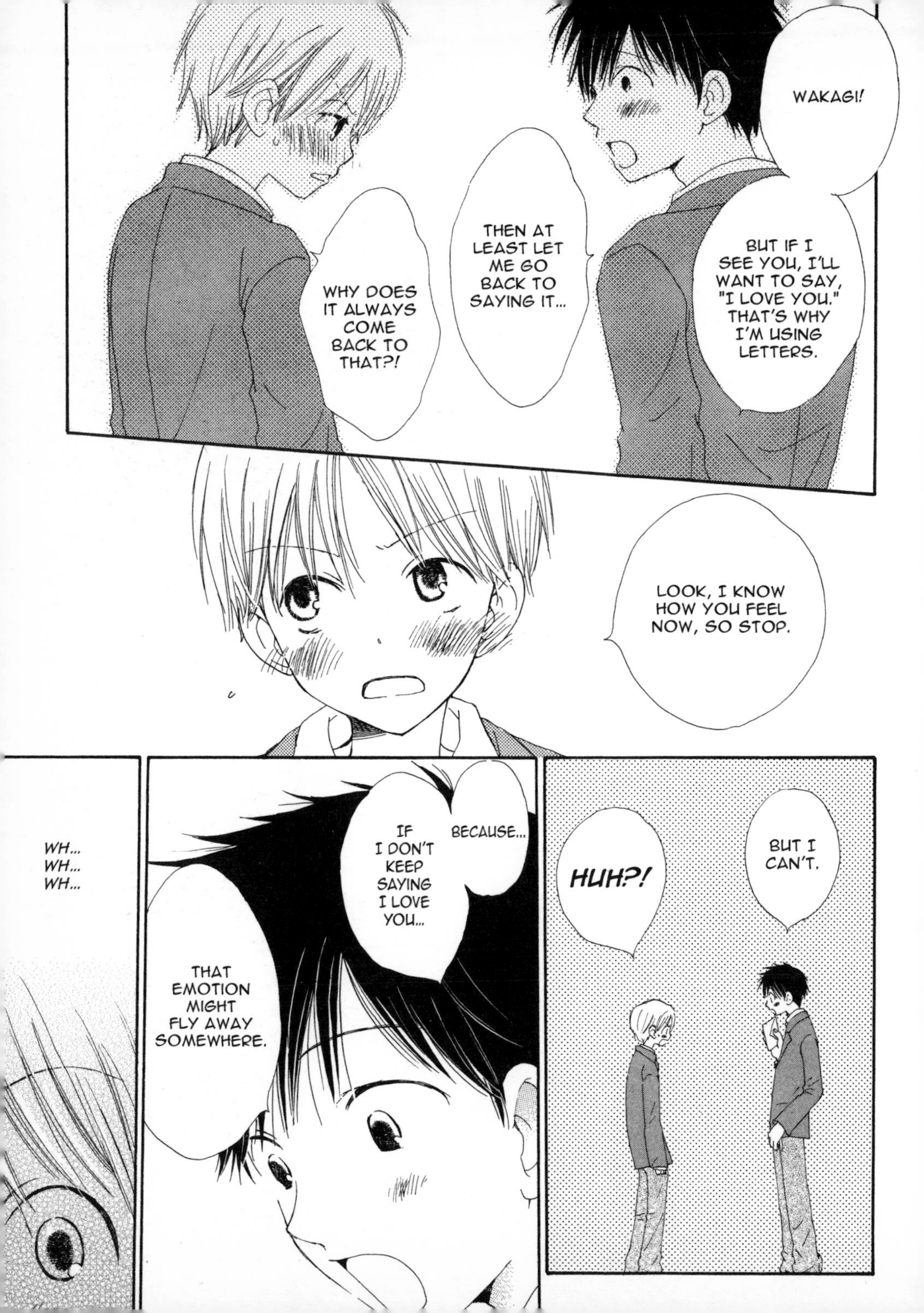
WAKAGI!
BUT IF I SEE YOU, I'LL WANT TO SAY, "I LOVE YOU." THAT'S WHY I'M USING LETTERS.
THEN AT LEAST LET ME GO BACK TO SAYING IT...
WHY DOES IT ALWAYS COME BACK TO THAT?!
LOOK, I KNOW HOW YOU FEEL NOW, SO STOP.
BUT I CAN'T.
HUH?!
BECAUSE...
IF I DON'T KEEP SAYING I LOVE YOU...
THAT EMOTION MIGHT FLY AWAY SOMEWHERE.
WH... WH... WH...

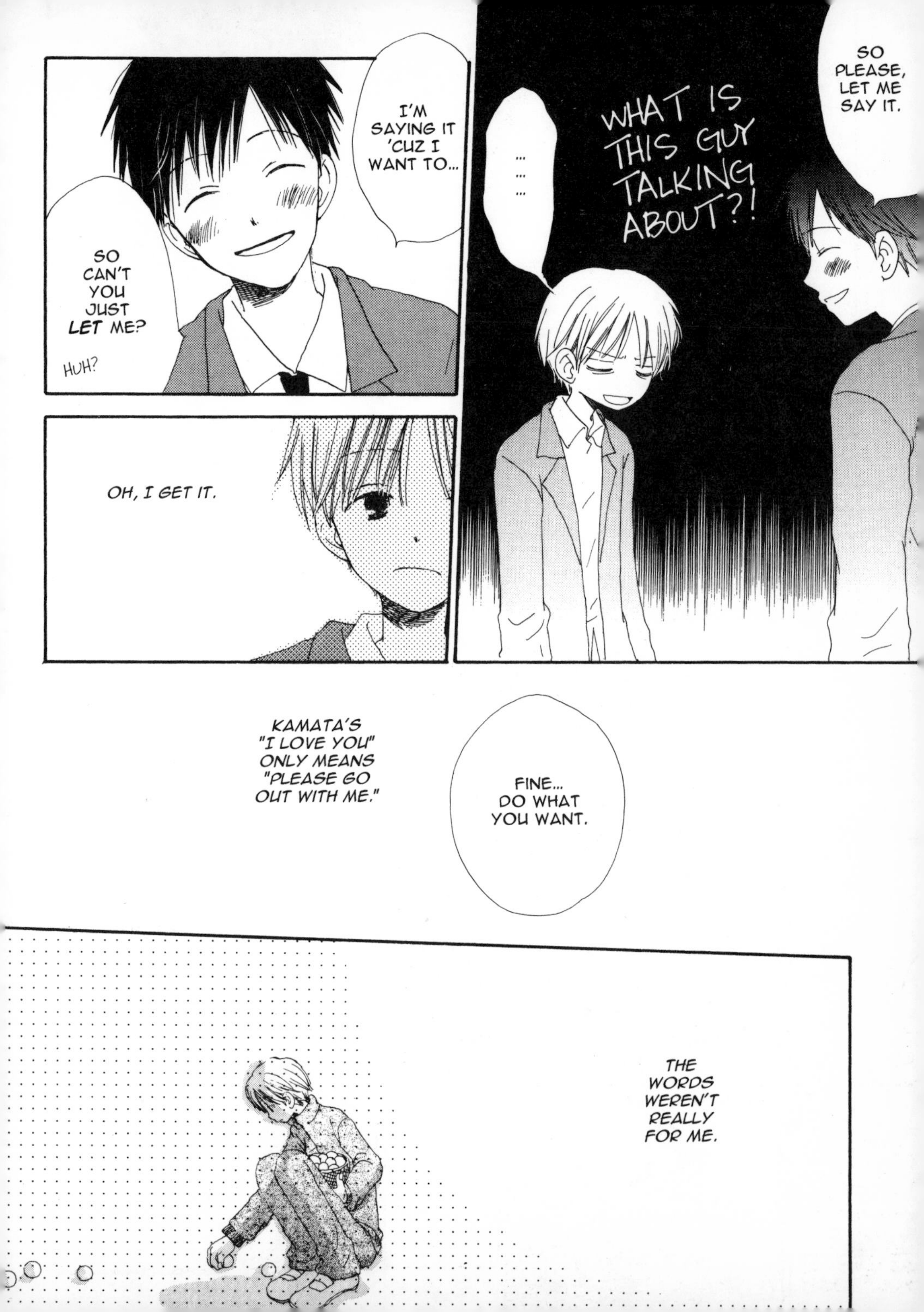
SO PLEASE, LET ME SAY IT.
WHAT IS THIS GUY TALKING ABOUT?!
... ...
I'M SAYING IT 'CUZ I WANT TO...
SO CAN'T YOU JUST **LET** ME?
HUH?
OH, I GET IT.
FINE... DO WHAT YOU WANT.
KAMATA'S "I LOVE YOU" ONLY MEANS "PLEASE GO OUT WITH ME."
THE WORDS WEREN'T REALLY FOR ME.

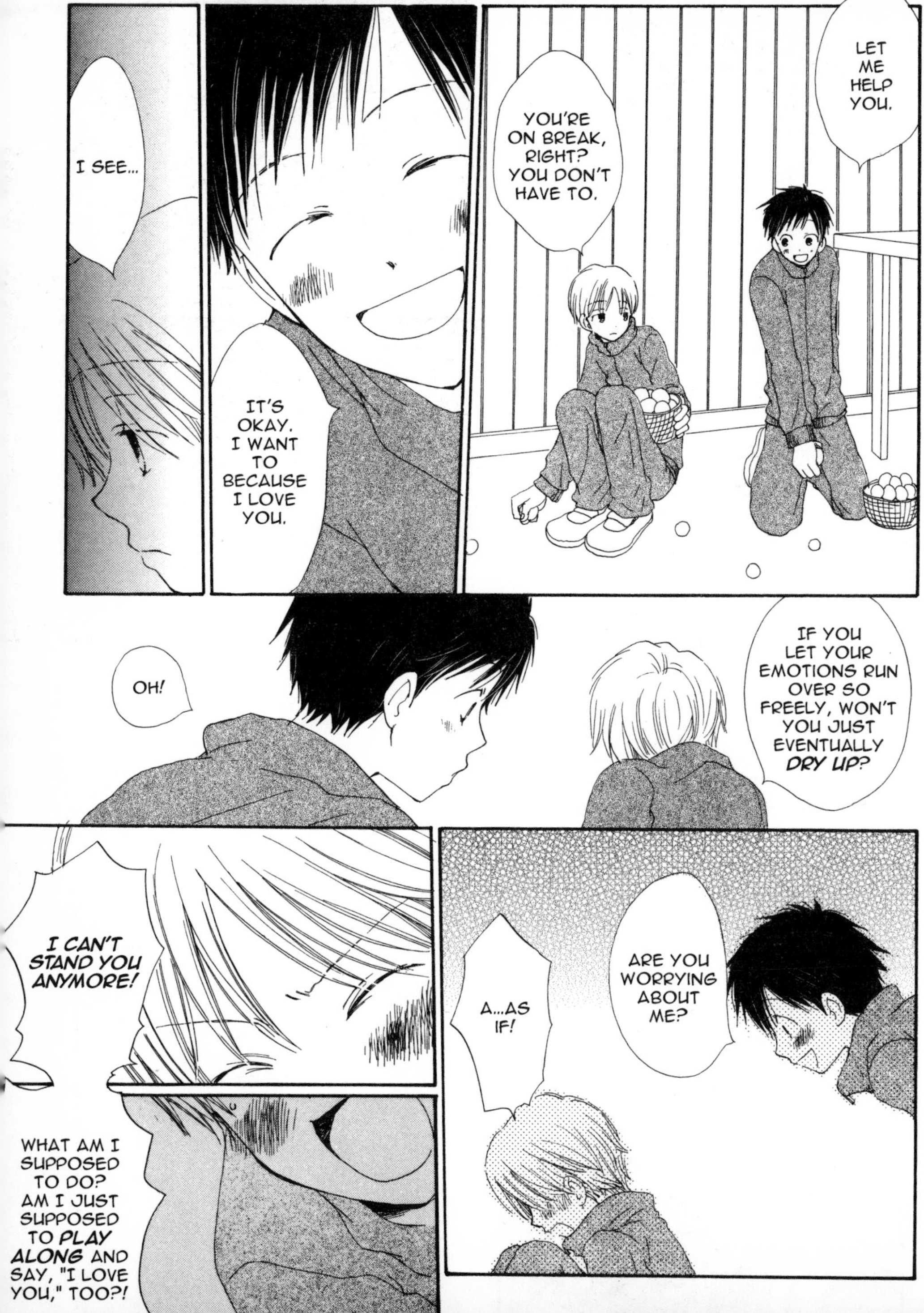
LET ME HELP YOU.
YOU'RE ON BREAK, RIGHT? YOU DON'T HAVE TO.
IT'S OKAY. I WANT TO BECAUSE I LOVE YOU.
I SEE...
IF YOU LET YOUR EMOTIONS RUN OVER SO FREELY, WON'T YOU JUST EVENTUALLY DRY UP?
OH!
ARE YOU WORRYING ABOUT ME?
A...AS IF!
I CAN'T STAND YOU ANYMORE!
WHAT AM I SUPPOSED TO DO? AM I JUST SUPPOSED TO PLAY ALONG AND SAY, "I LOVE YOU," TOO?!

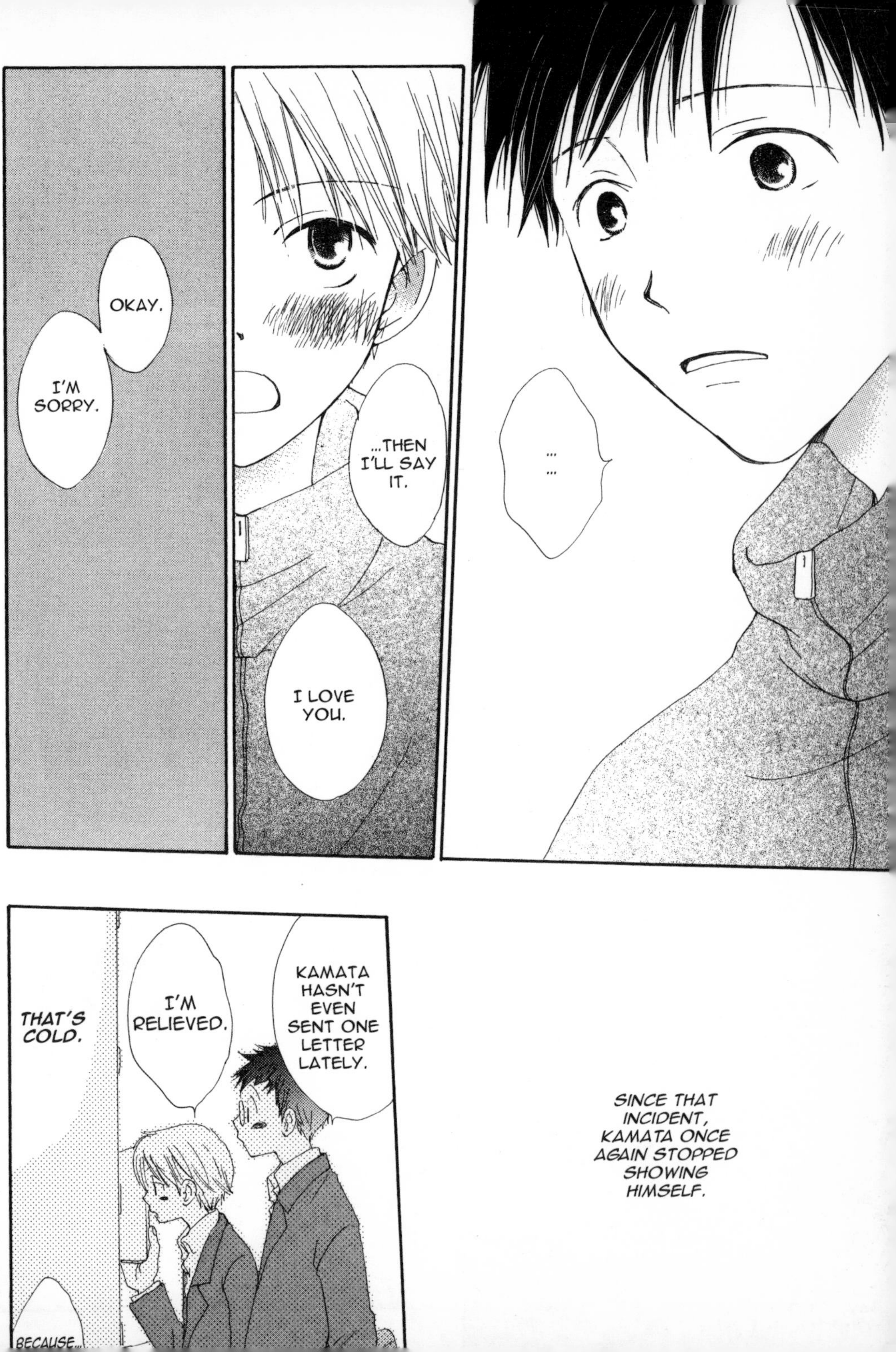
... ...
...THEN I'LL SAY IT.
I LOVE YOU.
OKAY.
I'M SORRY.
SINCE THAT INCIDENT, KAMATA ONCE AGAIN STOPPED SHOWING HIMSELF.
KAMATA HASN'T EVEN SENT ONE LETTER LATELY.
I'M RELIEVED.
THAT'S COLD.
BECAUSE...

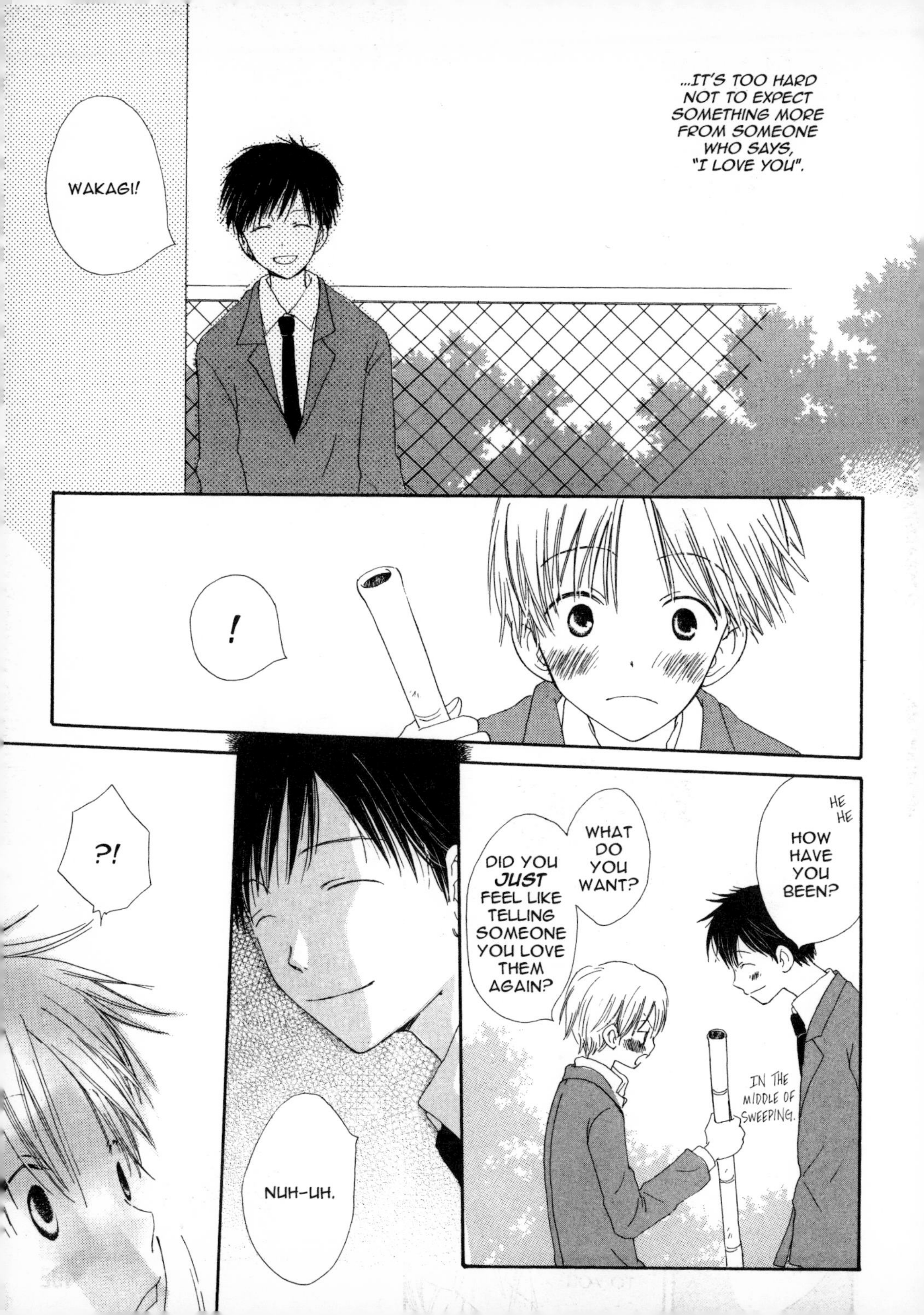
...IT'S TOO HARD NOT TO EXPECT SOMETHING MORE FROM SOMEONE WHO SAYS, "I LOVE YOU".
WAKAGI!
!
HE HE
HOW HAVE YOU BEEN?
WHAT DO YOU WANT?
DID YOU JUST FEEL LIKE TELLING SOMEONE YOU LOVE THEM AGAIN?
IN THE MIDDLE OF SWEEPING.
NUH-UH.
?!

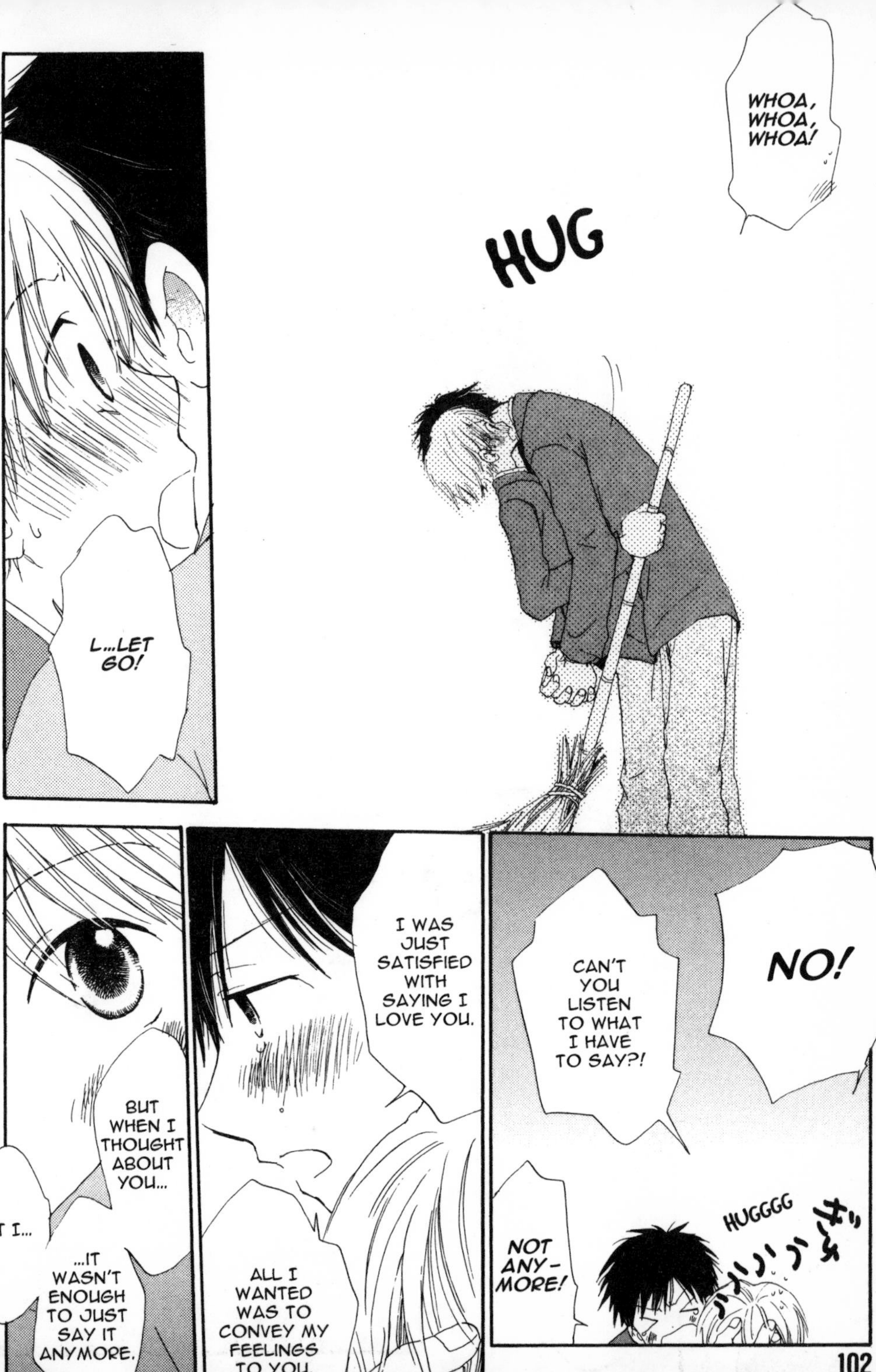
WHOA, WHOA, WHOA!
HUG
L...LET GO!
NO!
CAN'T YOU LISTEN TO WHAT I HAVE TO SAY?!
HUGGGG
NOT ANYMORE!
I WAS JUST SATISFIED WITH SAYING I LOVE YOU.
ALL I WANTED WAS TO CONVEY MY FEELINGS TO YOU.
BUT WHEN I THOUGHT ABOUT YOU...
BUT I...
...IT WASN'T ENOUGH TO JUST SAY IT ANYMORE.

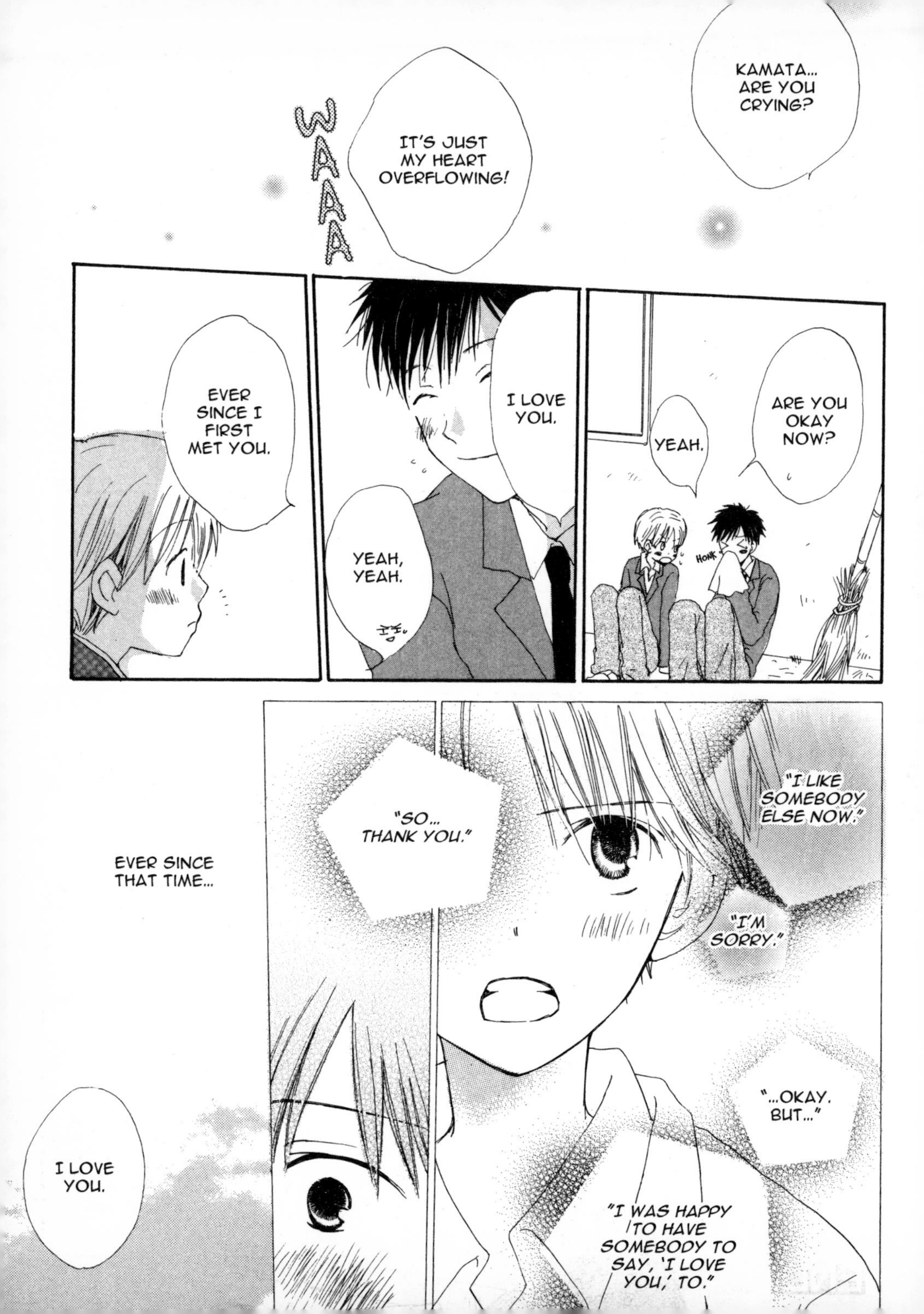
KAMATA... ARE YOU CRYING?
WAAAA
IT'S JUST MY HEART OVERFLOWING!
ARE YOU OKAY NOW?
YEAH.
HONK
I LOVE YOU.
YEAH, YEAH.
EVER SINCE I FIRST MET YOU.
"I LIKE SOMEBODY ELSE NOW."
"I'M SORRY."
"...OKAY. BUT..."
"I WAS HAPPY TO HAVE SOMEBODY TO SAY, 'I LOVE YOU,' TO."
"SO... THANK YOU."
EVER SINCE THAT TIME...
I LOVE YOU.

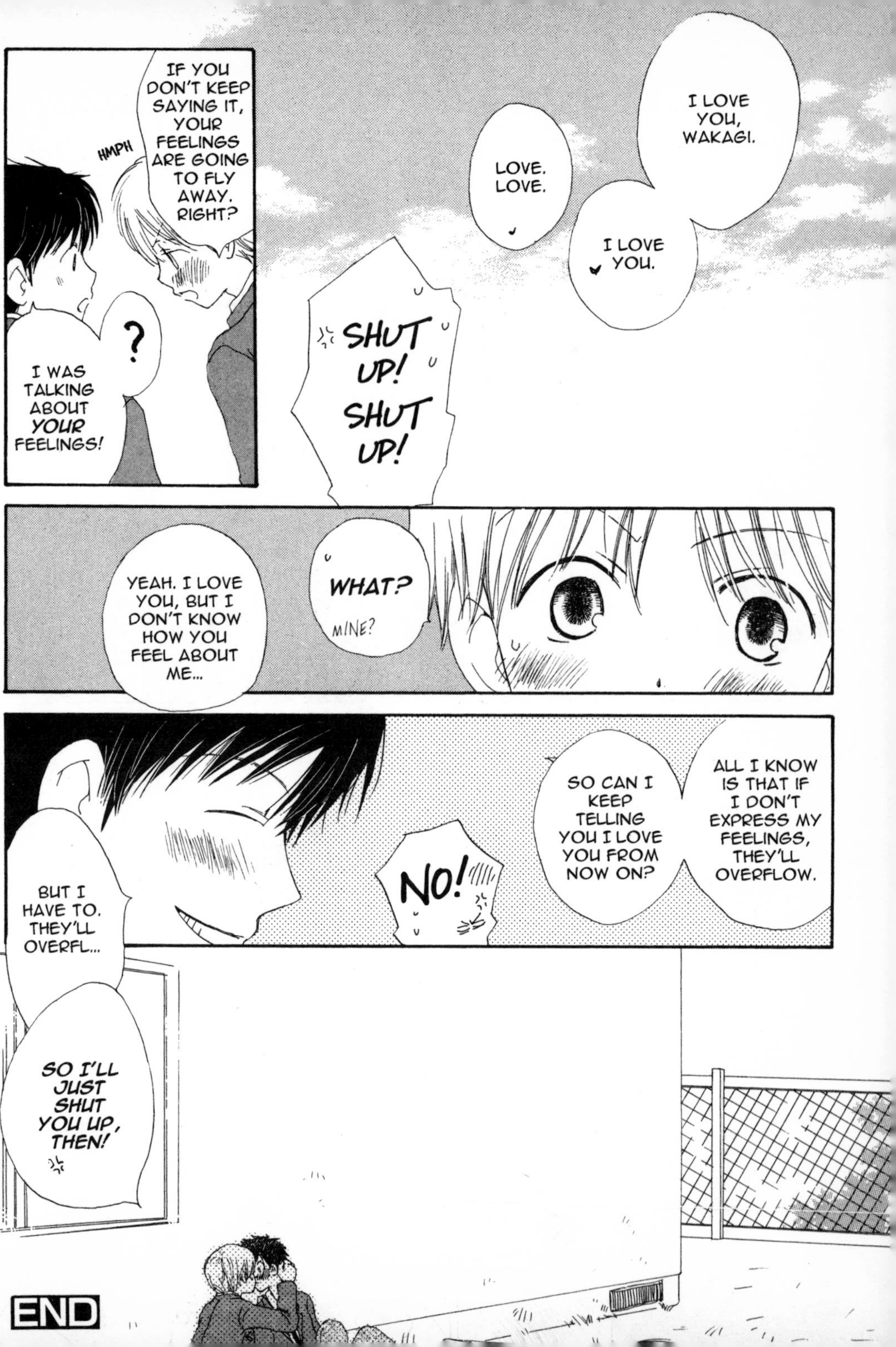
I LOVE YOU, WAKAGI.
LOVE. LOVE.
I LOVE YOU.
SHUT UP! SHUT UP!
IF YOU DON'T KEEP SAYING IT, YOUR FEELINGS ARE GOING TO FLY AWAY. RIGHT?
HMPH
?
I WAS TALKING ABOUT *YOUR* FEELINGS!
WHAT?
MINE?
YEAH. I LOVE YOU, BUT I DON'T KNOW HOW YOU FEEL ABOUT ME...
ALL I KNOW IS THAT IF I DON'T EXPRESS MY FEELINGS, THEY'LL OVERFLOW.
SO CAN I KEEP TELLING YOU I LOVE YOU FROM NOW ON?
NO!
BUT I HAVE TO. THEY'LL OVERFL...
SO I'LL JUST SHUT YOU UP, THEN!
END

CELLULOID CLOSET

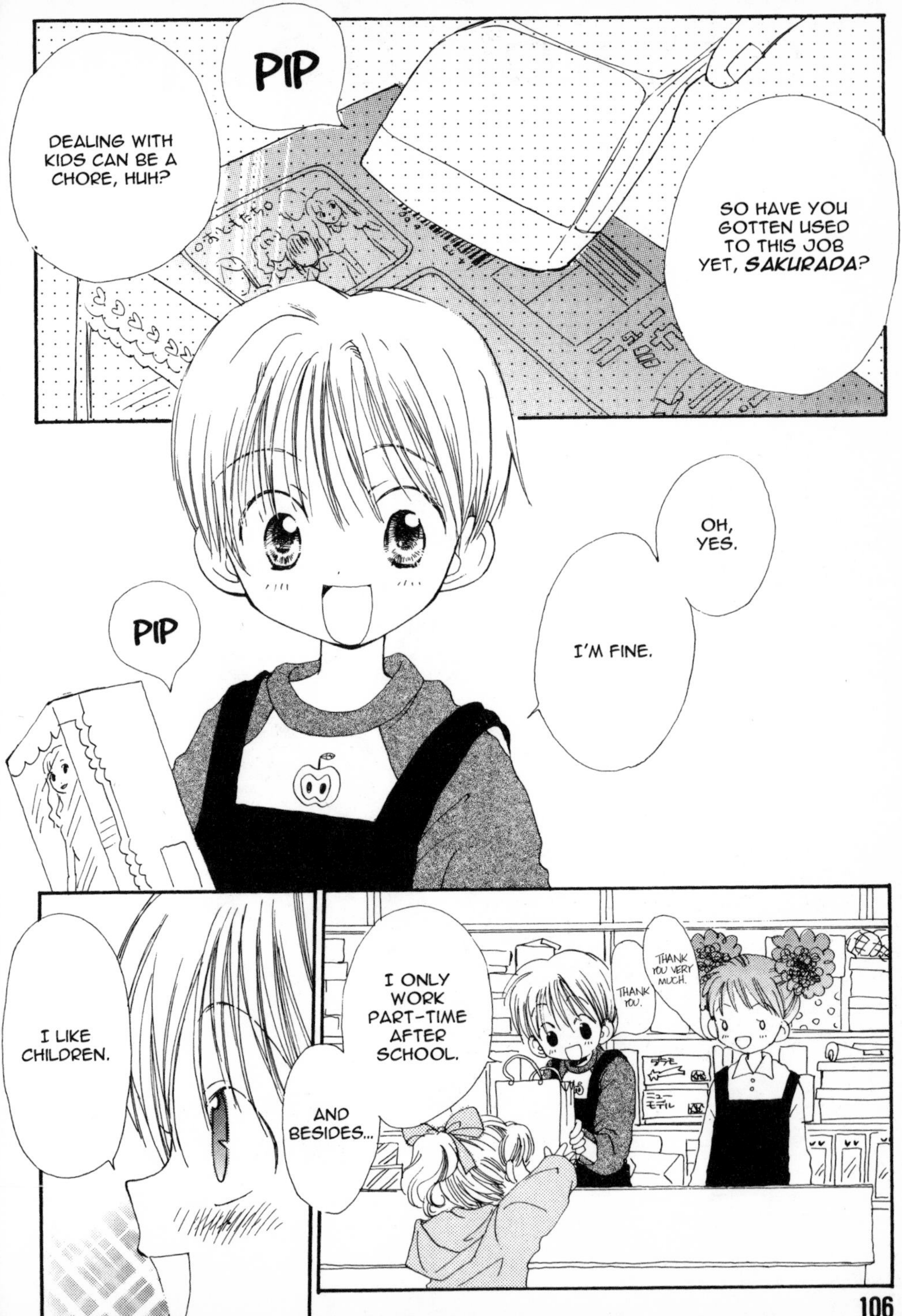
SO HAVE YOU GOTTEN USED TO THIS JOB YET, SAKURADA?
PIP
DEALING WITH KIDS CAN BE A CHORE, HUH?
OH, YES.
I'M FINE.
PIP
THANK YOU VERY MUCH.
THANK YOU.
I ONLY WORK PART-TIME AFTER SCHOOL.
AND BESIDES...
I LIKE CHILDREN.

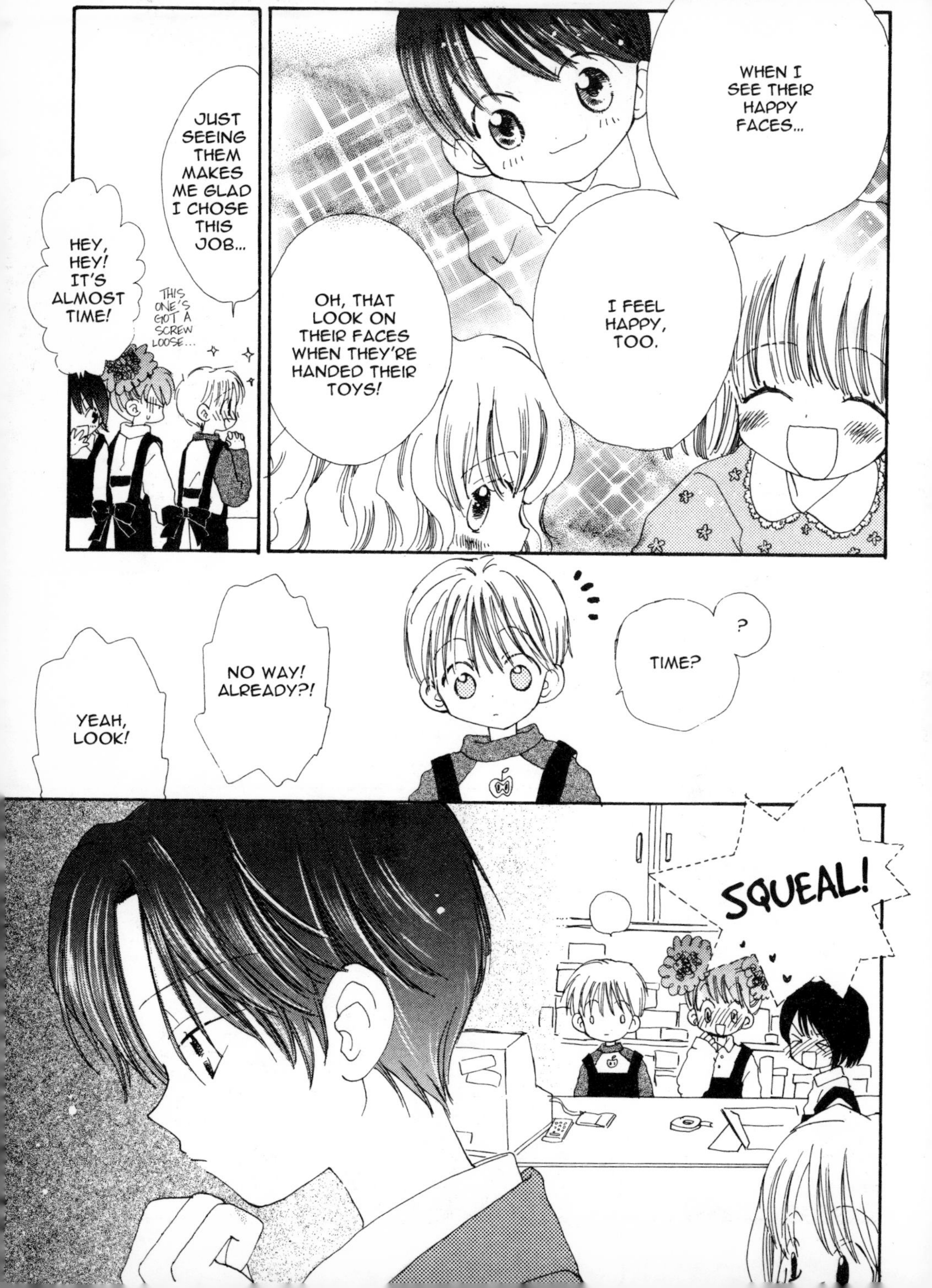
WHEN I SEE THEIR HAPPY FACES...
I FEEL HAPPY, TOO.
OH, THAT LOOK ON THEIR FACES WHEN THEY'RE HANDED THEIR TOYS!
JUST SEEING THEM MAKES ME GLAD I CHOSE THIS JOB...
HEY, HEY! IT'S ALMOST TIME!
THIS ONE'S GOT A SCREW LOOSE...
?
TIME?
NO WAY! ALREADY?!
YEAH, LOOK!
SQUEAL!

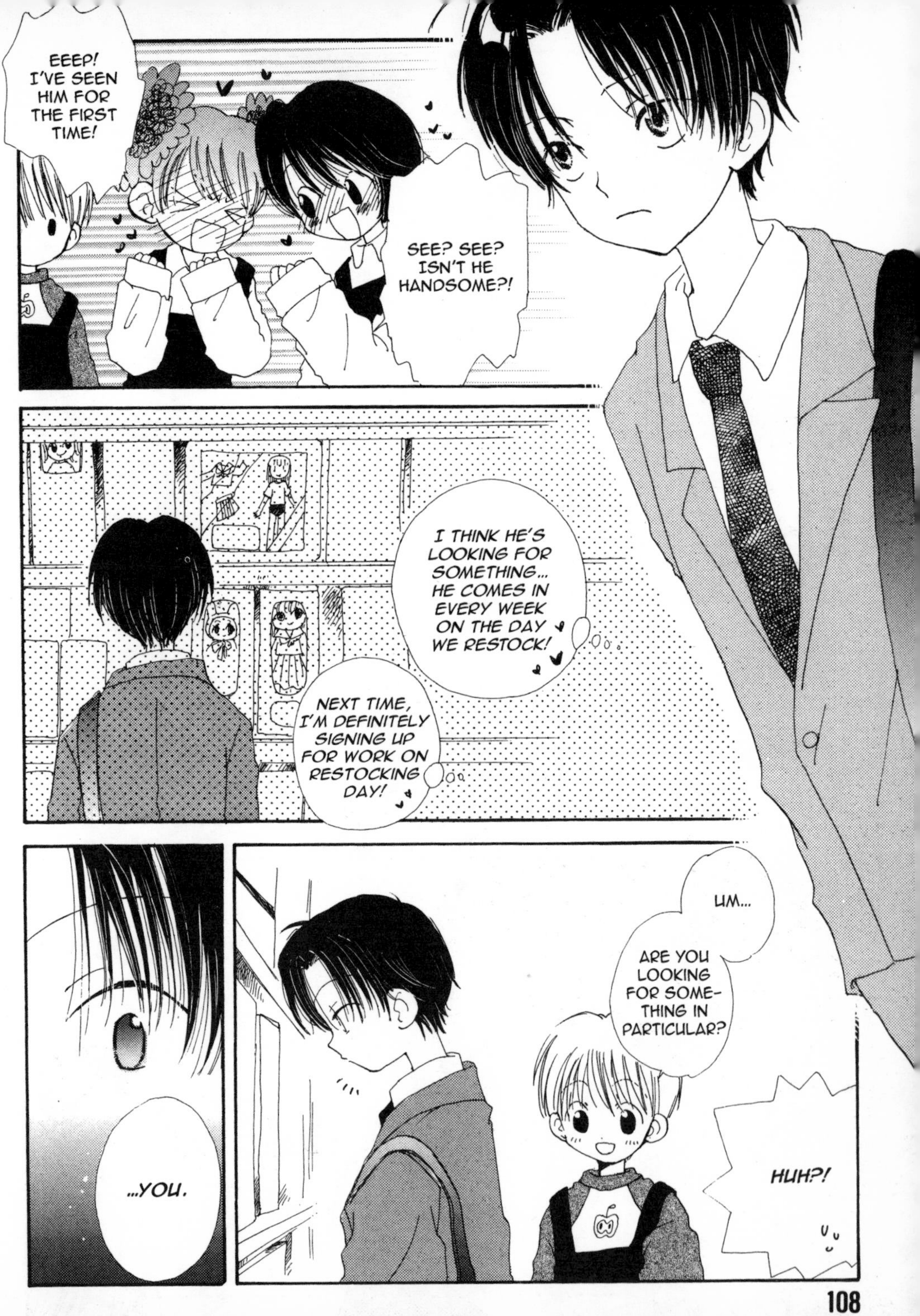
SEE? SEE? ISN'T HE HANDSOME?!
EEEP! I'VE SEEN HIM FOR THE FIRST TIME!
I THINK HE'S LOOKING FOR SOMETHING... HE COMES IN EVERY WEEK ON THE DAY WE RESTOCK!
NEXT TIME, I'M DEFINITELY SIGNING UP FOR WORK ON RESTOCKING DAY!
UM...
ARE YOU LOOKING FOR SOME-THING IN PARTICULAR?
HUH?!
...YOU.

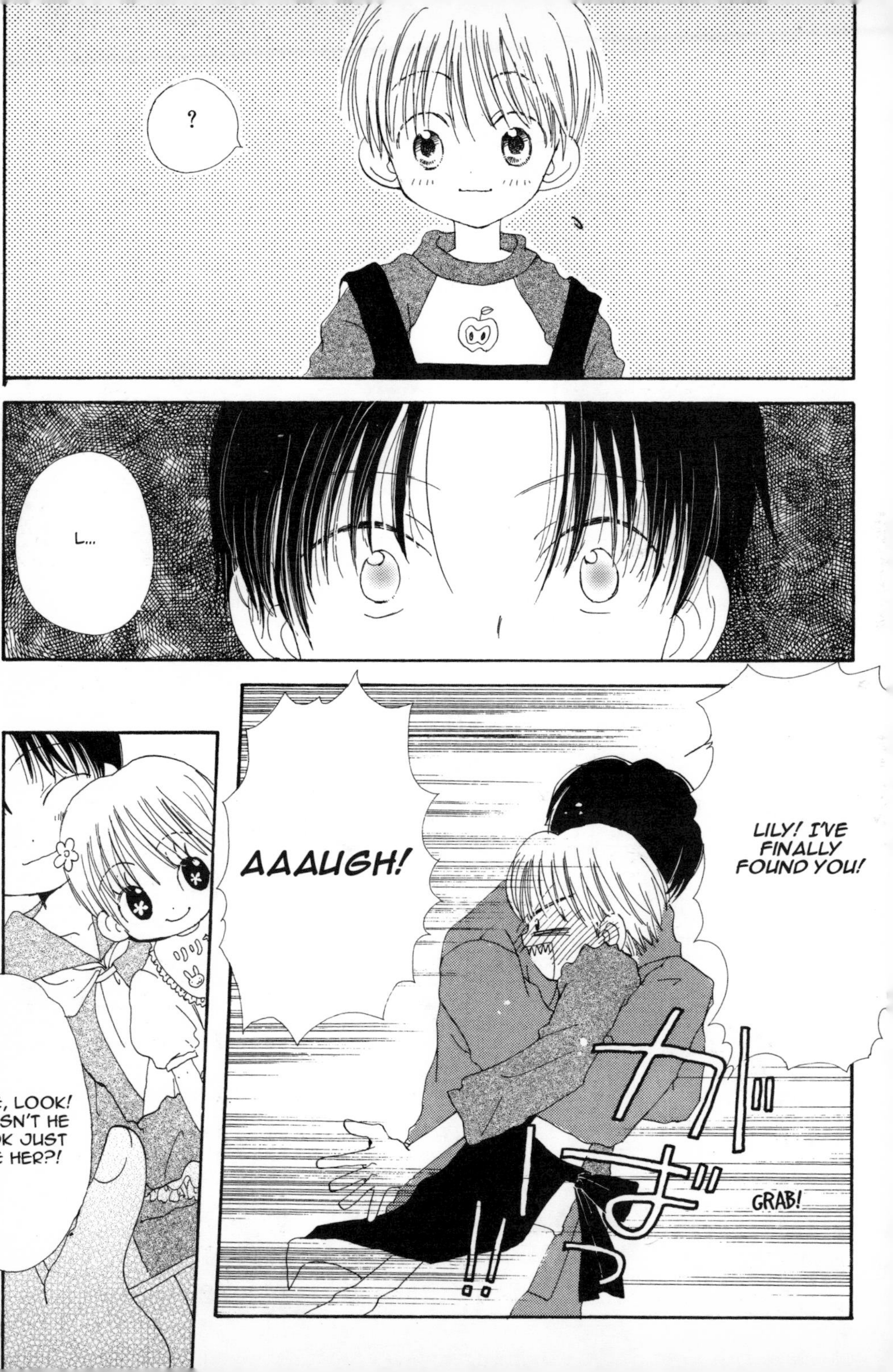
?
L...
LILY! I'VE FINALLY FOUND YOU!
AAAUGH!
GRAB!
HERE, LOOK! DOESN'T HE LOOK JUST LIKE HER?!

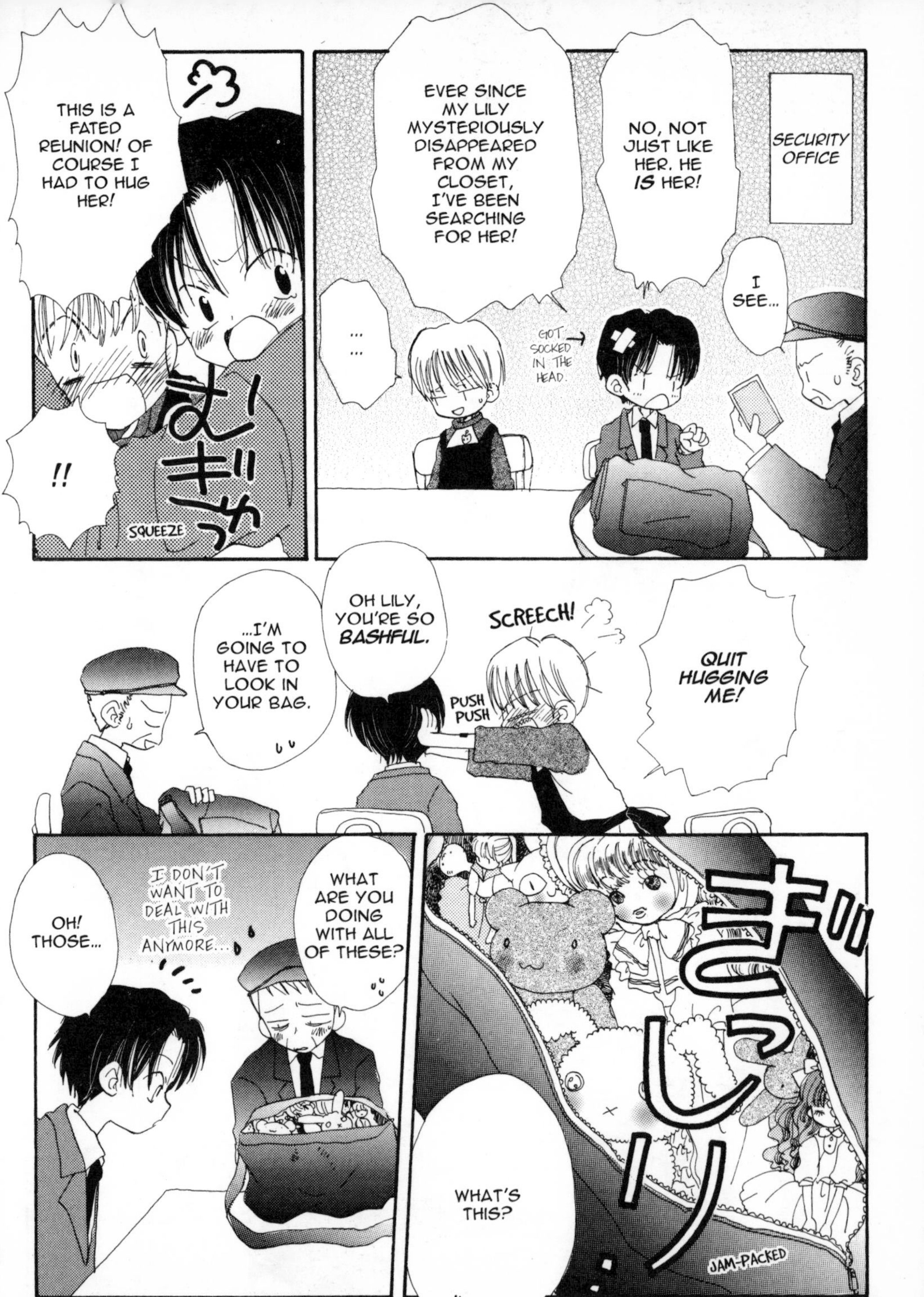
SECURITY OFFICE
I SEE...
NO, NOT JUST LIKE HER. HE IS HER!
EVER SINCE MY LILY MYSTERIOUSLY DISAPPEARED FROM MY CLOSET, I'VE BEEN SEARCHING FOR HER!
GOT SOCKED IN THE HEAD.
... ...
THIS IS A FATED REUNION! OF COURSE I HAD TO HUG HER!
!!
SQUEEZE
QUIT HUGGING ME!
SCREECH!
OH LILY, YOU'RE SO BASHFUL.
PUSH PUSH
...I'M GOING TO HAVE TO LOOK IN YOUR BAG.
JAM-PACKED
WHAT'S THIS?
WHAT ARE YOU DOING WITH ALL OF THESE?
I DON'T WANT TO DEAL WITH THIS ANYMORE...
OH! THOSE...

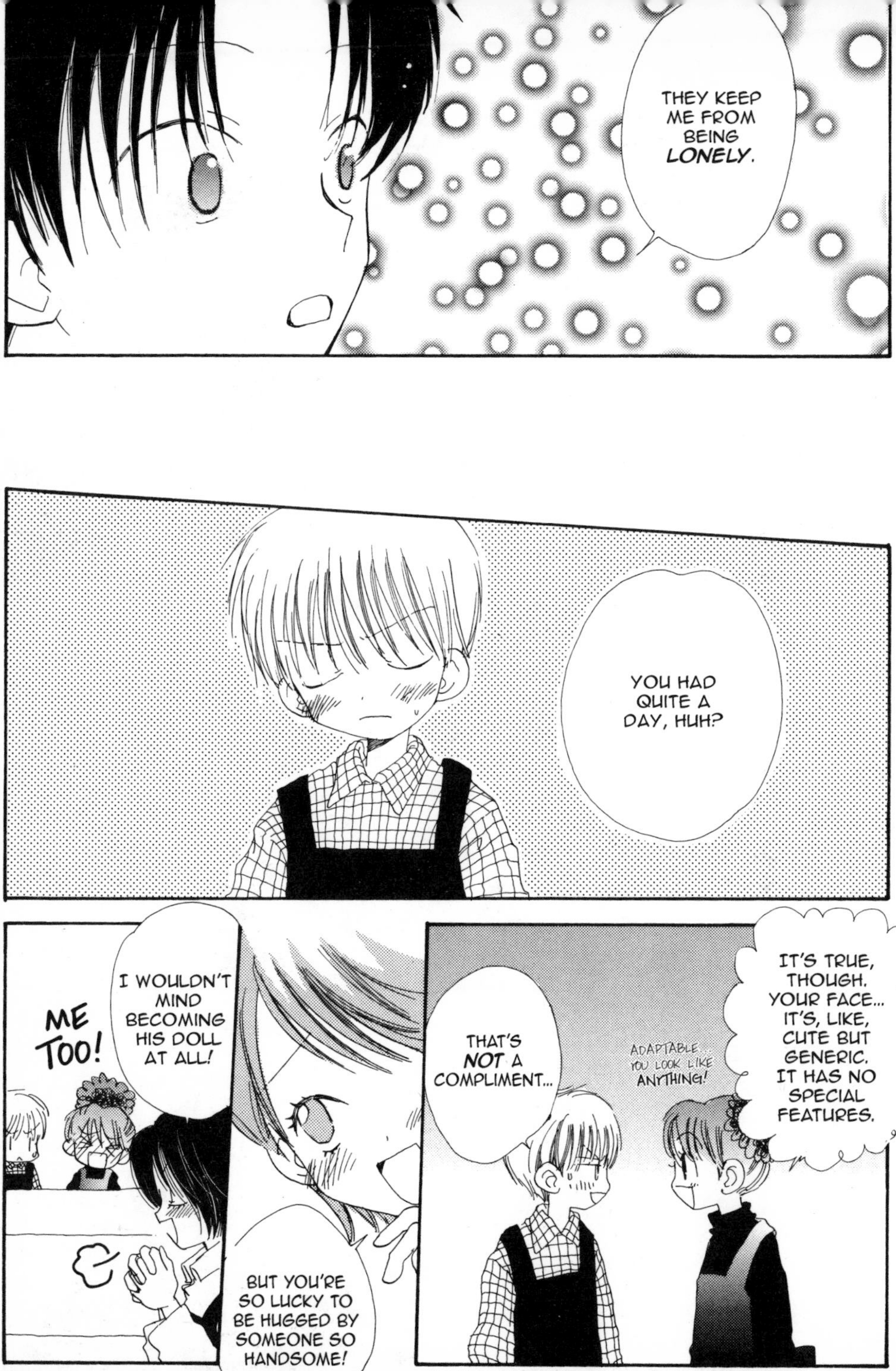
THEY KEEP ME FROM BEING LONELY.
YOU HAD QUITE A DAY, HUH?
IT'S TRUE, THOUGH. YOUR FACE... IT'S, LIKE, CUTE BUT GENERIC. IT HAS NO SPECIAL FEATURES.
ADAPTABLE... YOU LOOK LIKE ANYTHING!
THAT'S NOT A COMPLIMENT...
I WOULDN'T MIND BECOMING HIS DOLL AT ALL!
ME TOO!
BUT YOU'RE SO LUCKY TO BE HUGGED BY SOMEONE SO HANDSOME!

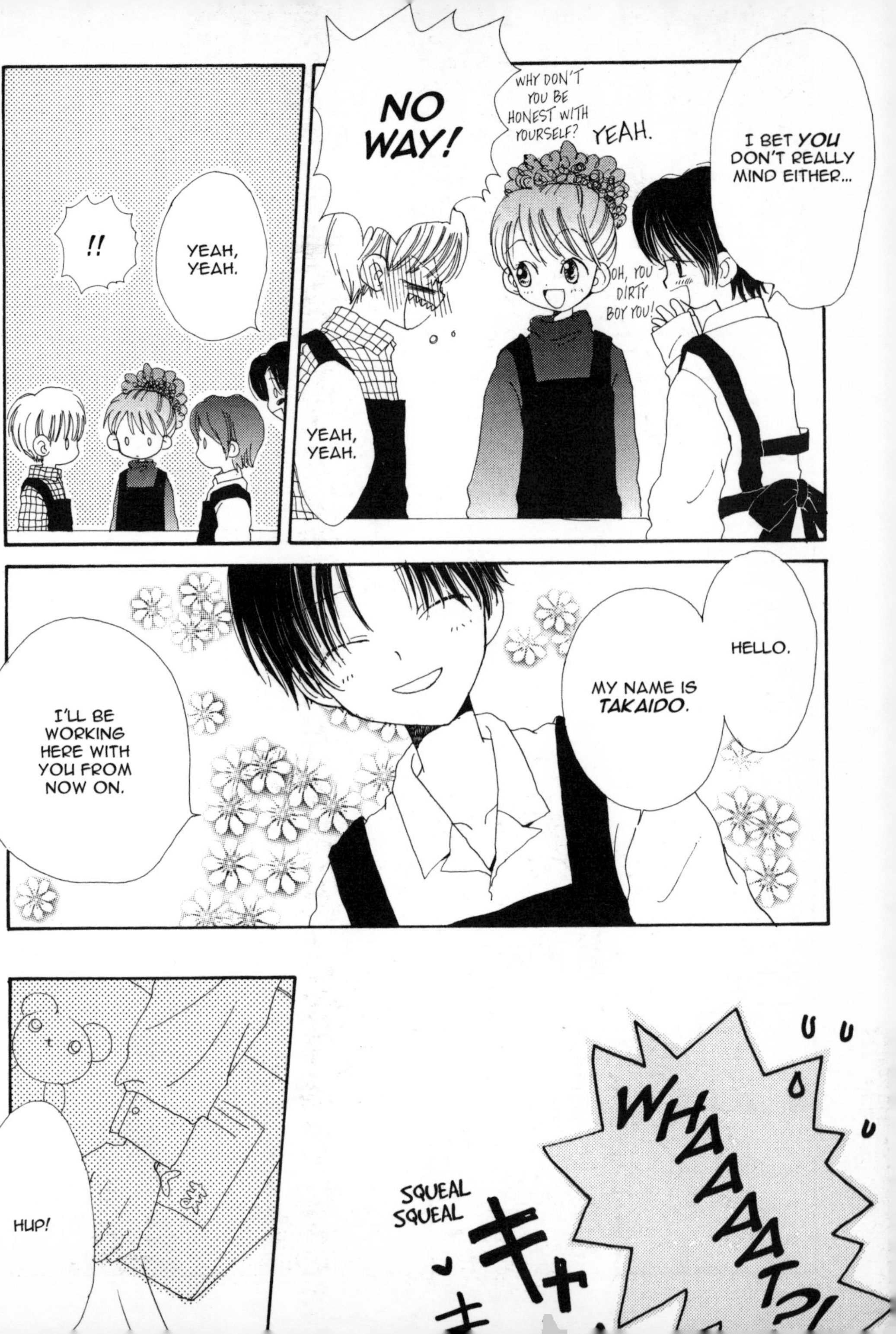
I BET YOU DON'T REALLY MIND EITHER...
WHY DON'T YOU BE HONEST WITH YOURSELF?
YEAH.
NO WAY!
OH, YOU DIRTY BOY YOU!
YEAH, YEAH.
YEAH, YEAH.
!!
HELLO.
MY NAME IS TAKAIDO.
I'LL BE WORKING HERE WITH YOU FROM NOW ON.
WHAAAAT?!
SQUEAL SQUEAL
HUP!

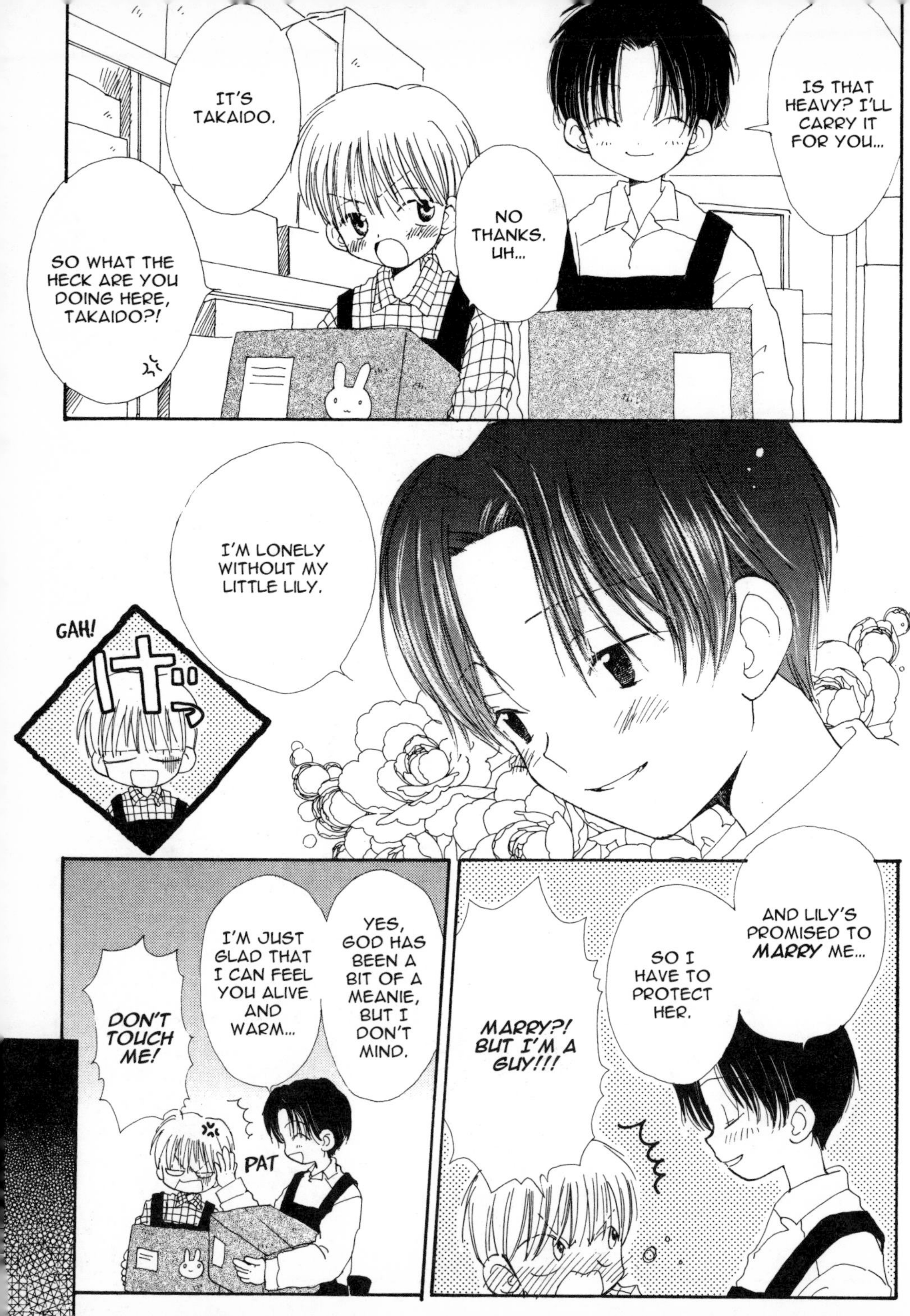
IS THAT HEAVY? I'LL CARRY IT FOR YOU...
NO THANKS. UH...
IT'S TAKAIDO.
SO WHAT THE HECK ARE YOU DOING HERE, TAKAIDO?!
I'M LONELY WITHOUT MY LITTLE LILY.
GAH!
AND LILY'S PROMISED TO *MARRY* ME...
SO I HAVE TO PROTECT HER.
MARRY?! BUT I'M A GUY!!!
YES, GOD HAS BEEN A BIT OF A MEANIE, BUT I DON'T MIND.
I'M JUST GLAD THAT I CAN FEEL YOU ALIVE AND WARM...
PAT
DON'T TOUCH ME!

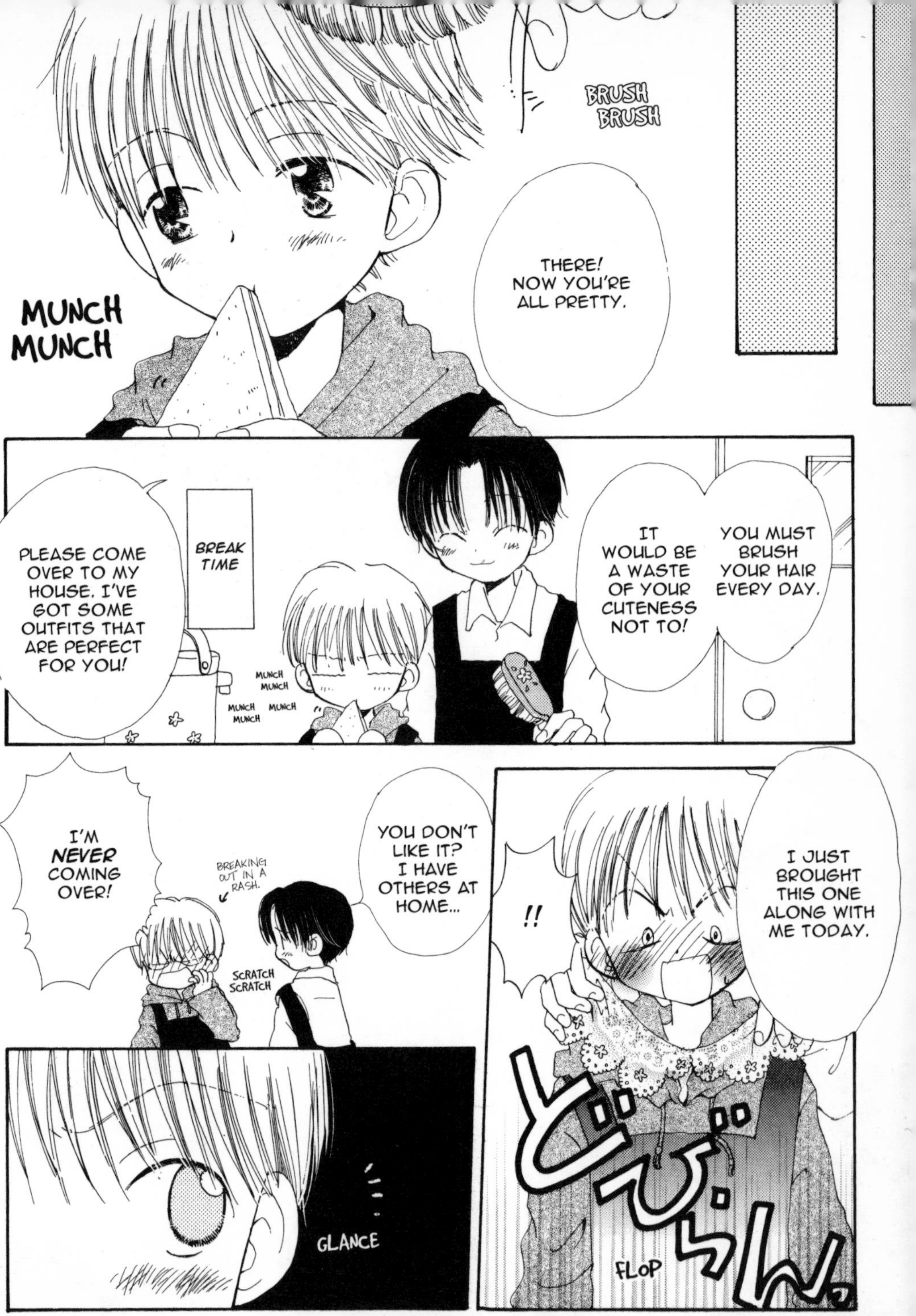
BRUSH BRUSH
THERE! NOW YOU'RE ALL PRETTY.
MUNCH MUNCH
YOU MUST BRUSH YOUR HAIR EVERY DAY.
IT WOULD BE A WASTE OF YOUR CUTENESS NOT TO!
MUNCH MUNCH
MUNCH MUNCH
MUNCH
BREAK TIME
PLEASE COME OVER TO MY HOUSE. I'VE GOT SOME OUTFITS THAT ARE PERFECT FOR YOU!
I JUST BROUGHT THIS ONE ALONG WITH ME TODAY.
!!
FLOP
YOU DON'T LIKE IT? I HAVE OTHERS AT HOME...
BREAKING OUT IN A RASH.
SCRATCH SCRATCH
I'M ***NEVER*** COMING OVER!
GLANCE

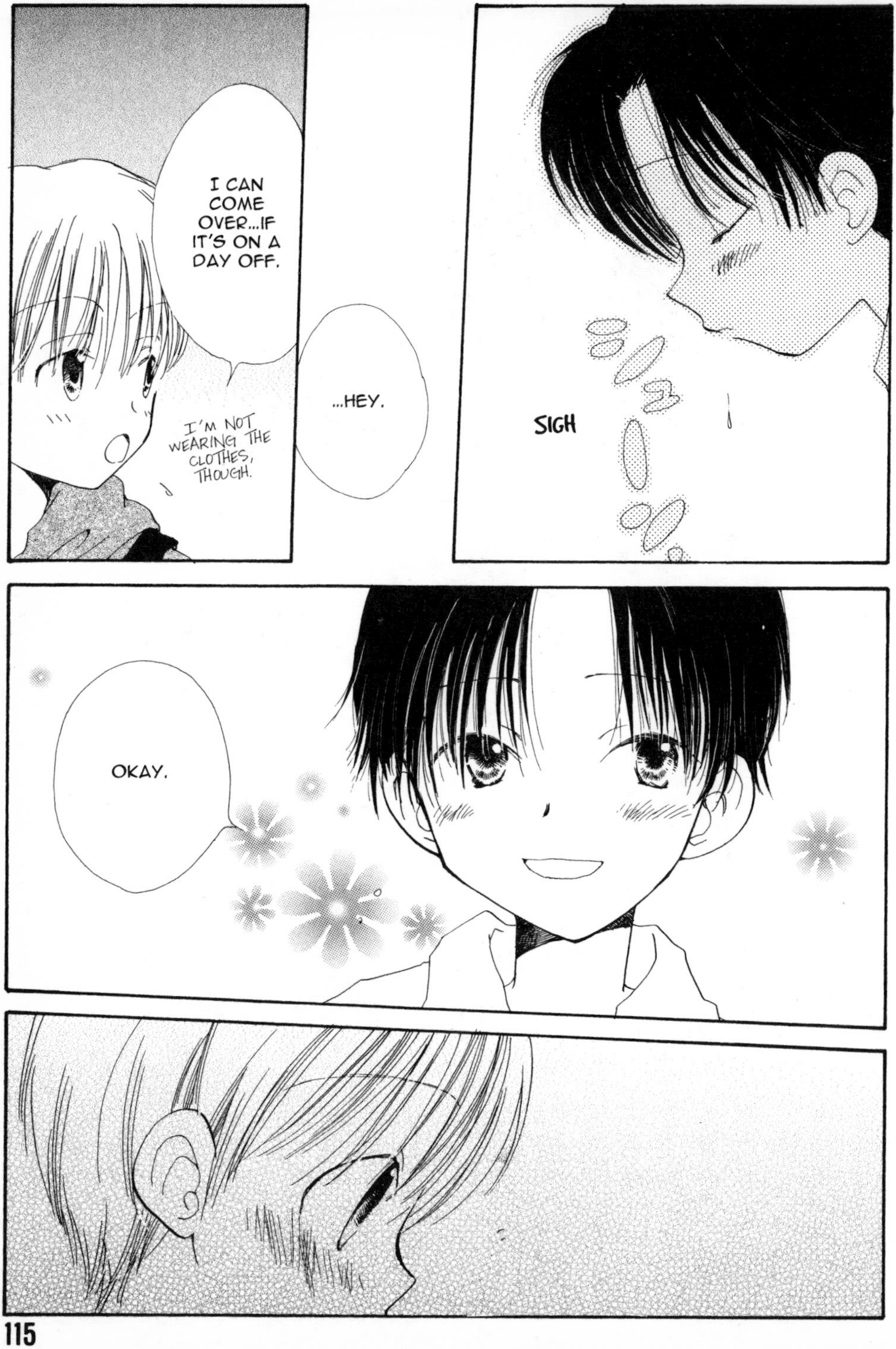
SIGH
I CAN COME OVER...IF IT'S ON A DAY OFF.
I'M NOT WEARING THE CLOTHES, THOUGH.
...HEY.
OKAY.

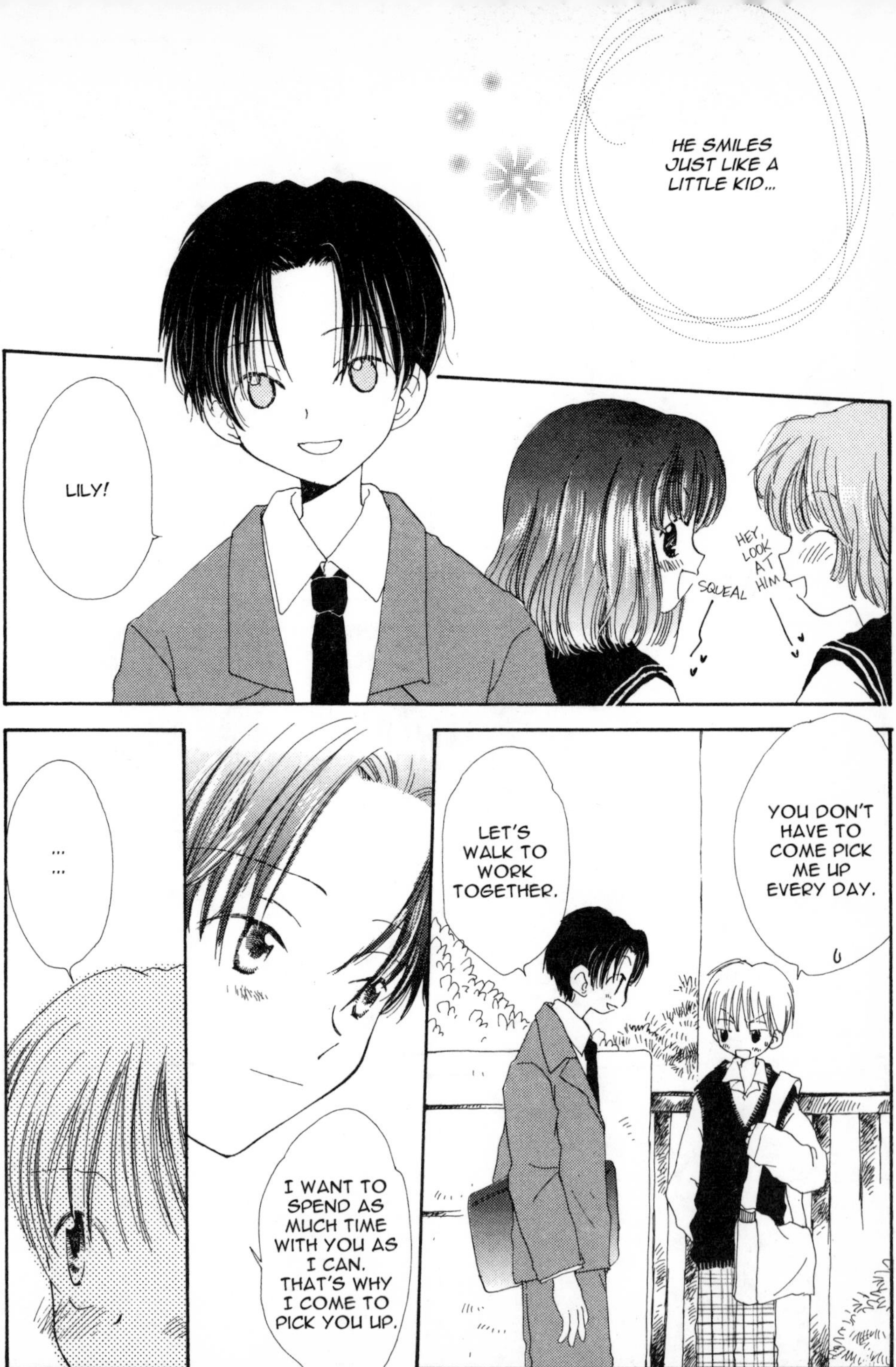
HE SMILES JUST LIKE A LITTLE KID...
LILY!
HEY, LOOK AT HIM
SQUEAL
YOU DON'T HAVE TO COME PICK ME UP EVERY DAY.
LET'S WALK TO WORK TOGETHER.
... ...
I WANT TO SPEND AS MUCH TIME WITH YOU AS I CAN. THAT'S WHY I COME TO PICK YOU UP.

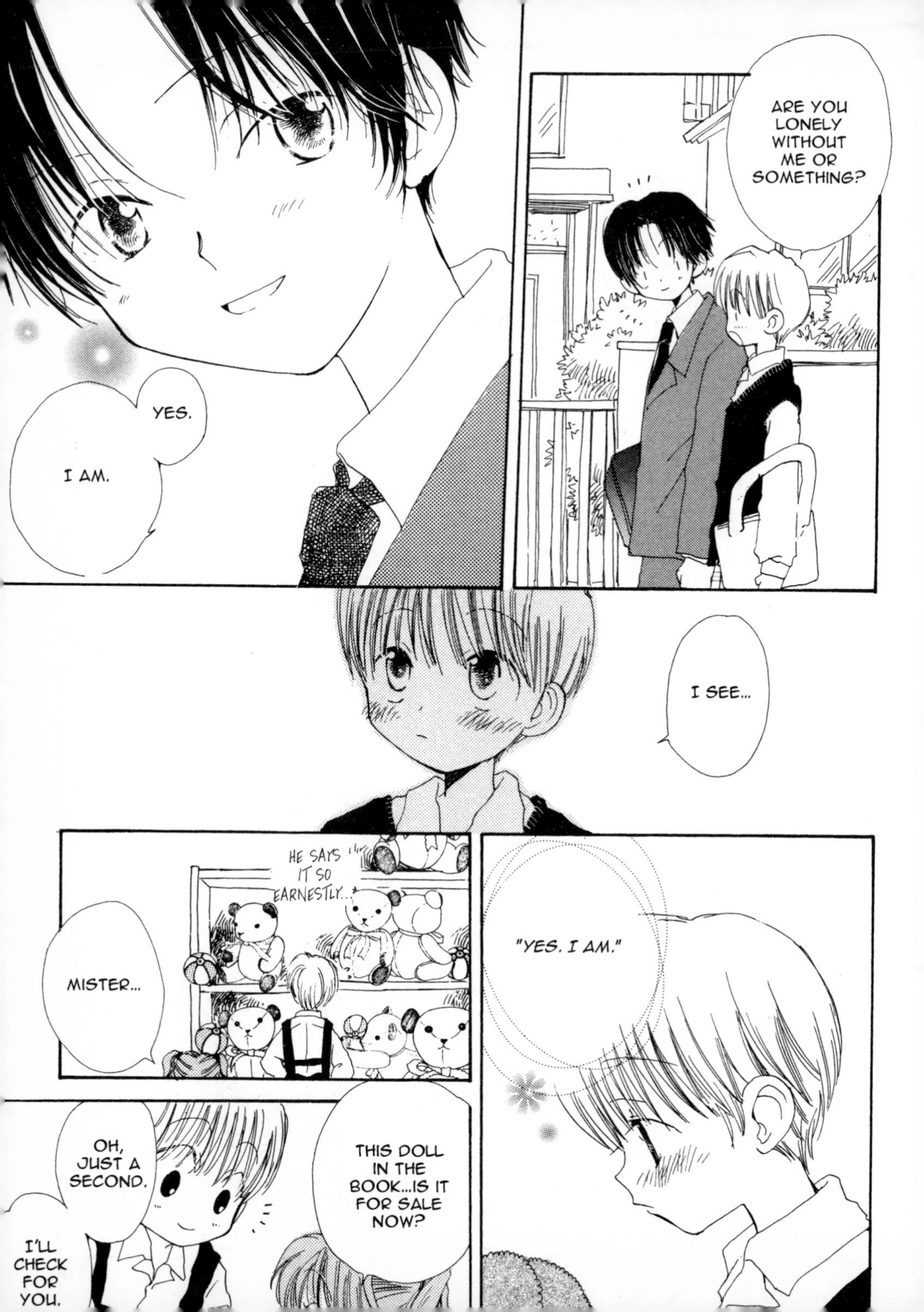
ARE YOU LONELY WITHOUT ME OR SOMETHING?
YES.
I AM.
I SEE...
"YES. I AM."
HE SAYS IT SO EARNESTLY...
MISTER...
THIS DOLL IN THE BOOK...IS IT FOR SALE NOW?
OH, JUST A SECOND.
I'LL CHECK FOR YOU.

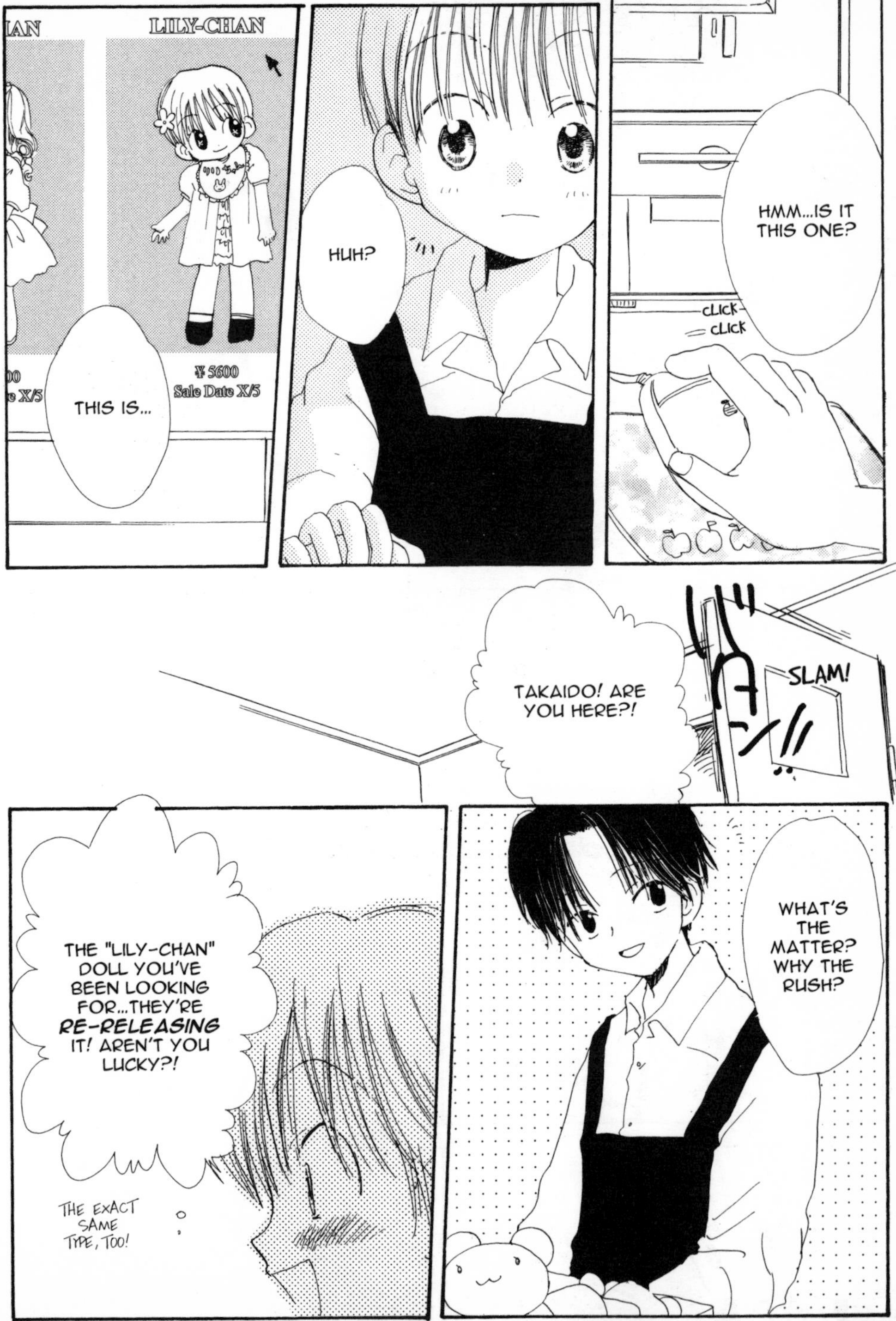
HMM...IS IT THIS ONE?
CLICK
CLICK
HUH?
LILY-CHAN
¥5600
Sale Date X/5
THIS IS...
SLAM!
TAKAIDO! ARE YOU HERE?!
WHAT'S THE MATTER? WHY THE RUSH?
THE "LILY-CHAN" DOLL YOU'VE BEEN LOOKING FOR...THEY'RE ***RE-RELEASING*** IT! AREN'T YOU LUCKY?!
THE EXACT SAME TYPE, TOO!

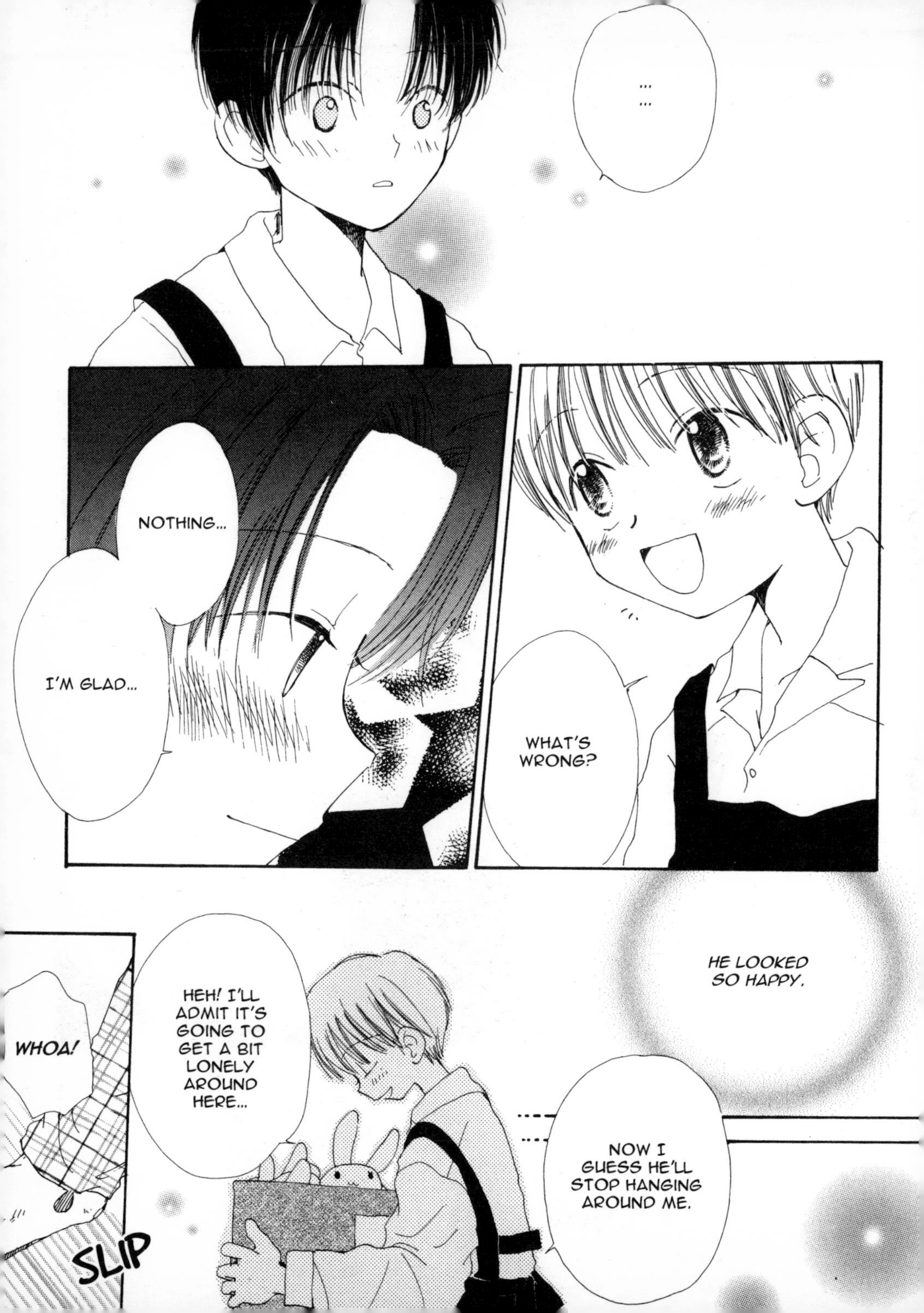
......
WHAT'S WRONG?
NOTHING...
I'M GLAD...
HE LOOKED SO HAPPY.
NOW I GUESS HE'LL STOP HANGING AROUND ME.
HEH! I'LL ADMIT IT'S GOING TO GET A BIT LONELY AROUND HERE...
WHOA!
SLIP

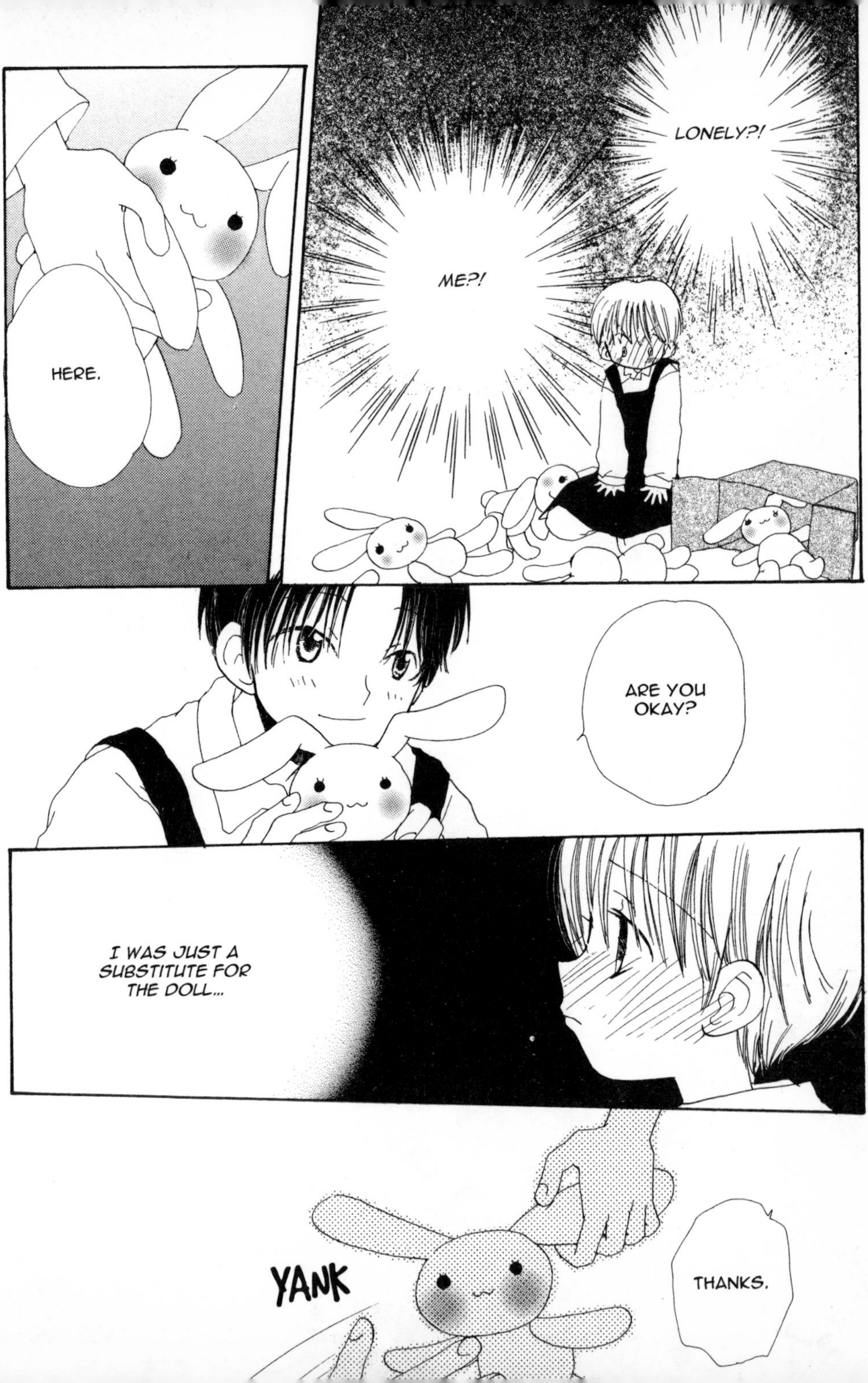
LONELY?!
ME?!
HERE.
ARE YOU OKAY?
I WAS JUST A SUBSTITUTE FOR THE DOLL...
THANKS.
YANK

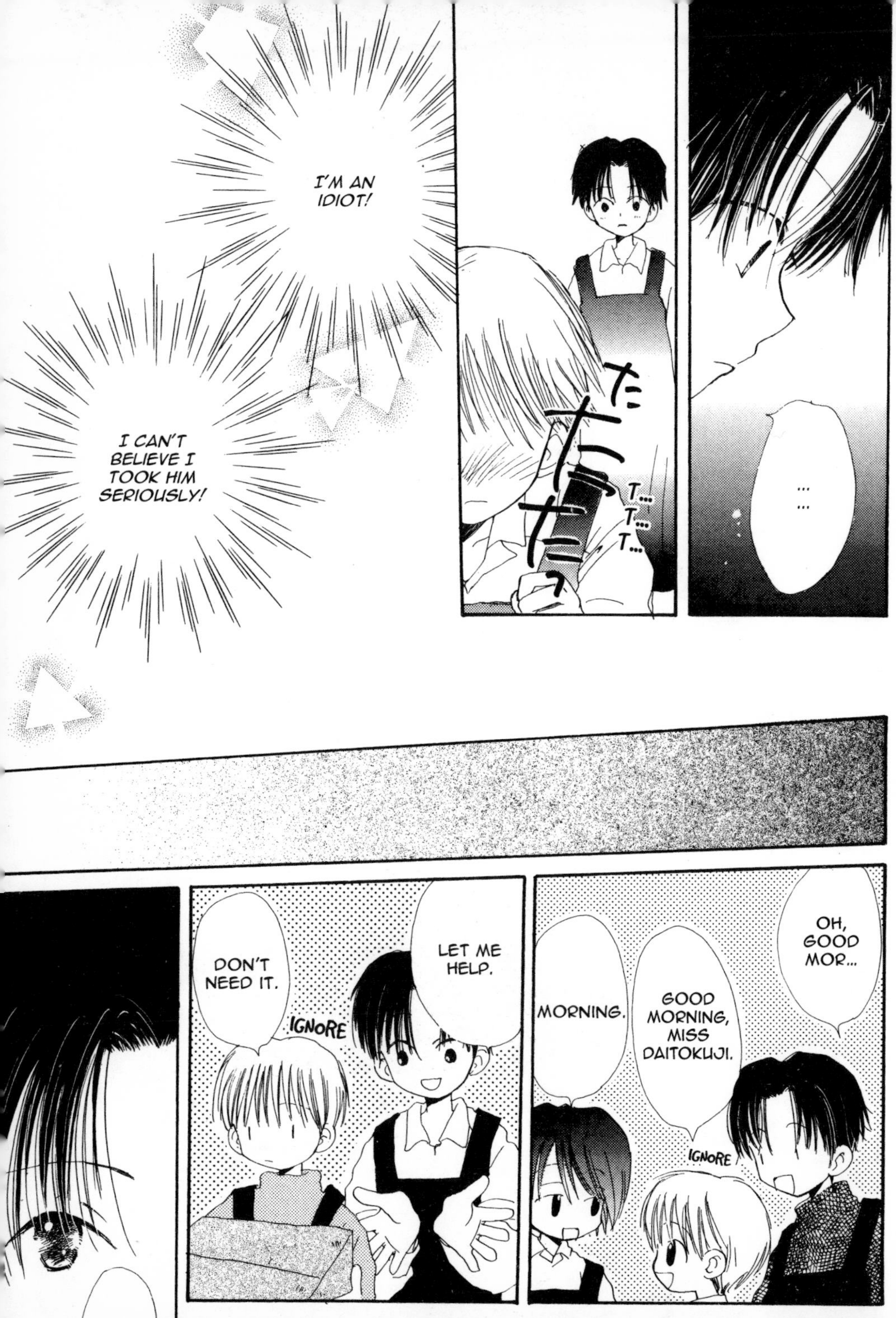
... ...
たたたっ
T... T... T...
I'M AN IDIOT!
I CAN'T BELIEVE I TOOK HIM SERIOUSLY!
OH, GOOD MOR...
GOOD MORNING, MISS DAITOKUJI.
IGNORE
MORNING.
LET ME HELP.
DON'T NEED IT.
IGNORE
...

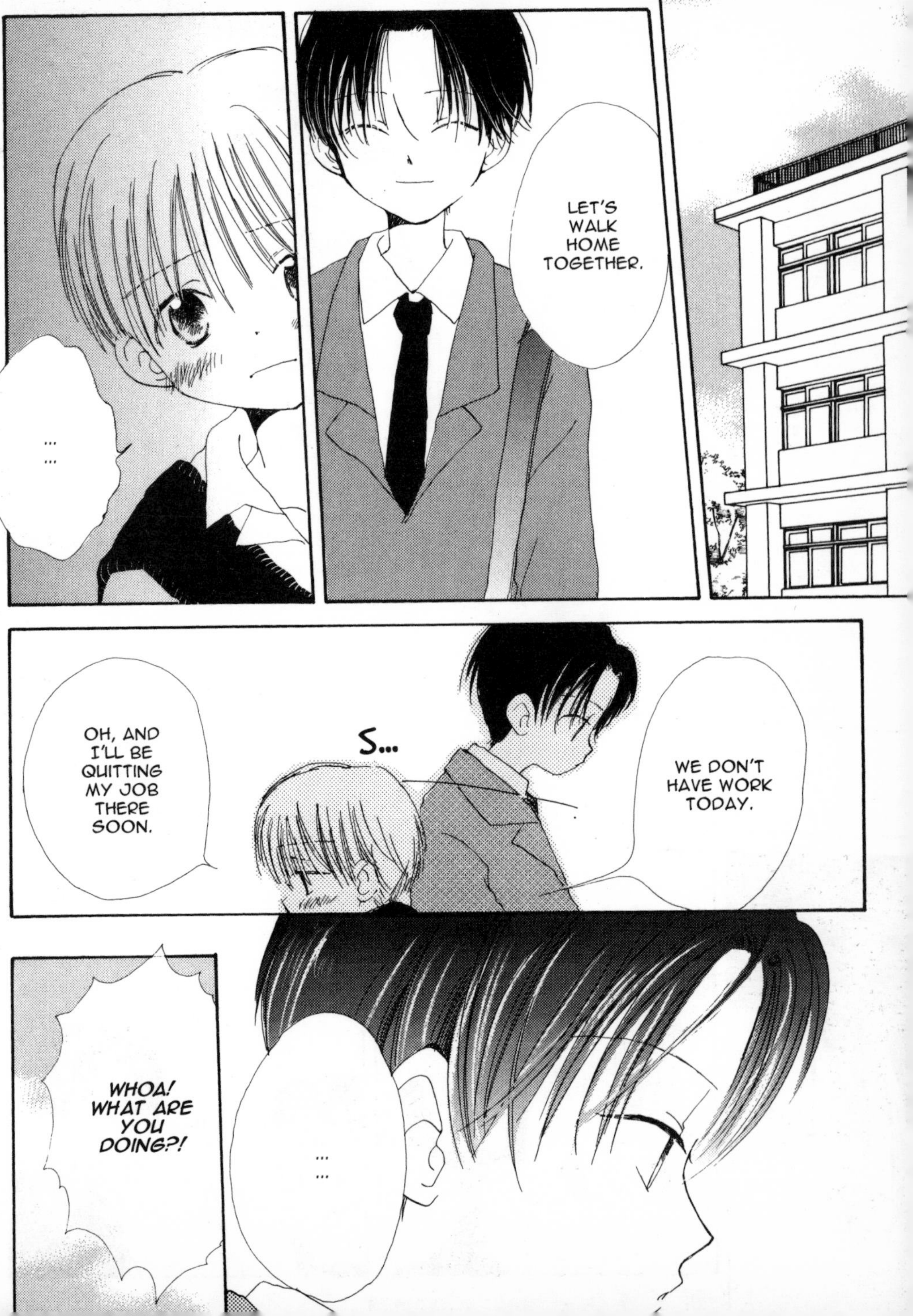
LET'S WALK HOME TOGETHER.
……
WE DON'T HAVE WORK TODAY.
S...
OH, AND I'LL BE QUITTING MY JOB THERE SOON.
……
WHOA! WHAT ARE YOU DOING?!

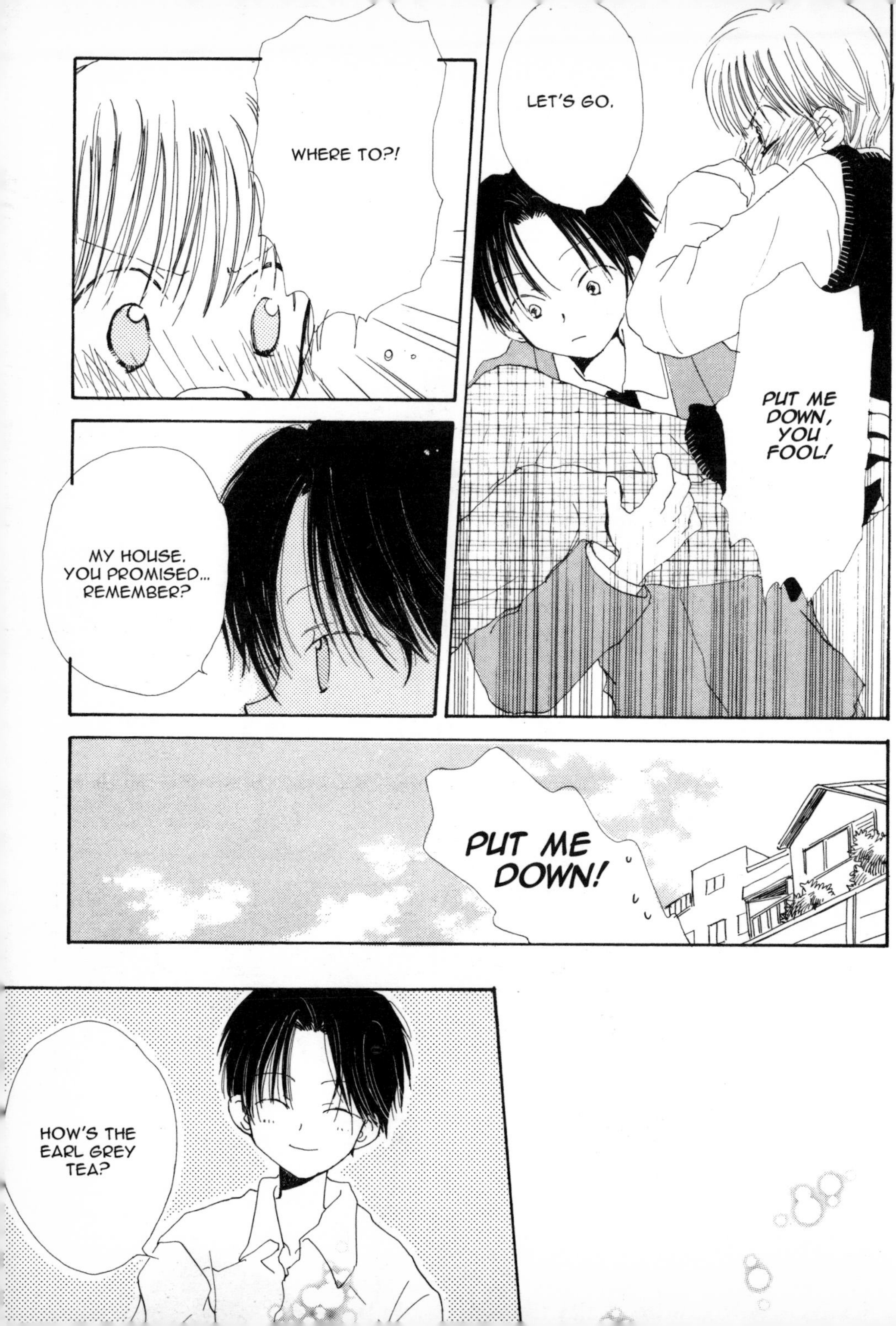
LET'S GO.
PUT ME DOWN, YOU FOOL!
WHERE TO?!
MY HOUSE. YOU PROMISED... REMEMBER?
PUT ME DOWN!
HOW'S THE EARL GREY TEA?

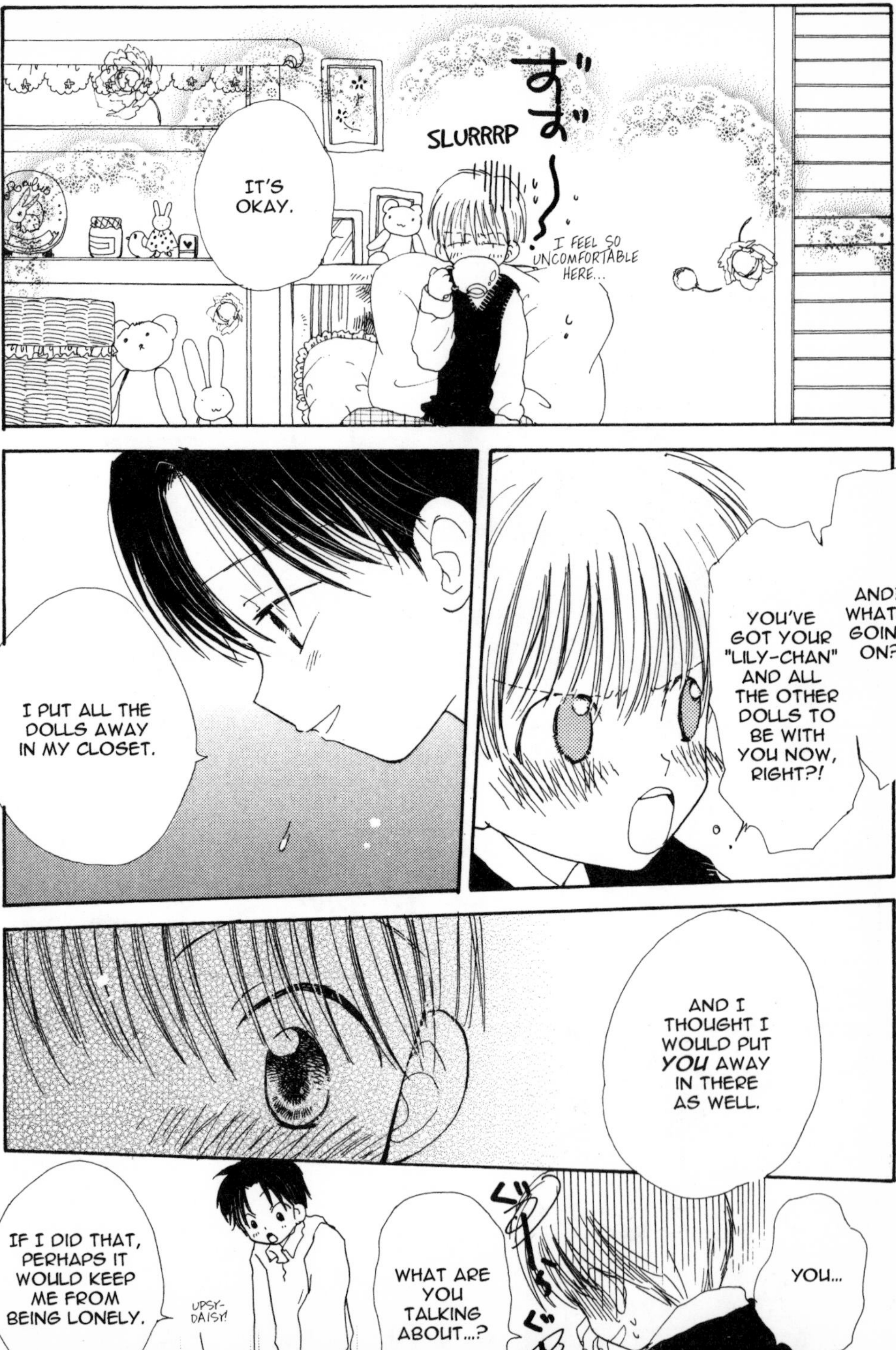
ずず~
SLURRRP
I FEEL SO UNCOMFORTABLE HERE...
IT'S OKAY.
AND? WHAT'S GOING ON?
YOU'VE GOT YOUR "LILY-CHAN" AND ALL THE OTHER DOLLS TO BE WITH YOU NOW, RIGHT?!
I PUT ALL THE DOLLS AWAY IN MY CLOSET.
AND I THOUGHT I WOULD PUT ***YOU*** AWAY IN THERE AS WELL.
YOU...
WHAT ARE YOU TALKING ABOUT...?
UPSY-DAISY!
IF I DID THAT, PERHAPS IT WOULD KEEP ME FROM BEING LONELY.

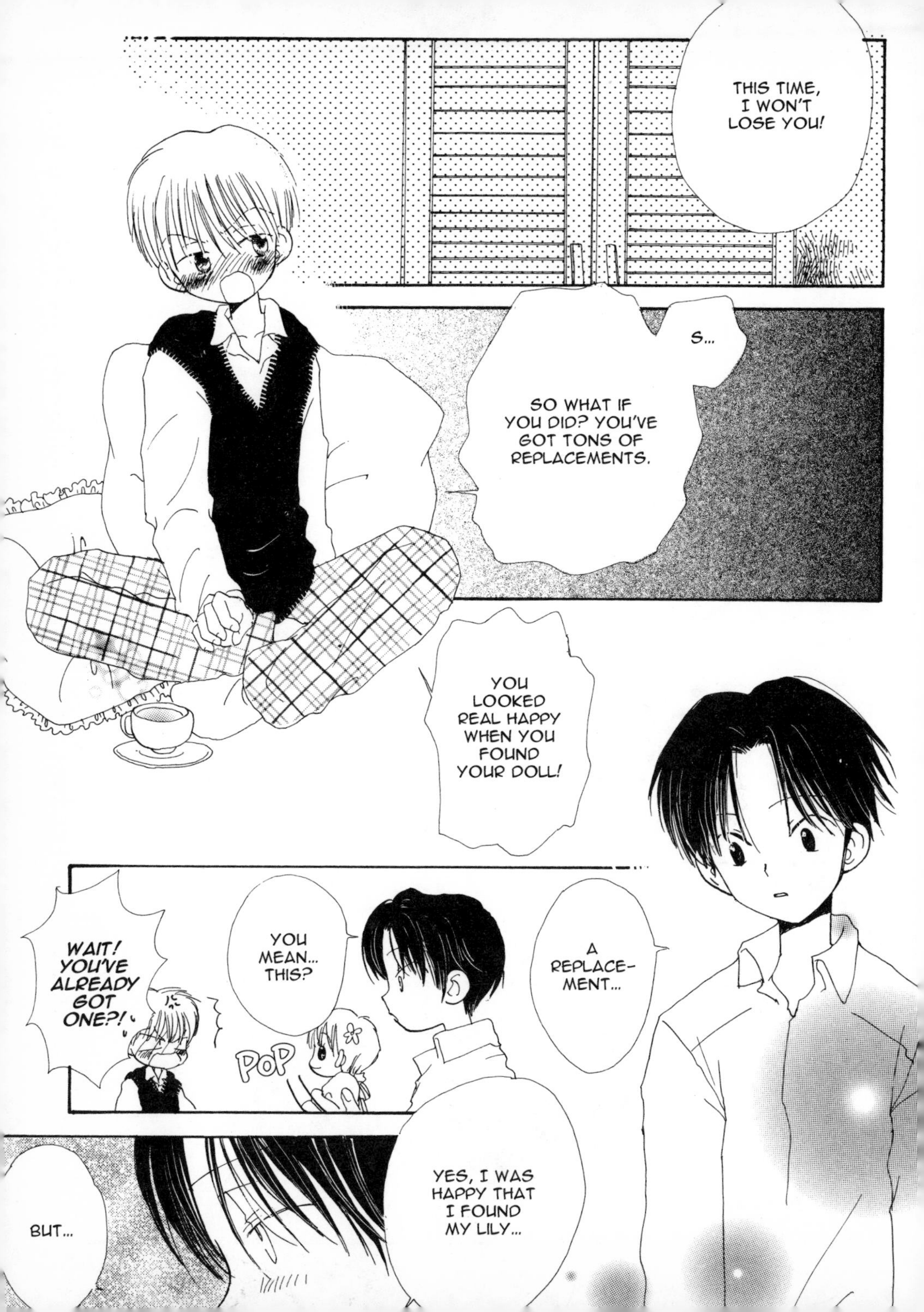
THIS TIME, I WON'T LOSE YOU!
S...
SO WHAT IF YOU DID? YOU'VE GOT TONS OF REPLACEMENTS.
YOU LOOKED REAL HAPPY WHEN YOU FOUND YOUR DOLL!
A REPLACE-MENT...
YOU MEAN... THIS?
POP
WAIT! YOU'VE ALREADY GOT ONE?!
YES, I WAS HAPPY THAT I FOUND MY LILY...
BUT...

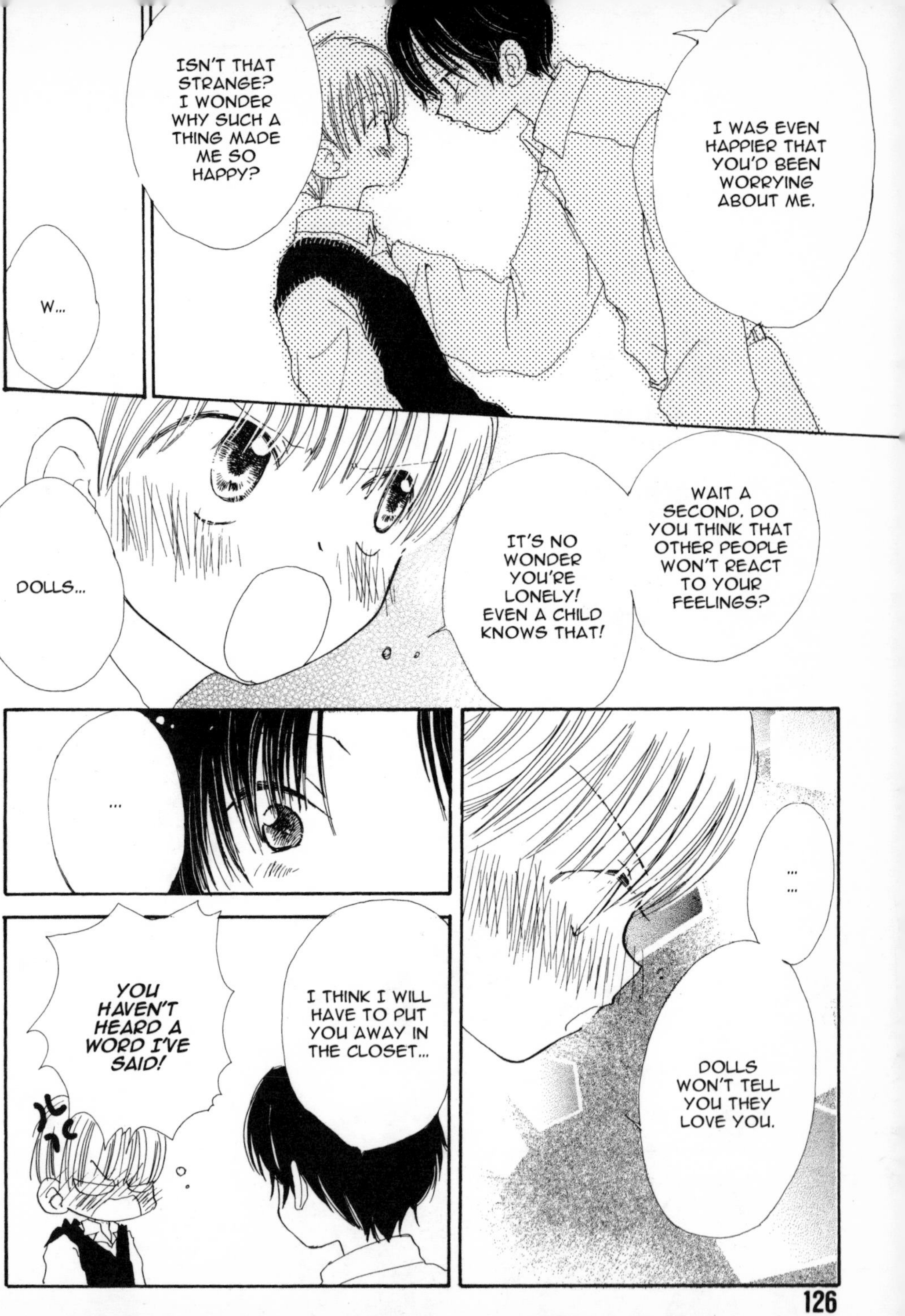
I WAS EVEN HAPPIER THAT YOU'D BEEN WORRYING ABOUT ME.
ISN'T THAT STRANGE? I WONDER WHY SUCH A THING MADE ME SO HAPPY?
W...
WAIT A SECOND. DO YOU THINK THAT OTHER PEOPLE WON'T REACT TO YOUR FEELINGS?
IT'S NO WONDER YOU'RE LONELY! EVEN A CHILD KNOWS THAT!
DOLLS...
... ...
DOLLS WON'T TELL YOU THEY LOVE YOU.
...
I THINK I WILL HAVE TO PUT YOU AWAY IN THE CLOSET...
YOU HAVEN'T HEARD A WORD I'VE SAID!

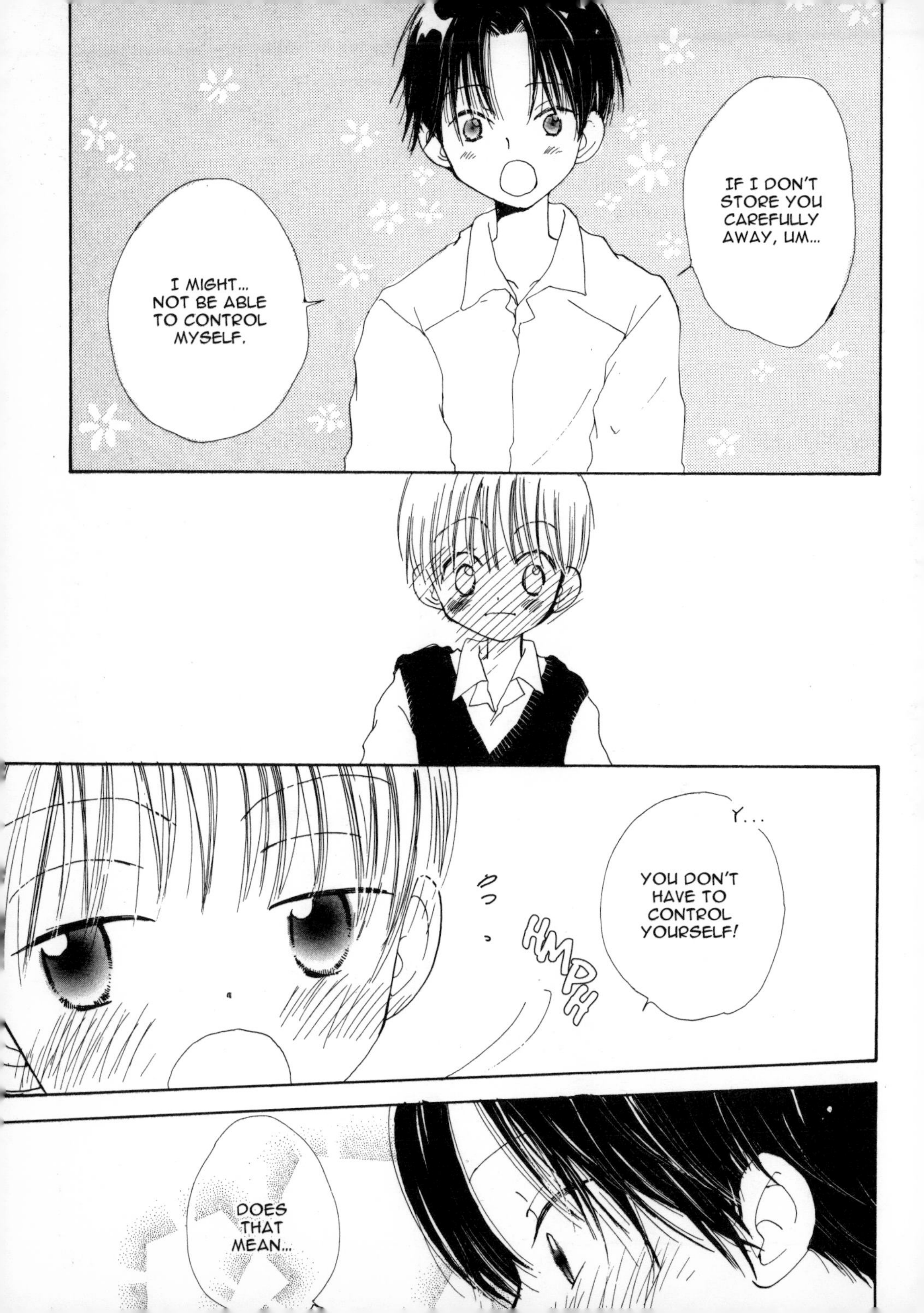
IF I DON'T STORE YOU CAREFULLY AWAY, UM...
I MIGHT... NOT BE ABLE TO CONTROL MYSELF.
Y...
YOU DON'T HAVE TO CONTROL YOURSELF!
HMPH
DOES THAT MEAN...

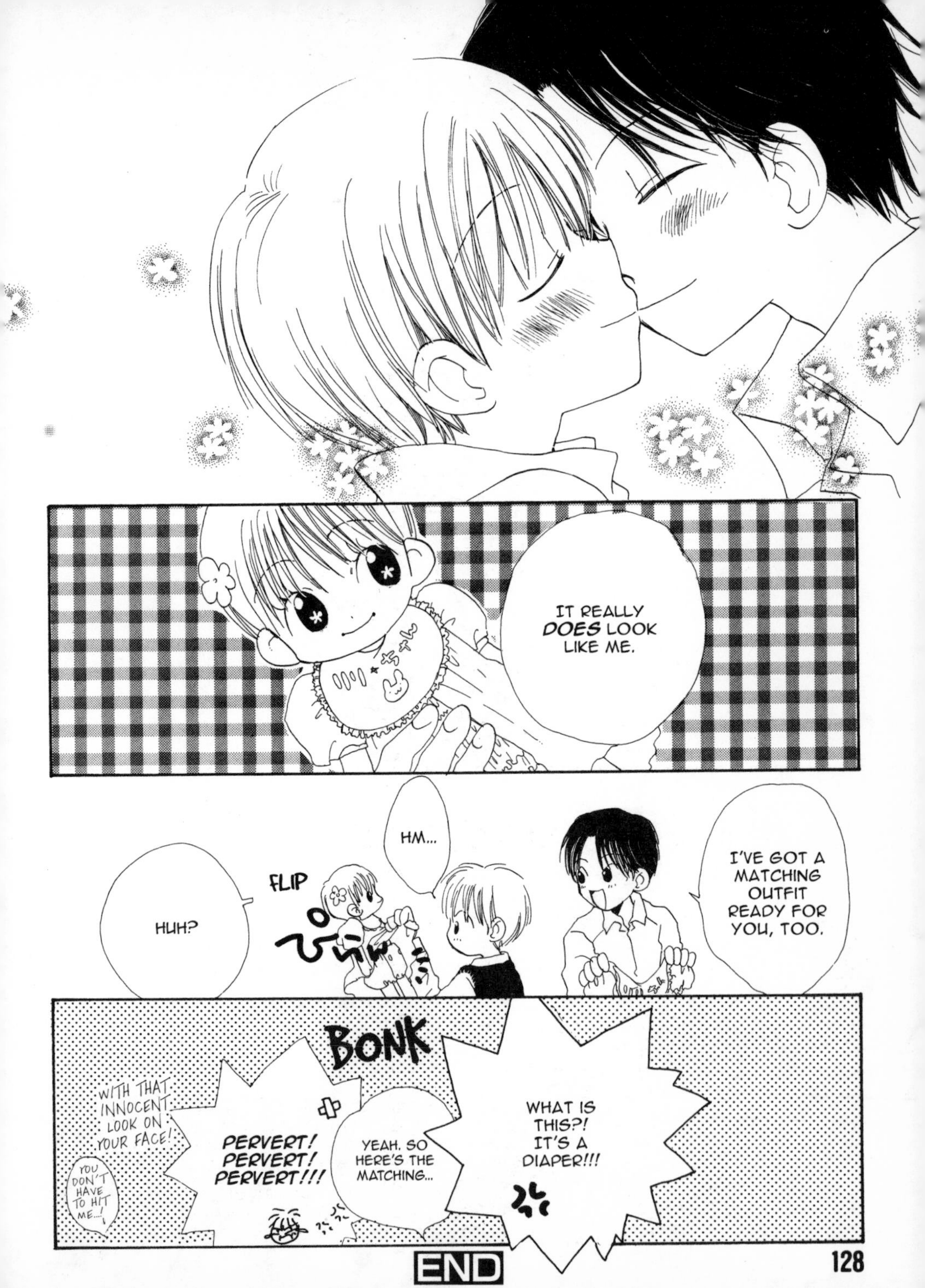
IT REALLY DOES LOOK LIKE ME.
I'VE GOT A MATCHING OUTFIT READY FOR YOU, TOO.
HM...
FLIP
HUH?
BONK
WHAT IS THIS?! IT'S A DIAPER!!!
YEAH. SO HERE'S THE MATCHING...
PERVERT! PERVERT! PERVERT!!!
WITH THAT INNOCENT LOOK ON YOUR FACE!
YOU DON'T HAVE TO HIT ME...!
END

ALMOST CRYING

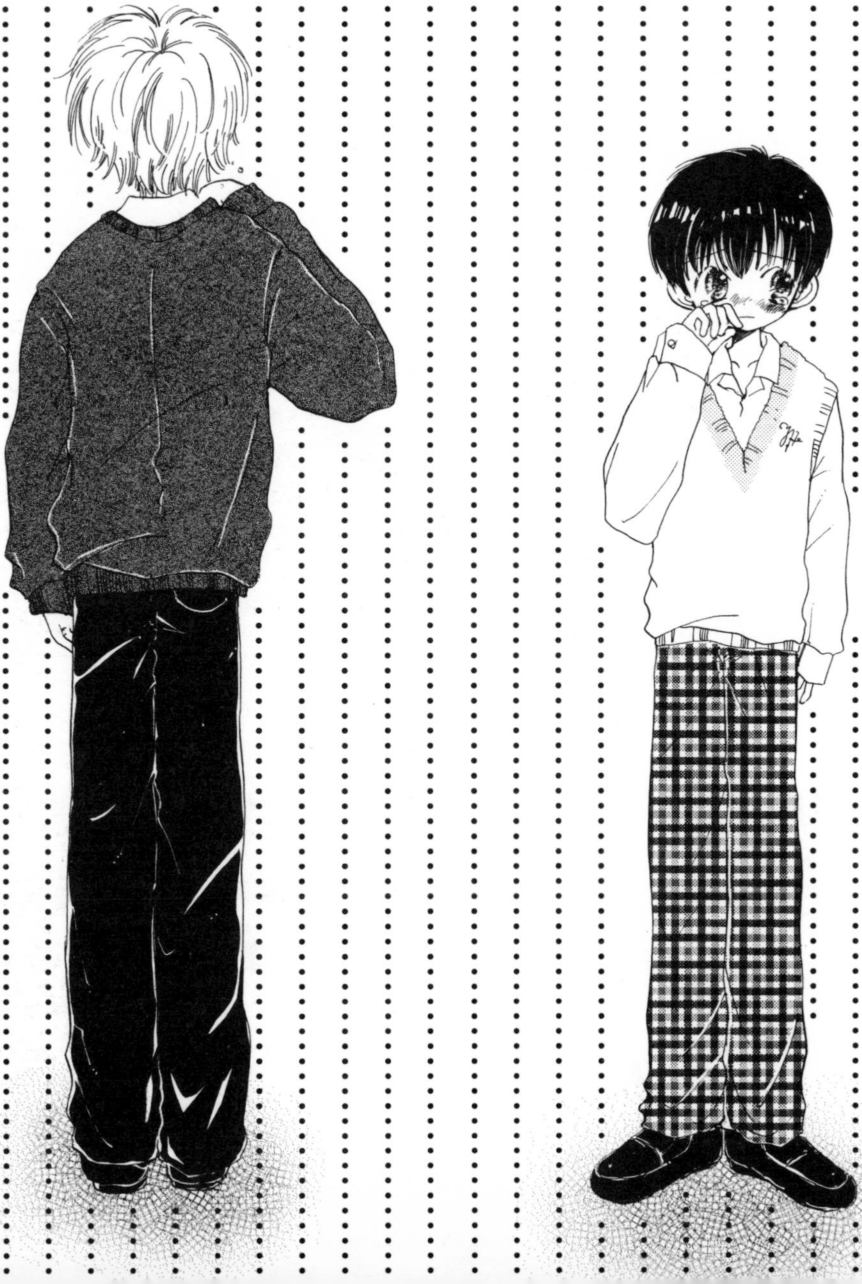

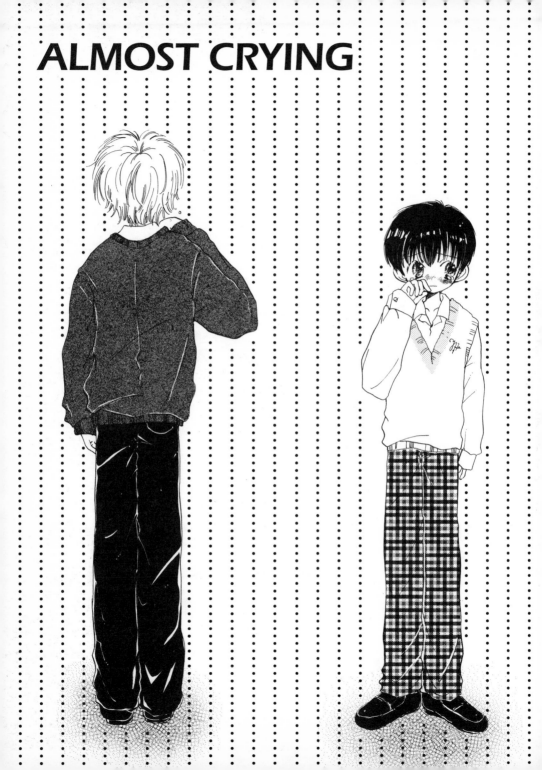

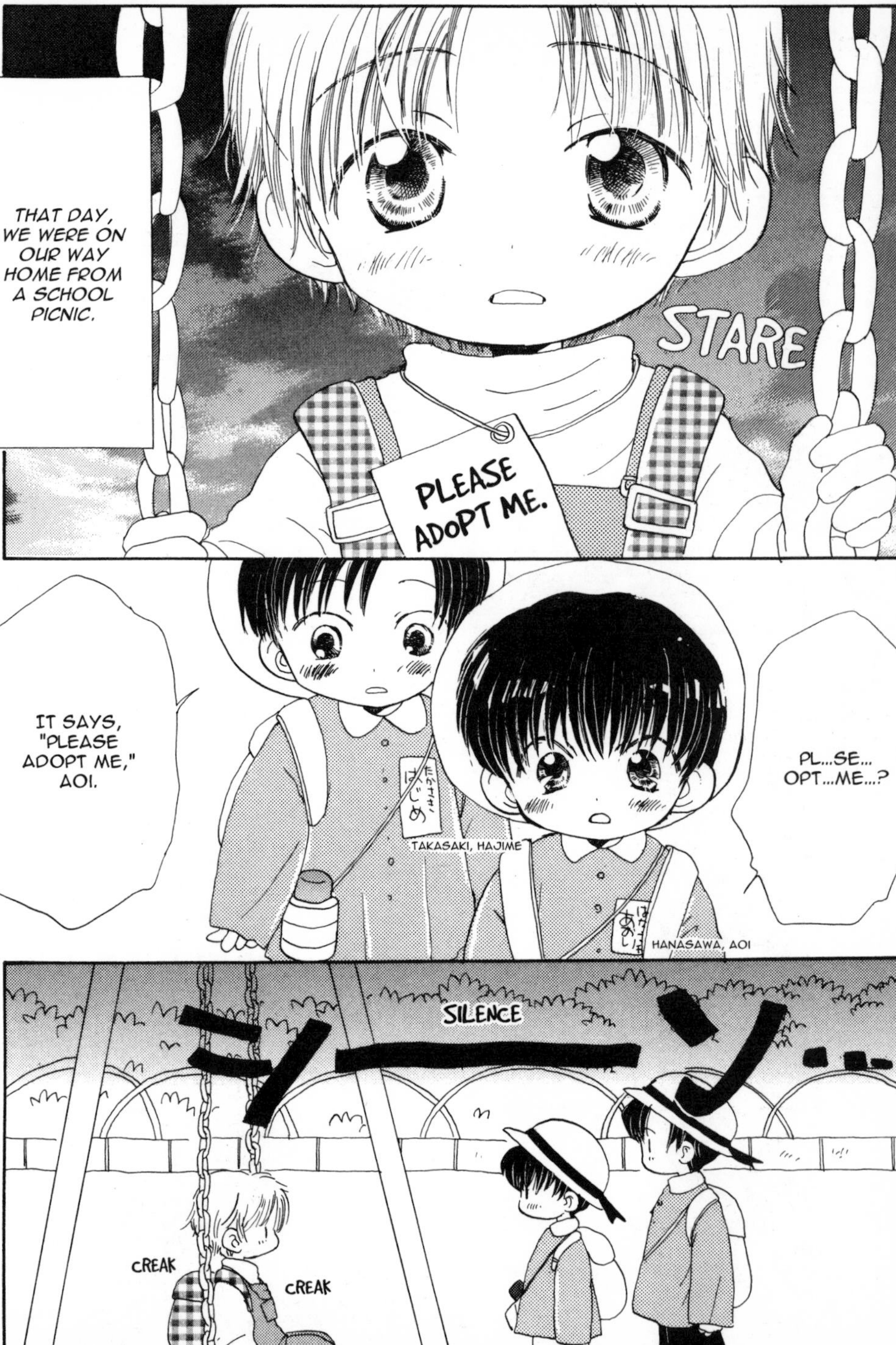

THAT DAY, WE WERE ON OUR WAY HOME FROM A SCHOOL PICNIC.
STARE
PLEASE ADOPT ME.
PL...SE... OPT...ME...?
HANASAWA, AOI
IT SAYS, "PLEASE ADOPT ME," AOI.
TAKASAKI, HAJIME
SILENCE
シーン..
CREAK
CREAK

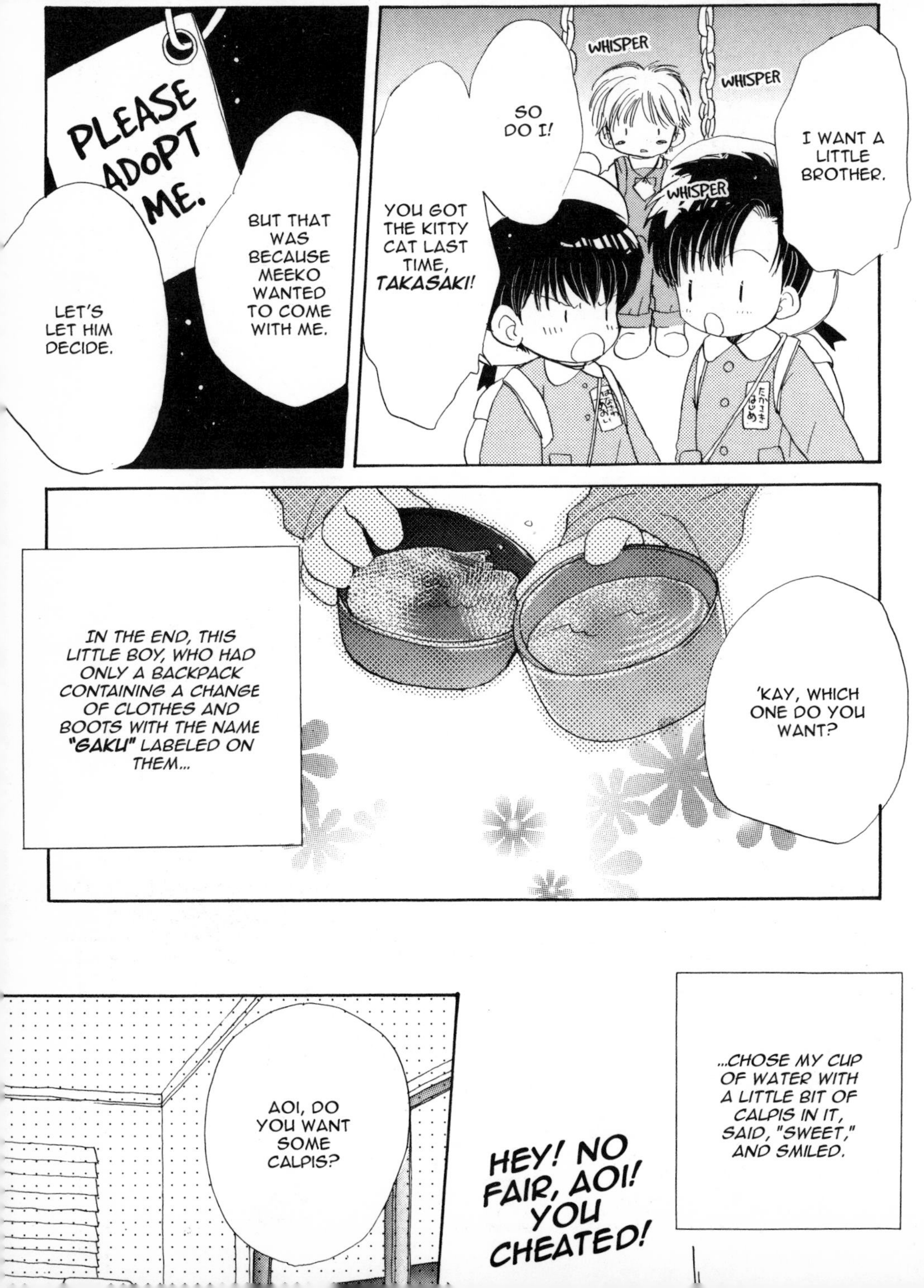
I WANT A LITTLE BROTHER.
WHISPER
WHISPER
WHISPER
SO DO I!
YOU GOT THE KITTY CAT LAST TIME, TAKASAKI!
PLEASE ADOPT ME.
BUT THAT WAS BECAUSE MEEKO WANTED TO COME WITH ME.
LET'S LET HIM DECIDE.
'KAY, WHICH ONE DO YOU WANT?
IN THE END, THIS LITTLE BOY, WHO HAD ONLY A BACKPACK CONTAINING A CHANGE OF CLOTHES AND BOOTS WITH THE NAME "GAKU" LABELED ON THEM...
...CHOSE MY CUP OF WATER WITH A LITTLE BIT OF CALPIS IN IT, SAID, "SWEET," AND SMILED.
HEY! NO FAIR, AOI! YOU CHEATED!
AOI, DO YOU WANT SOME CALPIS?

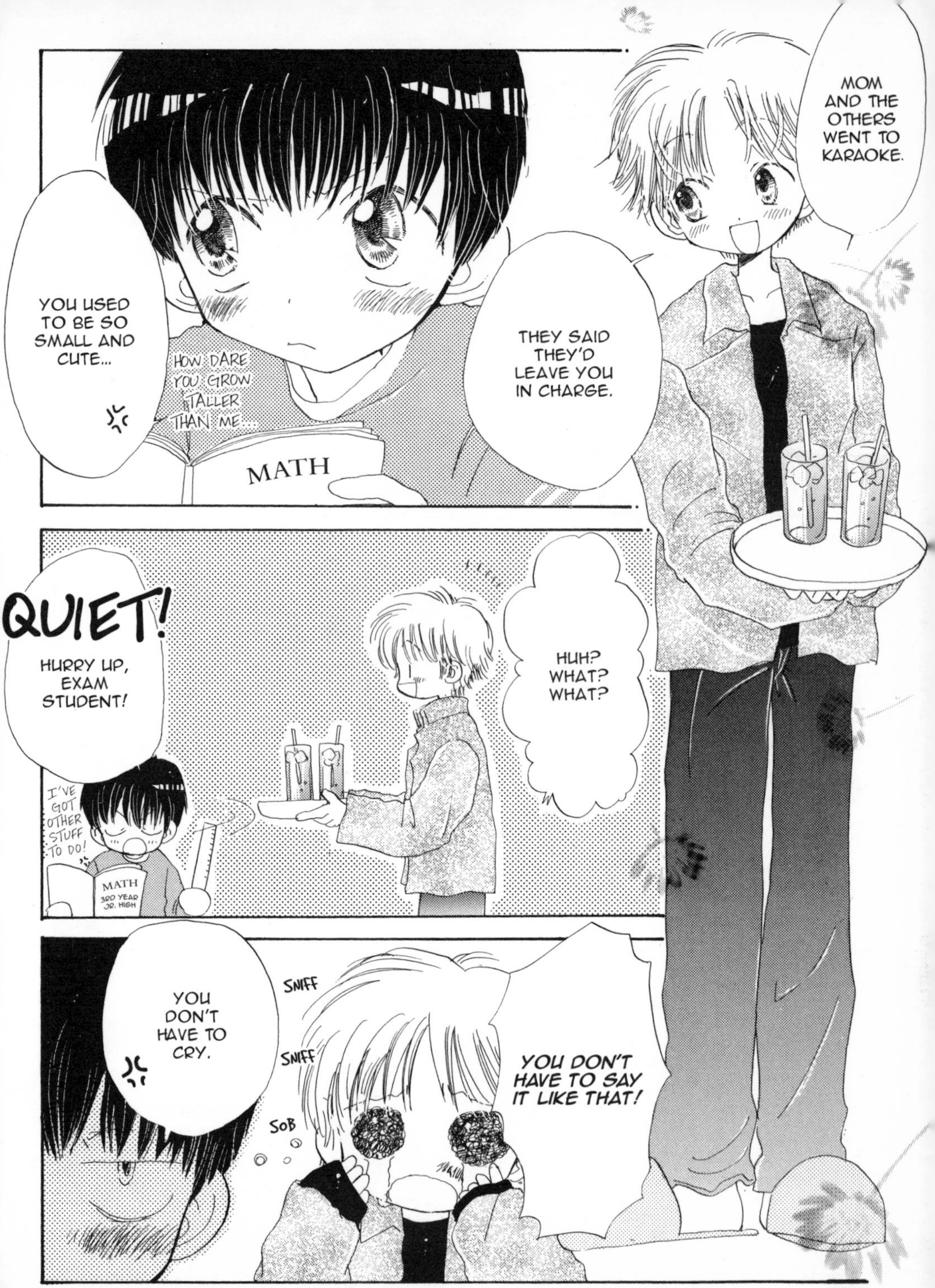
MOM AND THE OTHERS WENT TO KARAOKE.
THEY SAID THEY'D LEAVE YOU IN CHARGE.
YOU USED TO BE SO SMALL AND CUTE...
HOW DARE YOU GROW TALLER THAN ME...
MATH
HUH? WHAT? WHAT?
QUIET!
HURRY UP, EXAM STUDENT!
I'VE GOT OTHER STUFF TO DO!
MATH 3RD YEAR JR. HIGH
YOU DON'T HAVE TO SAY IT LIKE THAT!
SNIFF
SNIFF
SOB
YOU DON'T HAVE TO CRY.

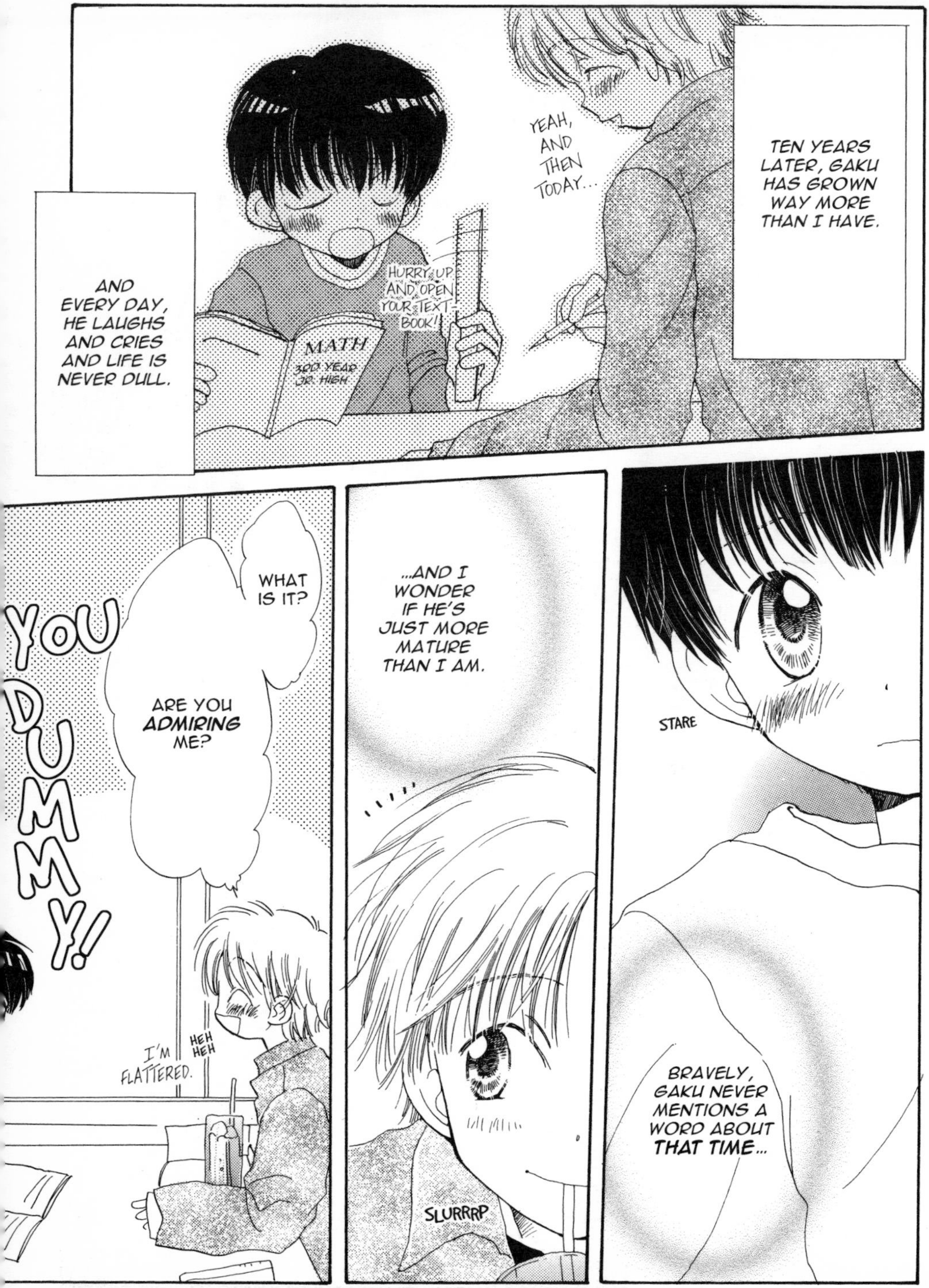
TEN YEARS LATER, GAKU HAS GROWN WAY MORE THAN I HAVE.
YEAH, AND THEN TODAY...
HURRY UP AND OPEN YOUR TEXT-BOOK!
MATH
3RD YEAR JR. HIGH
AND EVERY DAY, HE LAUGHS AND CRIES AND LIFE IS NEVER DULL.
STARE
BRAVELY, GAKU NEVER MENTIONS A WORD ABOUT **THAT TIME**...
...AND I WONDER IF HE'S JUST MORE MATURE THAN I AM.
SLURRRP
WHAT IS IT?
ARE YOU **ADMIRING** ME?
HEH HEH
I'M FLATTERED.
YOU DUMMY!

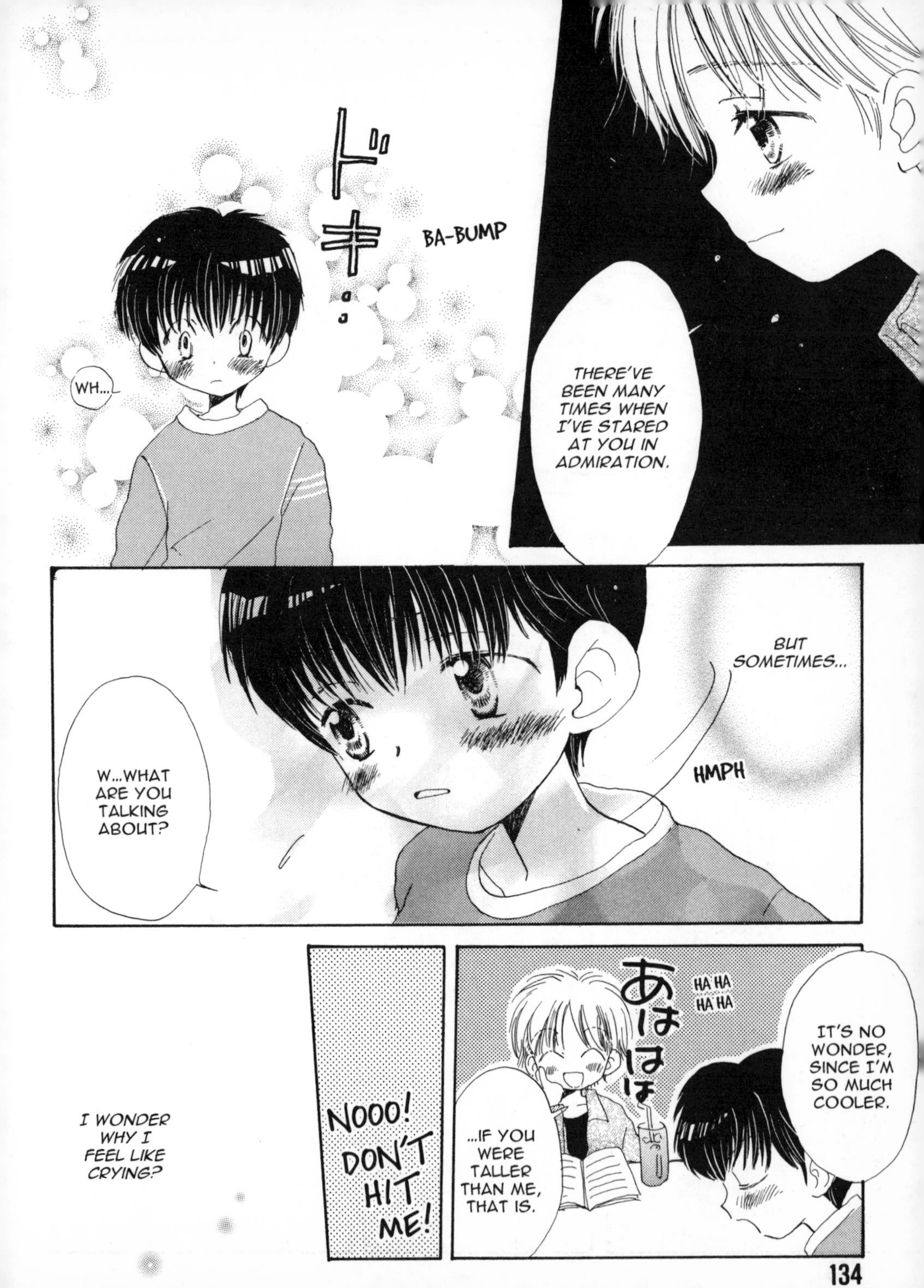
THERE'VE BEEN MANY TIMES WHEN I'VE STARED AT YOU IN ADMIRATION.
ドキッ
BA-BUMP
WH...
BUT SOMETIMES...
HMPH
W...WHAT ARE YOU TALKING ABOUT?
IT'S NO WONDER, SINCE I'M SO MUCH COOLER.
あははは
HA HA HA HA
...IF YOU WERE TALLER THAN ME, THAT IS.
NOOO! DON'T HIT ME!
I WONDER WHY I FEEL LIKE CRYING?

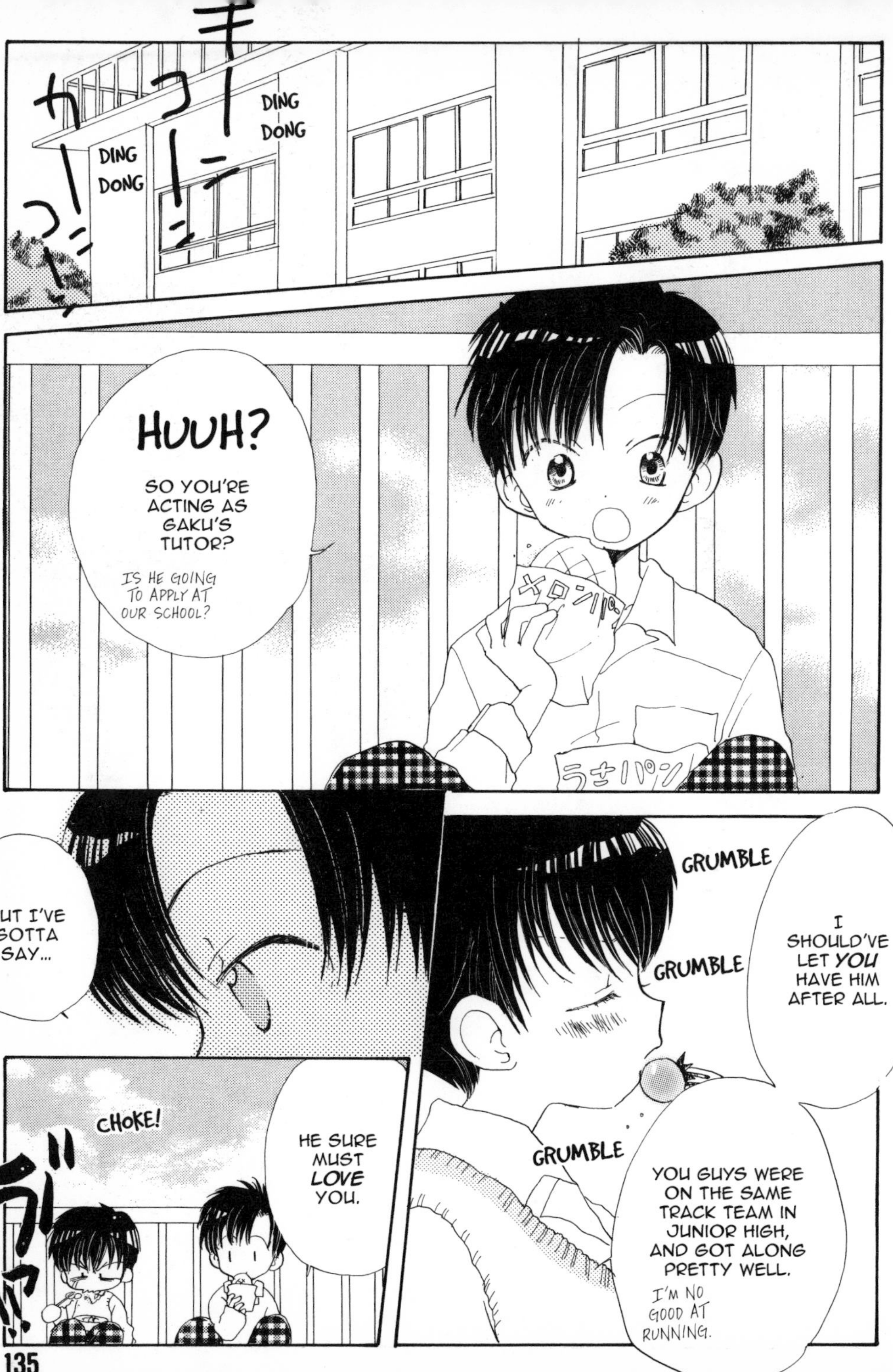
キーンコーン
DING DONG
カーンコーン
DING DONG
HUUH?
SO YOU'RE ACTING AS GAKU'S TUTOR?
IS HE GOING TO APPLY AT OUR SCHOOL?
GRUMBLE
I SHOULD'VE LET *YOU* HAVE HIM AFTER ALL.
GRUMBLE
GRUMBLE
YOU GUYS WERE ON THE SAME TRACK TEAM IN JUNIOR HIGH, AND GOT ALONG PRETTY WELL.
I'M NO GOOD AT RUNNING.
BUT I'VE GOTTA SAY...
HE SURE MUST *LOVE* YOU.
CHOKE!
ブッ!!

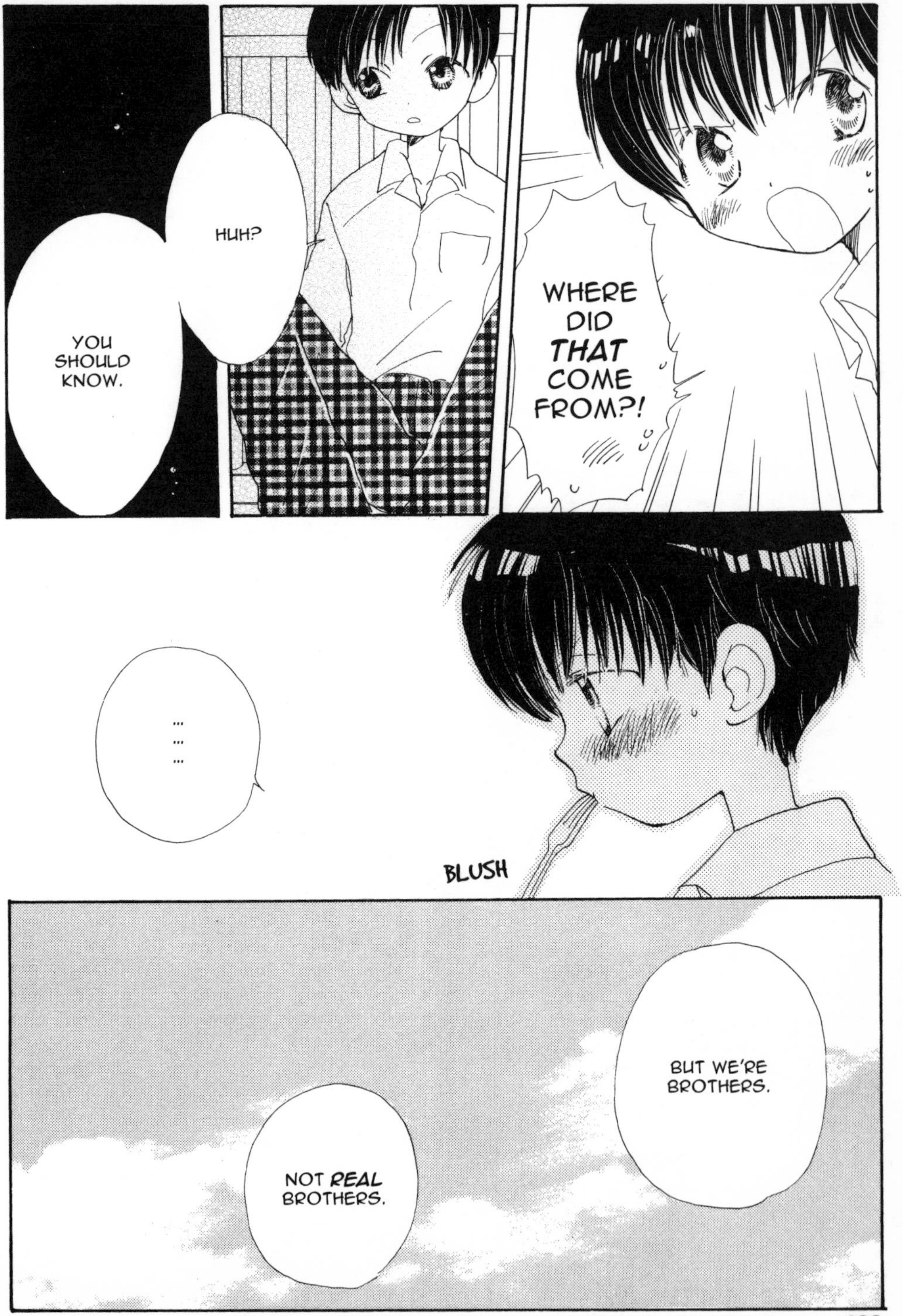
WHERE DID THAT COME FROM?!
HUH?
YOU SHOULD KNOW.
... ...
BLUSH
BUT WE'RE BROTHERS.
NOT REAL BROTHERS.

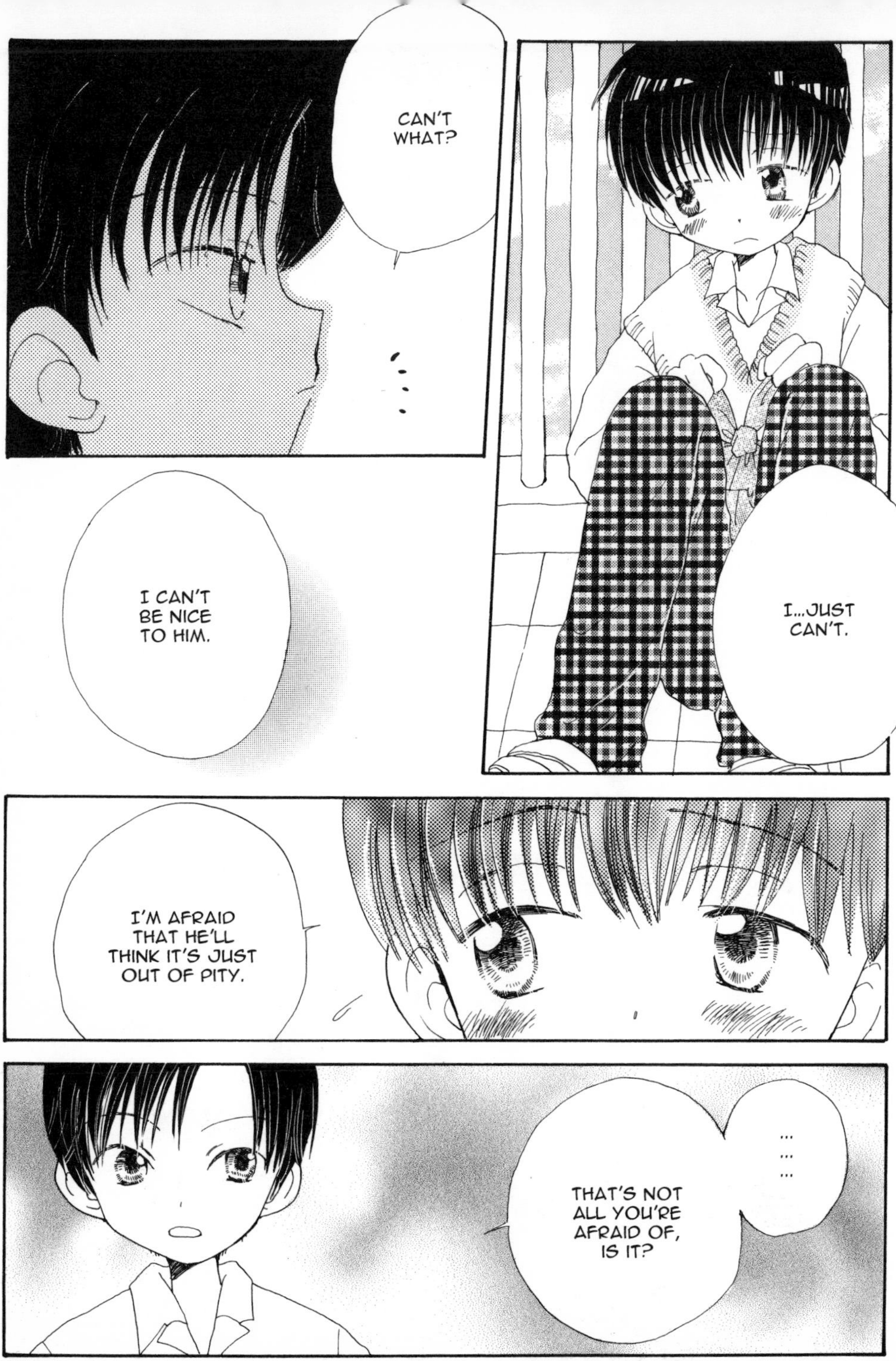

I...JUST CAN'T.
CAN'T WHAT?
...
I CAN'T BE NICE TO HIM.
I'M AFRAID THAT HE'LL THINK IT'S JUST OUT OF PITY.
... ...
THAT'S NOT ALL YOU'RE AFRAID OF, IS IT?

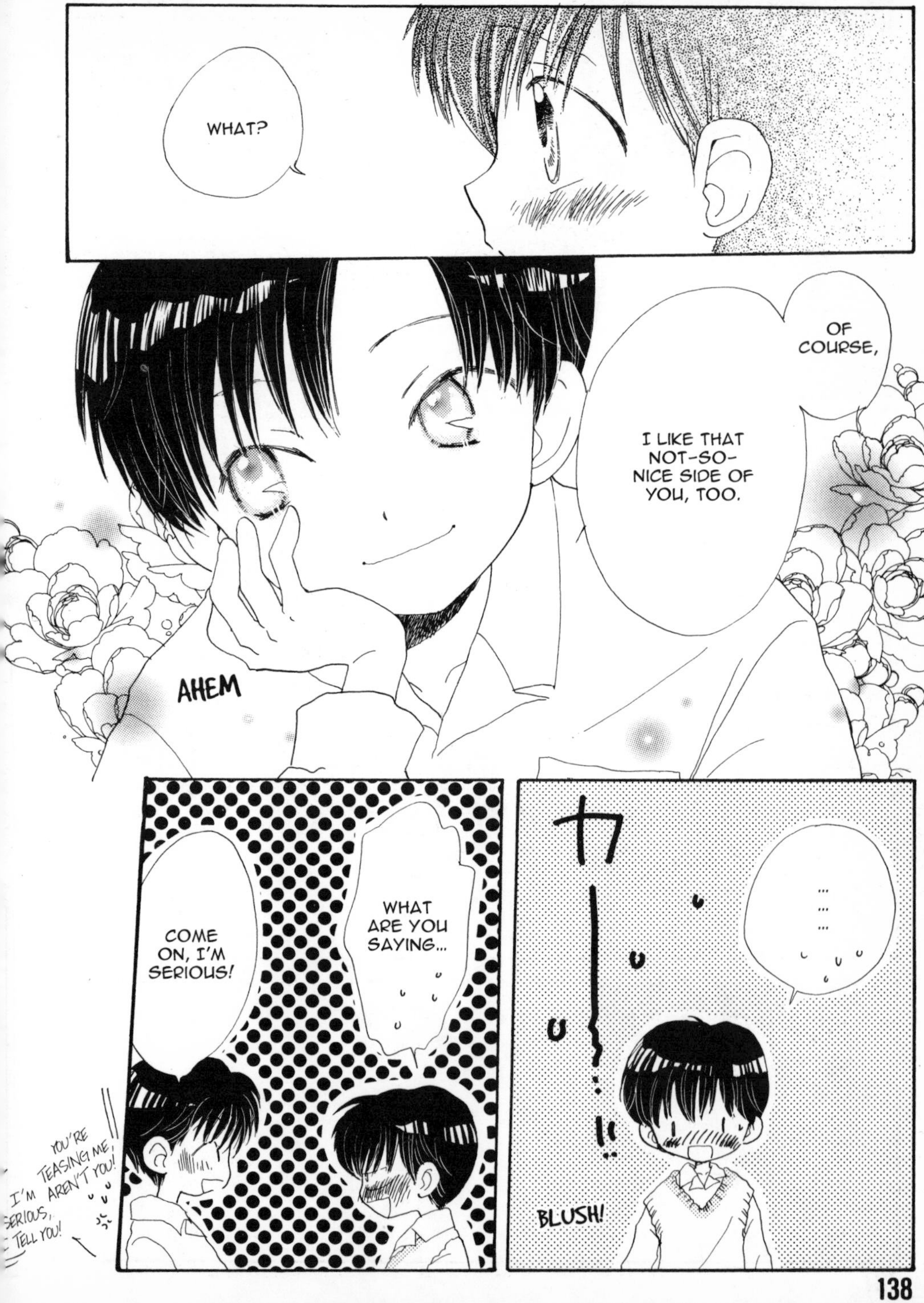
WHAT?
OF COURSE,
I LIKE THAT NOT-SO-NICE SIDE OF YOU, TOO.
AHEM
カー!!
......
BLUSH!
WHAT ARE YOU SAYING...
COME ON, I'M SERIOUS!
YOU'RE TEASING ME, AREN'T YOU!
I'M SERIOUS, TELL YOU!

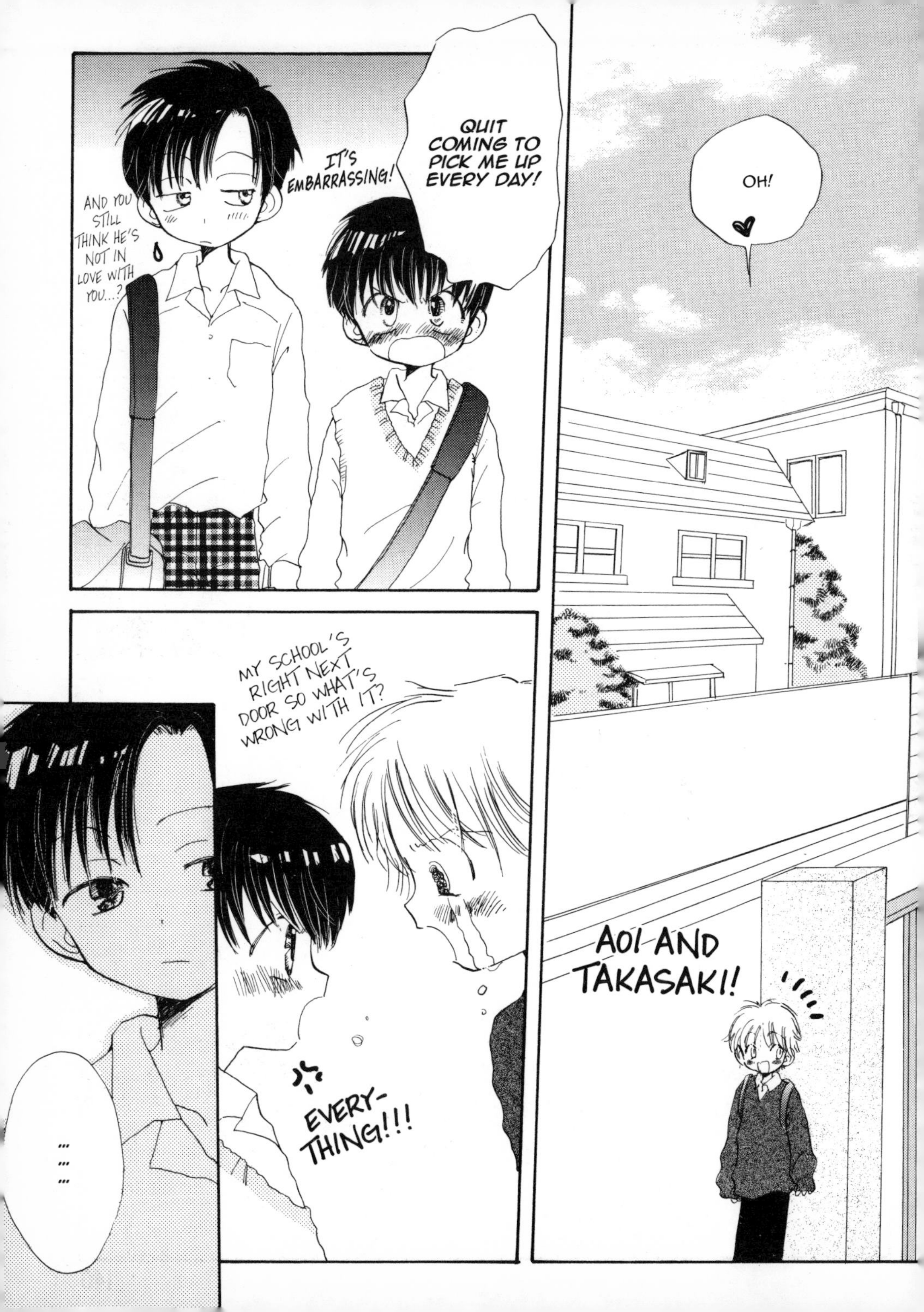
OH! ♥
AOI AND TAKASAKI!
QUIT COMING TO PICK ME UP EVERY DAY!
IT'S EMBARRASSING!
AND YOU STILL THINK HE'S NOT IN LOVE WITH YOU...?
MY SCHOOL'S RIGHT NEXT DOOR SO WHAT'S WRONG WITH IT?
EVERY-THING!!!
... ...

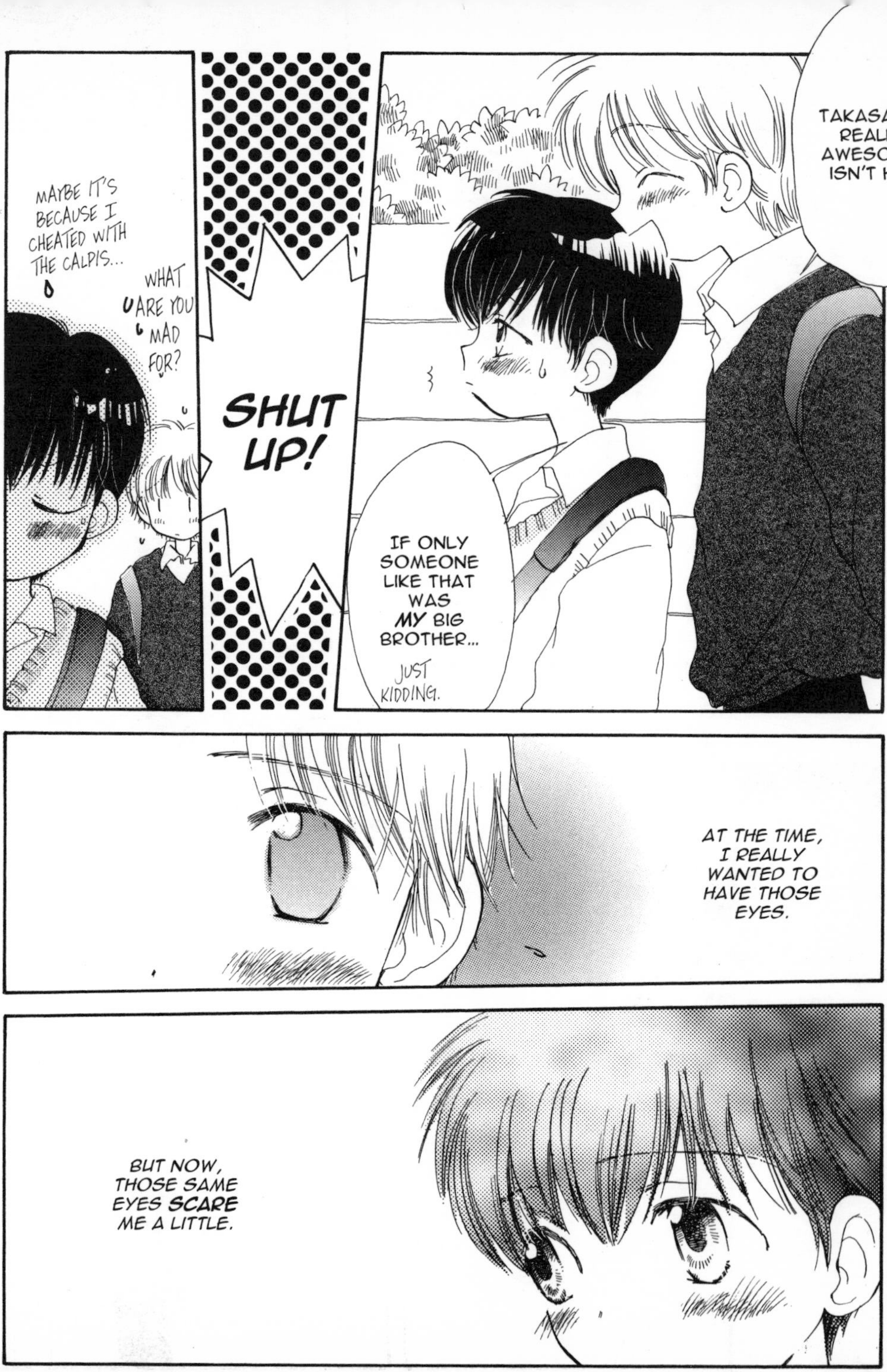
TAKASAKI'S REALLY AWESOME, ISN'T HE?
IF ONLY SOMEONE LIKE THAT WAS MY BIG BROTHER...
JUST KIDDING.
SHUT UP!
MAYBE IT'S BECAUSE I CHEATED WITH THE CALPIS...
WHAT ARE YOU MAD FOR?
AT THE TIME, I REALLY WANTED TO HAVE THOSE EYES.
BUT NOW, THOSE SAME EYES SCARE ME A LITTLE.

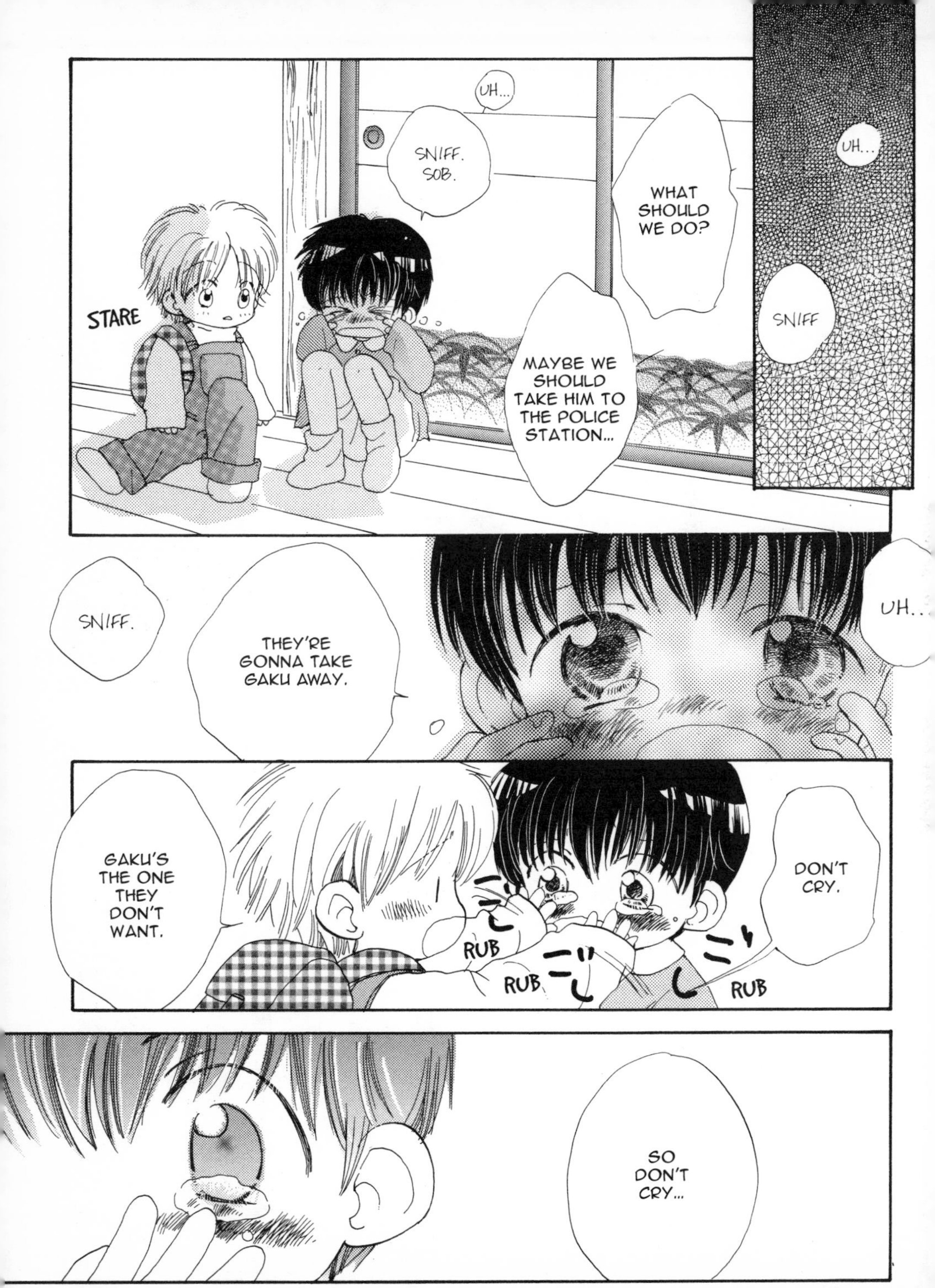
UH...
SNIFF
WHAT SHOULD WE DO?
MAYBE WE SHOULD TAKE HIM TO THE POLICE STATION...
UH...
SNIFF. SOB.
STARE
UH...
THEY'RE GONNA TAKE GAKU AWAY.
SNIFF.
DON'T CRY.
RUB
RUB
RUB
GAKU'S THE ONE THEY DON'T WANT.
SO DON'T CRY...

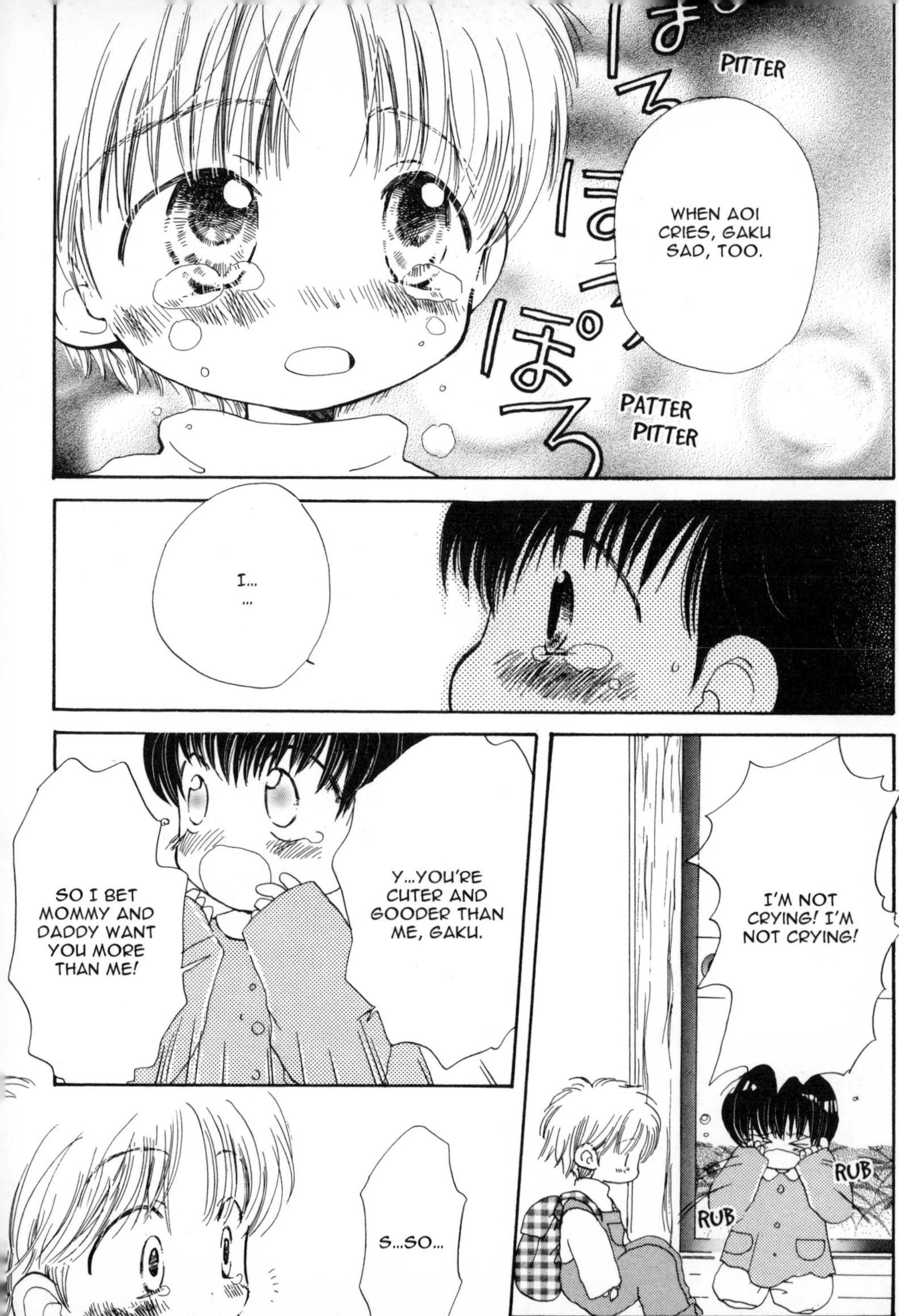
PITTER
WHEN AOI CRIES, GAKU SAD, TOO.
PATTER PITTER
I... ...
I'M NOT CRYING! I'M NOT CRYING!
RUB
RUB
Y...YOU'RE CUTER AND GOODER THAN ME, GAKU.
SO I BET MOMMY AND DADDY WANT YOU MORE THAN ME!
S...SO...

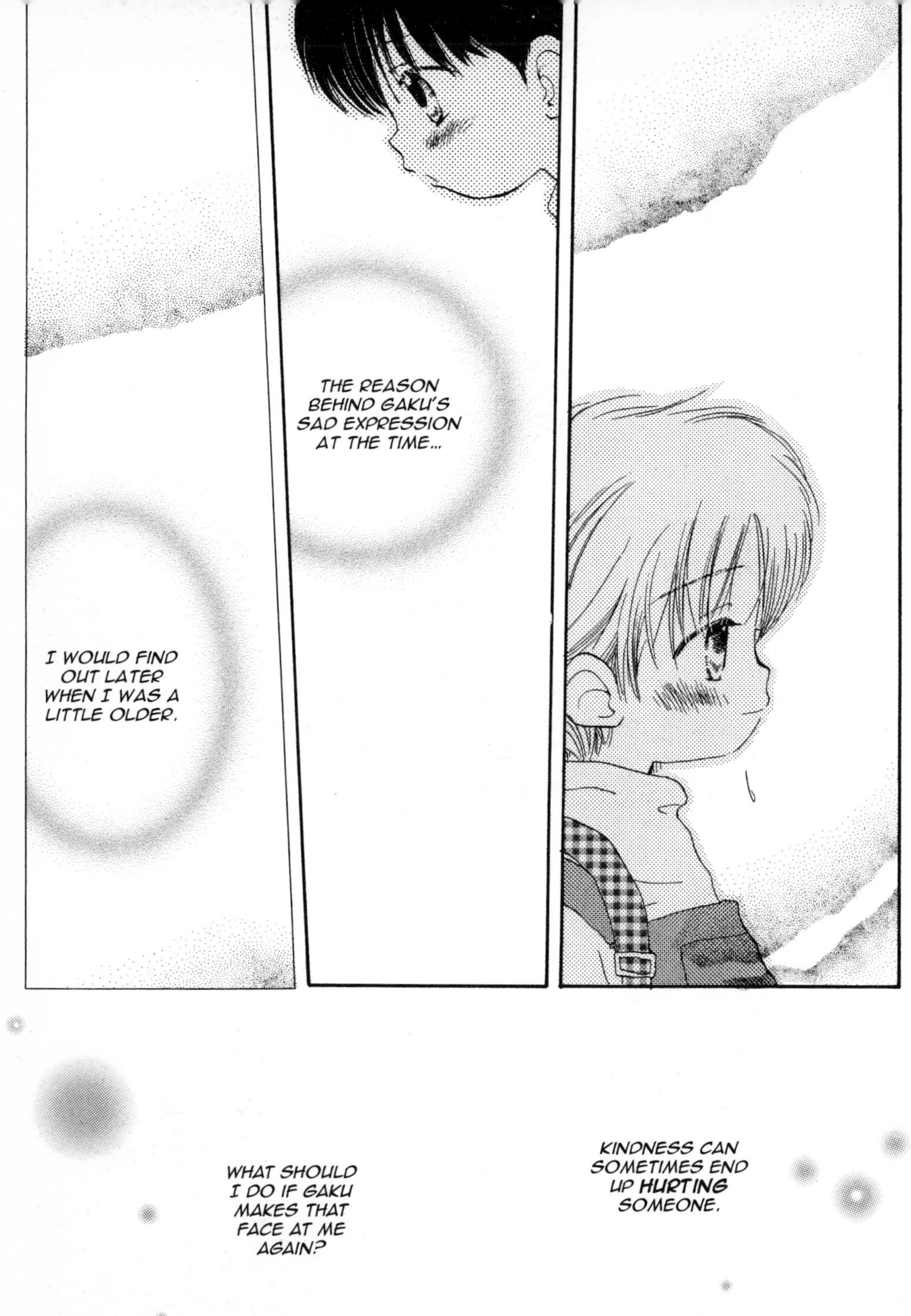
THE REASON BEHIND GAKU'S SAD EXPRESSION AT THE TIME...
I WOULD FIND OUT LATER WHEN I WAS A LITTLE OLDER.
KINDNESS CAN SOMETIMES END UP **HURTING** SOMEONE.
WHAT SHOULD I DO IF GAKU MAKES THAT FACE AT ME AGAIN?

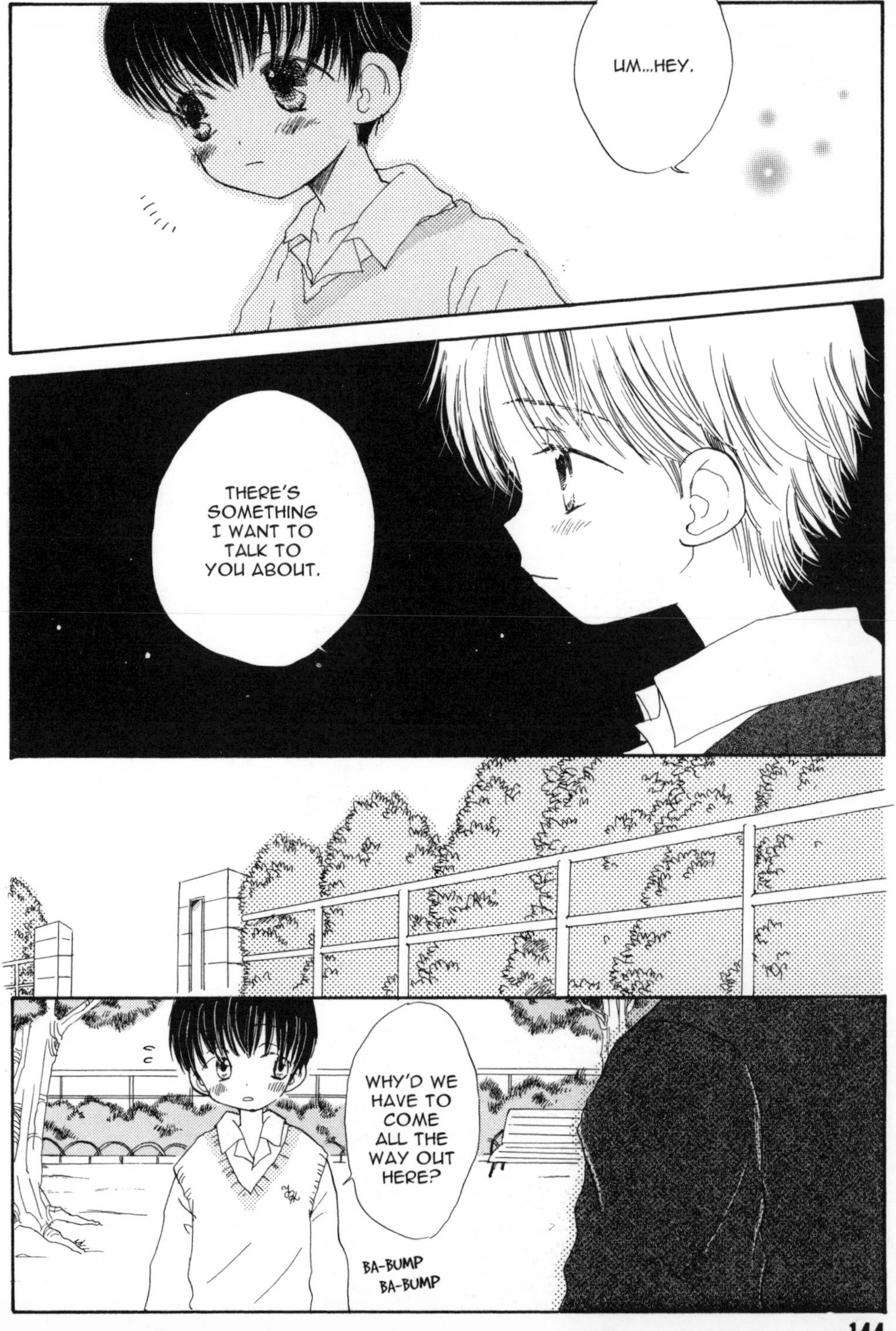
UM...HEY.
THERE'S SOMETHING I WANT TO TALK TO YOU ABOUT.
WHY'D WE HAVE TO COME ALL THE WAY OUT HERE?
BA-BUMP BA-BUMP

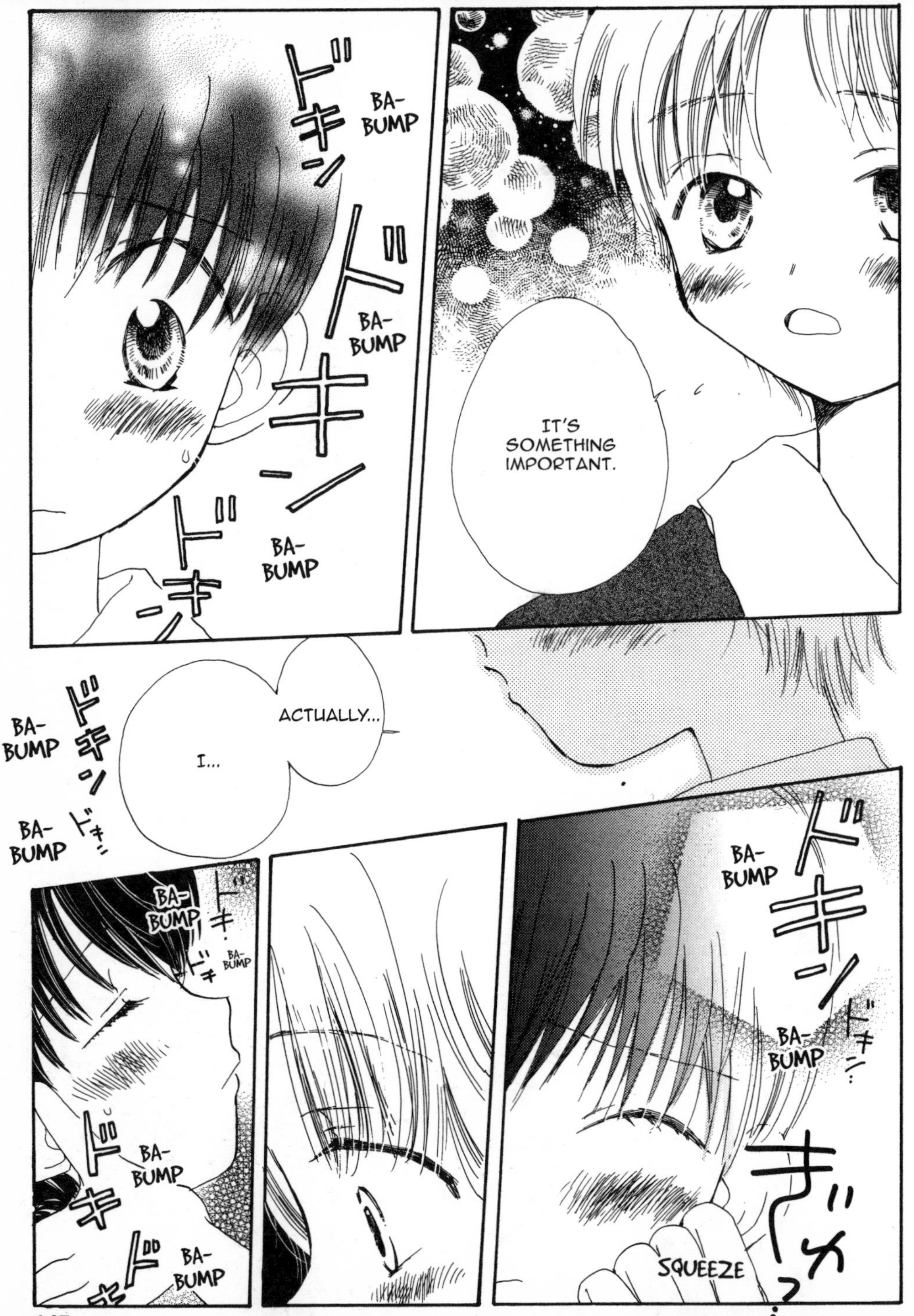
IT'S SOMETHING IMPORTANT.
ドキン
BA-BUMP
ドキン
BA-BUMP
ドキン
BA-BUMP
ACTUALLY...
I...
ドキッ
BA-BUMP
ドキ...
BA-BUMP
ドキン
BA-BUMP
ドキ...
BA-BUMP
ぎゅっ
SQUEEZE
BA-BUMP
BA-BUMP
BA-BUMP
BA-BUMP

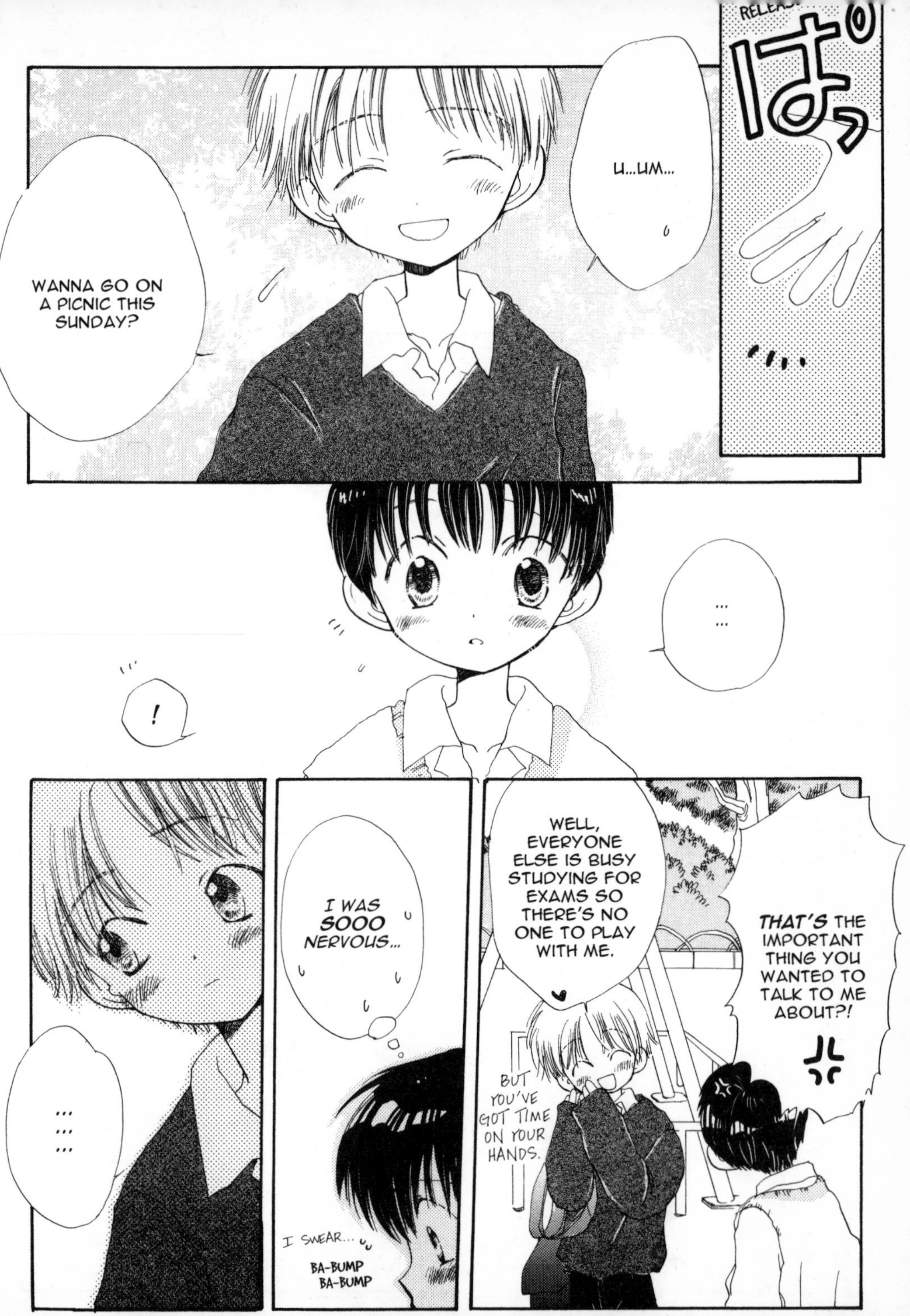

RELEAS
ぱっ
U...UM...
WANNA GO ON A PICNIC THIS SUNDAY?
...
...
!
WELL, EVERYONE ELSE IS BUSY STUDYING FOR EXAMS SO THERE'S NO ONE TO PLAY WITH ME.
THAT'S THE IMPORTANT THING YOU WANTED TO TALK TO ME ABOUT?!
BUT YOU'VE GOT TIME ON YOUR HANDS.
I WAS **SOOO** NERVOUS...
I SWEAR...
BA-BUMP
BA-BUMP
...
...
...

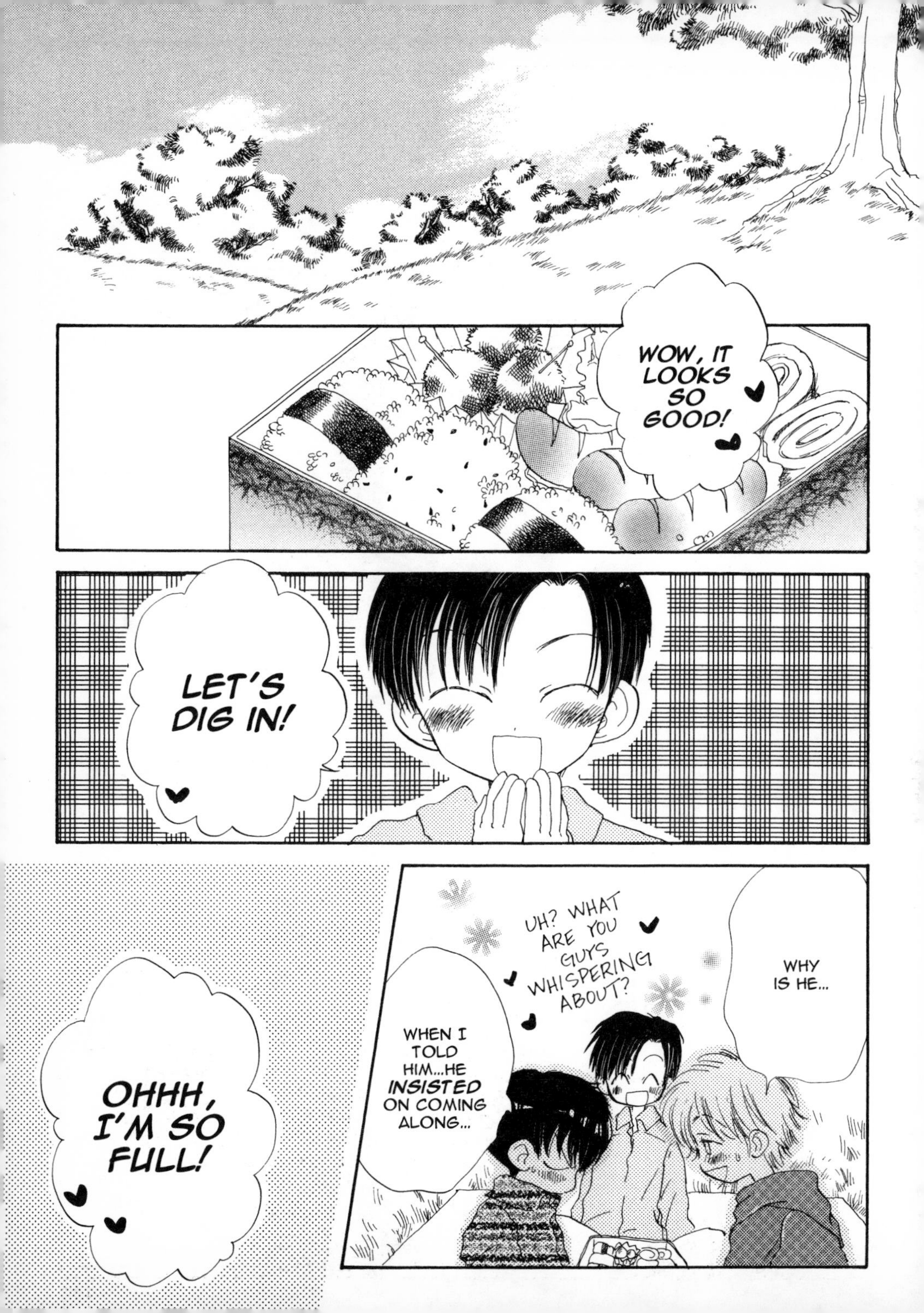
WOW, IT LOOKS SO GOOD!
LET'S DIG IN!
WHY IS HE...
UH? WHAT ARE YOU GUYS WHISPERING ABOUT?
WHEN I TOLD HIM...HE *INSISTED* ON COMING ALONG...
OHHH, I'M SO FULL!

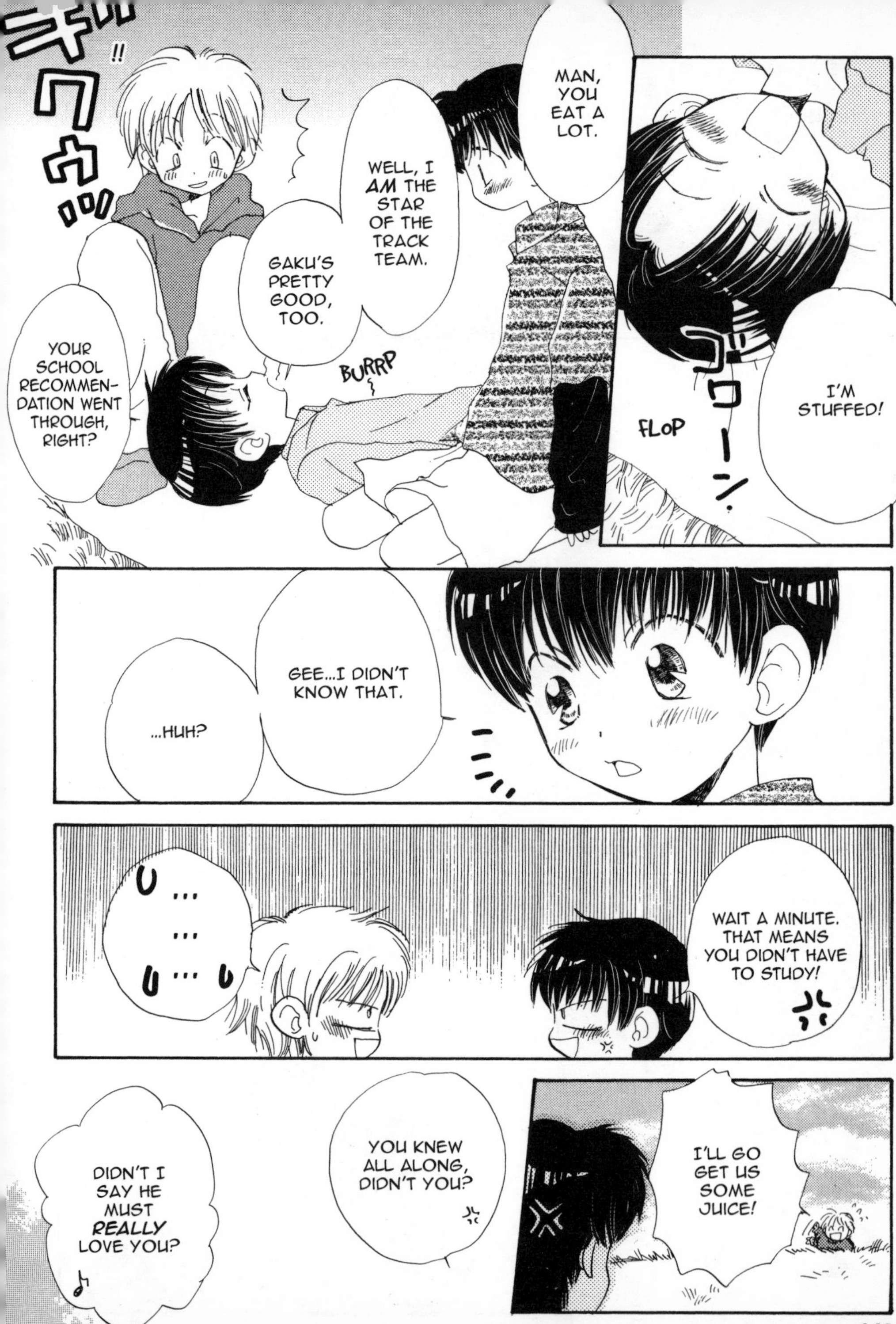
I'M STUFFED!
ゴローン
FLOP
MAN, YOU EAT A LOT.
WELL, I **AM** THE STAR OF THE TRACK TEAM.
GAKU'S PRETTY GOOD, TOO.
BURRP
YOUR SCHOOL RECOMMENDATION WENT THROUGH, RIGHT?
ギクゥ!!
GEE...I DIDN'T KNOW THAT.
...HUH?
WAIT A MINUTE. THAT MEANS YOU DIDN'T HAVE TO STUDY!
U... ... U... U
I'LL GO GET US SOME JUICE!
YOU KNEW ALL ALONG, DIDN'T YOU?
DIDN'T I SAY HE MUST **REALLY** LOVE YOU?

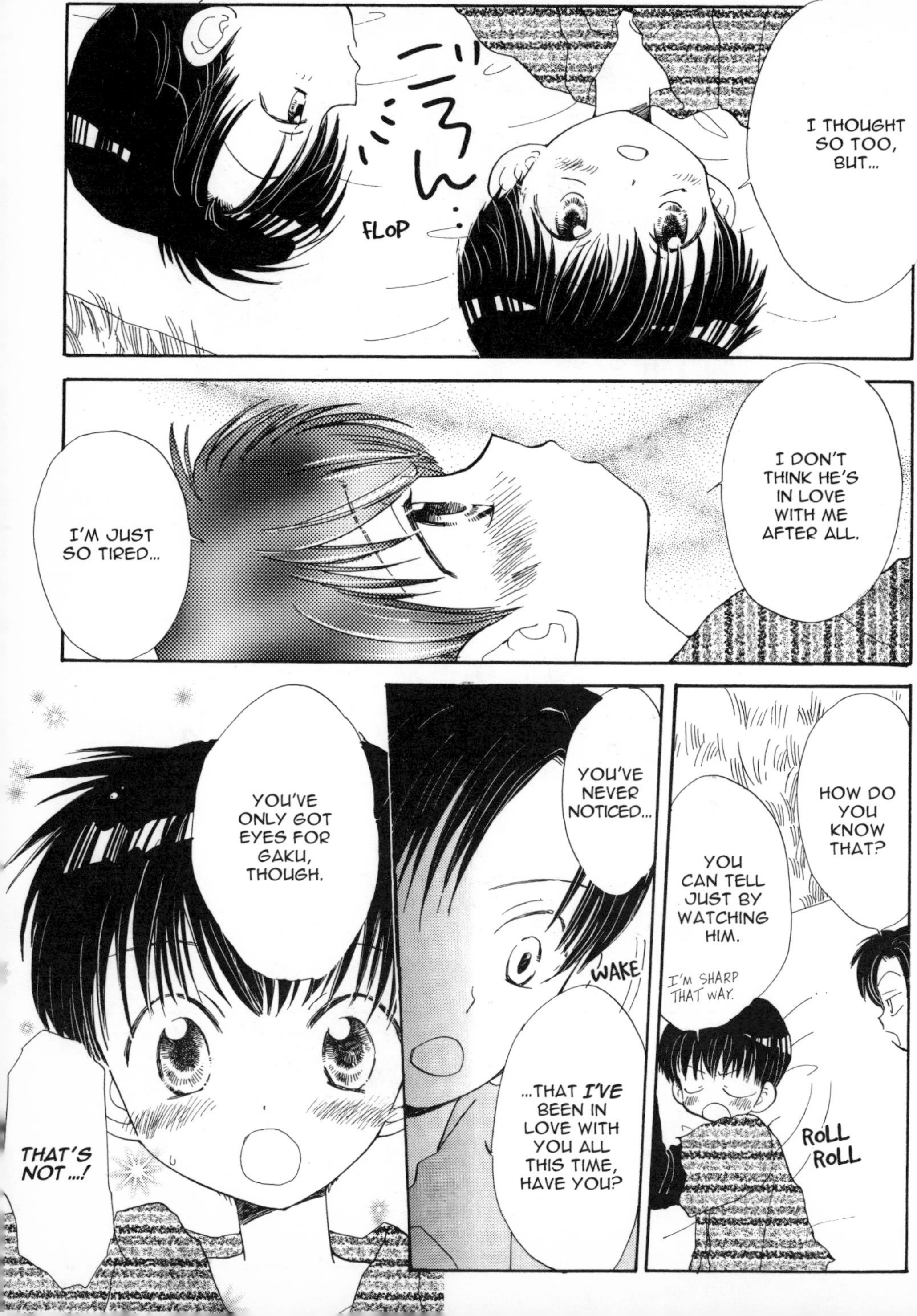
I THOUGHT SO TOO, BUT...
ごろん
FLOP
I DON'T THINK HE'S IN LOVE WITH ME AFTER ALL.
I'M JUST SO TIRED...
HOW DO YOU KNOW THAT?
YOU CAN TELL JUST BY WATCHING HIM.
I'M SHARP THAT WAY.
ROLL ROLL
YOU'VE NEVER NOTICED...
WAKE
...THAT *I'VE* BEEN IN LOVE WITH YOU ALL THIS TIME, HAVE YOU?
YOU'VE ONLY GOT EYES FOR GAKU, THOUGH.
THAT'S NOT...!

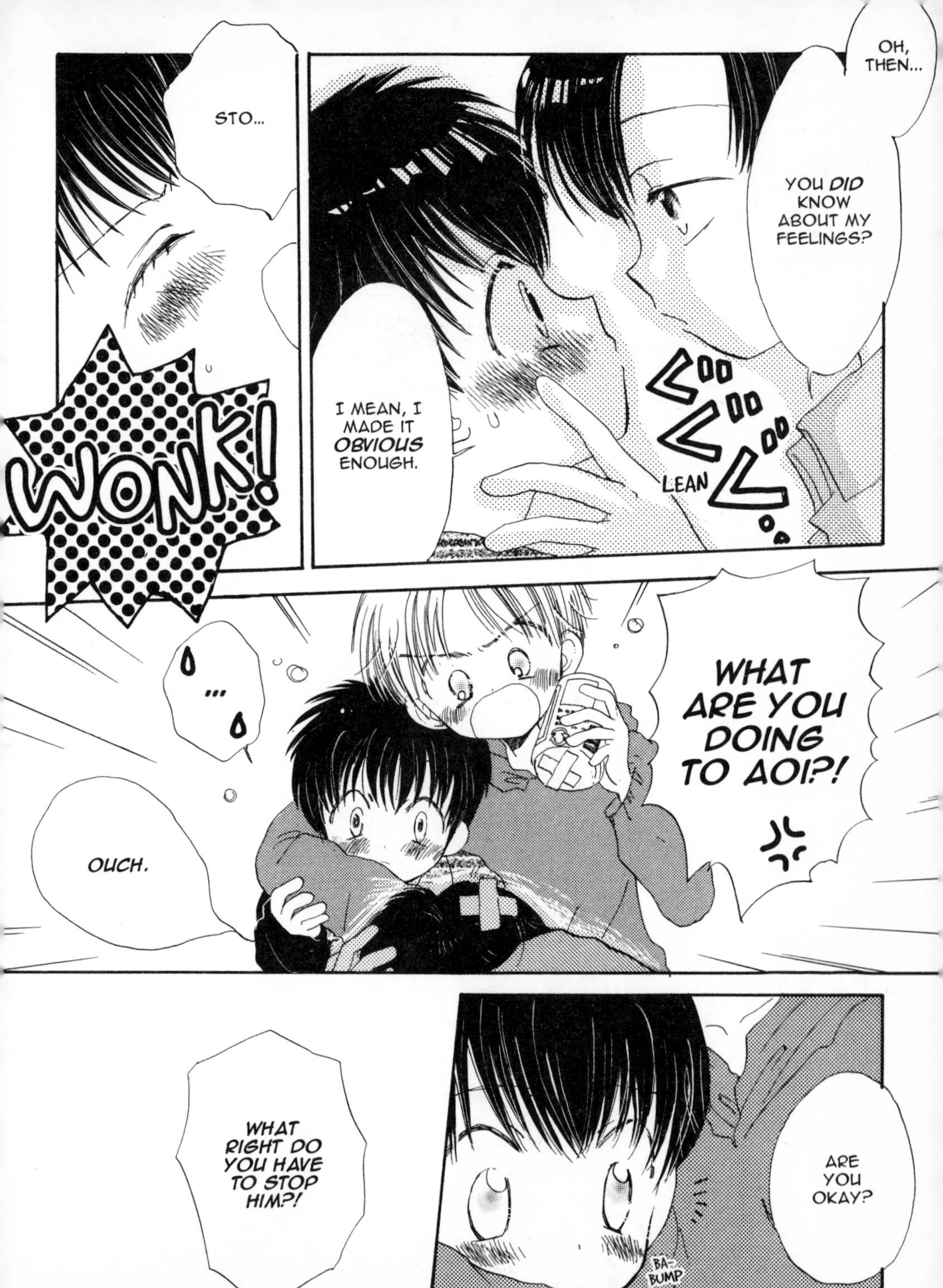
OH, THEN...
YOU DID KNOW ABOUT MY FEELINGS?
I MEAN, I MADE IT OBVIOUS ENOUGH.
LEAN
STO...
WONK!
WHAT ARE YOU DOING TO AOI?!
...
OUCH.
ARE YOU OKAY?
BA-BUMP
WHAT RIGHT DO YOU HAVE TO STOP HIM?!

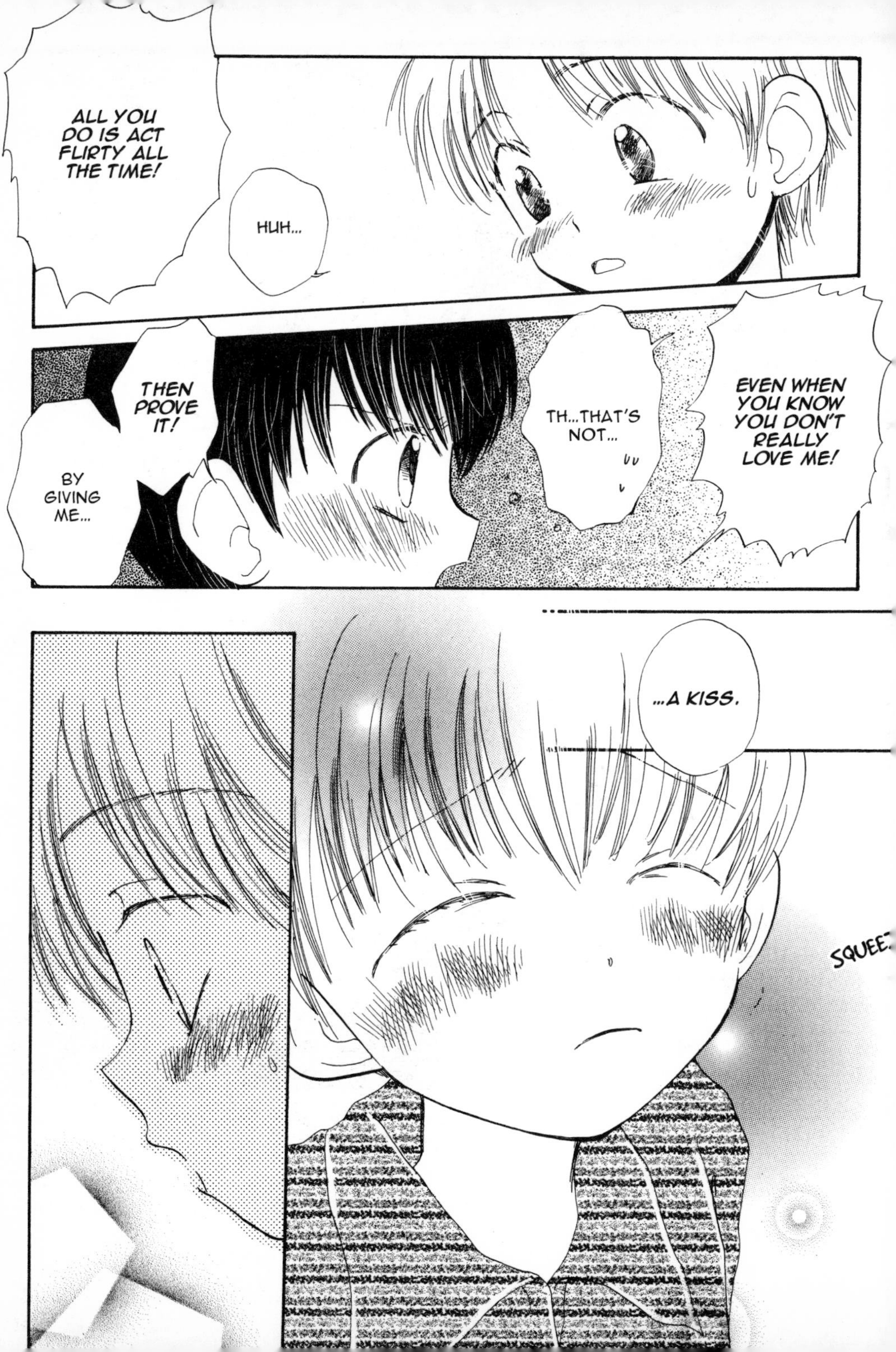
ALL YOU DO IS ACT FLIRTY ALL THE TIME!
HUH...
EVEN WHEN YOU KNOW YOU DON'T REALLY LOVE ME!
TH...THAT'S NOT...
THEN PROVE IT!
BY GIVING ME...
...A KISS.
SQUEEZ

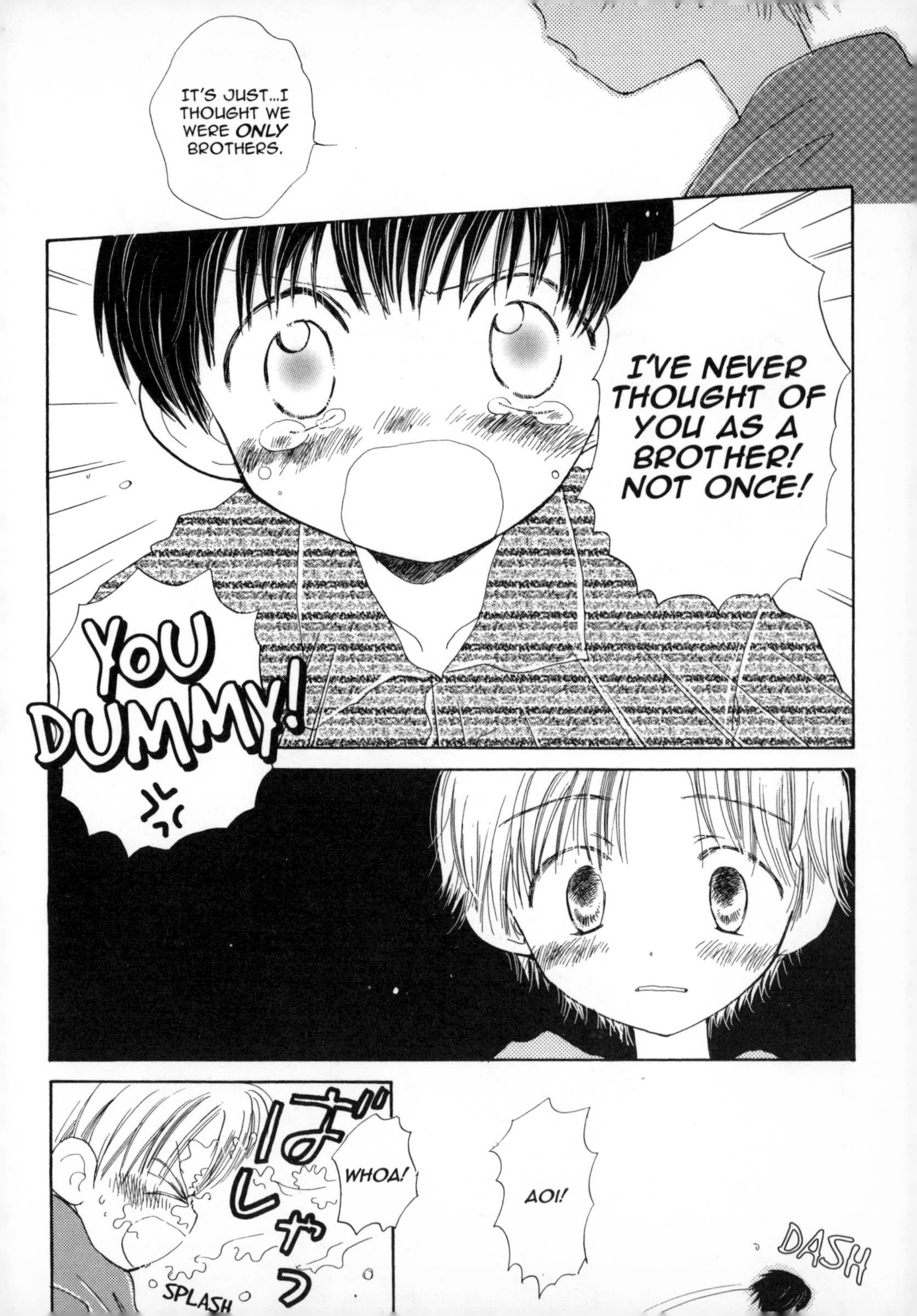
IT'S JUST...I THOUGHT WE WERE *ONLY* BROTHERS.
I'VE NEVER THOUGHT OF YOU AS A BROTHER! NOT ONCE!
YOU DUMMY!
AOI!
DASH
ばしゃっ
WHOA!
SPLASH

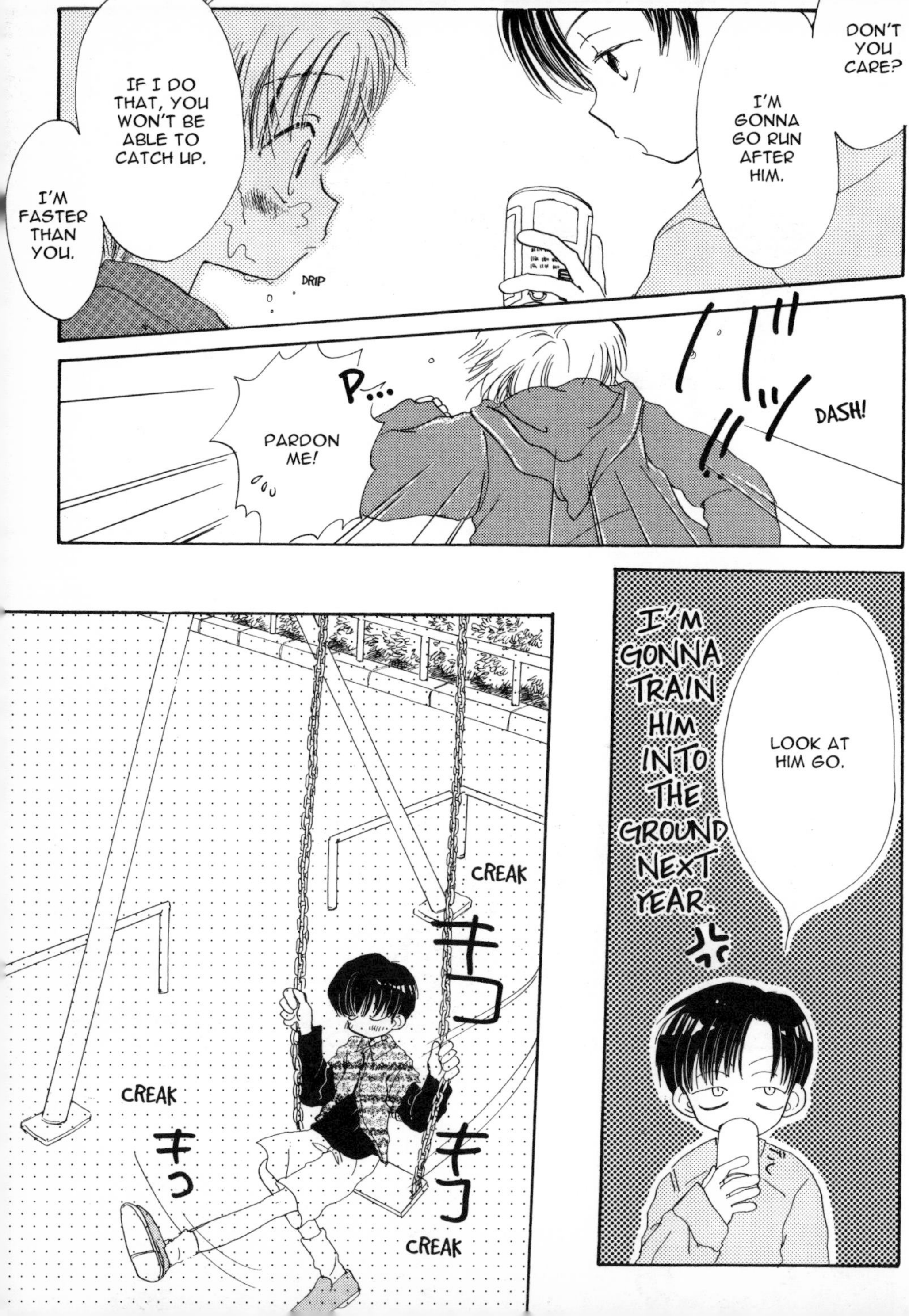
DON'T YOU CARE?
I'M GONNA GO RUN AFTER HIM.
IF I DO THAT, YOU WON'T BE ABLE TO CATCH UP.
I'M FASTER THAN YOU.
DRIP
DASH!
P...
PARDON ME!
LOOK AT HIM GO.
I'M GONNA TRAIN HIM INTO THE GROUND NEXT YEAR.
CREAK
キコ
CREAK
キコ
CREAK
キコ

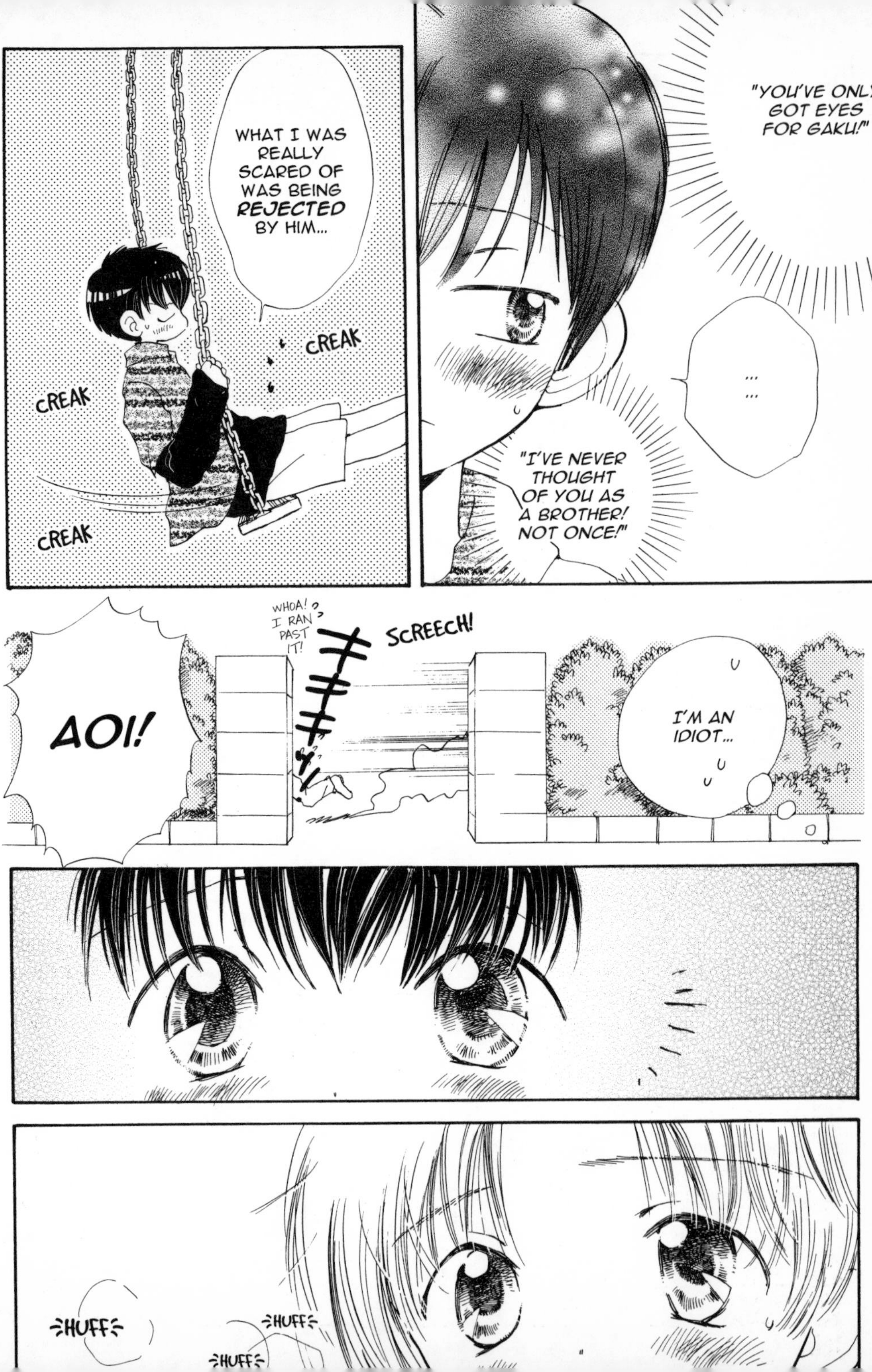
"YOU'VE ONLY GOT EYES FOR GAKU!"
... ...
"I'VE NEVER THOUGHT OF YOU AS A BROTHER! NOT ONCE!"
WHAT I WAS REALLY SCARED OF WAS BEING REJECTED BY HIM...
CREAK
CREAK
CREAK
I'M AN IDIOT...
SCREECH!
WHOA! I RAN PAST IT!
AOI!
HUFF
HUFF
HUFF

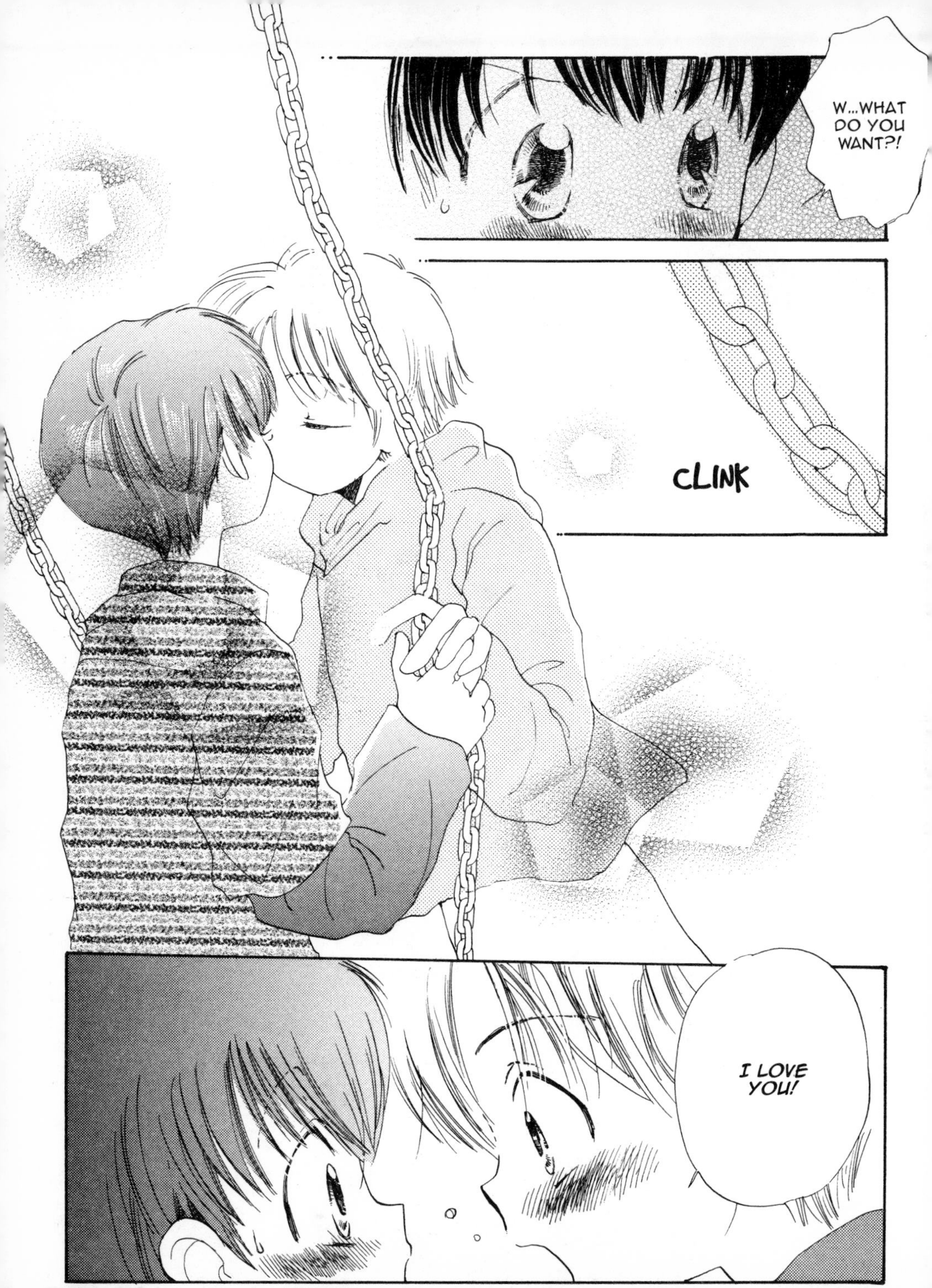
W...WHAT DO YOU WANT?!
CLINK
I LOVE YOU!

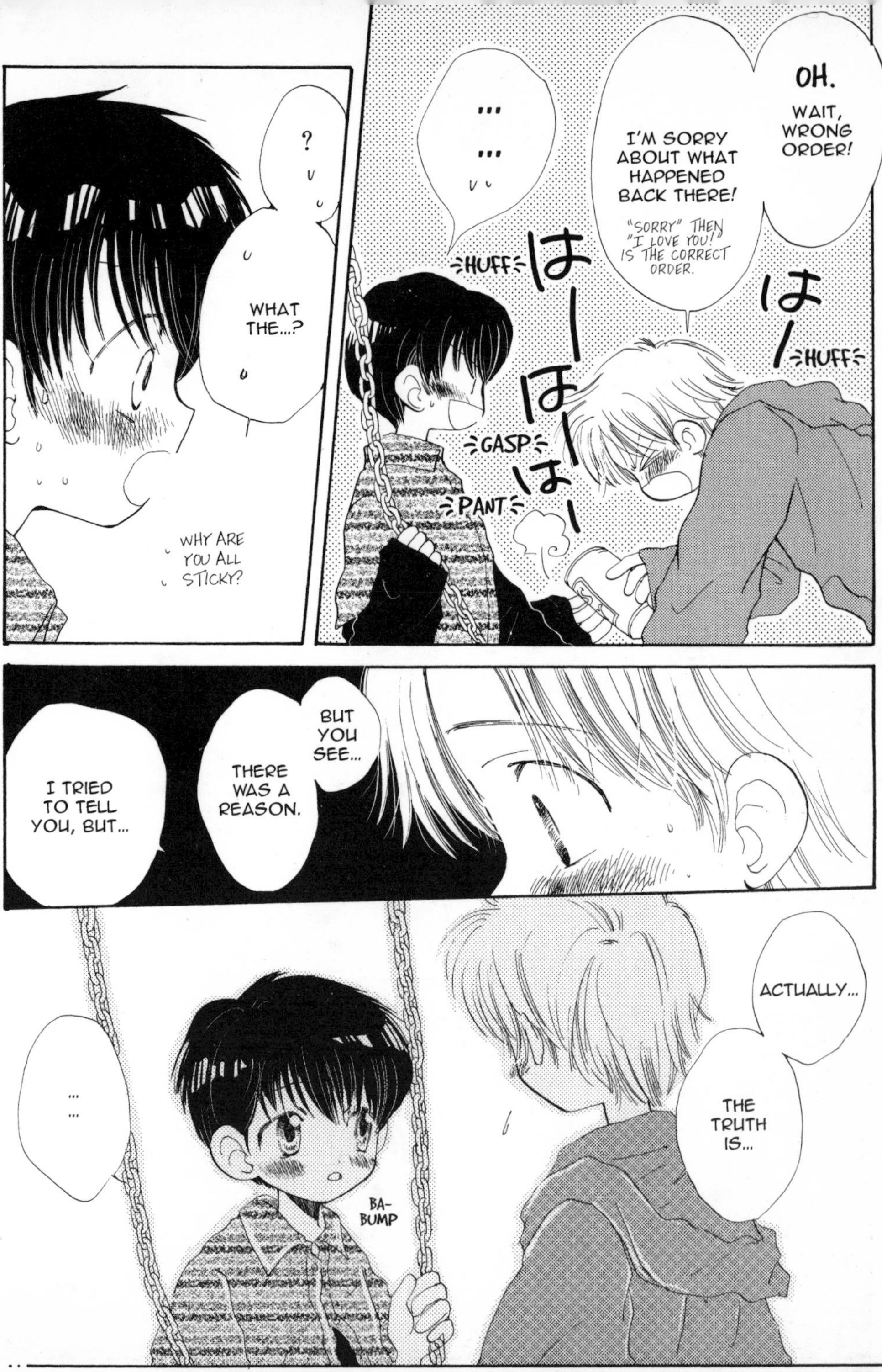
OH.
WAIT, WRONG ORDER!
I'M SORRY ABOUT WHAT HAPPENED BACK THERE!
"SORRY" THEN "I LOVE YOU!" IS THE CORRECT ORDER.
はー
HUFF
はーはーはー
HUFF
GASP
PANT
...
...
?
WHAT THE...?
WHY ARE YOU ALL STICKY?
BUT YOU SEE...
THERE WAS A REASON.
I TRIED TO TELL YOU, BUT...
ACTUALLY...
THE TRUTH IS...
BA-BUMP
...
...

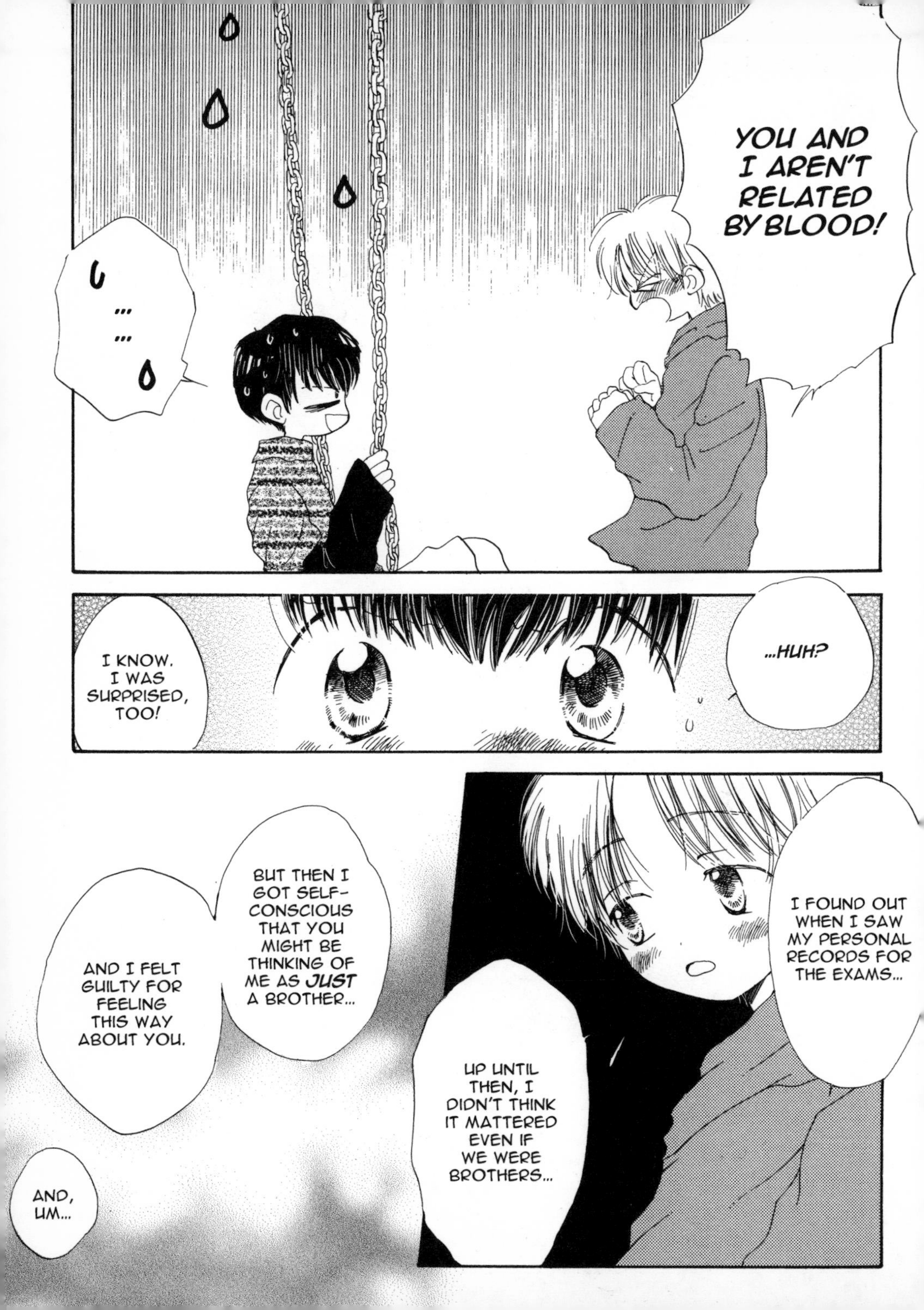
YOU AND I AREN'T RELATED BY BLOOD!
...
...
...HUH?
I KNOW. I WAS SURPRISED, TOO!
I FOUND OUT WHEN I SAW MY PERSONAL RECORDS FOR THE EXAMS...
UP UNTIL THEN, I DIDN'T THINK IT MATTERED EVEN IF WE WERE BROTHERS...
BUT THEN I GOT SELF-CONSCIOUS THAT YOU MIGHT BE THINKING OF ME AS *JUST* A BROTHER...
AND I FELT GUILTY FOR FEELING THIS WAY ABOUT YOU.
AND, UM...

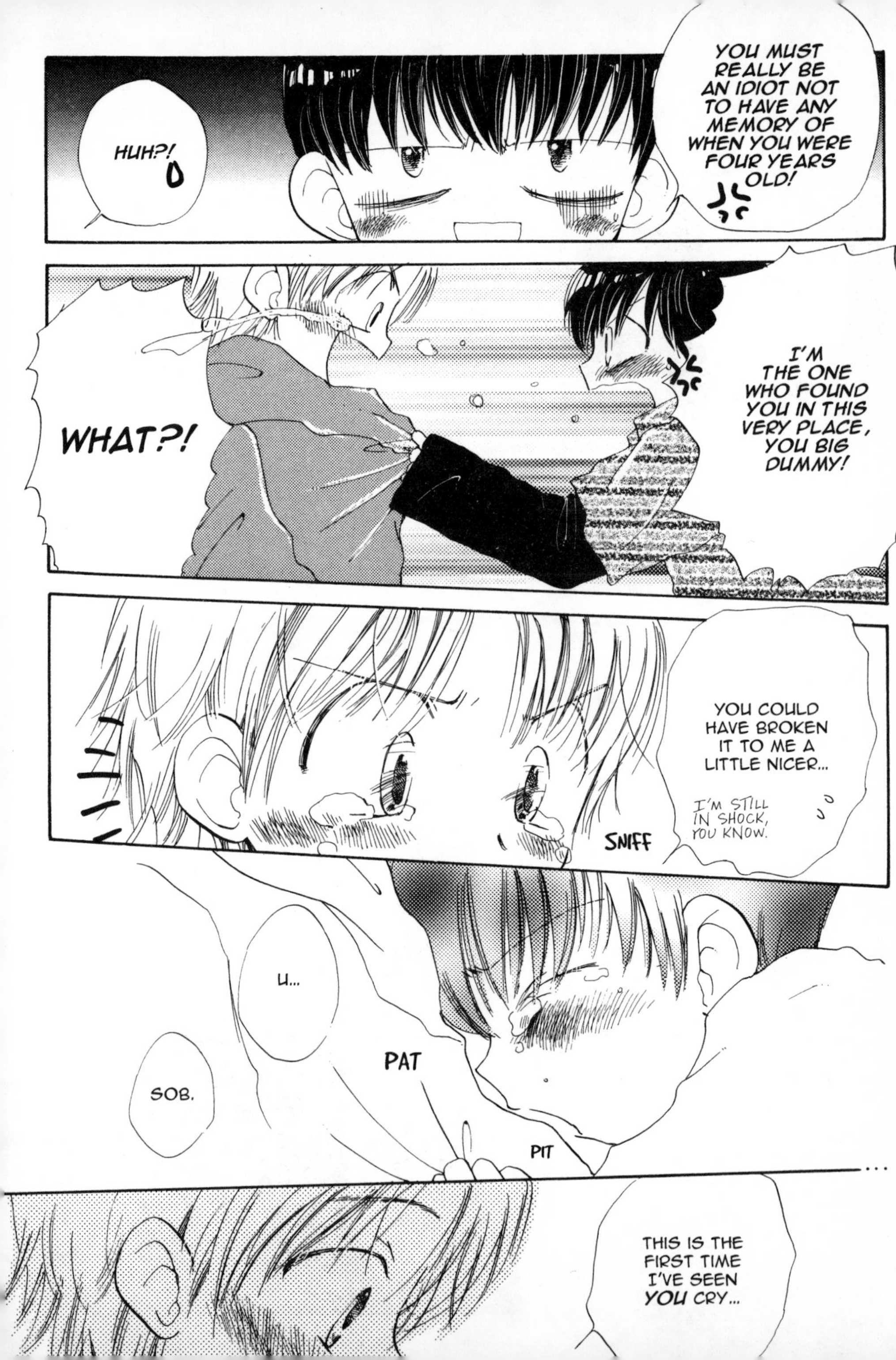
YOU MUST REALLY BE AN IDIOT NOT TO HAVE ANY MEMORY OF WHEN YOU WERE FOUR YEARS OLD!
HUH?!
I'M THE ONE WHO FOUND YOU IN THIS VERY PLACE, YOU BIG DUMMY!
WHAT?!
YOU COULD HAVE BROKEN IT TO ME A LITTLE NICER...
I'M STILL IN SHOCK, YOU KNOW.
SNIFF
U...
PAT
SOB.
PIT
...
THIS IS THE FIRST TIME I'VE SEEN YOU CRY...

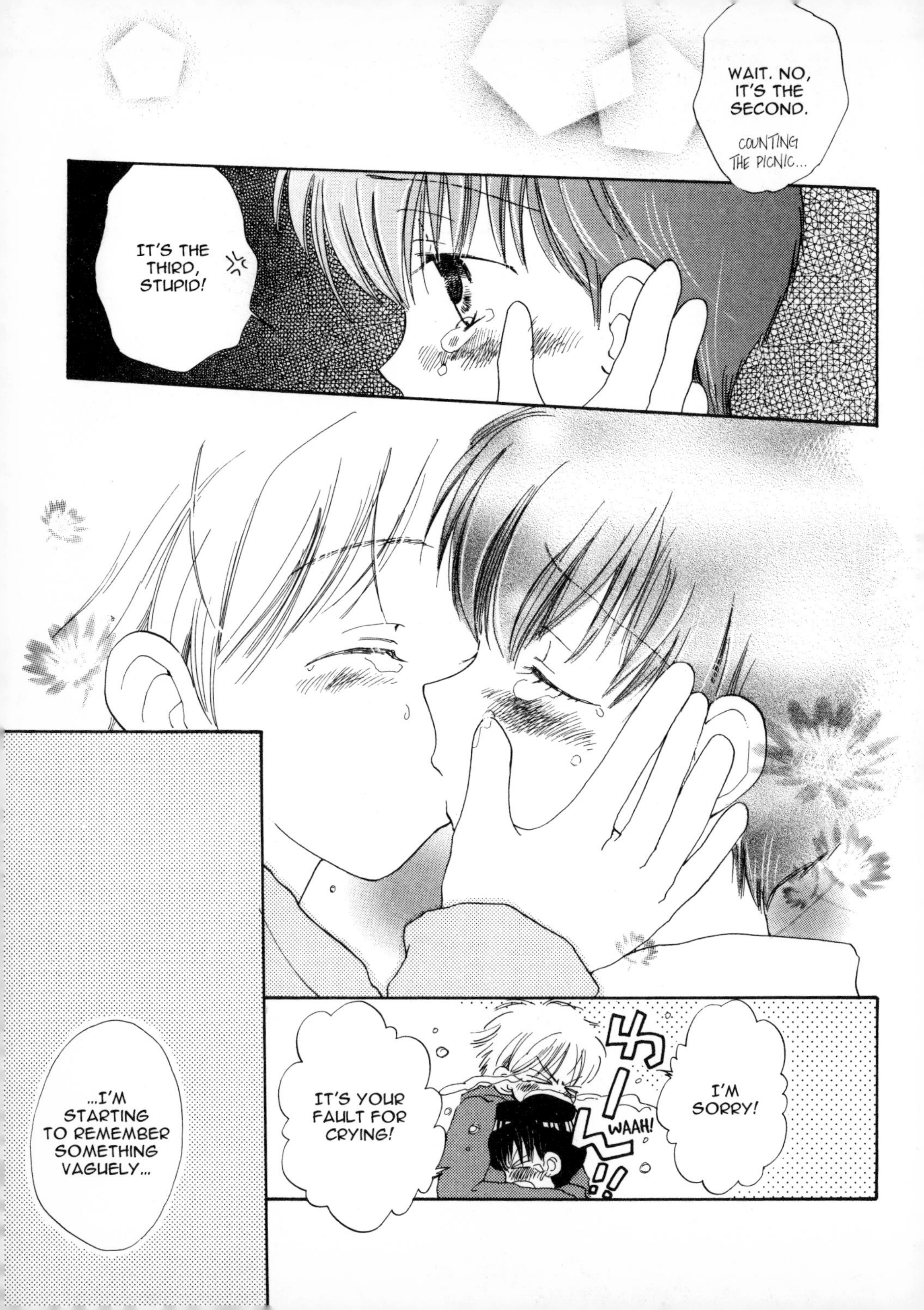
WAIT. NO, IT'S THE SECOND.
COUNTING THE PICNIC...
IT'S THE THIRD, STUPID!
I'M SORRY!
わーん!!
WAAH!
IT'S YOUR FAULT FOR CRYING!
...I'M STARTING TO REMEMBER SOMETHING VAGUELY...

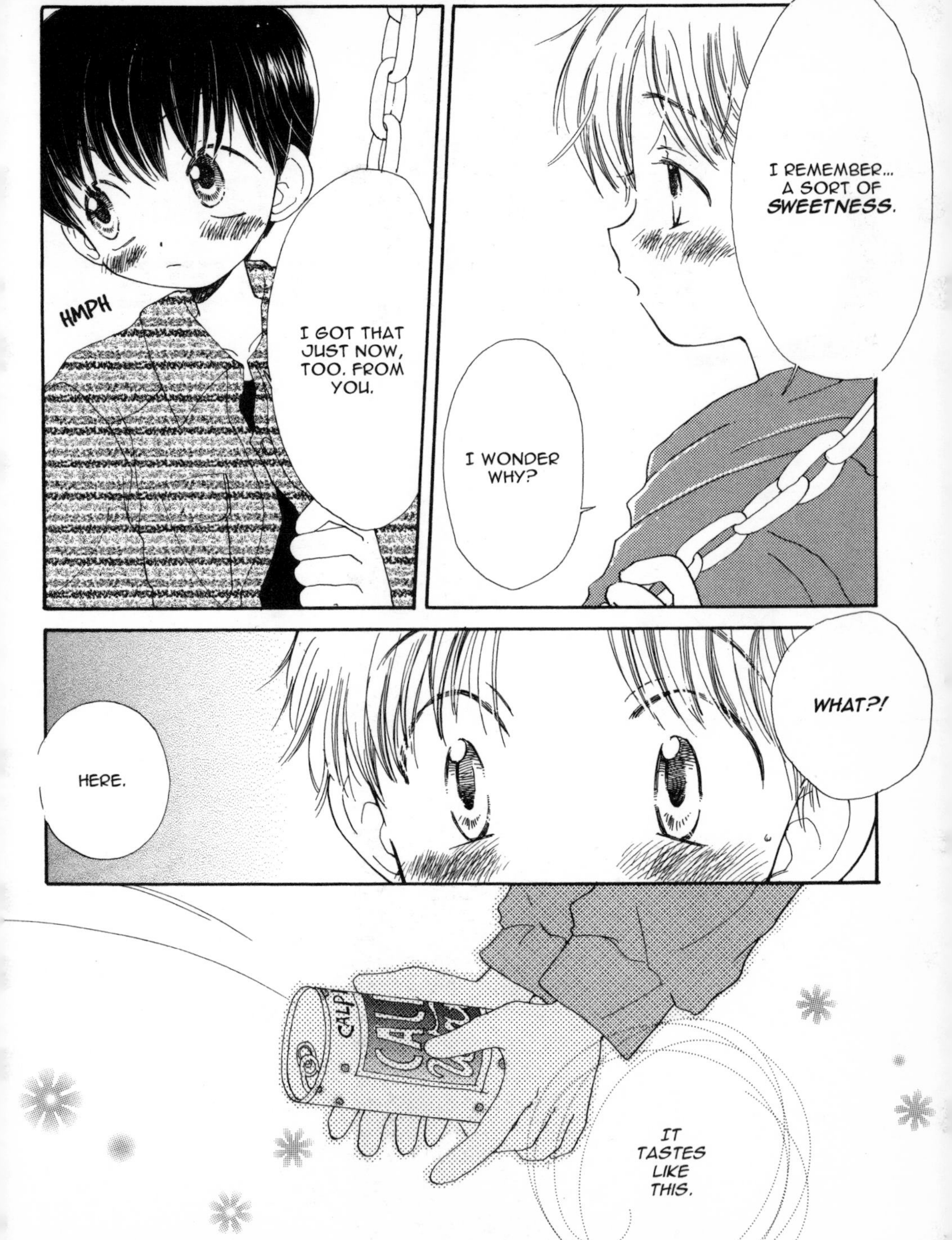
I REMEMBER... A SORT OF SWEETNESS.
I WONDER WHY?
I GOT THAT JUST NOW, TOO. FROM YOU.
HMPH
WHAT?!
HERE.
IT TASTES LIKE THIS.

END

THE TASTE OF FIRST LOVE

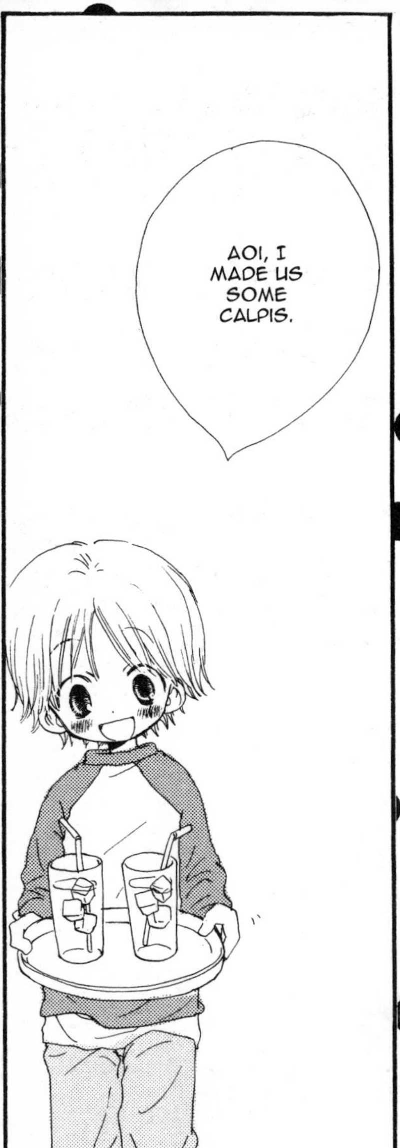
AOI, I MADE US SOME CALPIS.

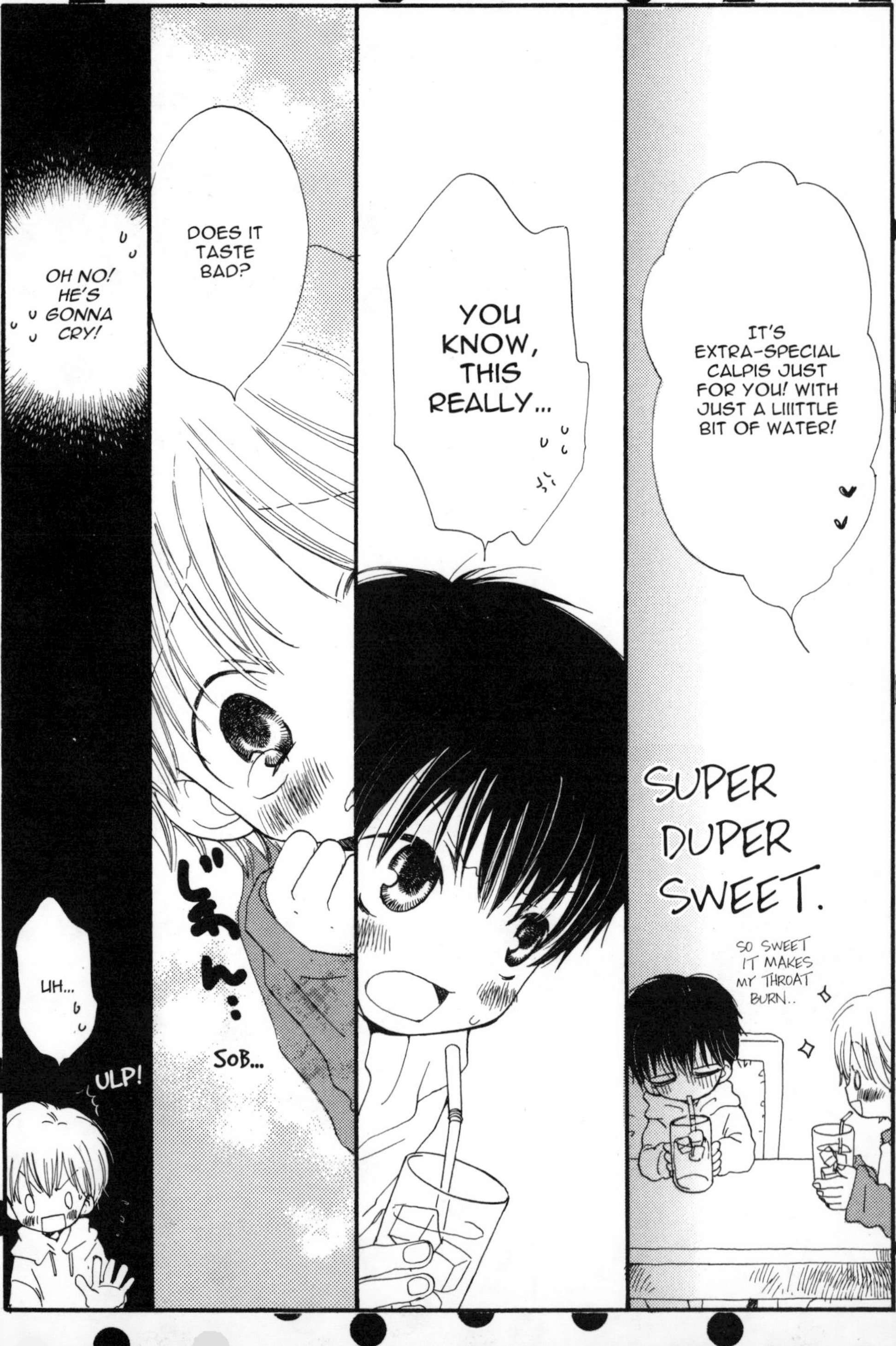
IT'S EXTRA-SPECIAL CALPIS JUST FOR YOU! WITH JUST A LIIITTLE BIT OF WATER!
SUPER DUPER SWEET.
SO SWEET IT MAKES MY THROAT BURN..
YOU KNOW, THIS REALLY...
DOES IT TASTE BAD?
じわん…
SOB...
OH NO! HE'S GONNA CRY!
UH...
ULP!

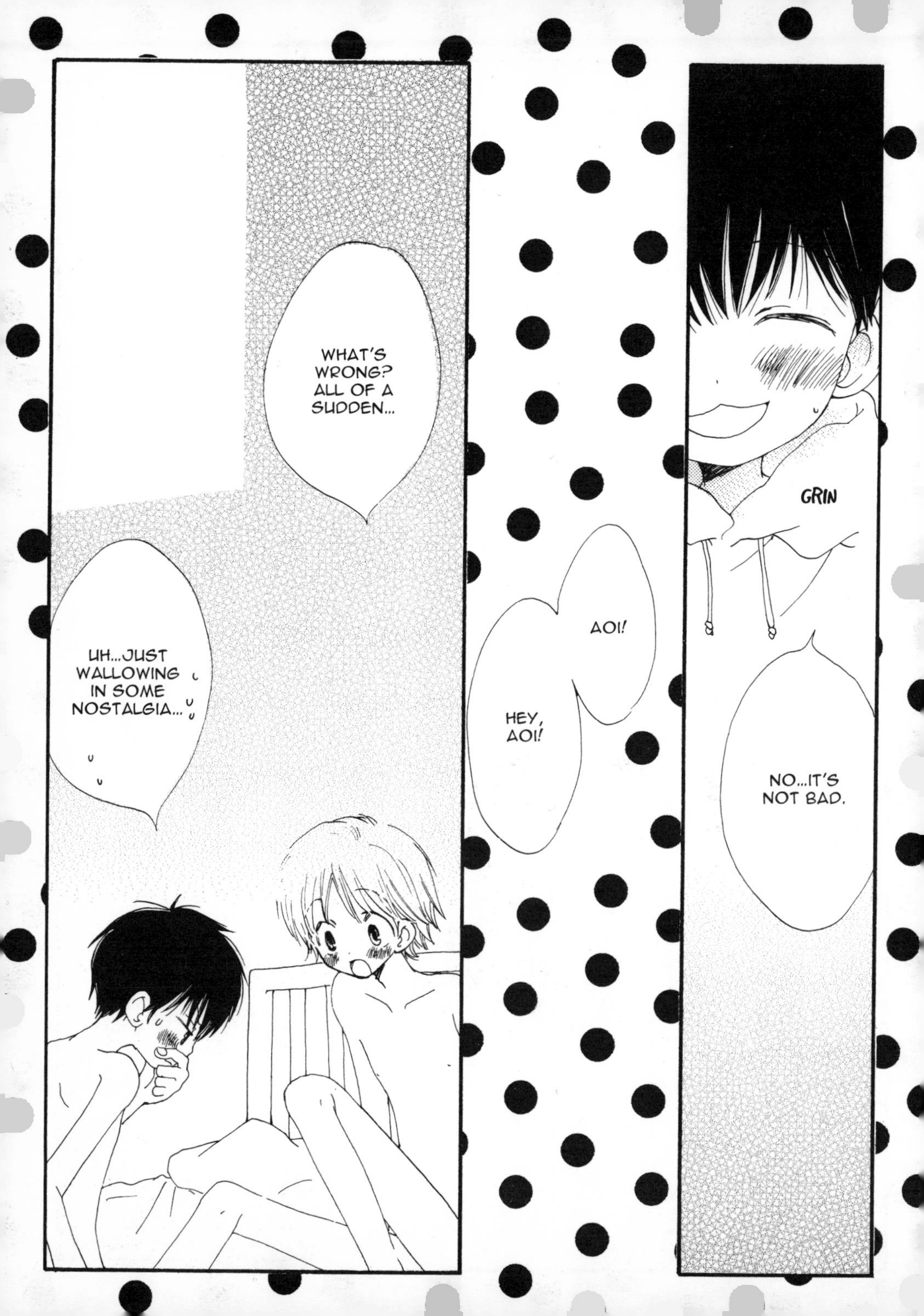
GRIN
NO...IT'S NOT BAD.
AOI!
HEY, AOI!
WHAT'S WRONG? ALL OF A SUDDEN...
UH...JUST WALLOWING IN SOME NOSTALGIA...

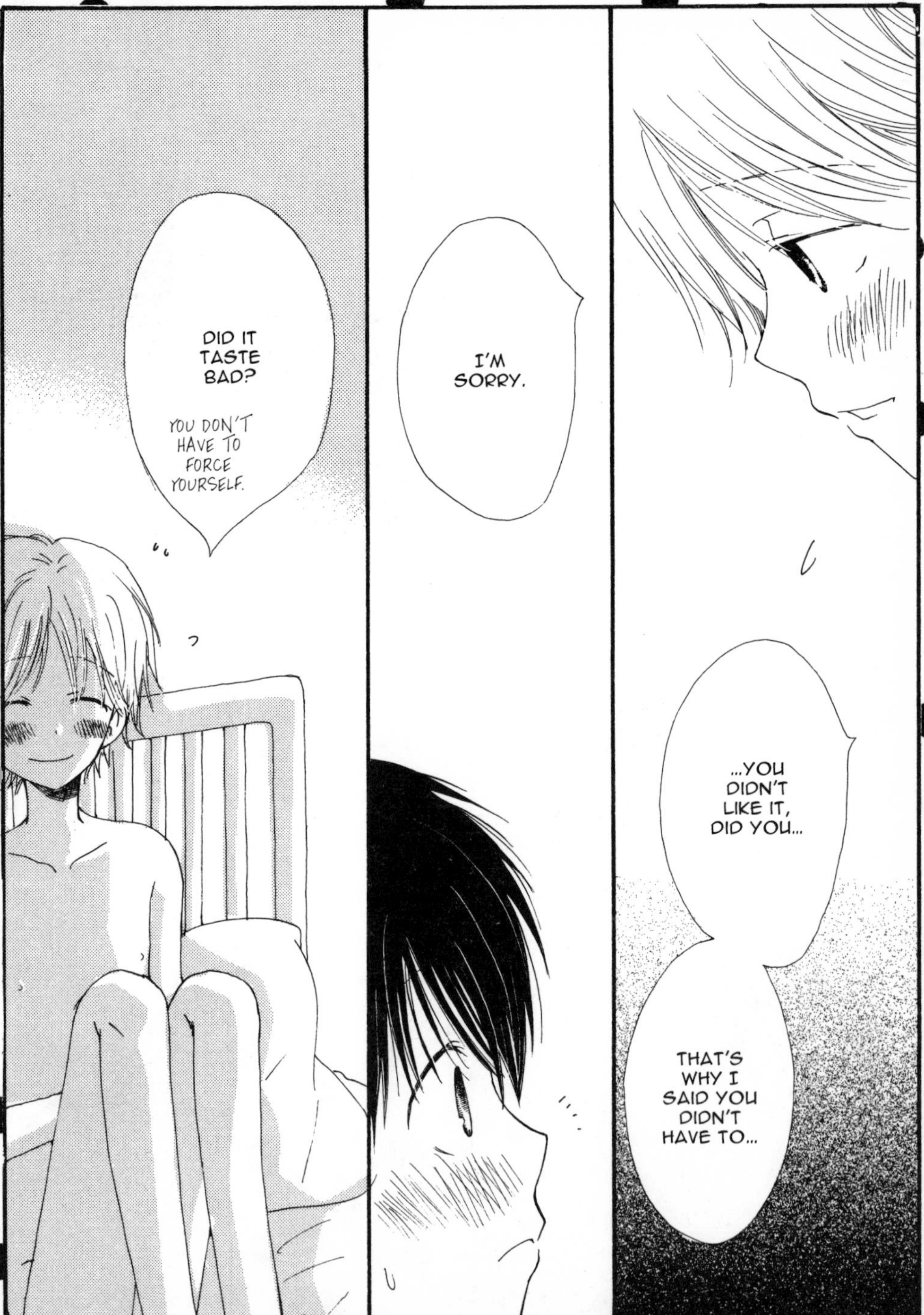
...YOU DIDN'T LIKE IT, DID YOU...
THAT'S WHY I SAID YOU DIDN'T HAVE TO...
I'M SORRY.
DID IT TASTE BAD?
YOU DON'T HAVE TO FORCE YOURSELF.

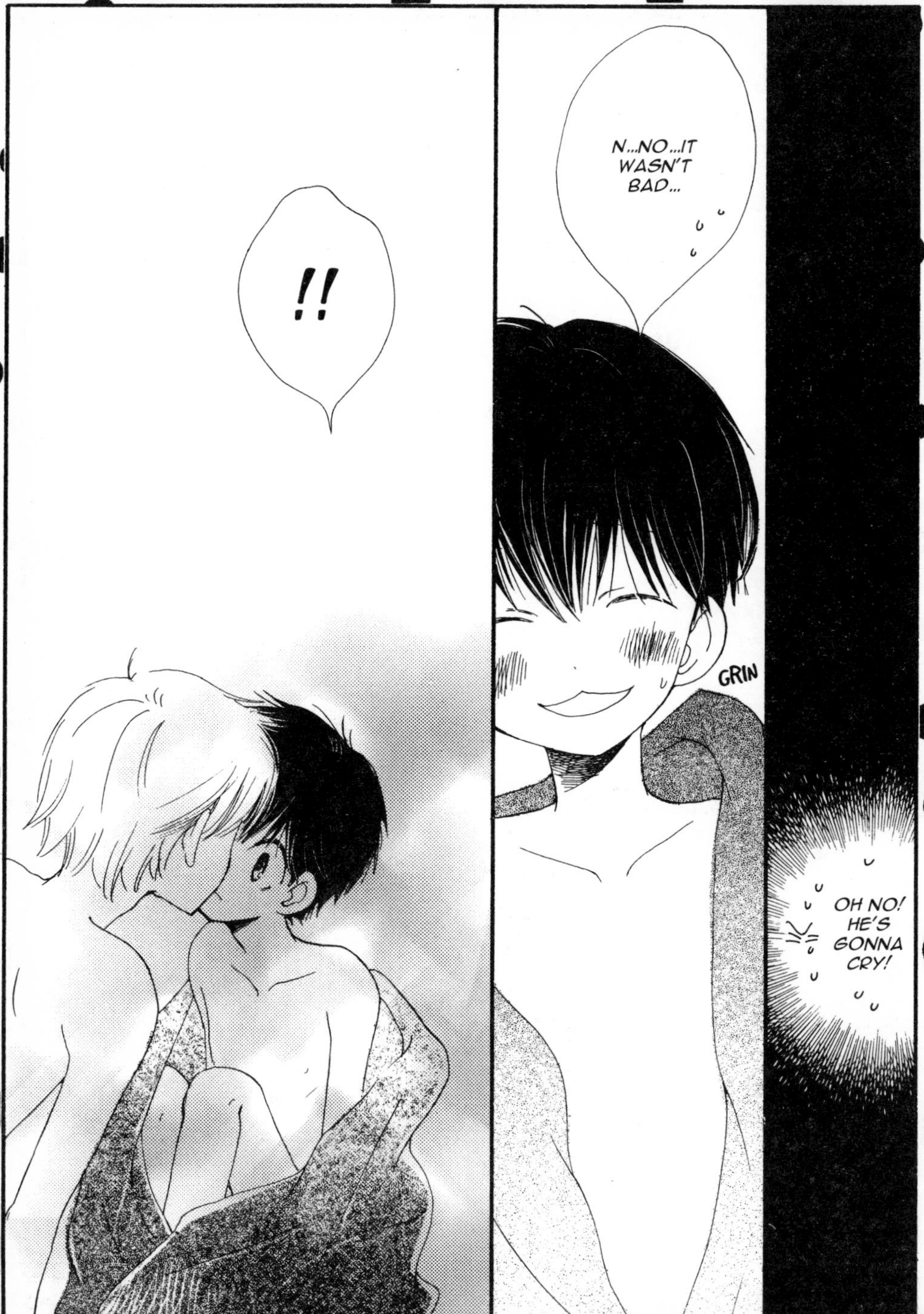
N...NO...IT WASN'T BAD...
GRIN
OH NO! HE'S GONNA CRY!
!!

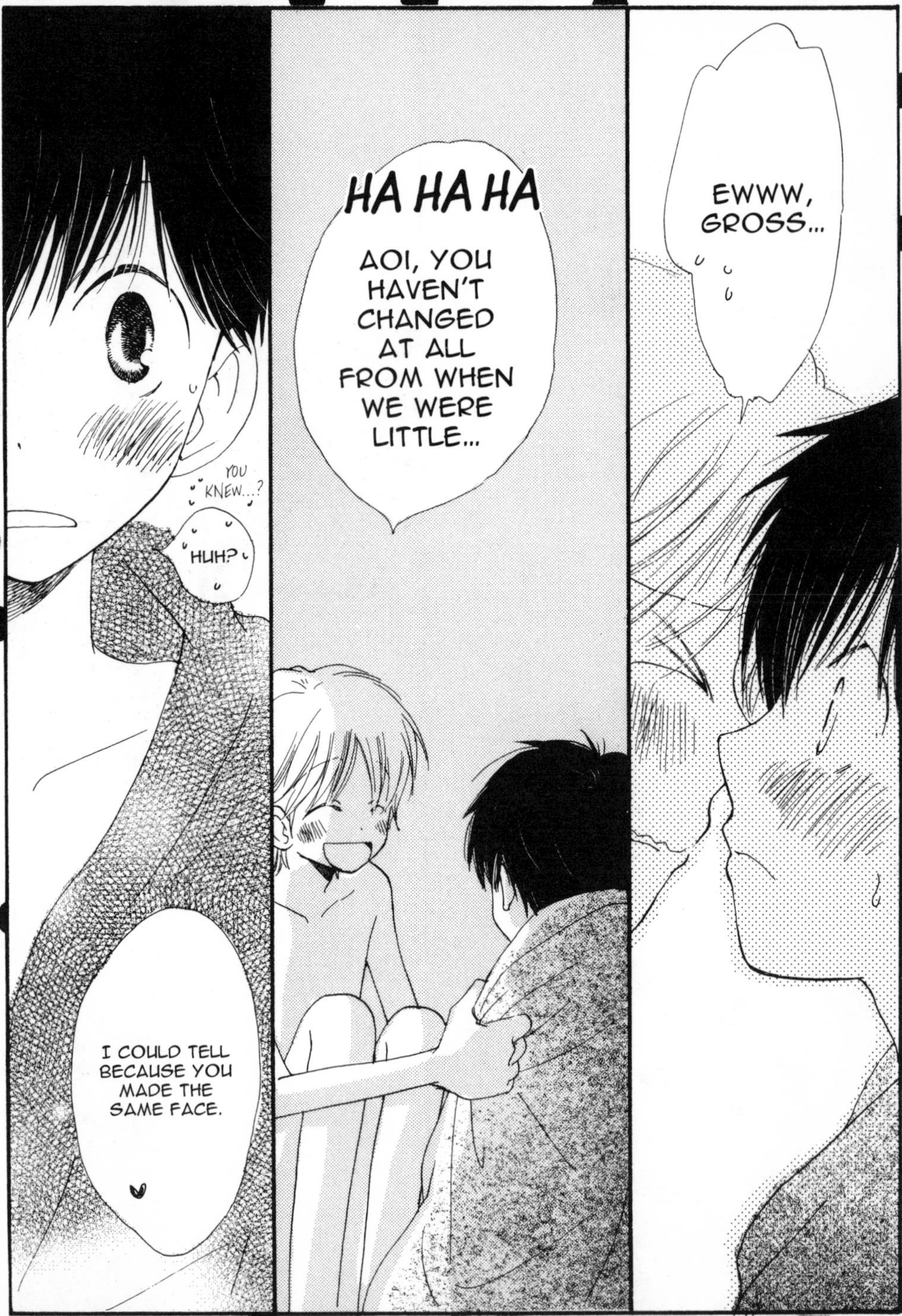
EWWW, GROSS...
HA HA HA
AOI, YOU HAVEN'T CHANGED AT ALL FROM WHEN WE WERE LITTLE...
YOU KNEW...?
HUH?
I COULD TELL BECAUSE YOU MADE THE SAME FACE.

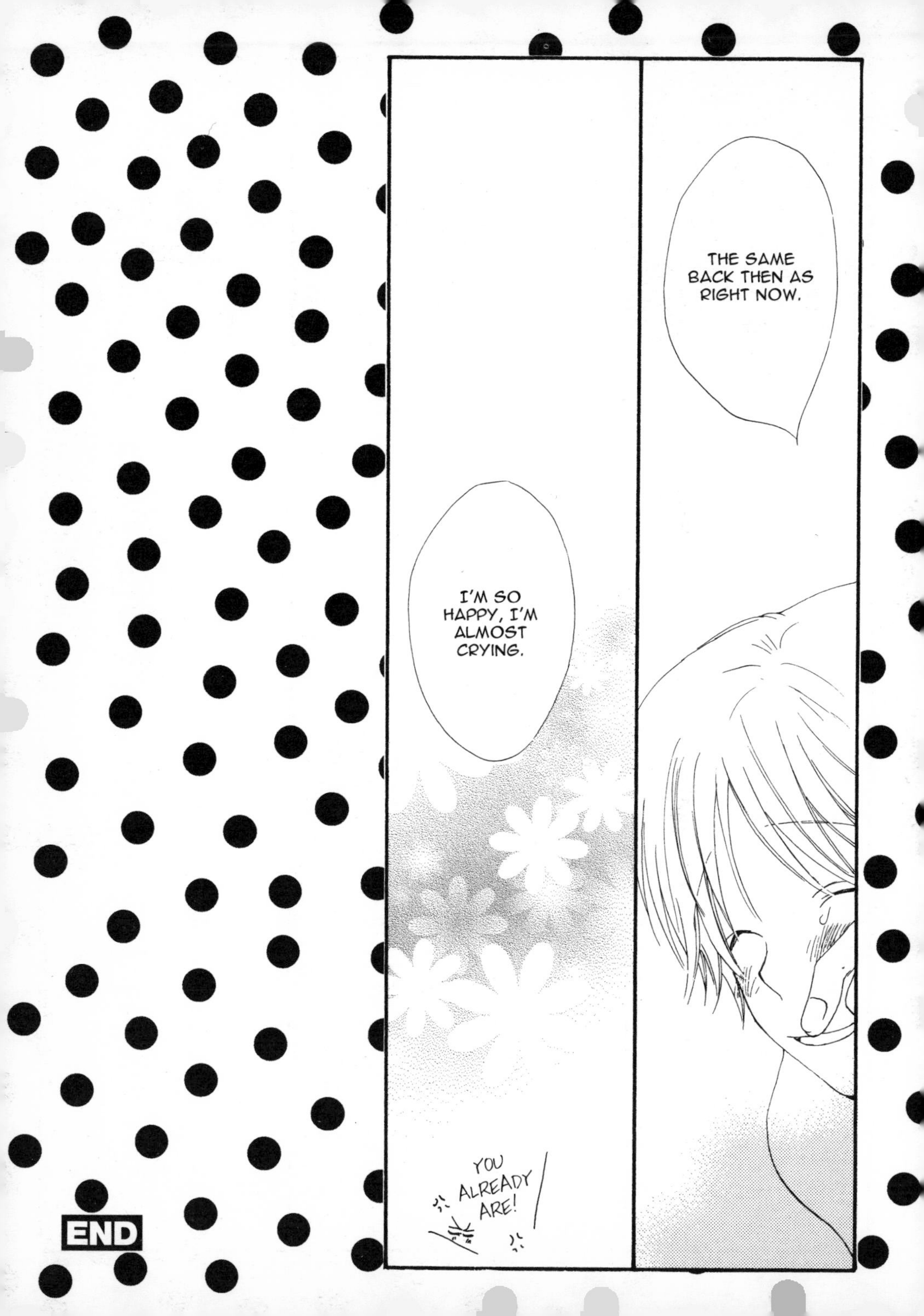
THE SAME BACK THEN AS RIGHT NOW.
I'M SO HAPPY, I'M ALMOST CRYING.
YOU ALREADY ARE!
END

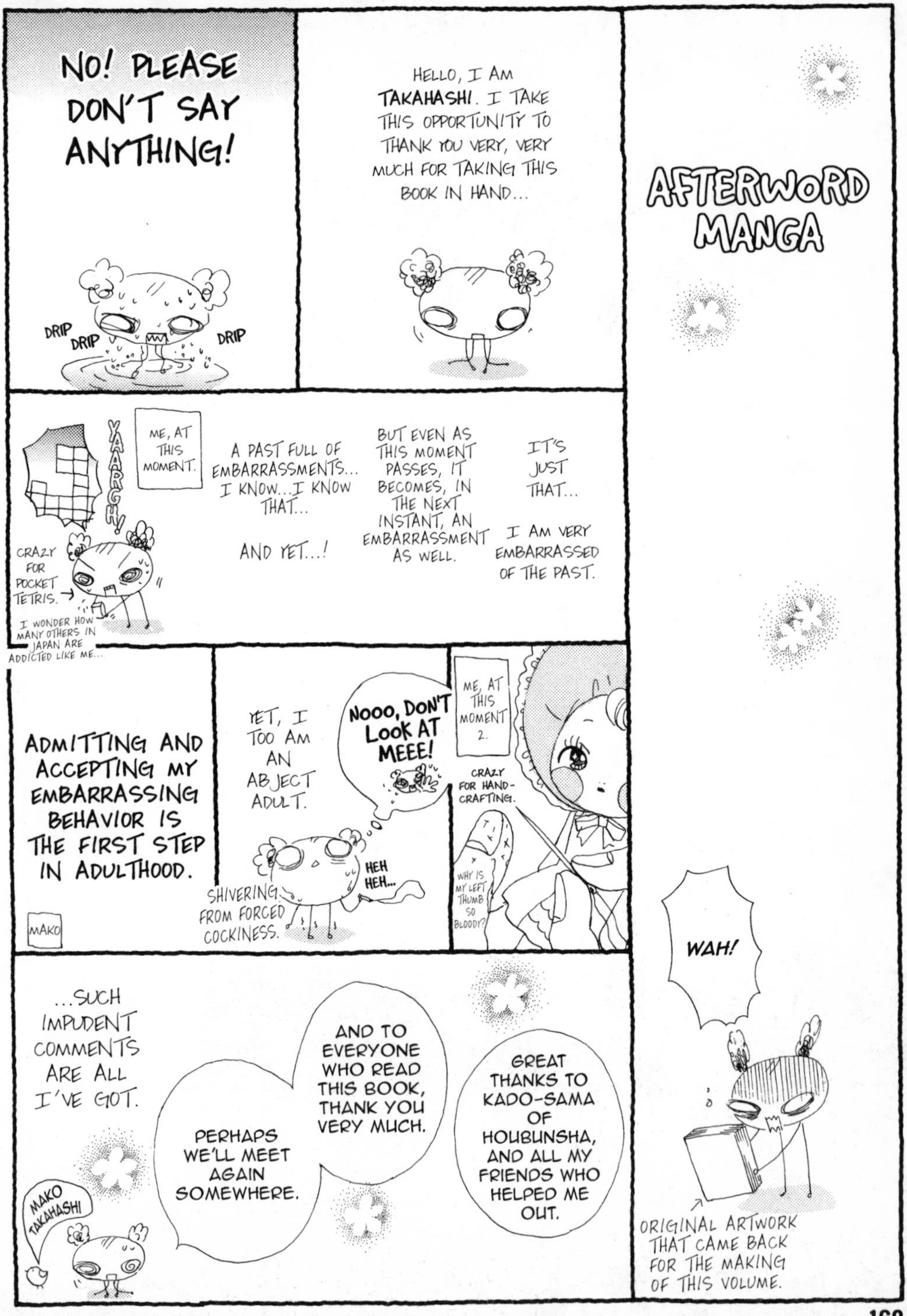
AFTERWORD MANGA
WAH!
ORIGINAL ARTWORK THAT CAME BACK FOR THE MAKING OF THIS VOLUME.
HELLO, I AM TAKAHASHI. I TAKE THIS OPPORTUNITY TO THANK YOU VERY, VERY MUCH FOR TAKING THIS BOOK IN HAND...
NO! PLEASE DON'T SAY ANYTHING!
DRIP
DRIP
DRIP
IT'S JUST THAT...
I AM VERY EMBARRASSED OF THE PAST.
BUT EVEN AS THIS MOMENT PASSES, IT BECOMES, IN THE NEXT INSTANT, AN EMBARRASSMENT AS WELL.
A PAST FULL OF EMBARRASSMENTS... I KNOW...I KNOW THAT...
AND YET...!
ME, AT THIS MOMENT.
YAAARGH!
CRAZY FOR POCKET TETRIS.
I WONDER HOW MANY OTHERS IN JAPAN ARE ADDICTED LIKE ME...
ME, AT THIS MOMENT 2.
CRAZY FOR HAND-CRAFTING.
WHY IS MY LEFT THUMB SO BLOODY?
YET, I TOO AM AN ABJECT ADULT.
NOOO, DON'T LOOK AT MEEE!
HEH HEH...
SHIVERING FROM FORCED COCKINESS.
ADMITTING AND ACCEPTING MY EMBARRASSING BEHAVIOR IS THE FIRST STEP IN ADULTHOOD.
MAKO
GREAT THANKS TO KADO-SAMA OF HOUBUNSHA, AND ALL MY FRIENDS WHO HELPED ME OUT.
AND TO EVERYONE WHO READ THIS BOOK, THANK YOU VERY MUCH.
PERHAPS WE'LL MEET AGAIN SOMEWHERE.
...SUCH IMPUDENT COMMENTS ARE ALL I'VE GOT.
MAKO TAKAHASHI

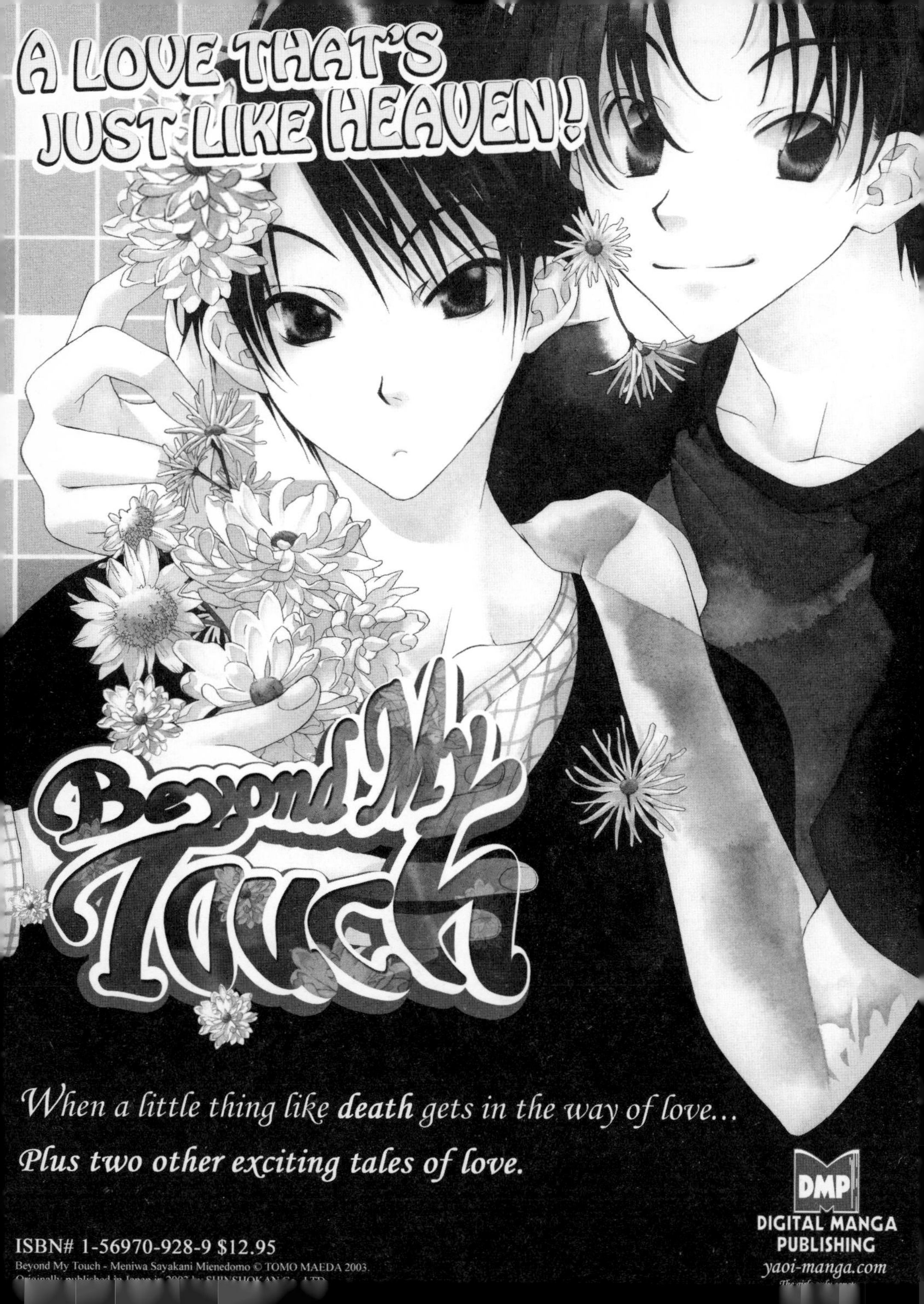
A LOVE THAT'S JUST LIKE HEAVEN!
Beyond My Touch
When a little thing like death gets in the way of love...
Plus two other exciting tales of love.
DMP
DIGITAL MANGA PUBLISHING
yaoi-manga.com
ISBN# 1-56970-928-9 $12.95
Beyond My Touch - Meniwa Sayakani Mienedomo © TOMO MAEDA 2003.

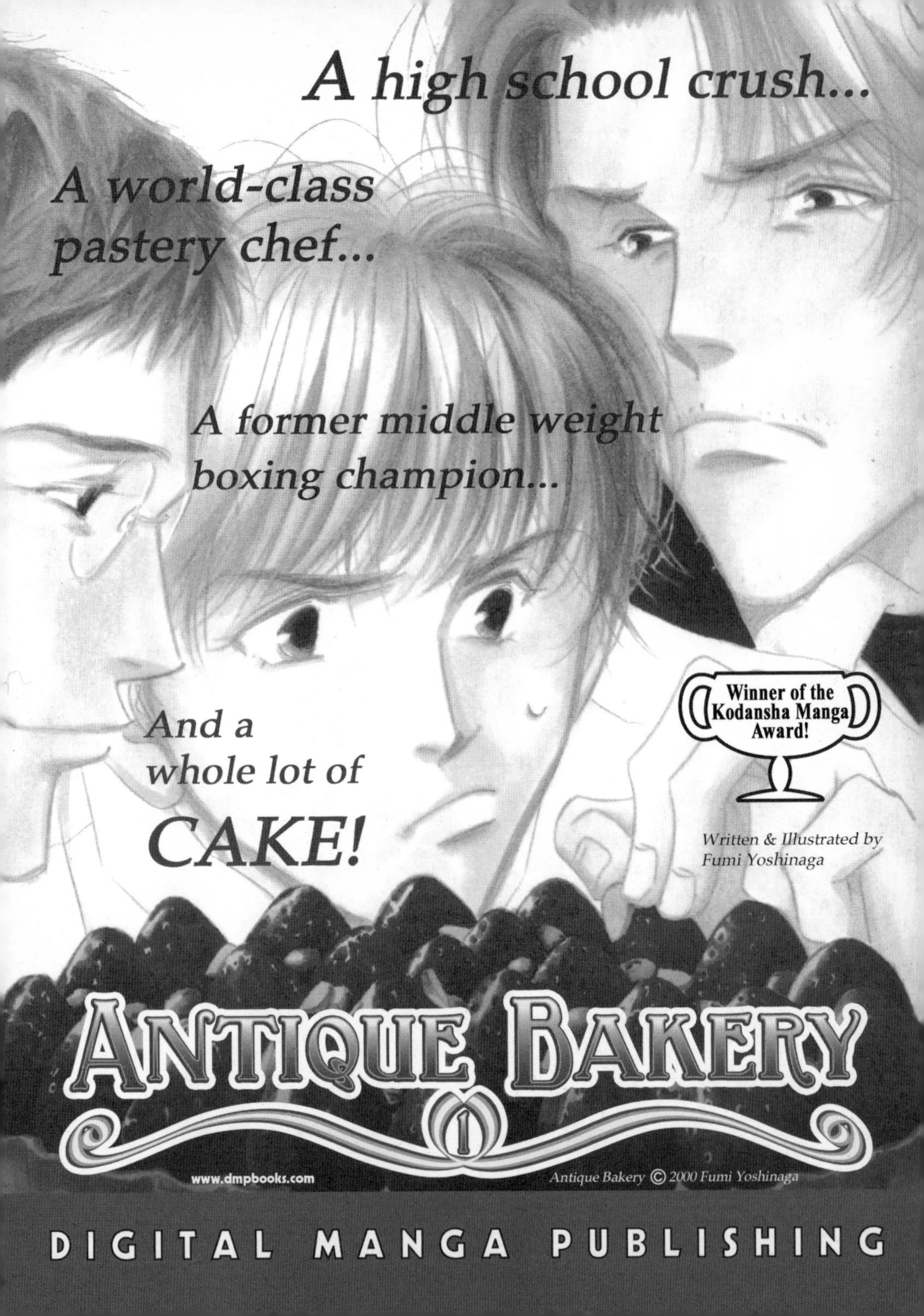
A high school crush...
A world-class
pastery chef...
A former middle weight
boxing champion...
And a
whole lot of
CAKE!
Winner of the
Kodansha Manga
Award!
Written & Illustrated by
Fumi Yoshinaga
ANTIQUE BAKERY
1
www.dmpbooks.com
Antique Bakery © 2000 Fumi Yoshinaga
DIGITAL MANGA PUBLISHING

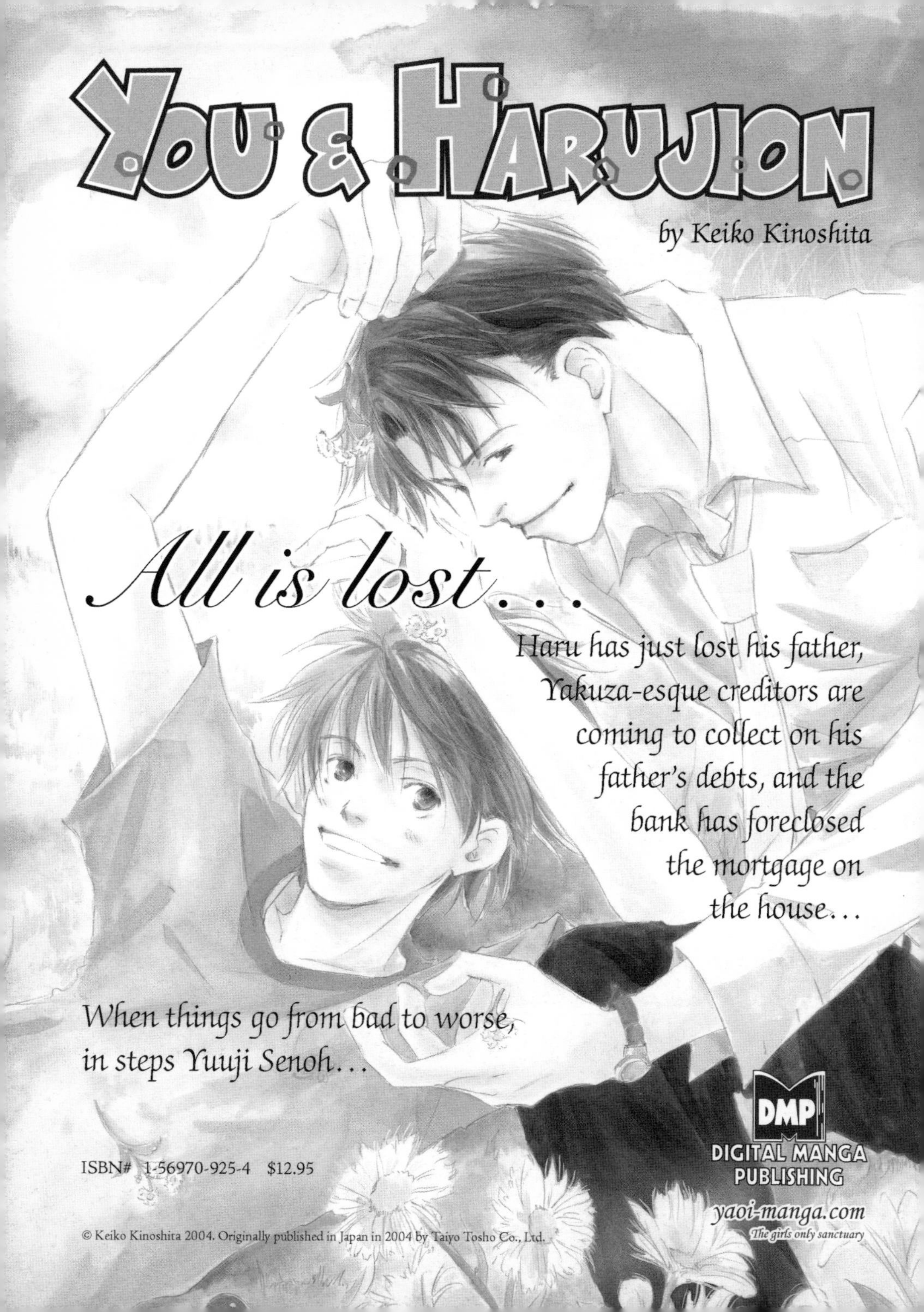
You & Harujion
by Keiko Kinoshita
All is lost . . .
Haru has just lost his father, Yakuza-esque creditors are coming to collect on his father's debts, and the bank has foreclosed the mortgage on the house…
When things go from bad to worse, in steps Yuuji Senoh…
DMP
DIGITAL MANGA PUBLISHING
yaoi-manga.com
The girls only sanctuary
ISBN# 1-56970-925-4 $12.95
© Keiko Kinoshita 2004. Originally published in Japan in 2004 by Taiyo Tosho Co., Ltd.

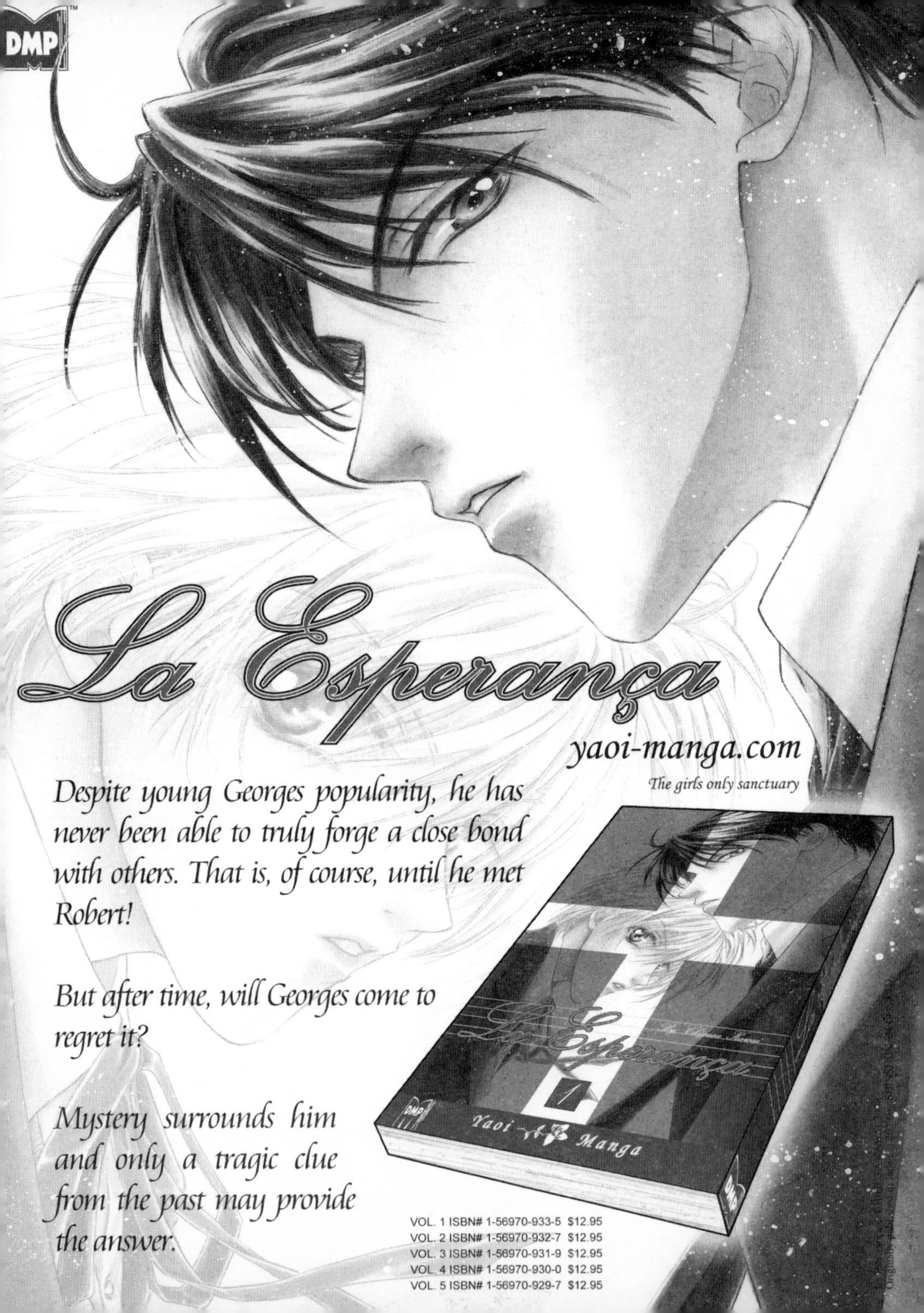

DMP
La Esperança
yaoi-manga.com
The girls only sanctuary
Despite young Georges popularity, he has never been able to truly forge a close bond with others. That is, of course, until he met Robert!
But after time, will Georges come to regret it?
Mystery surrounds him and only a tragic clue from the past may provide the answer.
La Esperança
1
DMP
Yaoi Manga
VOL. 1 ISBN# 1-56970-933-5 $12.95
VOL. 2 ISBN# 1-56970-932-7 $12.95
VOL. 3 ISBN# 1-56970-931-9 $12.95
VOL. 4 ISBN# 1-56970-930-0 $12.95
VOL. 5 ISBN# 1-56970-929-7 $12.95

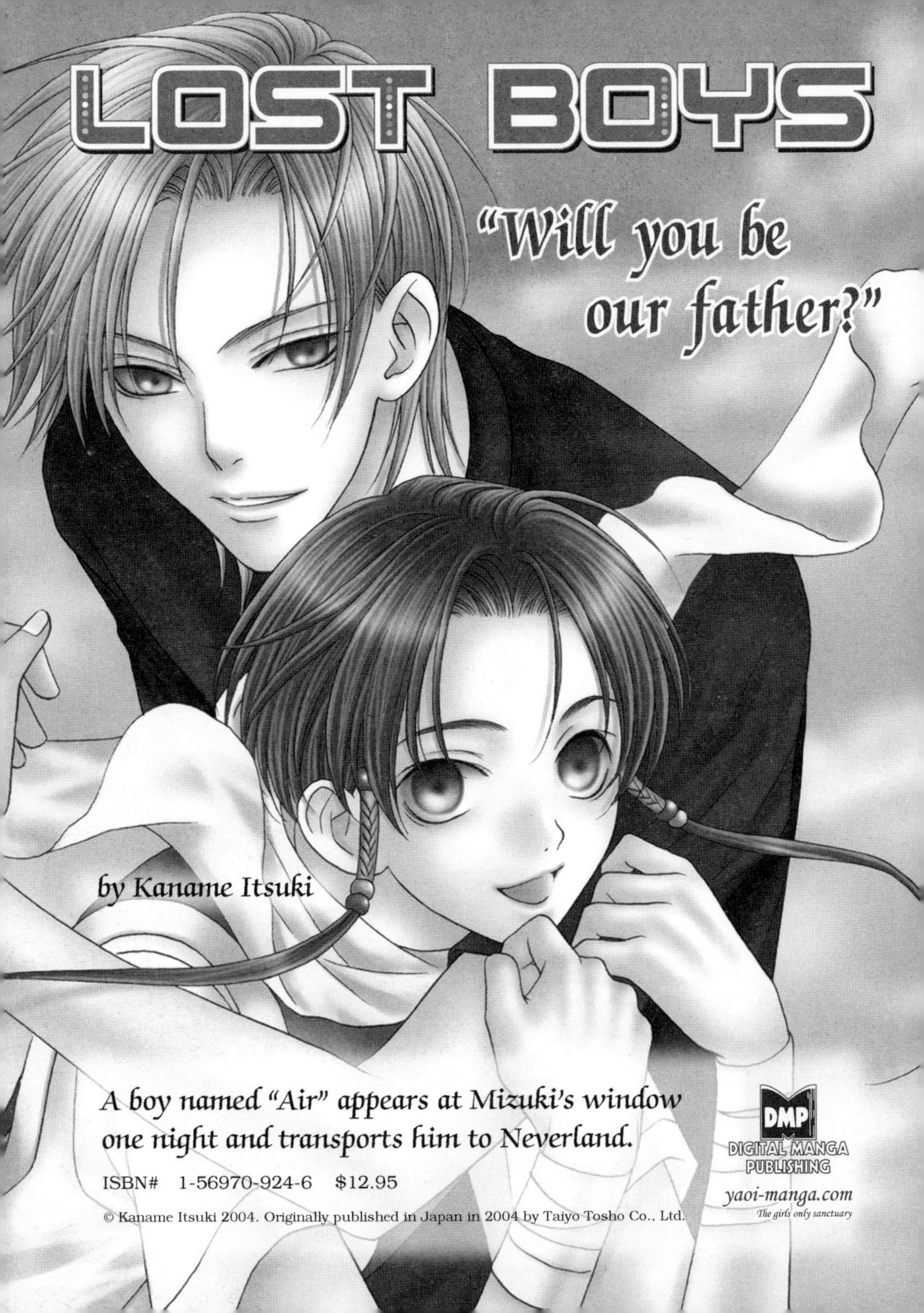
LOST BOYS
"Will you be our father?"
by Kaname Itsuki
A boy named "Air" appears at Mizuki's window one night and transports him to Neverland.
ISBN# 1-56970-924-6 $12.95
© Kaname Itsuki 2004. Originally published in Japan in 2004 by Taiyo Tosho Co., Ltd.
DMP
DIGITAL MANGA PUBLISHING
yaoi-manga.com
The girls only sanctuary

DMP

Kimi Shiruya- Dost thou Know?

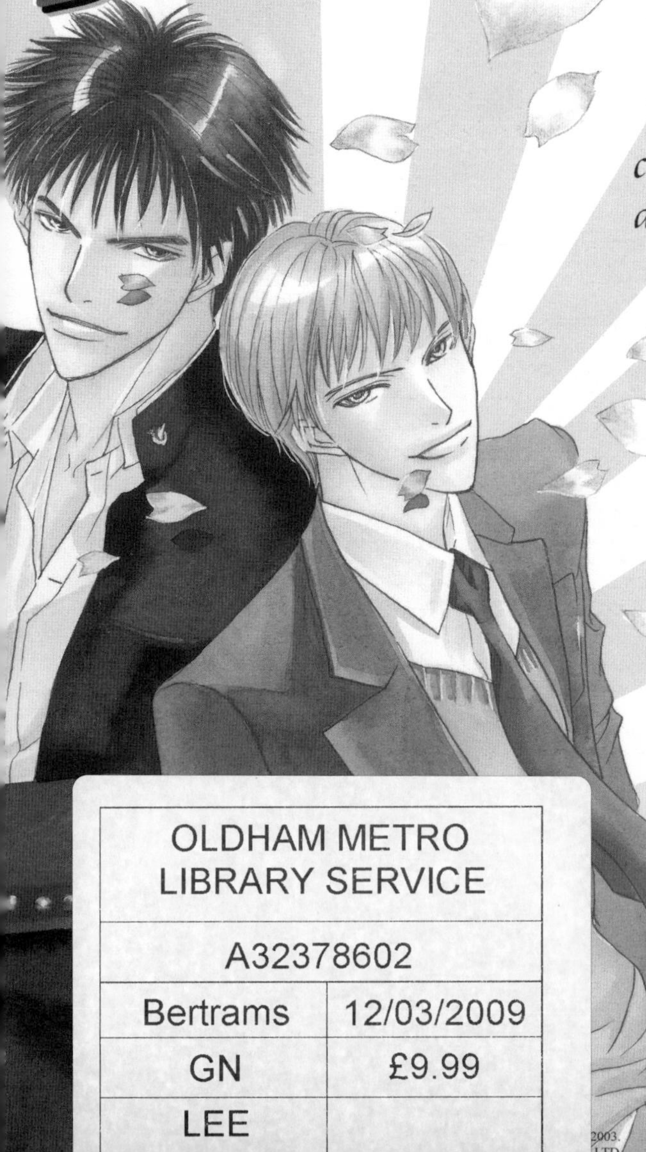

When Katsuomi and Tsurugi's wooden swords collide, sparks will fly, but as pride gets in the way of love, Tsurugi's brother Saya will profess his love to Katsuomi...

...Will jealousy drive Tsurugi to battle it out with Katsuomi one last time?

ISBN# 1-56970-934-3 $12.95

yaoi-manga.com

The girls only sanctuary

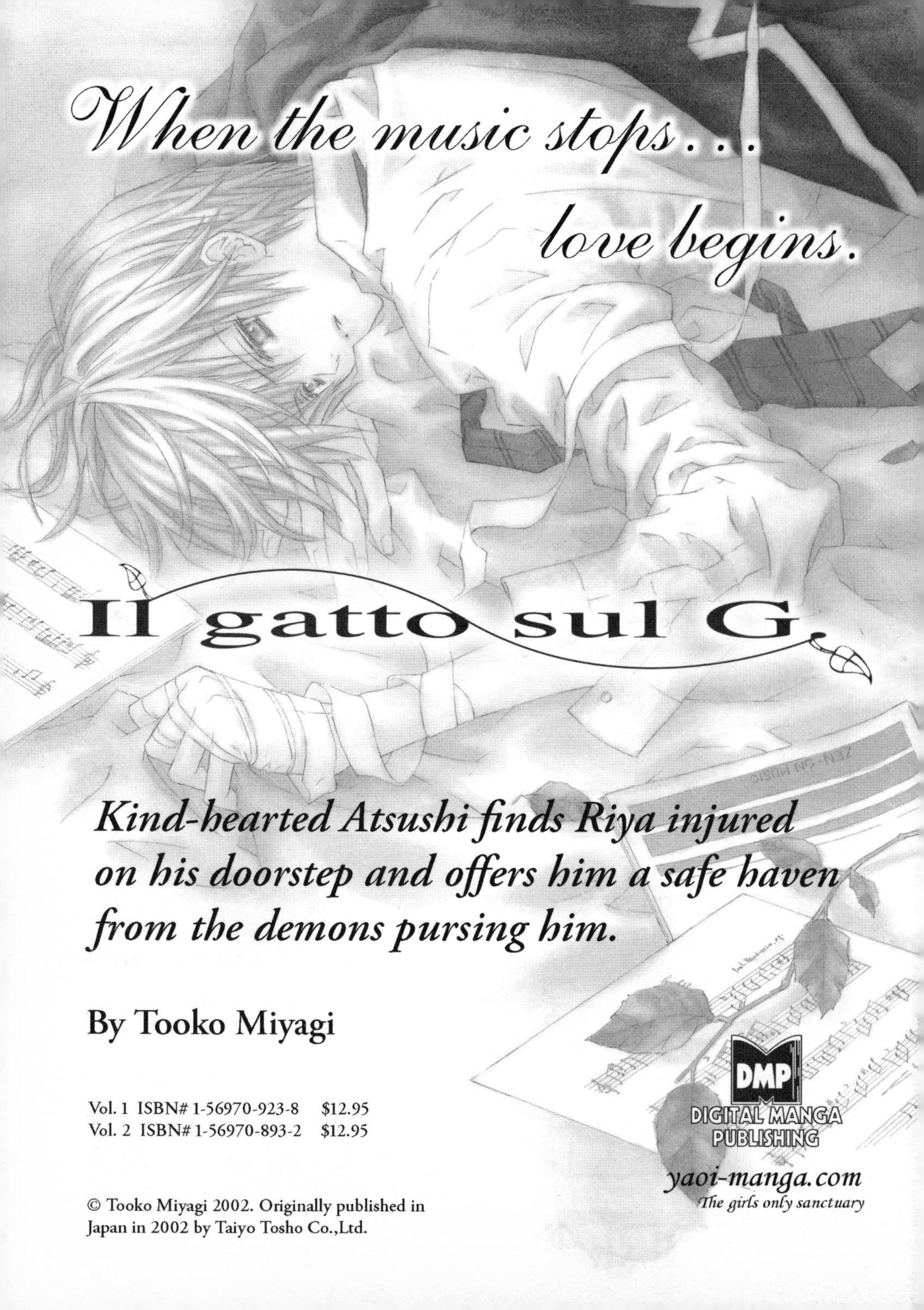
When the music stops . . .
love begins.
Il gatto sul G
Kind-hearted Atsushi finds Riya injured on his doorstep and offers him a safe haven from the demons pursing him.
By Tooko Miyagi
Vol. 1 ISBN# 1-56970-923-8 $12.95
Vol. 2 ISBN# 1-56970-893-2 $12.95
© Tooko Miyagi 2002. Originally published in Japan in 2002 by Taiyo Tosho Co.,Ltd.
DMP
DIGITAL MANGA PUBLISHING
yaoi-manga.com
The girls only sanctuary

STOP

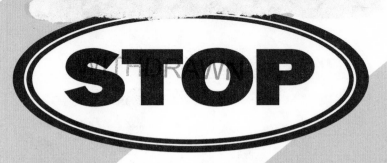

This is the back of the book! Start from the other side.

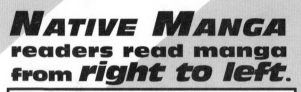

NATIVE MANGA readers read manga from *right to left*.

1
2
1
3
2
3
5
4
6
5
8
6

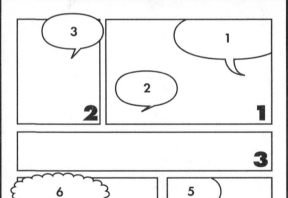

If you run into our ***Native Manga*** *logo on any of our books... you'll know that this manga is published in it's true original native Japanese right to left reading format, as it was intended. Turn to the other side of the book and start reading from right to left, top to bottom.*

Follow the diagram to see how its done.
Surf's Up!

NATIVE MANGA
RIGHT TO LEFT

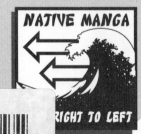